Passing On the Faith

Passing On the Faith:
A Radical Model for Youth and Family Ministry
Revised

Merton P. Strommen, PhD
Richard A. Hardel, DMin

saint mary's press

The acknowledgments continue on page 369.

The publishing team for this book included Ron Klug and Robert P. Stamschror, development editors; Maura Thompson Hagarty, revision development editor; Lorraine Kilmartin, reviewer; prepress and manufacturing coordinated by the production departments of Saint Mary's Press.

Printed in the United States of America

3463

ISBN 978-0-88489-970-9

Library of Congress Cataloging-in-Publication Data

Strommen, Merton P.
    Passing on the faith : a radical model for youth and family ministry / Merton P. Strommen, Richard A. Hardel. — Rev. ed.
        p. cm.
Includes bibliographical references and index.
ISBN 978-0-88489-970-9 (pbk.)
    1. Church work with youth. 2. Church work with families. 3. Parent and teenager. 4. Family—Religious life. 5. Youth—Religious life. 6. Christian education. I. Hardel, Dick. II. Title.
BV4447.S7265 2008
259'.1—dc22

                                                    2008017133

Contents

Foreword to First Edition   7

Preface to First Edition   9

Preface to Revised Edition   12

Chapter 1: What Is Youth and Family Ministry?   15

Chapter 2: Strengthening Family Relationships   40

Chapter 3: Fostering Close Relationships with God   76

Chapter 4: Faith-Focused Christian Education   111

Chapter 5: Congregations As Family   164

Chapter 6: Creating a Christian Youth Subculture   195

Chapter 7: Healthy Communities, Healthy Children   237

Chapter 8: Transforming Today's Culture   268

Chapter 9: The Circle of Creation   296

Chapter 10: From Vision to Action   316

Chapter Notes   339

Resource List   360

Selected Bibliography   365

Index   371

Foreword to First Edition

Families have extraordinary power to shape the lives of their children. This is so obvious that one would think it unnecessary to say. Unfortunately, a conspiracy of social forces has diminished the influence of family. Take, for example, the importance of a child's educational achievement. Educators know that the highest level of learning occurs when family and school interact as partners, moving in the same direction during a child's educational development. Families create positive learning environments at home—modeling, encouraging, and rewarding learning, while schools respect and encourage this family engagement. The family-school partnership is reinforced by frequent parent-teacher dialogues and parent engagement in school policies and programs.

This partnership is essential. Unfortunately, it is also uncommon. National studies tell us that all too often families give away their power and depend on schools alone to promote their children's achievement. And then the finger pointing begins. Teachers blame parents for being too busy with work and personal agendas to be attentive to the family role in learning. Parents blame schools for being out of touch with family pressures. Certainly, the reasons for parents' lack of involvement are complicated. But the reality is that family influence on learning has gone underground; it has become a latent, dormant power.

Families' influence on faith development parallels this reality. We know from documented studies and from our own intuition that parents are essential actors in their children's faith journey. Theoretically, congregations should support families in activating and using this power. Just as quality learning results from a strong family-school partnership, family strength results from a solid congregation-family partnership. Again, the ideal gets sabotaged. The trend is for families to depend solely on congregations to nurture faith just as they tend to depend solely on schools to nurture academic achievement.

Now is the time to awaken a sleeping giant—the power of parents to teach and nurture in partnership with the institutions designed to support them in their efforts rather than replace them. *Passing On the Faith* is a timely, urgently needed guide for awakening the considerable power of family life in the faith journey of children. Weaving together the wisdom of its authors, stories from the field, and recent research, this book offers a compelling case for rethinking the role of congregations and for unleashing the capacity to trigger the faith-building capacity of families. Offering clear and doable steps to guide families through the transformation, *Passing On the Faith* proves to be very practical.

I recommend this book with the highest enthusiasm. It represents an important paradigm shift. Someday, because of this wise treatise, congregational leaders will evaluate their successes as much against the standard of how well they have empowered families as against the standard of how well they have "programmed" the precious and fleeting time they have with children and adolescents. And as family empowerment grows, faith will blossom far beyond the limits of the congregations.

Peter L. Benson, PhD
President
Search Institute

Preface to First Edition

This book addresses a major concern of Christian parents and congregational leaders: How can we increase the likelihood that our children will be committed to Jesus Christ and a life of service when they graduate from high school? We, the authors, address this concern with a new paradigm—a partnership between congregation and family in which primary responsibility for faith development is assumed by parents. We are passionately committed to this paradigm, arriving at similar convictions despite our contrasting orientations.

I, Merton Strommen, founder of Search Institute, have served thirty years as a research scientist at Search Institute and at other serving institutions. Search Institute has garnered knowledge on church youth through national frontier studies involving youth, congregations, colleges, seminaries, schools, and youth-serving community organizations. Because Search Institute is an independent agency, it is free to focus its studies on matters of faith, beliefs, and values. Psychologists and sociologists ignored these subjects in 99 percent of the studies they carried out in the early 1900s.

These three foci reflect my years of working with students and youth, both as a college pastor and as national youth director for the Lutheran Free Church. My work in these ministries raised questions that I thought research could answer and provided a theological setting for interpreting the research information.

The most influential and shaping influences of my life, however, are my two families. One family is my parental family, which is headed by a clergy father and mother of deep faith. This family helped me find my life direction. My other family is the family formed by me, my loving wife, and our five wonderful sons. This family has deepened my faith in Jesus Christ, inspiring me and providing me with much wisdom and spiritual insight.

I, Dick Hardel, was raised by a meddling Methodist mom and a hardworking German-Lutheran dad, who loved the Lord and loved the church. I attended Lutheran Church-Missouri Synod schools for twenty years, from first grade through seminary. This classic education has helped me throughout my twenty-plus years of ministry as a parish pastor with a focus on youth and family ministry. I have also served as a pastor of smaller and yoked (connected) rural congregations in South Dakota and larger suburban congregations in South Dakota and Florida. One of the congregations in which I served as pastor also had a parochial school.

In addition to my ministry training and experience, I have also been trained by older Ringling Brothers Barnum and Bailey Circus clowns to be a clown myself. For more than twenty-five years, I have been a Christ clown. I established Christ Clown College and have taught hundreds of youth and adults the art of clown ministry, traveling throughout North America and Europe.

For about three-and-a-half years I served as an assistant to the bishop of the Nebraska Synod of the Evangelical Lutheran Church in America. Because I was such a right-brained, creative thinker, I had no administrative responsibilities; rather I was a creative resource for the 274 congregations in the synod at that time.

My passion for ministry with children, youth, and their families connected me to the research of Dr. Strommen at Search Institute and the Youth and Family Institute of Augsburg College, where I have served as the executive director for the past five years.

Dr. Strommen and I both grew up in homes where the Christian faith was expressed and practiced. We both have a passion for strengthening families to nurture faith in the home. Merton is definitely a left-brained, sequential thinker. I am a playful right-brained person who thinks in pictures. Thus, this combination of our minds has produced a book that includes both research and stories.

Major research studies form the basis of the many facets of the conceptual model in this book (see page 14). We draw on four decades' worth of studies conducted by Search Institute, which are broadly enhanced by corroborative research from other sources.

Although some of the studies are from past decades, we still use them because their information is significant. Many of the older studies used multivariate analyses of data to identify underlying variables. This type of in-depth study is quite different from studies that involve simple polling efforts. Information from studies based on nothing more than percentages from polls has a much shorter life.

To illustrate the strength of our older studies, a fifteen-year trend analysis of data from a study called *Five Cries of Youth* showed almost no change in four of its five major facets of church youths' life. The study showed that over the years, the facets were scarcely affected by cultural determinants such as national events, increased media exposure, or national shifts in value orientations. This is the type of bedrock research information that we share in this publication.

This book is also filled with a wealth of examples of what dynamic congregations are doing to nurture faith among their people. Many of these examples come from unpublished material that resulted from a unique follow-up to Search Institute's *Effective Christian Education* study. In the follow-up study, researchers visited thirty congregations that were labeled "exemplary" and twenty-four ethnic minority congregations that were not involved in the original study to identify characteristics of congregational life contributing to their dynamic faith life.

Through our research and analyses of personal experiences, we intend to show why congregations should adopt our radical paradigm of youth and family ministry—a paradigm that will help congregations move from vision to action.

Preface to Revised Edition

At a pastor's conference a few years after the first edition of *Passing On the Faith* was written, I gave a presentation on the radical model for the twenty-first century for discipleship and evangelization. Afterward, a participant came up to me, thanked me for my presentation, and said, "But you forgot one circle of relationship with God." Before he could speak it, I said, "The circle of creation." "Exactly," he responded. I invited him to tell me more.

The man was Dr. Edward J. P. Hauser, who at the time was on the faculty of the University of North Carolina in Asheville and also was chairperson of the North Carolina Synod Bishop's Task Force for Caring for Creation. Since then I have learned much from him and many others about the environment and the need for Christians to care for creation. As a result we have revised both the radical model for youth and family ministry and Passing On the Faith. This new edition presents the expanded model, which includes the circle of creation (see chapter 9), and has also been updated throughout in light of new ideas and research that have emerged during the past decade. This includes research reported in *Soul Searching* (Oxford University Press, 2005), by Christian Smith, and the *Exemplary Youth Ministry Study* done at Luther Seminary in St. Paul, Minnesota, which confirm and update the focus and themes of this book.

This book is about passing on the faith from generation to generation, throughout the milestones of a person's life. Faith is created and nurtured by the Holy Spirit through the gospel. The vision underlying the radical model was developed in light of the theological principle that faith is formed by the Holy Spirit working through personal, trusted relationships, often, but not always, in our own homes.

Each concentric circle in the diagram that describes this vision represents a category of relationships in which the Holy Spirit nurtures and forms faith. The original circles of children and youth, family, congregation, community, and culture are now surrounded by the new circle of creation. The cross of Jesus Christ is in the center and connects to each circle. A youth and family ministry for the twenty-first century connects all the generations in the total ministry of the congregation and, through the cross of Christ, recognizes the work of the Holy Spirit shaping faith in all the circles of relationships.

What is radical about the model is putting children and youth in the center of the ministry and surrounding them with the primary church, which is the family, or household. The word *radical* does not mean "far out." It means "to go back to basic principles." That is what we are doing in this book.

The foundational theology of this holistic vision is a radical theology of the cross. A theology for the twenty-first century must bring radical good news. It must be realistic about the human condition in our world; it must clarify the relationship between God and human beings, bring people together, and enable them to live in a close relationship with God, one another, and all creation; it must bring freedom, justice, and mercy; and it must give and sustain life. This vision calls on members of the Body of Christ, the Church, and especially those who are trained as leaders within the communities of faith, to be agents of transformation in the world. A theology of the cross is a theology of faith and revelation. Faith is necessary in order to see God's hidden revelation. Through faith, human beings are able to recognize God in the Incarnation, in creation, in humility, in the shame of the cross, in suffering, in the empty cross and the empty tomb, in Resurrection, and in "the least of these."

Only through faith can people see God's love, mercy, gracious will, and marvelous saving acts in Christ. Through the cross, God reframes how people see God active in everyday life and in all the circles of relationships. The cross of Jesus Christ calls people of faith to live in the world, in a relationship with God and with all creation, so others can see the grace of God.

Dr. Dick Hardel

Conceptual Model
Youth and Family Ministry

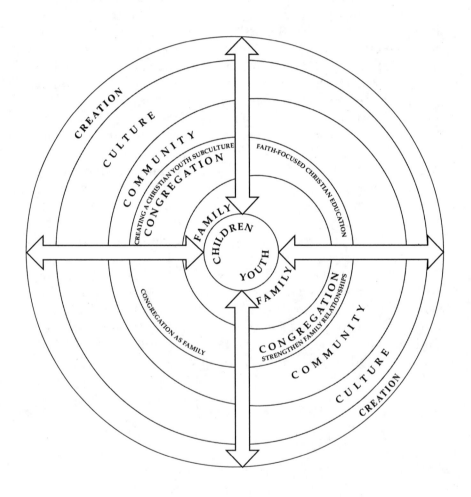

Chapter 1

What Is Youth
and Family Ministry?

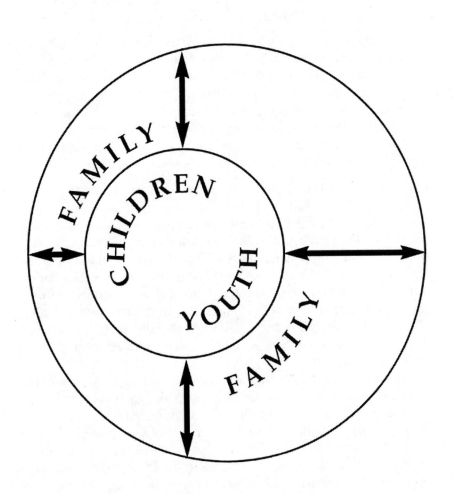

Thirty-five years of research in the Church shows that the relationship of faith to daily life has changed in our culture. According to major studies Search Institute has conducted in all the largest church bodies in America, fewer church families are producing the kind of youth whose hearts are committed to the mission of Jesus Christ. The studies conclude that we are losing our youth from the church and the faith as they turn to at-risk behaviors.[1]

In the book *Soul Searching,* Christian Smith explains that a large number of young people in the United States value religion not for the sake of God nor for its offer of life-transforming truth that brings eternal salvation. Rather, they value religion because it helps them be happy and make good choices.[2]

> It appears that only a minority of U.S. teenagers are naturally absorbing by osmosis the traditional substantive content and character of the religious traditions to which they claim to belong. For, it appears to us, another popular religious faith, Moralistic Therapeutic Deism, is colonizing many historical religious traditions and, almost without anyone noticing, converting believers in the old faiths to its alternative religious vision of divinely underwritten personal happiness and interpersonal niceness.[3]

Why are we losing these children? Because the tradition of passing on the faith in the home is disappearing for many members of Protestant and Catholic congregations. A study conducted in 1980 called *Young Adolescents and Their Parents* involved a national random sample of eight thousand adolescents whose parents were members of congregations in eleven different Protestant and Catholic denominations. The study showed that "God, the Bible, or religious things" are seldom discussed in church homes. Only 10 percent of church families discusses its faith with any degree of regularity; in 43 percent of the homes in these denominations, faith is never discussed.[4]

A similar study conducted in 1986 involved 7,551 students from 196 randomly selected Catholic schools. When asked how often their family talks about religious things, only 17 percent of the students claimed to discuss such topics at least once a week.[5]

In 1990 a national sample of youth and adults from six major Protestant denominations was asked the same question. Their response was no better: 35 percent of the youth, ages sixteen to eighteen, said they rarely, if ever, talked about faith or God with their mother, and 56 percent reported not ever having such discussions with their father. When asked how often they have devotions or worship as a family, 64 percent reported that their family rarely or never did so. Only 9 percent reported holding family devotions with any degree of regularity.[6]

As is obvious from these percentages, faith sharing is not happening today in most families of the church. It seems as though parents do not recognize their role in the faith growth of their children. As a result, children lack the undergirding that comes from being raised in homes that take matters of faith seriously. The effects of this lack are being noticed. A 1997 national study entitled *Kids These Days: What Americans Think About the Next Generation* reported that two-thirds of the two thousand adults surveyed came up with negative adjectives like *rude, wild,* and *irresponsible* when they were asked to describe teenagers. Nearly half of those surveyed described younger children as spoiled, and only 37 percent believed today's youngsters might eventually make this country a better place.

This study clearly demonstrates a fundamental concern about teenagers' moral and ethical values: "Americans are convinced that today's adolescents face a crisis—not in their economic or physical well-being but in their values and morals."[7] Only a minority of families today are orienting their children to a life of faith, service, and responsible living. This does not have to be our future. Strong, ethically oriented, life-shaping families are indeed as possible today as they were decades ago.

God's Vision for Today's Families

Two basic concepts in the Bible reveal God's desire for families. The first has to do with *relationships*. The Scriptures focus not on the family as a collective unit but on how the relationship with a gracious God is passed on from parents to children; hence, what is written applies equally well to single-parent households, blended-family households, or any configuration that makes up a family. The Scriptures focus on the grace of God, no matter the family.

To children, Paul writes: "Honor your father and mother . . . that it may be well with you and you may live long on the earth." To parents, Paul writes: "And, fathers, do not provoke your children to anger, but bring them up in the discipline and instruction of the Lord" (Ephesians 6:2–4, NRSV). Paul preaches that mutual love and respect between adult and child is an important part of a family relationship. Each member of a family is to treat the others with the same love God shows us. As Jesus says, "Love one another as I have loved you" (John 15:12, NRSV).

A second requirement for families involves *priorities*. Christ says: "Seek first his kingdom and his righteousness and all these things will be given to you" (Matthew 6:33, NIV). "These things" includes family life. In case we fail to get that point, Jesus spells out his claim for being the center of our lives when he says:

> Anyone who loves father and mother more than me is not worthy of me; and anyone who loves his son or daughter more than me is not worthy of me; and anyone who does not take his cross and follow me is not worthy of me. Whoever finds his life will lose it, and whoever loses his life for my sake shall find it. (Matthew 10:37–39, NIV)

According to the Scriptures, a strong, life-shaping family needs to build and maintain two key relationships—a strong family relationship and a strong relationship with God. These relationships are two sides of the same coin. One side encourages bonding between parents and children. The other side encourages bonding with Jesus, the Christ—a relationship that enables the gospel of grace and forgiveness to be lived out. When these two types of relationships characterize a family, the family indeed becomes strong and life shaping. This is only possible, however, if parents seek to develop these essential relationships.

An important question to ask is, How can the congregation most faithfully and effectively encourage and support faith formation in the home, intentionally attending to its critical role in the family-congregation partnership?

A New Paradigm Is Needed

Church leaders increasingly realize that a child's life is directly affected by what happens in the home. Leaders recognize that to pass on the faith from generation to generation, a new paradigm of ministry is needed—one that is holistic and connects children, youth, family, congregation, community, culture, and creation. These are all areas of relationships where the Holy Spirit works and shapes faith. Faith formation is for everyone, not just children. The journey of faith is a community activity that connects to all the concentric circles of relationships. To effectively pass on faith from generation to generation, the domestic church (home) and the public church (congregation) must work in partnership.

The current paradigm has subtly conveyed the impression that faith is nurtured only in the church buildings. This has ultimately institutionalized the faith, a phenomenon found in both the Roman Catholic and Protestant churches.

Fr. Robert Stamschror describes how this has come to characterize the Roman Catholic Church:

> The common understanding of the role of the family as a partner with the institution in faith formation was to give birth to the child, present it for baptism, enroll it in a Catholic school or CCD program, and make sure that the child attended Mass and received all the appropriate sacraments. It is important again to note here that the operative perspective of Faith during these times was primarily focused on the content and forms of Faith, that is, the beliefs that the church taught about God and what a Catholic practice should be in the light of those beliefs.[8]

In parallel fashion, the teaching and nurturing of faith in Protestant congregations today is associated primarily with the church building, or what is often called the "Godbox." When people talk about God and faith only in the buildings of the congregation, then God is in a box. Over the years the message has been, "Let the professionals do the teaching. They know best." So, parents send their children to the church for Sunday school or other religious instruction, handing the responsibility of faith education to the teachers.

Parents who believe their responsibility has ended when they have transported their children to church schools are not bad parents, however. They simply do not know how to nurture the faith, because it probably was not modeled in their own homes when they were growing up. The good news is that some parents want to learn how to form and nurture faith in their children; they want to participate in the family-congregation partnership.

In this book we use the term *family* in its broadest definition. A single person has a family, because she or he converses with at least two or three people two or three times a week if not daily. This unit, then, constitutes family. Some families may have children, whereas others may not. Like families in the Scriptures, we include friends and mentors, as well as relatives, in our definition of *family*. Our family is those people with whom we share our faith, values, and purpose as they relate to a life of hope and love.

A Realistic Vision: Ten Characteristics of Committed Youth

The vision we authors present in this book is a partnership between family and congregation that will encourage and support the Ten Characteristics of Committed Youth that mark a life of commitment to Jesus Christ and a life of witness and service. We have identified the following ten characteristics:

1. Trusting in a personal Christ
2. Understanding grace and living in grace
3. Communing with God regularly
4. Demonstrating moral responsibility
5. Accepting responsibility in a congregation
6. Demonstrating unprejudiced and loving lives
7. Accepting authority and being personally responsible
8. Having a hopeful and positive attitude
9. Participating in the rituals of a Christian community
10. Engaging in mission and service

Dare we pray that God can accomplish these characteristics in the lives of youth and adults? Knowing that God has accomplished them in the lives of many former youth and adults, we must now determine how we can help increase the probability that these characteristics will become a reality for the youth and adults currently in our congregations.

The answer presented in this book considers the interactive effect of six levels of influence: peer (youth to youth), family, congregation, community, culture, and creation. Each level of influence significantly contributes to the characteristics we desire for our children and youth, and each level needs to be part of our ministry.

Though six levels of influence are involved, the most powerful influence comes from the family, especially parents. The evidence is overwhelming that the probabilities of seeing committed youth are greatest when family members are bonded to one another in close relationships and bonded to God in close relationships. Recent research on the religious and spiritual lives of American teenagers confirmed the importance of parents and extended family in faith formation.

> Contrary to popular misguided cultural stereotypes and frequent parental misperceptions, we believe that the evidence clearly shows that the single most important social influence on the religious and spiritual lives of adolescents is their parents. Grandparents and other relatives, mentors, and youth workers can be very influential as well, but normally, parents are most important in forming their children's religious and spiritual lives.[9]

The term *probability* is one we use advisedly, because we cannot guarantee that specific children will mature with a committed faith. Faith is a gift from God to be received and nurtured by sinful human beings, and although the Christian faith is given to children in Baptism, not all children are willing to retain this gift through daily renewal. Not all parents who have their children baptized teach and nurture this faith in the lives of their children. The influence of family, peers, congregation, community, culture, and creation determines whether children and youth become people of mature faith. Faith is formed by the Holy Spirit through personal, trusted relationships in all six of these areas.

A New Paradigm for Faith Formation

A faith-formation paradigm limited to religious instruction for children and a youth group for high school students no longer equips one generation to pass on the faith effectively to the next generation. A paradigm shift is needed—one that results in a more comprehensive approach and fosters faith through relationships with peers, family, the congregation, the community, culture, and creation (see fig. 1).

Figure 1

Our Desired Outcomes

The need for this shift is widely felt. In September 1976 the United States Catholic Conference's (USCC's) Department of Education published *A Vision of Youth Ministry*. Now, more than three decades later, new challenges confront the Roman Catholic Church's ministry with adolescents. In 1997 *Renewing the Vision: A Framework for Catholic Youth Ministry* was published as a comprehensive and holistic ministry with younger and older adolescents. It includes an emphasis on the church of the home, or the family, as the first community and the most basic way in which God gathers us, forms us, and acts in the world. This vision, also emphasizing extended family, the parish, the positive building blocks of the whole community, and the present culture, helps congregations move into a new paradigm of youth and family ministry.[10]

John Roberto, founder of the Center for Ministry Development, created an approach to faith formation that embraces the vision of moving beyond a schooling paradigm to a "whole Church" paradigm. Called *Generations of Faith,* the approach stresses lifelong faith formation centered on the events of Church life, on faith growth in the home, and on connecting all the generations.[11]

Such a paradigm shift connects silent generations (people over sixty-five years of age), perhaps the most-churched group of people in the history of our country, to the millennial kids, who do not know the stories of God's gracious love and how these stories relate to their lives. This new vision identifies the family as God's domestic church and the congregation as God's communal Church. The peer relationships, home, congregation, community, culture, and creation are viewed as providing the context within which faith-lives are shaped.

As the first and most basic community, the family acts as a model for other, larger faith-learning communities. Diana Garland, director of the Family Ministry Project located at Louisville Presbyterian Theological Seminary, in Kentucky, defines *family.* According to her, the model of family that Jesus endorses is the adoptive family. The last act of Jesus' earthly ministry recorded in the Gospel of John enacts that adoptive model. Jesus turns to his mother and says, "Woman, behold your son." Then turning to the beloved disciple he says, "Behold your mother." The Church follows Christ by ensuring that no one in the family of faith is familyless—everyone is adopted into the family.[12]

A Partnership Between Family and Congregation

In her book *Family: The Forming Center,* Marjorie Thompson raises the all-important question "What if the family were not merely an object of the church's teaching mission, but one of the most basic units of the church's mission to the world?" She continues, saying, "What I am suggesting is that the communal church and the domestic church need to recapture a vision of the Christian family as a sacred community. This will require an awareness of the 'sacred' in the 'secular,' of God in the flesh of human life."[13] Wendy Wright, in her book *Seasons of a Family's Life: Cultivating the*

Contemplative Spirit at Home, gives lessons on gaining awareness of discovering the sacred that is present in the busyness of everyday family life.[14]

Stamschror, former editor for Saint Mary's Press Family Faith-Life Resources, identifies this awareness as an important part of family life, saying, "A personal and trusting adherence to God is the proper aspect of faith to be nourished in the family setting."[15]

In its latest conceptual model, *Passing On Faith,* The Youth & Family Institute presents a partnership of family and congregation in which the home is viewed as the primary place for teaching and nurturing the faith. Because the beginning years for this are pre-birth to age six, and most Sunday schools do not begin instruction until a child is age three, half the primary years for nurturing faith are lost for children who do not receive this guidance at home. The congregation is available simply to strengthen parents and other primary caregivers in their ability to evangelize the children whom God has placed in their lives.[16]

Many congregations already have begun faith formation ministries based on the suggestions and concepts of Marjorie Thompson, John Roberto, and The Youth & Family Institute. In 1991 Our Lady of Guadalupe, a Roman Catholic church in Helotes, Texas, adopted an alternative model to religious education called family-centered catechesis. Their approach is based on a "Family Perspective" document prepared by the United States bishops in 1988, which includes the following four principles:

1. *A Christian Vision of Family Life*
   The family has a unique identity and mission that permeates its tasks and responsibilities.

2. *The Family As a Developing System*
   The family is not a collection of individuals but a living and developing system whose members are essentially interconnected.

3. *Family Diversity*
   Diversity in structure, economic status, special needs, ethnic and religious heritages, and the influence of societal trends affect the roles and activities of families today.

4. *The Partnership Between Families and Social Institutions*
   Partnerships need to be formed between families and the institutions that share family responsibilities.[17]

Cynthia Tejeda, coordinator of Family Faith Development and Social Concerns at Our Lady of Guadalupe, remembers the benefits that came to her home from a family life program in her congregation when she was a ninth grader. Curious about how these ideas could affect the parish she now served, she introduced family-centered catechesis to several families gathered in a home. Out of this small pilot effort has emerged a family-centered approach that has established a new paradigm for religious education.

To provide resources and support for parents involved, her congregation introduced three options for families to choose from. The first is a type of family Sunday school for all ages: a parish-based, intergenerational faith-formation experience for the whole family offered one Sunday a month. In addition to a thirty-minute gathering and family activity period, there is a forty-five-minute learning time for each age-group: children through adults.

The second option is a program called *Seasons of Faith*. It is for all ages, and it uses a home-based approach to a family-centered catechesis. Each household is provided a home resource book (with lectionary-based lessons for each week) and an adult workbook along with an age-appropriate book for children and youth. Parents are instructed how to use these materials in settings other than the classroom.

The third option focuses on a parish-based experience that is offered three times a month for different age-groups. The classes are facilitated by an adult, high school peer minister, or mentor. Parents can choose to be involved in one, two, or all three of these options.

As might be expected, this revolutionary innovation took time to establish, and it received resistance at first. Some said: "We hired you to teach our children and youth. That is your job, not ours. You have the training and expertise." Others said: "We can't be responsible for the faith development of our children. We don't know what to say. We have had no training in Christianity since childhood." A few families actually left their churches to find other parishes to be responsible for their children's religious education.

But Our Lady of Guadalupe has not suffered. When the family-centered catechesis was introduced in 1990, there were seven hundred families in the parish. By 1998, there were 2,400 families, with 65 percent of the members under thirty-five years of age. Obviously, parents with children have been joining this parish.

Although much of the growth has to be credited to the congregation's location in a quickly growing area, the paradigm shift has not deterred people from joining. On the contrary, parents have expressed enthusiasm for this approach, saying:

- "We appreciate being involved in our child's learning."
- "We appreciate the availability of options and the flexibility this approach gives our family."
- "We have closer family relationships."
- "We are getting acquainted with the Bible and learning how to use it."
- "We are having prayer together as a family."

Tejeda, who has had the full support of her pastor and church council, identifies the following assumptions underlying the paradigm they have adopted:

- The family is the domestic church.
- Family life is sacred and holy.
- Both parish and family have responsibilities in promoting family faith growth.
- Because family life has changed significantly, approaches to religious education must reflect, respect, and embrace the contemporary family.
- Parents are the primary educators of their children in faith.
- Families and the parish need time to adjust to change; fear and resistance should be expected.
- Parents and guardians need resources and support to build confidence in their ability to form their children in faith.[18]

Another congregation has also shifted responsibility. Concordia Lutheran Church in Kirkwood, Missouri, decided to shift the responsibility for faith formation to the family. Ben Freudenburg, former minister of Christian Home, took sabbatical visits to various congregations only to realize that the congregation of which he was director of Christian education was church-centered and home-supported. Excited to take on the challenge of developing a home-centered, church-supported congregation, he introduced the idea to his senior pastor and the governing board. The idea gained full support. To reflect this shift, the congregation revised its mission statement to read as follows:

Concordia-Kirkwood is a sending community called together by the Spirit of Christ—celebrative and imaginative in worship, *SEEKING TO MAKE THE CHRISTIAN HOME THE PRIMARY AGENCY FOR FAITH FORMATION*—shaping, nurturing and equipping the people of God for the ministry for which they have been gifted and to which they have been called.[19]

This mission statement, the result of a long process, is undergirded by the following basic assumptions:

- Our world has changed from a "churched" to an "unchurched" society.
- The critical unit to hand on the faith and its resulting values is the Christian home.
- The Christian congregation is a most valuable community for meeting an unchurched society through the Christian home.

This particular congregation decided to use the phrase *Christian home* rather than the word *family,* because many people feel excluded by the word *family.* The word *agency* refers to home because it is to be seen as a "God-ordained place." The phrase *primary agency* draws attention to the fact that the home is to receive the primary attention and energy of the congregation.

The mission statement also identifies the areas in which the shift of responsibility is to occur: worship, home, and training. The shift to becoming family centered is seen in such programs and activities as family daily vacation Bible school, family Bible hour, and family worship services. Parents shift from being cooks and taxi drivers to being equippers of faith. For Freudenburg, a program of training parents to communicate, show caring, and become involved in faith building is at the heart of a congregation's ministry.

Convinced by his studies and observations that faith should be taught and modeled in the home, Freudenburg decided he should begin in his own home. Over a period of time, he tried to create in his own home what he would like to see become a reality in the homes of his congregation. In a book based on his experiences, *The Family-Friendly Church,* Freudenburg lays the groundwork for a shift in thinking from a church-centered, home-supported ministry to a home-centered, church-supported ministry.[20] This shift, however, requires families to be strong, receiving encouragement from many areas.

Bethlehem Lutheran Church in Aberdeen, South Dakota, has experienced phenomenal growth as a faith community by using the model of The Youth & Family Institute that focuses on a partnership of home and congregation in nurturing faith, living well in Christ, and passing on the faith. They are responding to basic questions people ask: "What does it mean to be family? Could it be about God? To whom do we turn for help?" The buildings of Bethlehem Church have become a training center to equip uncles, aunts, godparents, neighbors, friends, grandparents, and parents in how to nurture faith and pass it on to the children in their lives. They gather people of all generations to help with this discipleship training.

Many faith communities of the Roman Catholic Church are experiencing the joy of new growth through the work of John Roberto and the leaders of *Generations of Faith*. Their work includes a focus on the partnership of domestic church (home and family) and public church (congregation) in lifelong learning of faith.[21]

Strategies for Strengthening Family

Assist Parents in the Baptismal Journey

To help congregations shift the responsibility of religious instruction, Dr. Roland D. Martinson, professor of pastoral theology at Luther Seminary; Dr. Richard Hardel, senior fellow and former executive director of The Youth & Family Institute; and David W. Anderson, program director of The Youth and Family Institute, have developed a strategy for ministry that fosters a partnership between the communal and domestic churches. They call it *Passing On Faith*.

The partnership is introduced by a home visitation team made up of a male and a female, one of them being from the most-churched generation, those over age sixty-five. The teams meet with families at various milestones (e.g., Baptism, the start of school, driver's license, Confirmation, graduation, new job, retirement). Before a Baptism, for example, the team prepares the family and child for the upcoming milestone by presenting information on baptismal grace, the importance of prayer, faith communication in the home, child development, and faith-informed child rearing, as well as ideas and resources for maintaining faith life in the household. During the visit, the families are given a *FaithChest* and a *FaithLife in the Home Resource and Gift Guide*.[22]

Stored in the *FaithChest* and listed in the *FaithLife in the Home Resource and Gift Guide* might be the following items: musical CDs, a Bible, faith-in-daily-life storybooks, a baptismal candle and other remembrances of one's Baptism, *FaithTalk with Children* cards, games, and DVDs. These items can be used for communicating faith at times when family members intersect with one another—bedtime, car time, lap time, sick time, mealtime, vacation time, and other significant family times.

The *Passing On Faith* model presents six strategies that connect the milestones in a family's life with God. The milestones are to be celebrated not only in the home but also in a congregational festival worship service followed by a reception for the child and the family members. These worship celebrations and all other worship services are designed to be friendly for children and youth as well as adults.

During these contacts the congregation informs the parents of positive, Christian parenting support and resources available in a variety of forms, varying from moms' and dads' days out, to parent support groups, to DVDs, to classic parenting books, to family counseling, to parenting mentors and networks.

Recent research confirms that if we want Christian children practicing faith, then we must have practicing Christian adults. If our desired outcomes are nurturing faith and passing on the faith, then it is more important for children to be worshiping in corporate worship (Mass) with their parents and family than to be in Sunday school without their parents or family.

Congregations in the *Passing On Faith* model also sponsor intergenerational training events to equip uncles, aunts, moms, dads, grandparents, godparents, and other caregivers with the skills and understanding needed to nurture faith at a specific milestone in a young person's life. To assist congregations in sponsoring intergenerational training events that connect faith with specific milestones, The Youth & Family Institute has created a *Milestones Ministry Manual* that includes intergenerational helps within corporate worship and also activities for other intergenerational events. You can find this resource on their Web site.

Work for Long-Lasting Marriages

In their book *A New Day for Family Ministry,* Richard Olson and Joe Leonard conclude that congregations must have an active ministry that focuses on strengthening existing marriages. A partnership between household and congregation requires stable and long-lasting marriages. It is important to counter the shattering effect of divorce by helping couples make their relationships enduring and by helping divorced people develop new relationships, healed, healthy, and hope filled.[23]

To help the Church realize this objective, Mike McManus and his wife, Harriet, of Fourth Presbyterian Church in Bethesda, Maryland, developed a "Marriage Savers" movement. They introduced the idea of citywide agreements about marriage preparation and marriage agreements to pastors and congregations. According to McManus, the divorce rate in Modesto, California, the first city to adopt such an agreement, dropped 40 percent during one decade. Obviously other factors could have contributed to this drop, but the contribution of "Marriage Savers" to the drop is evident. A 12 percent drop was noted in Fairbanks, Alaska, over seven years; a 28 percent drop in Peoria, Illinois, over six years; and a 35 percent drop in Modesto, California, over eleven years.[24]

When St. Paul and Minneapolis adopted the Twin Cities Community Marriage Policy in 1997, they became the largest metropolitan community to have adopted a marriage agreement. The signers included bishops and denominational executives from a diverse Christian spectrum, along with representatives of the Jewish and Islamic communities. The policy calls for a minimum of four months of marriage preparation and a minimum of four premarital counseling sessions that involve use of the Bible, a premarital inventory, and intensive education. In addition, the faith leaders are expected to do the following:

- strongly encourage additional retreats, classes, and marriage enrichment opportunities designed to build and strengthen marriages
- train mature couples to serve as mentors to engaged couples, newlyweds, or couples experiencing marriage difficulties
- use or develop programs for couples with troubled marriages, allowing some mentoring to be done by couples whose own marriages were once in trouble

- use or develop support systems for couples with stepfamilies and couples of different religious backgrounds[25]

Greater care in preparing couples for marriage and in strengthening these marriages will enhance the partnership between family and congregation in the faith formation of children and youth. Preparation can address the growing phenomenon of couples living together before marriage. By 1990, 45 percent of unmarried adults had cohabited, and 39 percent of married couples had lived with their spouse before marriage.[26] But living together before marriage is no guarantee of marital success; in fact, couples who live together first divorce at higher rates (38 percent) than couples who live separately before marriage (27 percent).

A study entitled *The Relationship Between Cohabitation and Divorce,* by researchers William Axinn and Arland Thornton of UCLA, confirms this data. They found that marriages preceded by cohabitation were 50 to 100 percent more likely to end than those marriages not preceded by cohabitation.[27]

Encourage Parents to Be Spiritual Leaders

In "The Role of Work and Family in the Faith and Value Formation of Children," Dr. Roland D. Martinson notes the central role parents have played in passing on faith to their children.[28] The parental role was established by Moses when he instructed parents to keep the theological and ethical core of God's word at the center of Israel's life:

> Keep these words that I am commanding you today in your heart. Recite them to your children and talk about them when you are at home and when you are away, when you lie down and when you rise. Bind them as a sign on your hand, fix them as an emblem on your forehead, and write them on the doorposts of your house and on your gates. (Deuteronomy 6:6–9, NRSV)

This is *radical.* This is going back to basic principles. Note in the text above that the home is the primary place of faith formation, not the temple or synagogue. The responsibility to teach and nurture faith is that of the parents and extended family.

Walter Brueggemann, theologian and seminary professor, notes that in the biblical world, the family is the primary unit of meaning, shaping and defining reality: "One major function of intergenerational life is to transmit the stories and promises which identify the family, so that each new generation has an inheritance that gives both identity and roots, purpose and vocation."[29]

The major ritual and tradition through which families in the Old Testament celebrated God's story and Israel's identity was the seder meal (ceremonial dinner) held every Friday evening when the family gathered at the table. During this and other family rituals, the father and mother functioned as priest, spiritual teacher, and leader.

In the *Passing On Faith Conference Participant's Manual,* David W. Anderson notes that Martin Luther, in his sermon "The Estate of Marriage," reflected his convictions about the role of father and mother in these words:

> Most certainly father and mother are apostles, bishops, and priests to their children, for it is they who make them acquainted with the Gospel. In short there is no greater or nobler authority on earth than that of parents over their children, for this authority is both spiritual and temporal.[30]

There are, of course, many families in which only one parent is able to serve as a spiritual leader. Though the task is more difficult for that parent, the objective of making the home a center for nurturing the faith and experiencing the presence of God should remain the same.

An important aspect to consider in fostering the family as God's domestic church is the role of father. Organizations such as the Promise Keepers, the National Center for Fathering, and the National Fatherhood Initiative emphasize that fathering is one of the most important and challenging tasks men face. These and other organizations have worked to revitalize congregational men's groups and return men to a greater sense of responsibility for their roles as spiritual leaders in their homes. Many denominational men's organizations, as well as local congregations, have responded to the need to strengthen the father's role as a nurturer of faith in the home through spiritual renewal retreats, workshops on developing spiritual disciplines, and seminars on spiritual leadership in the home. Lyman Coleman, working with The Youth & Family Institute, has developed a powerful ministry with men, Men Marked with the Cross of Christ, to help them grow in faith and become strong spiritual leaders in the home and congregation. He first began working with some Roman Catholic men's ministries and then with Lutheran and Presbyterian men. In the book *Coming of Age,* the authors, Dr. David Anderson, Dr. Paul Hill, and Dr. Roland Martinson, encourage congregations to mentor young men to be faithful fathers and pass on the faith to their children.[31]

This important role of spiritual leader is increasingly neglected as the presence of fathers in many families diminishes. Wade F. Horn, director of the National Fatherhood Initiative, says that in 1960 the total number of children living in fatherless families was fewer than eight million. By 1997 the total had risen to nearly twenty-four million. Today nearly four out of ten children in America are being raised in homes without fathers, and authorities predict that soon it will be six out of ten.[32]

In addition to the absence of fathers, the absence of mothers is also increasing. Mothers seem to be abandoning their children, turning the responsibility over to the grandparents. Across the country more than 633,000 grandparents have become the primary caregivers for more than one million children.

Connie Booth, a counselor with Lutheran Social Service in Minneapolis, has witnessed this increase in Minneapolis. "It seems to be connected with the rise of the crack cocaine epidemic," she says.

> [Mothers] got involved with drugs or alcohol and because of that they are no longer able to parent. In some cases, the kids were just dropped off on the grandparents' doorstep. In other cases, the grandparents had to really fight to get the kids out of the home.

> [This problem] crosses all socioeconomic bounds. We have grandparents in the inner city and in our wealthy suburbs who are raising their grandchildren. Nobody seems to be immune to this. Many are caring for their grandchildren in an unofficial capacity. They don't want to report their children to the county social workers, so they simply step in and do what needs to be done.[33]

The statistics show the increasing number of parents—mothers and fathers alike—who renounce their responsibility to be spiritual leaders in the home. This lack of responsibility comes at a high cost not only to the children being neglected but also to society as a whole.

Consider the High Cost of Neglect

Jack Westman, child psychiatrist at the University of Wisconsin, used calculations based on the cost of public services in Wisconsin in 1994 to create a worst-case scenario. He chose a child born to an incompetent single parent on welfare who grows into a habitual criminal and spends forty years of his life in prison. The cost to society is two million dollars. This stands in contrast to the one million dollars contributed by a productive child raised by a competent parent.

Westman believes that the right to parent should be earned, because parenting is a responsibility and a privilege. His argument is that incompetent parents cost society enormous amounts of money; therefore, some requirements should be placed on parents. In his controversial book, *Licensing Parents: Can We Prevent Child Abuse and Neglect?* he suggests the following three requirements:

1. Parents must be at least eighteen years of age.
2. Parents must make a written commitment to rearing a child (similar to applying for a marriage license).
3. Parents must attend parenting classes before the birth of their child.

Westman says his requirements encompass three key predictors of bad parenting:

- being too young to control one's life
- having no commitment to child rearing
- having no knowledge of child rearing

He is joined in his argument by David Lykken, a professor at the University of Minnesota, who since 1970 has worked on a world-renowned study of twins. His research on psychopathic personalities has led him to examine the link between children born out of wedlock and violent crime. Out of his research has come the book *The American Crime Factory: How It Works and How to Slow It Down.* Lykken notes that the "American Crime Factory" is turning out potential sociopaths at an ever-increasing rate. Instead of building more and more prisons, we should be trying to stop the assembly line.

Hennepin County officials in Minneapolis have estimated that in terms of 1988 dollars, they have spent more than $2 million dealing with the seventy offenses committed by seven children of one family. A total of twenty-nine institutions and programs have been used in an attempt to rehabilitate members of this family—to no avail, however.

Reviewing the records of ten other such families, a probation officer, David Seeler, said, "It's baffling to see how ineffective all these programs are, and it's disturbing to see the court throw all this money at these kids with no results. The flip side is: What else can one do?"[34]

The difficulty of changing the lives of young people raised by incompetent parents is discussed in the book *Castaways: The Penikese Island Experiment.* The author, George Cadwalader, a Marine veteran of Vietnam, established an Outward Bound–type program for juvenile delinquents on Penikese Island off Massachusetts. He hoped that the delinquent kids would learn self-worth by living in a pure environment and would grow in self-confidence by participating in outdoor activities. After fifteen years of experimenting with this, he tried to evaluate the results of his effort. Of the first 106 boys who came to Penikese out of troubled homes, only sixteen turned themselves around. The other ninety went on to live lives of destruction.[35]

Although these cases are extreme, they do illustrate how vital it is for children to be raised by loving, responsible parents if they are to develop the Ten Characteristics of Committed Youth.

The importance of family life is being identified by many voices. Knut Andresen, then general director of the Church of Norway's National Council and author of "Youth in the Church of Norway," asked why 85 percent of youth are losing contact with the church after eight months of Confirmation classes, after one year in a church youth group, or in better cases, after six years as a member of a youth organization. After examining the data of an extensive survey, he came to the following conclusion:

> One explanation is the family. We never talk about faith at home. That goes for regular churchgoers. They are mostly leaving it to the professionals—that means the pastors, the lay staff, and other church officials—or to grandmothers. They might worship in the church on Sunday, but they don't have family devotions, prayer, or Bible reading. They might talk about faith with other members of the congregation, but they are very seldom talking about faith at home.[36]

Figure 2

Change in Family Closeness

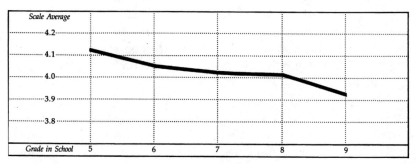

Item: "Members of my family get along well with each other." Based on the average of 5 items. 5 = almost always true; 4 = often true; 3 = sometimes true; 2 = true once in a while; 1 = never true

From *Young Adolescents and Their Parents: A National Portrait,* copyright ©1984 by Search Institute®. Reprinted with permission of Search Institute®. All rights reserved.

Provide Help in Parenting

People learn by experience. For this reason it is easy to assume that the new parents, not the older ones, need instruction and ministry. Research shows, however, that experience does not necessarily equip parents for the responsibilities they face in this role.

Evidence from two major studies shows that family relationships decline in closeness as parents gain experience. Family unity and closeness decline steadily from the childless stage to the adolescent-raising stage in the family cycle. Relationships are at their lowest ebb when children are adolescents.

This was discovered in a national study of eight thousand early adolescents and ten thousand parents randomly chosen from congregations in eleven major denominations. Youth and parents, independent of one another, both reported less unity and closeness as the children moved in age from fifth to ninth grade (see fig. 2). There was a discernible decline in parental harmony, communication, parental control, and expressions of love as children approached adolescence.[37] It is apparent that parents need more than experience to develop the kind of families that are life shaping.

Though premarriage counseling, family counseling, and youth counseling are made available, people still may seek divorce, have children out of wedlock, or remarry to form a stepfamily. In other words, a ministry is sharply limited in its ability to alter the nature of family structures other than to emphasize the importance of long-lasting marriages and to model such marriage relationships.

Nor can much be done about the resources people bring into a marriage such as income or level of education. True, some things can be done to improve the level of income or to encourage further education, but as a whole, little can be done to alter these factors in family happiness. The same applies to such background variables as race, gender, and age. These are givens that do affect family happiness, but little can be done to change them.

What, then, is within the scope of a ministry to parents? The one area of possibility can be labeled *family relationships*. At least five such variables are open for ministry:

1. marital relations or parental harmony
2. children's relationships with their residential fathers
3. children's relationships with their residential mothers
4. children's relationships with their nonresidential mothers
5. children's relationships with their nonresidential fathers

These variables are the most important in determining whether there are close relationships and happiness in a family. What is our basis for saying that?

In 1994 Alan Acock, sociologist at Oregon State University, and David Demo, professor of family studies at the University of Missouri, conducted a study called *Family Diversity and Well-Being*. They surveyed 13,017 households, collecting information on four thousand variables that would represent American families and households in their full breadth.[38]

From this study, Acock and Demo have been able to identify which factors are most influential in shaping the happiness, well-being, and emotional adjustment of children and parents. They studied the simultaneous effects of family structure, family resources, background variables, and family relationship variables. They found that family structure has a modest effect; family resources such as income and education have little effect; background variables have very little effect; and family relationship variables have an enormous effect on family happiness, irrespective of family structure, family resources, or background variables.

Family relationship variables are the aspects of family that can be influenced by congregational ministries. In the following list,

Dr. David Stoop summarizes what many counselors and psychologists have defined as characteristics of a healthy family:
- It is balanced; it can adapt to change.
- It handles problems on a family basis, not just an individual basis.
- It has solid cross-generational connections.
- It maintains clear boundaries between individuals.
- Its individuals deal with one another directly.
- It accepts and encourages differences.
- It accepts the thoughts and feelings of others.
- Its members know what they can give to others and what they can receive from others.
- It maintains a positive emotional climate.
- Its members value the family as "a good place to live."
- Its members learn from one another and encourage feedback.
- Its members are allowed to experience their own emptiness.

In short, the well-adjusted family has found a balance between two seemingly contradictory dynamics—being close and being separate. When either of these two dynamics gets seriously out of balance, the result is family dysfunction.[39]

God's desire for close family relationships can be viewed as a goal for closeness without possessiveness. It is a dimension of family life that a pastor can address.

A Vision for a Christian Family

We are aware, however, that a family is a complex organism in which the attitudes, values, and actions of each member interact with one another. Changes do not come easily, because of the unpredictable reaction of different members to any proposed change. Each individual family and each congregational family is unique. Though we recognize the family as a system in which each member often lives out a designated role, we believe changes are possible where there is both intention and willingness to live by God's promises in the Bible.

Eight desired outcomes (to be described in chapters 2 and 3) combine to shape the lives of children and youth. Each desired outcome contributes to the Ten Characteristics of Committed Youth. The more factors found in a family, the greater the likelihood that these ten characteristics will describe its youth.

We believe that these eight desired outcomes can be developed over time and that strong, life-shaping families are as possible today as they were fifty years ago. Many of today's families can prove this to be true. The one difference for today's families is that parents must become more intentional about what they do or don't do as a family. Becoming more intentional means doing for our families what we do in the area of health: stop doing the things that make for ill health (e.g., eating unhealthy foods, using drugs, smoking) and begin doing those things that make for good health (e.g., exercising, praying, eating healthy foods).

Chapters 2 and 3 identify those aspects of family life that make for good health and strength; chapter 2 identifies four factors that make for close family relationships, and chapter 3 identifies four factors that make for close relationships with God. If these factors are made a part of family life, they will vastly increase the probability that children will demonstrate the Ten Characteristics of Committed Youth at high school graduation.

The Ten Characteristics are best established in a young person's life when home and congregation partner in nurturing faith, living well in Christ, and passing on the faith.

Chapter 2

Strengthening Family Relationships

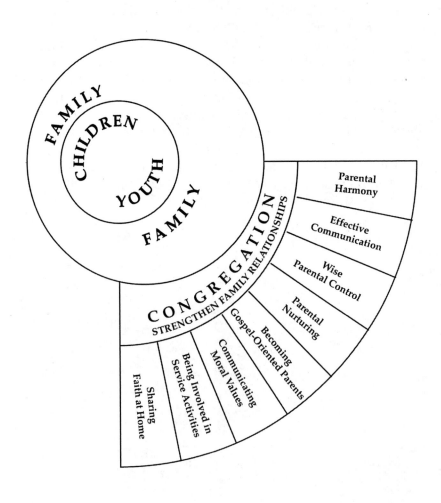

Close family relationships are important because faith is formed by the Holy Spirit through personal, trusting relationships. Healthy relationships within families can be developed and strengthened in four ways, each contributing to the formation of committed children and youth:

- parental harmony
- effective communication
- wise parental control
- parental nurturing

A Christian congregation can minister to families in all four ways because it is the one institution where membership and programs include all ages; it is the one organization whose purpose and message is to affect close family relationships; it is the one place where parents can experience the redemption found in a personal relationship with God. Through God, parents can find an inner sense of personal harmony that is essential for close relationships.

Parental Harmony

Parental harmony is the starting point. Of all the factors contributing to family disunity, marital discord is the strongest; it is at least twenty times more powerful a predictor of family disunity than is divorce.[1]

Parents set the tone and establish the atmosphere within a home. Their feelings about each other determine the climate of a home, establishing an atmosphere of love, trust, and security that nurtures the Ten Characteristics of Committed Youth and Children. Parental warmth and affection are important factors in healthy child adjustment and in turn are linked to the quality of marital relationships.[2]

Acock and Demo find a direct relationship between children's well-being and parents' marital adjustment. Marital stability, specifically the mother's marital happiness, shapes the context in which children live.[3] Parental harmony is far more important than family structure in contributing to children's adjustment, self-esteem, and various measures of psychological well-being.[4] It enhances their happiness, bolsters their academic performance, and plays a pivotal role in their socioemotional adjustment. The quality of family relationships accounts for much of the variation seen in the emotional adjustment of adolescents.[5]

Effects of Marital Discord

The importance of parental harmony in contributing to close relationships is seen in the long-lasting effects on children exposed to marital discord. In her fifteen-year study on the long-term effects of divorce on children, Judith Wallerstein found that almost half the children raised in families characterized by marital conflict, upon reaching young adulthood, were described as "worried, underachieving, self-deprecating, and sometimes angry young men and women. Many were involved in multiple relationships and impulsive marriages that ended in early divorce."[6]

A follow-up study conducted in 1993 to check the validity of Wallerstein's findings used longitudinal data from a national sample of American children born between 1965 and 1970. The study found that among eighteen- to twenty-two-year-olds from disrupted families, 65 percent had poor relationships with their fathers, and 30 percent had poor relationships with their mothers. A total of 25 percent had dropped out of high school, and 40 percent had received psychological help. Although the study was controlled for demographic and socioeconomic differences, it nonetheless shows that youth from disrupted families are twice as likely to exhibit these problems as youth from nondisrupted families.[7]

The research evidence from a number of studies is overwhelming. Parental harmony contributes enormously to the emotional health of children, whereas marital conflict is devastating in its long-lasting effects. Without question, an important ministry of a congregation is to promote parental harmony.[8]

Dynamics That Erode Parental Harmony

Those who conduct discussion groups with parents report that most parents find it difficult to acknowledge there are any difficulties in their family. Many will say their family is very loving and caring when it is not so. Others will refer to their family as quite religious when there is little evidence of this quality. The one thing a family is most ashamed of is often the very thing they try to cover over with a myth.

When parents were asked to characterize themselves in the *Young Adolescent-Parent National Survey,* the adjectives that the ten thousand parents favored to describe their relationships with others were *gentle, kind, confident,* and *warm.* Though fathers saw themselves as less able to devote themselves completely to other people than did mothers, they still regarded themselves as strongly helpful and somewhat aware of the feelings of others. Mothers considered themselves able to devote themselves completely to others, aware of people's feelings, and very warm in interpersonal relationships.[9]

Few parents realize that their behavior may be altered by emotional dynamics hidden from their conscious awareness that can subtly cloud their understanding and perception. If this happens, otherwise loving and insightful parents lose their ability to see that certain actions are inappropriate and at times hurtful to family relationships.

Unhealthy Behaviors Experienced in One's Family of Origin

As children grow into adults, they often become more and more like their parents, repeating behaviors their parents displayed at home. This can be a major deterrent to parental harmony. A pastor's wife once said, "What can I do about this habit of yelling at my kids? I don't believe that's the way to handle a situation, but it was the way Mom did it at home. It frightens me to think my children will do the same unless I change."

Repeating past behaviors can result in perpetuating verbal or physical abuse of one's spouse. If a father is critical, abusive, or at times violent with his wife, his son may be inclined to similar behaviors as an adult.

The behavior adopted from one's parental home, of course, may not be as obvious as verbal or physical abuse. It may be as subtle as the tendency not to express one's feelings, not to say "I love you," not to take an interest in the children, or not to pay attention to household responsibilities.

I (Merton Strommen) was influenced by my father, a Lutheran pastor who had a reputation of being strict. I had no idea I would repeat his behavior when, at age eighteen, I became a schoolteacher responsible for twenty-eight rural students in seven grades. I was determined to be a good teacher, and I worked hard at it, but, as I soon learned, my approach needed changing.

One night at the farmhouse where I roomed, I received a visit from the chairman and a member of the school board. They wanted to talk privately with me. They told me that some of the children were afraid of me and did not want to go to school. At first I was shocked, but the more I thought about it, the more I realized that my dad's strictness was surfacing in me and my teaching.

With this new insight, I set out to make changes that would positively affect the atmosphere of the school. Instead of pressing for perfection and correct responses from students, I began to concentrate on building relationships with them. I invited the students to help me put on the play *A Christmas Carol,* and I proposed the formation of a melody and rhythm band. In a short time, the students and I had developed an atmosphere conducive to working and learning as a team.

Because my strict demeanor was brought to my attention early on, I was able to recognize the pattern and make some important changes in how I related to the students. As a result we developed an atmosphere of working and learning together.

Wounded Memories, Hurtful Remembrances

A second deterrent to parental harmony is found in traumatic past events. Past experiences can profoundly affect how a person perceives and relates to a spouse and children. Unhealed and wounded memories can hinder people from developing close, long-lasting relationships. For this reason, mothers and fathers need to take time to recall and share experiences of their past with their spouse and their children. Doing so can help a spouse better understand a current reaction to an unhappy situation.

I (Merton Strommen) have a friend who told of an experience that haunted her throughout the few years of her married life. When she was in her early twenties, her mother died suddenly. No longer living in her hometown, my friend had to rush home for the funeral and hadn't had a chance to grieve. Her family gathered in the church basement prior to the service, and at the sight of their grief my friend began to unleash her feelings. The pastor, noticing her sobs, took her aside and sternly told her to stop grieving lest she unnerve her father. In response, she stuffed her feelings inside and buried her grief.

In the years that followed, she was haunted by a recurring nightmare in which her mother dug herself out of the grave, walked disheveled to the window of her father's house, and saw the woman to whom he was now married. Angered, her mother went to the door and pounded with her fists.

It was not until my friend's marriage had ended in divorce that she was finally able to shed some tears. Reverting back to the role of a daughter who had cried in her mother's lap, she cried for four hours over both the loss of her mother and the loss of her husband. After this period of grief, she felt a sense of peace, and never again did her nightmarish dreams recur.

Many people are hindered from developing close, long-lasting relationships because of unhealed, wounded memories. That is why a ministry that enables people to uncover such memories and become free of them is so releasing and redeeming.

Unmet Personal Needs, Unfulfilled Ambitions

A third deterrent to parental harmony occurs when parents try to live out unfulfilled dreams through their children. In doing so, they become prey to emotional upheavals every time their children show an inadequacy or fail to live up to the parents' expectations. This often shows up in youth soccer or baseball games when a father who never made it in athletics yells in disgust, trying to coach his child to succeed in doing what he never succeeded in doing. Or, a father-coach expects his child to do better than the others simply so the father can look good as coach.

Feelings of Failure

A fourth deterrent is found in parents who feel like failures. Half the parents in the *Young Adolescent-Parent National Survey* carry a nagging thought that they are not as good a parent as they should be. A national study of church women shows that this feeling of having failed as a parent increases with age and is strongest in widowed women over sixty-five.[10]

It is difficult to realize how deep and pervasive are the feelings of inadequacy that trouble many parents. Fathers thinking they have not succeeded in the work world are especially sensitive to how they are regarded as a parent. Mothers who try to maintain a job and care for household duties are particularly conscious of how their children respond at home or school. Of the fourteen concerns that surfaced in a national study of church women, the top ranked concern is worry over children.[10]

Parents who have been self-critical and troubled with low self-esteem since their youth are especially susceptible to feelings of failure; hence, they are likely to overreact when their children fail to obey or show proper respect. They interpret this as another sign of failure. Their natural reaction to the misbehaving child is to become more controlling and rule-oriented parents.

Each of the four deterrents to parental harmony can cause parents to become extremely angry about insignificant incidents. In some cases parents become so angry they are afraid they might hurt their spouse or children. Others react by becoming depressed and withdrawing into a lonely and condemning silence the whole family experiences but does not understand. Either reaction creates marital conflict and establishes a climate troubling to the children.

Stresses That Intensify Underlying Dynamics

Stress intensifies the effects of the four deterrents to parental harmony and further disturbs other relationships within the family. This stress is created by such things as work overload, the loss of a job, financial hardship, a major illness, a tragic accident, a natural disaster, a disability for a family member, a move to a new community, or an arrest.

A well-documented factor in the lives of working mothers is *multiple-role stress.* Although many mothers today are part of the work force, most of their husbands have not significantly increased their own household and child care responsibilities.

Since 1965 John Robinson, a professor of sociology at the University of Maryland, has conducted four studies on how Americans use their time. Every ten years he has asked a group of several thousand randomly selected adults to keep a diary for one day, requiring them to record what they did at particular times throughout the day. From these studies Robinson has concluded that the proportion of time parents spend with their children hasn't changed much in thirty years: mothers continue to spend about four times as much time with their children as fathers do.[11]

Other studies support Robinson's conclusion. In her study of fifty families, social scientist A. Hochschild reported that this unequal sharing of responsibility is the single most important cause of marital conflict.[12]

Another stress factor that disturbs family relationships is the loss of a child. Psychologist David M. Kaplan and his research team studied forty families that had lost a child to leukemia. Seventy percent of the parents showed evidence of serious marital problems. Forty percent of the families noticed the development of a serious drinking problem in at least one parent, and 43 percent of the mothers lost their ability to perform household duties. In addition to Kaplan's study, other studies show a high rate of divorce in families that lose a child.[13]

In most cases, the negative effects of any stress factor can be lessened by better communication between husband and wife. Because each partner experiences grief and handles emotional difficulties differently, it is important that couples share and listen to each other's deepest thoughts, feelings, and judgments. My wife and I (Merton Strommen) noticed the strong difference between our experiences when we compared first-draft copies of our account of the death of our son David. The difference was so marked that we retained these separate accounts in our book *Five Cries of Grief.*[14]

When good communication between husband and wife does not occur, the negative effects of stress can result in an even more stressful situation—divorce. As the divorce rate continues to increase—up 60 percent between 1980 and 1990—some parents and children continue to suffer from its effects.[15]

Parental roles differ substantially after divorce. Before parental separation, fathers usually carry major responsibility for the economic support of the family, but after divorce, the responsibility shifts substantially to mothers. This means that in single-parent families, the mother bears not only the load of household and parental responsibilities but also the pressing load of financial responsibility. This can often result in negative feelings toward the absent father, which can further affect the general climate of the home.

As the climate of the home changes, children become affected. In the first year after divorce, both boys and girls show more anxious, demanding, noncompliant, aggressive, and dependent behaviors with peers and adults than do children in nondivorced families. Young boys seem to be particularly affected. The result is a spiral of escalating hostility between mother and son.

The effects, nevertheless, are seen with all children, no matter their sex or age. The effects of marital discord and family disruption resulting from divorce are still visible in children some twelve to twenty-two years later. Children of divorced parents often develop poor relationships with their parents and high levels of problem behavior.[16]

> Parental separation and divorce are disruptive life course events that usually restructure relational networks and generally depress religious participation. Divorce and the death of a parent can also precipitate emotional crises for parents and children alike, which can be expressed as resentment or anger toward God.[17]

If remarriage occurs after a divorce, another stressful situation is introduced—stepparenting. Initially children can be resistant to the entrance of a stepfather or stepmother, because they view this person as an intruder who broke up their parents' marriage. Consequently, it takes longer for trust and acceptance to become established in a stepfamily. However, over time a sense of well-being can develop. In their study of American households, Acock and Demo found that mothers in stepfamilies exhibit a sense of well-being that is considerably higher than mothers who divorce but do not remarry. In fact, the sense of well-being is almost as high for remarried mothers as for mothers in first-marriage families. The initial stress apparently mitigates after the first three years of a newly formed family.[18]

What Congregations Can Do to Promote Parental Harmony

What about the dark side of family life in a congregation? To what extent are divorce, domestic violence and abuse, AIDS, suicide, and incest taking a toll on family life? That is what members of the Family Ministry Committee for the Southeastern California Conference of the Seventh-day Adventist Church wondered. For seven years they had been addressing the easy family issues. They had scheduled seminars on preparing for marriage, enriching marriage, developing parenting skills, and learning to evaluate family history. They had built an extensive resource library of videos, seminar workbooks, and audiotapes. They wanted to keep a positive attitude, yet they felt uneasy. If bad things are happening, they thought, and we pretend not to notice, are we really fulfilling our congregational ministry? How does this affect church members? If we avoid the dark side of family life, will the congregation think the church is completely out of touch with reality?

With the help of the Center for Health Research at Loma Linda University, the committee decided to carry out a scientifically designed survey of families. Sixteen hundred names were randomly selected from the conference membership rolls. The committee then contacted each chosen member by mail or in person. Unfortunately the survey yielded a response rate of only 35 percent, too small a return rate to accurately generalize the findings. The survey results do demonstrate, however, that there is indeed a dark side to family life in congregations. It even exists in a church body (Seventh-day Adventist) known for its promotion of high standards and biblically oriented lifestyle.

The list of percentages that follow reflects only the experiences of those who responded to the survey. (Note: one can assume that if all who were asked to complete the survey had responded, the percentages would be lower. It is likely that many who did not respond felt the questions did not apply to them and hence did not participate.)

- Twenty-four percent have been divorced or permanently separated.
- Thirty percent were physically abused at home before age eighteen.
- Forty-three percent were emotionally abused at home before age eighteen.
- Sixteen percent were victims of incest before age eighteen.
- Thirteen percent have abused drugs or alcohol.
- Thirty-seven percent have lived with a drug or alcohol abuser.
- Thirty-five percent know someone who is HIV positive (has the virus that causes AIDS) or has AIDS.
- Twenty-seven percent have had suicidal inclinations.

The Family Ministry Committee published the results of the survey in a book called *Resources for Family Ministry*.[19] The book also addresses such issues as domestic violence, eating disorders, suicide, unwed pregnancies, child abuse, and rape, giving a description of each behavior, symptoms of each behavior, and suggestions for controlling each behavior—both immediately and over time.

In addition to providing this printed resource, the Family Ministry Committee has also established an anonymous counseling service for clergy families out of the conviction that marital conflict in a pastor's home can create unhealthy congregations. The need for this service is indicated by the fact that in a conference of 180 pastors, seventy made use of this counseling service.

What did those experiencing crises view as helpful and redemptive? According to the authors of *Resources for Family Ministry*, Fred Kasischke and Audray Johnson, here are the main suggestions survey respondents made:[20]

- Personal contact is most effective. Assistance with child care, calls on the telephone, or home visits are especially appreciated.
- Support groups are essential. Ninety-three percent of the survey respondents say the Church should provide support groups for people experiencing crises.
- Family training seminars help. Seminars that focus on family crises and equip individuals to communicate better are highly recommended.
- Pastoral counseling is helpful, but 92 percent of the respondents felt that pastors should be trained to be more effective in counseling.
- Printed material has limited effectiveness. Though viewed to be of some value, such materials are least effective in achieving personal healing.

The authors indicate that healing takes place when family crises are openly acknowledged, when families feel supported in a caring group setting, when families experience concrete acts of love and concern, and when all efforts are bathed in prayer.

The All Saints Church in Phoenix, Arizona, has made great efforts to build harmony between spouses in the community. Church members took a look at marriages and divorce rates and recognized the need for the congregation to be intentional about supporting marriages and strengthening families.

Under the leadership of Linda Staats, the minister of faith and daily life at All Saints, the congregation developed a marriage ministry. The church began by training married couples who have been married three or more years and who exhibit a strong faith to be marriage mentors to engaged couples. Each couple took the Prepare and Enrich Inventory, developed by David Olson of the University of Minnesota, and attended six weeks of two-and-a-half-hour classes on marriage enrichment, during which the couples became a support group for one another. The couples were asked how they could best use their gifts to mentor an engaged couple. Some chose to work one on one with a couple while others chose to lead support groups of engaged couples. In three years, six such support groups were formed.

As a policy, the congregation's family ministry works with any couple that wants to develop a strong, Christ-centered marriage. Each couple pays a fee of four hundred dollars that covers the various wedding expenses and the cost of premarriage preparations and postmarriage support services. Like their mentors, each couple must go through the Prepare and Enrich Inventory. They also must attend a daylong Marriage Marathon Retreat in which they participate in a communication workshop. Continuing support is offered for every newly married couple either through a small support group or an individual mentor couple.

The All Saints marriage ministry program works with young people before they become engaged. Mentors teach young people how to recognize a healthy relationship between spouses and how to choose a mate who will help foster a healthy relationship.

Effective Communication

A second factor in strengthening family relationships lies in the quality of communication between parents and their children. An important part of children's development and well-being is the relationships they have with their parents. The more time children spend with their fathers, the better their measures of well-being and emotional adjustment. Children's well-being is highest when mothers interact enjoyably with their children, and it is lowest when interaction becomes difficult and unenjoyable.[21]

Communication in the home is vital because it contributes so powerfully to these family relationships. When open communication is lacking between husband and wife, it usually is lacking between parent and child. Though easiest to establish when children are small, it becomes increasingly difficult to establish as

Figure 3

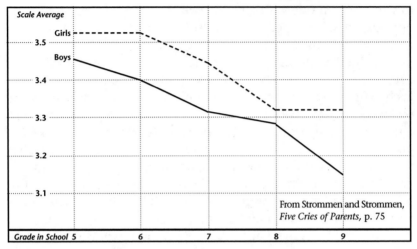

Change in Youth's Desire
for Communication with Parents

Question: "For each of the following five items, tell if it is something you want to talk about with your parents more, less, or the same as you do now." (Participants in the survey were then to answer this question for issues relating to drugs, friends, school, ideas of right and wrong, and sex.)
5 = much more; 4 = a little more; 3 = about the same; 2 = a little less; 1 = much less

the children move into early adolescence; usually after fifth grade, boys and girls begin to lose interest in communicating with their parents. Figure 3 shows the result of a study of eight thousand early adolescents, shows this decline.

Though this decline in interest is real, it does not indicate a complete loss of interest. The first study conducted by Search Institute (1960), a national study of Lutheran youth and adults, revealed the extent to which communication in the home was regrettably lacking for most church youth and parents. These youth and parents said they wished they could talk with one another about significant issues, but for some reason this was not a part of their family lives.

Thirty-two years later (1992), Search Institute probed further into this issue by conducting a national survey of youth and parents in eleven major Catholic and Protestant denominations. To gain insight into young people's desire for parent-youth commu-

nication, the institute described typical adolescent issues and then asked, "If you were in the following situations, to whom would you most likely turn for help or advice?" Here were their choices:
- a parent or guardian
- a friend my age
- an adult friend (not a relative)
- a priest, minister, or rabbi
- a teacher or school counselor
- nobody

One might expect that the majority would prefer their peer group and select the response "a friend my age." One also might expect that fewer youth would select "parent or guardian" if they thought their parents were serious about matters of faith. These expectations were tested.

A sample of one thousand parents was selected from the data bank of more than ten thousand parents who had participated in an earlier study called the *Early Adolescent Study*. Chosen were parents who considered religion important, who were service oriented, who were concerned about their child's views of right or wrong, who allowed their children to question rules, and who prayed.

After the parents were isolated, their adolescent children were selected from the data bank and their preferences noted regarding with whom they would prefer discussing particular problems. Here are the results:
- When having trouble in school, I would turn to . . .
  a parent or guardian = 55 percent
  a friend my agè = 15 percent
  a teacher = 17 percent
  all others = 12 percent
- When wondering how to handle my feelings, I would turn to . . .
  a parent = 51 percent
  a friend = 21 percent
  nobody = 9 percent
  all others = 18 percent
- If some of my friends start using drugs or alcohol, I would turn to . . .
  a parent or guardian = 45 percent
  a friend my age = 19 percent

a teacher = 10 percent
an adult friend = 9 percent
nobody = 9 percent
a minister or relative = 12 percent
- When having questions about sex, I would turn to . . .
a parent or guardian = 53 percent
a friend my age = 19 percent
nobody = 10 percent
all others = 17 percent
- When feeling guilty about something I have done, I would turn to . . .
a parent or guardian = 40 percent
a friend my age = 25 percent
a minister or priest = 11 percent
nobody = 9 percent
all others = 15 percent
- When deciding what to do with my life, I would turn to . . .
a parent or guardian = 66 percent
nobody = 10 percent
a friend my age = 6 percent
all others = 18 percent

Although the percentage of adolescents who chose "a parent or guardian" diminished as the adolescents moved from fifth to ninth grade, never did the percentage of those who chose "a friend my age" equal or exceed the percentage of those who chose "a parent or guardian." It should be noted, however, that parents in this study are members of a congregation and may be seen as more trustworthy because of this.

This study, just like Search Institute's first study done in 1960, reveals that both youth and parents want to communicate with one another on issues that are more than superficial. Youth prefer to discuss their problems and concerns with their parents rather than their peer group even though they may see their parents as being serious about their faith.

In spite of this declared interest in communicating with one's parents on sensitive issues, again only a minority of youth reports that this actually happens. When I (Merton Strommen) was listening to a group of young people evaluate a videotape called *Learning the Language of Faith in the Home,* I noticed that they spoke appreciatively of the family devotions they saw, wishing their parents had started this with them when they were young. When asked about starting family devotions now, they responded negatively, saying that because their family had never discussed important issues, it would seem phony and unnatural. When asked to identify what they deemed necessary for communication to be established in their home, they came up with three excellent suggestions for parents:

1. Take time to share ideas and listen to what we have to say.
2. Initiate discussions using current world events. Such discussions will build a bridge of communication over which religious subjects can more easily move.
3. Give us the freedom to disagree with you and to hold a position that differs from yours.

This third suggestion was given with some feeling. The young people wanted the freedom to explore various positions in order to arrive at a position they could feel was theirs.

These youth, whose parents were leaders in the church, appeared convinced that once communication had been established about ordinary events, discussions of faith could become natural in their homes. This was indicated by their willingness to pray together with their family and to use the Bible in discussions of current events and issues.

Communication, a key to close family relationships, needs to be improved in most families. We (the authors) see this every time we do a congregational survey in preparation for a *Vision-to-Action* workshop (an eight-hour event to establish priorities for youth and family ministry). In this survey youth and adults are asked to rank the importance of several family functions and to tell how well each is being achieved in their own families. The function that invariably draws one of the highest ratings of importance is "to encourage parent-youth communication through classes on discussing adolescent issues with youth." This function, however, usually ranks among the lowest for achievement; the gap between the rating of importance and the rating of achievement for this function is usually one of the largest found among the thirty-two items in the survey.

How Communication Might Be Encouraged

H. D. Grotevant and C. R. Cooper have studied the effect of different patterns of family communication on adolescent identity formation. They have found that boys are more likely to achieve a sense of identity when their father initiates compromise, inquires about their feelings, and allows for differences of opinion. They also found that all family interactions are important to a girls' identity formation.[22]

Congregations can help parents do a better job of communicating with one another and their children, but one wonders to what extent this is being done. In the *Effective Christian Education* study, Christian education coordinators in each of the six major denominations were asked if their congregation was "providing classes for parents on effective parenting or communications." Only 8 percent indicated that their congregation was providing such assistance.[23]

To address this issue, The Youth & Family Institute has developed a training program, an adaptation of the Peer Ministry training program of Dr. Barbara Varenhorst, called *Faith and Skills for Parenting*. The program helps parents communicate better with their children, become more aware of the importance of good communication, and develop caring skills for their home settings.

The *Adoption Study* conducted by Search Institute further identifies the importance of communication in the home. It shows that a parental stance of openness and a willingness to talk are the two most important factors in determining whether adopted adolescents are referred for psychological counseling. The study also shows that adoptive parents are seemingly more aware of the importance of communication than are biological parents and therefore work harder at conversing with their adopted adolescent. A total of 65 percent of the adolescents in this study say, "I have lots of good conversations with my parents." Such communication helps bring about the needed close relationships.[24]

Verbal communication, however, is not the only form of communication that helps form these relationships. Communication also involves a ministry of presence in which parent and child spend time together. Dr. David Elkind, noted child and adolescent psychologist, stated in a 1997 conference to Christian educators in San Diego that "when children act up they probably do not need a time-out, but a time-in. They need to be with their parents and be included in a close family." As a man who loves sports, I (Merton Strommen) found that when I was a young parent, wonderful communication occurred when I played basketball or football or rode bikes with my children. We enjoyed these times together, and playing together helped us know one another better even though we exchanged very few words.

Starting Early with Communication in the Home

Communication between parents and children starts early. During the first three years of a child's life, connections between neurons are formed in the brain, leading to the development of language, emotion regulation, and academic ability. By talking and reading to their children during the first few months of life, parents establish the foundation for language development.

To test the effect of communication at an early age, two psychologists, Betty Hart and Todd Risley, recruited forty-two families with infants between seven and twelve months of age. Their parents were either welfare recipients, blue-collar workers, or professionals. Once a month for three years, observers visited the families' homes, recording how much communication between mother and child took place while the mothers cooked dinner, folded laundry, and watched television. The analysis of these observations, published in Hart and Risley's book *Meaningful Differences,* revealed a distinct correlation between social class and level of communication.[25]

"The differences were amazing," says Risley. "The welfare child heard six hundred words an hour, the working class child heard twelve hundred words an hour, and the professional child heard 2,100 words an hour—a staggering amount." Not only did children from highly verbal families hear more words, but also the parents asked them more questions and repeated or expanded upon comments the children made. This positive feedback reinforces children's verbal expression and learning and balances the more negative, controlling comments parents make, like, "Get your feet off the table" or "Put your shoes back on."

Risley found that by the time the children reached four years of age, the disparity in the number of words they knew showed up on IQ and vocabulary tests. Three-year-olds from the talkative families had higher IQ and vocabulary scores than three-year-olds from taciturn families. Similar results were found in the *Fullerton Longitudinal Study*, which tracked the development of 130 children from the time they were one year old until they were eight years old. The evidence clearly shows that communication in the home is vital for a number of reasons:

- It enhances the academic success of the child.
- It helps shape the child's self-image.
- It builds bridges for sustaining communication about personal issues.
- It creates close family relationships.

Deterrents to Husband-Wife Communication

If communication is so vital, why is it so often lacking? A large part of the answer lies in gender differences. Gender differences can create difficulties in communication between men and women. The *Boston Couples Study* revealed that females tend to disclose material that is personal and feeling-oriented, whether positive or negative. Males, on the other hand, tend to favor information that is factual, relatively neutral, and positive in tone.[26]

In addition to their difference in choice of subject matter, men and women differ in their reasons for avoiding self-disclosure. This became evident in a study conducted by Burke, Weir, and Harnson, in which a group of husbands and wives were asked why they avoid self-disclosure. Almost half the wives said "they did not want to burden or worry their spouse." Only 18 percent of the males chose this same response. More men identified their spouse's lack of knowledge of the situation and their own desire to keep home and work problems separate as the most important reasons for avoiding self-disclosure. None of the women gave these reasons.[27]

Gender differences in communication become most evident when a couple loses a child. Men and women grieve differently, and this contributes to their inability to understand each other. Because men favor the factual and more objective aspects of life, they often find it difficult to share their grief reactions. When my wife and I conducted grief sessions for parents who had lost a loved one, we noticed that usually only mothers attended. Privately they would confess that they had tried to bring their husbands but found them unwilling to participate.

A significant part of communication between husband and wife is the nonverbal aspect of communication. To illustrate, husbands of unhappy wives are typically less able to read their wives nonverbal cues than those of strangers. Where there is misinterpretation of facial expressions and an inability to sense the tone of one another, misunderstanding and ill will are more likely to occur.[28]

Deterrents to Parent-Youth Communication

Certain patterns of parental behavior serve as turn-offs to youths' interest in communication with their parents. These deterrents are rooted in parents' preoccupation with their own concerns. Some common patterns of parental behavior illustrate how parents fail in listening to their children:

• listening with half an ear
• listening with a judging attitude
• listening to recall a similar experience in their own life

A parent who listens with half an ear pretends to listen but continues doing whatever he or she is involved in. It doesn't take an adolescent long to realize that she or he does not have Mom's or Dad's full attention. This can cause the adolescent to walk away in anger.

A parent's judging attitude reveals itself when Mom or Dad says something like, "Yes, but . . ." or "Yes, I hear you, but I disagree with what you are saying." Instead of listening to understand what an adolescent is saying, the parent judges the attitudes or behavior of the youth. When a parent corrects or passes judgment on the attitudes or behaviors of an adolescent, he or she only stymies further conversation.

A parent who listens to recall a similar experience in his or her own life is making a well-meaning but self-centered effort to be reassuring. Instead of actually listening to the youth, the parent says, in effect, "I want you to listen to something that happened to me." This shifts attention away from the concern of the youth and refocuses it on the personal interest of the parent, causing the young person to feel that further conversation is useless.

These three listening mistakes hit home with a lot of parents. Unfortunately, these common deterrents to parent-youth communication prevent the close relationships that result from communication of the heart. Learning to listen with the heart is the only way parents can come to understand one another and their children.

What Congregations Can Do to Teach Effective Communication

Because listening is basic to communication, a useful ministry in a congregation is to help husband and wife learn to listen from the heart. Once this basic approach is mastered, parents can use it to develop closer relationships with their children. The three important guidelines for listening discussed below can be promoted by congregations and practiced in congregational events. They are not techniques, but they are stances to be learned over time as one shifts one's approach from being the superior person in the conversation to being one who listens and talks as a peer.

Guideline 1: Encourage Expression of Feelings

Listen in ways that encourage expression of feelings. Not until the speaker identifies feelings with words can there be any real communication. To encourage such expression, the listener needs to convey an attitude of warm interest, free from a spirit of judgment or criticism. A spouse or adolescent can quickly judge an attitude from the listener's tone of voice or facial expressions.

To encourage such expression of feelings, a listener can use verbal responses. *Affirming responses* such as "I can understand what you are saying" or "I appreciate your willingness to tell me that" make it easier for the speaker to continue. *General leads* that give the speaker freedom to share what he or she chooses work better than specific questions. Authority figures tend to use specific questions that can put a speaker on the defensive or in a dependency role. When specific questions are used repeatedly, answers tend to get shorter and shorter until eventually conversation stops. More general questions, such as "Do you mind telling me more about that event?" or "Could you give me an example?" convey an open-endedness that allows the other person to share what he or she wishes.

Guideline 2:
Listen to Discern the Other Person's Perspective

Trying to view a situation through the eyes of another is a deliberate effort to know the inner life and feelings of that person. A listener can help this active process along by using two additional kinds of *feedback responses.*

One feedback response is to convey that the listener is trying to understand what is being said. Such phrases and questions as, "Let me tell you what I am hearing to see if I am on target," or "In other words, this is how you view the situation. Does this sound accurate?" can allow the speaker to clarify any misconceptions and then continue with the conversation.

A second useful feedback response involves clarification or interpretation. Rather than just restating or summarizing what has been heard, the listener tries to interpret what she or he has heard. The interpretation comes from listening with a "third ear"—noticing the feelings being expressed along with the words and putting them together. A clarification offered in a tentative way could be as follows: "You feel you're being picked on. Is that right?" or "You feel blamed for everything that happens. Is that correct?" If the interpretation is off target, the other person is encouraged to continue talking and correct the impression. The net effect of this kind of listening from the heart is a closer relationship between the two involved in the conversation.

Guideline 3: Listen with a Sense of Hope

It is important to express the conviction that there is hope, regardless of the situation at hand. This hope can be based on the listener's faith in the speaker and in the possibilities seen in that individual. The ultimate source of hope, however, is centered in the belief that with God nothing is hopeless. The listener's confidence in God's power to transform gives the one struggling with a problem a sense of hope. Christ is present, reaching over the shoulder of the listener to transform the situation.

Wise Parental Control

A third contributor to close family relationships is wise parental control—that is, the way parents set boundaries and exercise discipline in their home. Parents' approach to discipline shapes not only the emotional climate of a family but also the child's personality, character, and response to the Gospel.

Three Types of Parental Discipline

Through a lifetime of careful studies, Diana Baumrind was able to identify three types of parental discipline:
• autocratic
• permissive
• democratic

Most parents tend to use one of these three types of discipline. Each approach is associated with contrasting kinds of behavior. Autocratic and permissive discipline create distance between parent and adolescent, whereas democratic discipline encourages family closeness. In other words, the way parents treat their children evokes either a positive response or a rebellious rejection of the very behavior parents idealize.

Parents who discipline their children autocratically—with rigid rules, harsh words, and cruel punishment—can expect to see their children involved in rebellious or at-risk behaviors. Parents who permissively give their children whatever they want can also expect to see negative effects. Parents who use a democratic approach, however—an approach that is flexible and Gospel-oriented—are likely to see their children developing the Ten Characteristics of Youth Committed to Christ and living a life of witness and service.[28]

Search Institute tested Baumrind's findings with data from one of its own studies of 10,467 parents drawn into a national random sample. The result of Search's studies are included in the descriptions that follow.[29]

Autocratic Discipline

This type of control characterizes one who values obedience as a virtue and favors punitive or forceful methods to curb the self-will of a child. As a method of discipline it is not foreign to church people. In Search Institute's *Early Adolescent Study*, four thousand of the ten thousand–plus parents leaned toward autocratic discipline. In response to the statement "I will not allow my child to question the rules I make," one in ten parents said they "often" take this stance, and another 30 percent admitted to taking this stance "sometimes."[30]

An even stronger indication of parents' tendency to be more rigid or controlling was their response to the statement "I expect my child to believe I am always right." A surprising 19 percent of the mothers and 25 percent of the fathers said this is "often" true for them. If we include the many who agreed that they "sometimes" take this position, we would find that half the parents of early adolescents try to give the impression that they are always right at various times.

Bradley Strahan, a psychologist at an Australian college, highlights the significance of control in parent-child relationships. When children reach adolescence, a major change they must make involves entering into a new relationship with their parents. The ways parents respond to this change are good indicators of whether the adolescents will achieve a sense of independence without disconnecting from the family. Strahan also points out that adolescents whose parents adopt an autocratic approach to parenting are less likely to engage in the vital exploration processes of adolescence and are therefore more likely to adopt external rather than internal moral standards. Generally, these adolescents are more prone to peer pressures because they have learned to rely on external sources of control and approval rather than internal self-control.[31]

In a two-year longitudinal study of adolescents' moral reasoning, L. J. Walker and J. H. Taylor found that when parents inquired about children's opinions, asked clarifying questions, and paraphrased the children's words to ensure understanding, the children were more likely to grow in their moral reasoning. Parents who directly challenged, lectured, or critiqued their children were most likely to have children who developed very little moral reasoning over the time of the study; in fact, the nature of parent-child interaction was more predictive of growth in moral reasoning than was the influence of the parents' own level of moral reasoning.[32]

In spite of its negative effects on close family relationships, many parents use autocratic discipline with increasing frequency as close relationships begin to decline. Search Institute discovered in a study of 7,050 adolescents (a national random sample of youth from several denominations) that in families of overly strict or controlling parents the greatest rebelliousness takes place.

A *Study of Generations* (a study based on a national random sample of Lutherans) found that parents who were autocratic in their approach to discipline tended to be law-oriented in their understanding of Christianity, viewing Christianity as basically a set of rules and standards that must be obeyed.[33] The sobering evidence is that adolescents raised under autocratic control are more likely to engage in stealing, lying, fighting, and vandalism, and to experience feelings of social alienation and age prejudice throughout their lives. In addition, these youth are more likely to reject traditional moral standards and involvement in a congregation and are less likely to relate well to people, instead adopting a prejudicial and judgmental spirit.

Permissive Discipline

Permissive parents see themselves as a resource to be used as children wish—not as the people responsible for shaping their children's future behavior. Strangely, this approach can be as negative in its effects on children (and on close family relationships) as an autocratic approach.

Children raised by permissive parents are less likely to go out of their way to help people and less likely to live by the moral standards of their parents. They are more likely, however, to become involved in such hedonistic behaviors as use and abuse of alcohol, drugs, and sex and are more likely to seek out movies that are sexually explicit and erotic. Children living in such homes have trouble believing their parents really care about them. They often interpret permissiveness as rejection.[34]

Despite its obvious negative effects, a significant number of church people lean toward permissive parenting. When asked how often they let their children do whatever they want to do, more than one-third (37 percent) of parents responded "often" or "very often." One-fifth of parents questioned admitted to being too lenient, often letting their children off easy. The significance here is that this failure to set boundaries contributes neither to close family life nor to adolescents' moral development.

Democratic Discipline

Democratic parents value both independence and disciplined conformity in their children. They combine firmness with the freedom of a democratic setting, affirming their children's individual qualities and style while at the same time setting standards for future conduct.

Search Institute's *Early Adolescent Study* found that when asked to respond to this statement—"I give my child a chance to talk over rules not liked or understood"—more than half the parents claimed to do this "often."

Adolescents raised under this type of discipline are far more likely to reflect positive characteristics; they are more likely to be service oriented, concerned about people, free from feelings of alienation, and committed to a religious faith. In addition to its positive effects on children, democratic discipline also fosters family closeness and parental affection.

A study designed to assess the possible connection between parents' use of social control and college students' use of marijuana reinforces the positive long-term effects of democratic discipline. Researchers found a high use of marijuana among students whose parents were permissive disciplinarians and a medium use among those whose parents were autocratic disciplinarians. The students who reflected a low use of marijuana were those raised by democratic disciplinarians. Researchers concluded that the quality of parent-child interaction, the parents' respect for the children's participation, and the mutual sharing and listening to one another, fostered a commitment to the parents' values.[35]

What Congregations Can Do to Encourage Wise Parental Control

The method of discipline a parent uses strongly influences the behavior of the children and the closeness of the family members. For a congregation wishing to further strong, life-shaping families, it is clear that an important aspect of congregational ministry is one that helps young parents adopt a democratic approach.[36]

Offering classes that teach young people (including young parents) how to establish clear rules and boundaries, how to be consistent in defining and applying clear consequences when boundaries are broken, how to discipline when not in the presence of others, how to handle conflict in a positive way, how to use good judgment to take a flexible stance, and how to avoid the use of sarcasm can be a good way to start.

The limits this type of approach places on children are very effective. Children and youth do best when they grow up with a strong sense of what is expected of them. Young people whose parents limit certain activities and place restrictions on where and when they may be involved are more likely to have positive attitudes about their God, their church, and their family.[37]

Parental Nurturing

A fourth contributor to strong family relationships is parental nurturing. This involves parental acts and attitudes of love that enhance and nurture the well-being of children and result in positive emotional bonds or relationships between parents and children.

Significance of Bonding and Attachment

A body of research has developed around what is called the attachment theory, which suggests that each individual has an attachment behavioral system that is active from cradle to grave and explains how children and parents form bonds with one another. The theory suggests that children constantly monitor the whereabouts of their parents. If parents are close, children feel secure. If parents are out of sight, children feel threatened. The ability of children to seek out their parents when threatened and the ability of parents to provide comfort when children feel this way is critical in the development of positive parent-child bonding.

Children whose parents are always emotionally available develop certain mental images of their parents and of themselves: they see their parents as trustworthy and themselves as worthwhile. Studies have consistently found that optimal adolescent development is fostered when parents combine high levels of care and support with attitudes and behaviors that promote growing autonomy and independence in their children.

When my (Merton Strommen's) grandson was born almost four months prematurely, he lay in his incubator weighing less than one pound. Doctors deemed it important that he receive as much physical contact as possible, so I would visit him often, sticking my hand through the glove in the incubator to let his tiny fingers curl around my little finger. I would sing to him, talk to him—I wanted him to know I was there.

When I was ready to leave and would start to withdraw my hand, I could feel his little fingers tighten around my little finger. He did not want me to go. A bond was being formed, and I was becoming important to him. Because he was sensing my love and feeling a sense of security, he was learning to trust and love me. Today a powerful bond exists between the two of us.

A four-year study of adoptees randomly selected from the adoption files of four states (Minnesota, Wisconsin, Illinois, and Colorado) provides evidence supporting the power and significance of this kind of bond. Search Institute calls it the key to healthy family relationships and the key to adolescents' well-being. When there is no emotional bonding, the picture changes. Twenty-five percent of adopted adolescents in this study who were not emotionally bonded to either parent showed signs of rebellion, rejection, and oppositional behavior (delinquency, drug abuse, etc.). Clearly, the lack of emotional bonding between parents and adolescents has serious consequences.[38]

On the positive side, youth who are affectionately bonded with both birth parents or both adoptive parents are most likely to abstain from at-risk behaviors. If an adolescent is attached to only one parent, involvement in at-risk behaviors increases.

When Attachment Weakens

According to the *Adoption Study,* the attachment or emotional bonding between parents and adolescents diminishes as children grow older. Almost 20 percent of the parents involved in this study indicated that the attachment they felt when their children were two years of age was gone by the time their children were adolescents.

Figure 4

Change in Demonstrative Affection by Parents

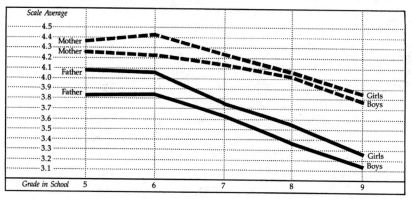

Item: "How often does your mother/father hug or kiss you?" Based on the average of 5 items. 5 = daily; 4 = couple of times a week; 3 = one to four times a month; 2 = less than once a month; 1 = never

This reduction in affection as children grow older agrees with the *Early Adolescent Study.* It shows a dramatic drop-off in affection as adolescents progress in school. The percentage of parents expressing verbal affection ("I love you") went from 50 percent for fifth graders to 30 percent for ninth graders. The percentage of parents showing physical affection (hugs or kisses) dropped from 73 percent to 40 percent within the same age-group (see fig. 4). As might be expected, fathers proved to be less demonstrative in showing affection than mothers. Although expressions of love and caring tend to diminish as children grow older, they remain essential elements in the development of close family relationships.[39]

A useful instrument for assessing the presence or absence of parental care and protection is found in the *Parental Bonding Instrument.*[40] One set of items assesses coldness, neglect, and rejection; a second set describes parental care and warmth; a third set identifies behaviors related to the promotion of autonomy and independence; and a fourth set describes parental intrusiveness.

These four scales make it possible to identify four quadrants. Those experiencing:

Figure 5

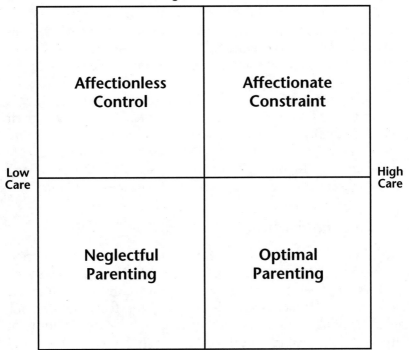

Parental Bonding

High Protection

Affectionless Control	**Affectionate Constraint**
Neglectful Parenting	**Optimal Parenting**

Low Care ... **High Care**

Low Protection

- high care and low protection
- high care and high protection
- low care and high protection
- low care and low protection

Youth who rate their parents high in care and low in protection are the most psychologically healthy individuals. On the other hand, those youth who describe their parents as high in protection and low in care are the most psychologically vulnerable. Figure 5 is based on Parker's *Parental Bonding Model*. Note in the figure how parents tend to fall into one of four quadrants with respect to providing care and protection.

In a national study of 1,115 randomly selected Australian youth of the Seventh-day Adventist Church, youth who scored in the optimal quadrant—high care and low protection—showed a distinct advantage in psychological adjustment over youth scoring in the other quadrants. They also were the most committed to the Christian faith.

The overwhelming conclusion from this carefully crafted study is stated in these words, "The nature and quality of the relationships between parents and their adolescents are of critical importance for an adolescent's adjustment and mature response to the Christian faith."

The author, Strahan, underscores this point when he says, "It is important for parents to recognize that *how* they engage their children in family religious activities is more important than *whether* children participate in family religion or not. It is quite possible for the *how* of religious practice to be destructive and thus deny what is presumably the real meaning and purpose of religion."[41]

A Caring Environment

The power of a caring environment is evident in the data collected in a massive study of twelve thousand parochial school adolescents (grades six to twelve) of the Seventh-day Adventist Church in the United States. The study included thirty-eight items that describe indicators of faith and ultimately measure the youth's maturity of faith. It also enabled the youth to describe their home, school, and church environments.

- Of those youth unable to report a caring environment, only 5 percent gave evidence of a mature faith.
- Of those reporting only one caring environment, 17 percent gave evidence of a mature faith.
- Of those reporting two caring environments, 30 percent gave evidence of a mature faith.
- Of those reporting three caring environments—home, school, and congregation—53 percent gave evidence of a mature faith.

These statistics clearly suggest that the more caring environments an adolescent experiences, the more he or she will grow in faith.[42]

After analyzing data from his study of Australian youth of the Seventh-day Adventist Church, Strahan emphasizes the significance of the parent-child bond in adolescent development (see fig. 6). He says, "The quality of the parent-child bond is more important than the parents' religious practice for predicting adjustment and support of a religious faith."[43]

Figure 6

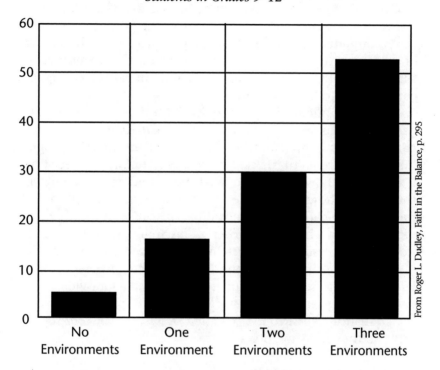

The Power in Caring Environments
Percentage of Youth with a Mature Faith
Students in Grades 9–12

From Roger L. Dudley, Faith in the Balance, p. 295

The quality of this bond depends upon the parents' capacity for warmth and affection. Developing this bond takes time; there are no shortcuts to close relationships built on mutual respect and affection. A strong commitment of time and energy is necessary.

Caring Parents

To pass on faith to our children, we need parents who are AAA (Triple A) road servants as described by David Anderson and Paul Hill in their book *Frogs Without Legs Can't Hear*. Parents are road servants because they serve children on the journey of faith. AAA parents are

- **Authentic.** They have integrity and character. They know they need forgiveness, and they place their trust in Jesus Christ. They do not try to be "cool" or to be their child's best friend.

- **Available.** They take the time to listen to their child and have caring conversations with her or him. They see every milestone in the child's life as an opportunity to connect with God.
- **Affirming.** They affirm the identity of their child as a child of God, that the love of God is in them, and that the child is to live in a way that makes a difference in the lives of others.[44]

As important as it is that caring lay adults work with the youth of a congregation, it is even more important that parents reflect three facets of Christian parenting: communication, caring, and commitment to faith-building.

Irene Strommen, former trainer of trainers in peer ministry, has developed a program called *Faith and Skills for Parenting* to train parents in these three facets of Christian parenting. The program introduces parents to the skills involved in family conversations, teaches them how to listen to what their children are saying, and shows them how to interpret nonverbal communication. This training helps parents build a healthy sense of worth in their children, establish a helpful approach to discipline, learn how to confront sensitive issues, and assist children in decision making.[45]

Seraphim Communications, Fairview Behavioral Services, and Lutheran Social Service of Minnesota produced a four-video Christian parenting series based on the asset development research of Search Institute entitled *It Takes More Than Love*. The four sessions focus on the following topics:

Intentional Parenting

This session begins by teaching parents to look at parenting as asset building rather than problem centered. This first session reiterates to parents that nothing can substitute for time and attention; building assets in children requires commitment and strong intention.

Value-Centered Parenting

This session aims at encouraging parents to instill a sense of worth and value in their children. Our culture's values are based on external factors such as wealth, beauty, and success, but parents must value their children as unique gifts. Children who feel valued tend to adopt the values their parents model, and to practice value-based behaviors.

Nurture-Centered Parenting

This session introduces boundaries as an extension of values. Because the purpose of parenting is to prepare children for confident adulthood, setting value-based boundaries both teaches and prepares children to be responsible and capable.

Inclusive Parenting

This session reminds parents that raising children is a complex and intense task that moms and dads can't do alone. They need a larger community to help in this task. Just as children need support and love from other adults, so do parents.

Saint Mary Catholic Community of Helena, Montana, has developed its own godparenting program that has had wonderful effects on the youth involved. Starting when they are freshmen in high school, groups of youth meet with an assigned volunteer couple once a week through the end of the youths' senior year. Meeting each week in a home, the youth come to know one another and their volunteer "godparents." At the end of the first four-year period of the program, all but one of the nineteen seniors who had originally joined were still participating. The director of Christian Formation and Youth Ministry in the Helena community was impressed by the effect the volunteer couples have had on the youth ministry. In a letter she writes, "In close to twenty years of working with youth, I have never seen such a 'good return' of seniors."

Close Family Relationships Foster the Ten Characteristics of Committed Youth and Children

The four family-strengthening characteristics—parental harmony, effective communication, wise parental control, and parental nurturing—contribute greatly to the development of committed youth when practiced regularly in the home. In its *Early Adolescent Study,* Search Institute divided the adolescents into two groups, separating those whose parents are seen by their adolescents as practicing family-strengthening techniques, Group A, from those whose parents rated low on these qualities, Group B. When the adolescents were asked to respond to character statements, more from Group A reflected the characteristics of committed youth than from Group B (see fig. 7).

Figure 7

Adolescents' Responses to Character Statements: Group A Versus Group B

Characteristic	Item	Group A	Group B
Demonstrating moral responsibility	"I do a lot of things I hope my parents never find out about."	26%	38%
Accepting responsibility in a congregation	"My church or synagogue is very important to me."	52%	36%
Demonstrating unprejudiced and loving lives	"I am kind to other people."	83%	67%
Reflecting self-esteem	"On the whole, I like myself."	71%	58%
Accepting authority and being personally responsible	"My parents almost always trust me."	72%	52%
Having a hopeful and positive attitude	"When things get tough, I keep trying."	68%	53%
Engaging in mission and service	"I help others often."	43%	28%

The comparison of these two groups indicates the power of parental harmony, effective communication, wise parental control, and parental nurturing. As more homes reflect these essentials, more adolescents exhibit the Ten Characteristics of Committed Youth. It is important to note that had *none* of the parents in Group B practiced at least some of the techniques under discussion, the contrasts would have been even greater.[46]

Self-Evaluation by Congregation

To determine how they contribute to the strength of family relationships, congregational leaders can ask themselves these questions:

1. Are we doing anything to enhance all-important parental harmony?
   - Do we make personal contacts by telephone or in person?
   - Do we provide opportunities for reflection?
   - Do we provide support groups for people experiencing a crisis?
   - Do we provide family training seminars to help families deal with crises?
2. Does our ministry encourage better communication between parents and between parents and children?
   - Do we openly address that communication drops in the home as children approach adolescence?
   - Do we help adolescents discuss issues with their parents?
   - Do we encourage communication between parents and children when children are infants?
   - Do we help parents learn to listen to each other and to their children?
3. Are the parents in our congregation aware that their styles of discipline shape their children's personality, character, and response to the Gospel?
   - Can parents distinguish between an autocratic, permissive, and democratic style of discipline? Do they know the first two have negative effects?
   - Do parents provide their adolescents with clear, firmly established rules and boundaries?
   - Do we encourage a flexible stance blended with good judgment?
   - Do parents need help understanding the power of a Gospel-oriented approach?
4. Do we stress the importance of families' demonstrating love and affection for one another?
   - Have we encouraged emotional bonding, emphasizing that it is one of the strongest predictors of adolescent well-being?
   - Do parents realize that they tend to demonstrate less affection as their children grow older?
   - Do we emphasize that the quality of family relationships is critical to adolescents' response to the Gospel?
   - Do we emphasize that close family relationships foster the Ten Characteristics of Committed Youth?

Chapter 3

Fostering Close Relationships with God

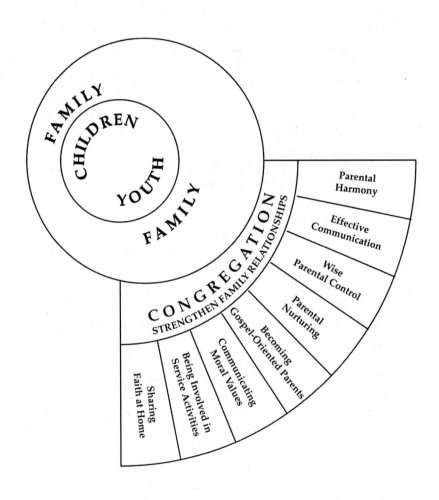

The question still before us is this: How can we increase the probability that the Ten Characteristics of Committed Youth and a life of witness and service become realities in our youth?

The previous chapter focused on one side of the coin and gave us an answer: namely by engendering close family relationships. This chapter, focusing on the other side of the coin, gives us another answer: namely by engendering close relationships with God.

When the congregation and the home are partners in nurturing faith and when there are both close family relationships and close relationships with God, the probability of the Ten Characteristics of Committed Youth, repeated below, becoming a reality are greatest.

1. Trusting in a personal Christ
2. Understanding grace and living in grace
3. Communing with God regularly
4. Demonstrating moral responsibility
5. Accepting responsibility in a congregation
6. Demonstrating unprejudiced and loving lives
7. Accepting authority and being personally responsible
8. Having a hopeful and positive attitude
9. Participating in the rituals of a Christian community
10. Engaging in mission and service

Faith and God

Faith: A Need for Intentional Nurture

Our culture, in contrast to former generations, no longer supports and encourages religious faith. Rather, it undermines it. Steven Carter, in his best-selling book *The Culture of Disbelief,* shows how religion is no longer given public recognition but rather is being trivialized. For an increasing number of people in our society, a religious faith is something to oppose. For example, a school board in Hillsborough, New Jersey, decided that too many students persisted in saying, "Saint Valentine's Day," so they renamed the occasion, "Special Person Day." They also rechristened Christmas as "December season" and banned classroom presents because they viewed the giving of gifts to be a "religious activity."[1]

Ellen T. Charry, professor of theology at Princeton Theological Seminary, insists that intentional Christian nurture is a necessity today. In her article "Raising Christian Children in a Pagan Culture," she observes that the church is the only institution that can rescue children from the deforming emphasis our culture places on money, sex, and power. She underscores the point that the most important ministry of the contemporary Church (and we add, of the family) is the intentional formation of young Christians.[2]

In 1996 a Family Ministries Initiative carried out by the Methodist Church in Minnesota used both focus groups and written surveys to interview parents. When asked what challenges or difficulties their families face, an overwhelming number of parents responded with "time stress." This response was given twice as many times as other stress factors such as economic pressure, mental and physical illness, social and political pressure, or family structure. When asked how the church helps with their strengths or challenges, an overwhelming number of parents answered "by being a network of people who care." Its welcome, support, intergenerational activities, small groups, sense of community, and relationships all provide a source of strength and identity. When asked how the church could better help their family, most parents responded with "Provide learning and support opportunities on matters of faith and spirituality. Help us teach faith at home to make God relevant."

When family ministry consultant Peggy Johaningsmeir summarized what the 247 parents who participated in focus groups said, she ended with these words: "We ask the church to help us integrate our faith values into our daily lives and to support and hold us accountable in our growth as disciples of Jesus Christ."[3]

One of the major roles of a congregation in faith formation is to strengthen families to grow in faith and nurture faith in the children. Even though they may not realize it, parents are very important in the shaping of faith in their teenage children.

> The importance of faith for teenagers fairly closely tracks the importance of faith for their parents. Parents for whom religious faith is quite important are thus likely to be raising teenagers for whom faith is quite important, while parents whose faith is not important to them are likely to be raising teenagers for whom faith is also not important.[4]

Faith: A New National Interest

Though the culture undervalues it, religious faith is returning as a public interest. For example, a number of major newspapers now include a Faith and Values section in their weekend editions. In 1996 *Time* magazine featured an article on faith and healing that acknowledged a growing body of scientific evidence that shows how faith and spirituality can improve physical health.

Also in 1996 the newsletter for the American Psychological Association carried the article, "Psychologists' Faith in Religion Begins to Grow." The article begins by stating that psychologists since Freud have generally regarded religious belief and practice as signs of weakness or even pathology. This outlook is changing now, as studies show that people who see God as a partner who loves them enjoy greater positive mental health outcomes.[5]

For many years, beginning in 1994, CBS featured a highly popular drama called *Touched by an Angel* during prime time on Sunday nights. This hour-long drama proved that a series about faith in God can attract a wide following.[6]

The high attendance figures for Mel Gibson's film *The Passion of the Christ* demonstrated that there is a lot of interest in faith and the Church. Books like Dan Brown's *The Da Vinci Code* quickly became best-sellers and triggered more films about the Church and faith. In the midst of a culture that has moved away from being founded in the Christian faith to more pluralistic expressions of faith, there is an interest to know more about the stories of faith.

Faith: A Close Relationship with God

How might a parent answer a child who asks for a definition or description of a living faith? The question is not an easy one to answer because faith is both complex and dynamic. Faith touches all dimensions of human life—the affective, cognitive, volitional, and behavioral. Martin Luther called faith "a living, active, busy, mighty thing."[7] In other words, a vibrant faith permeates every facet of our existence, manifesting itself in what we trust, value, and do.

Faith can be defined as something that involves three interrelated aspects:

- It is an affair of the heart.
- It is a commitment of the mind.
- It results in good actions.

Faith Is Each of These All the Time, Not One of Them Once in a While

Faith: An Affair of the Heart

Research on faith maturity and faith formation by Search Institute; by Christian Smith in the study Religion and Youth, out of the University of North Carolina; and by others has indicated that Church leaders in youth ministry and Christian education have fallen short in giving children and youth a heart for the gospel. We have tended to intellectual faith maturity instead of to helping children and youth experience it and live it.

Kenda Creasy Dean focuses on giving youth a heart, or passion, for God and the Church in her book *Practicing Passion*. A passionate faith is much more than an emotion.

Christians, therefore, came to view passion not simply as an emotion but also as the experience of being willingly "undone" by divine love. Passion, literally, is God's undoing. Out of love for

Figure 8

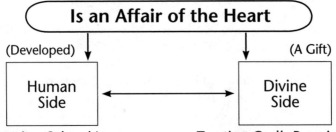

A Vibrant Faith

Is an Affair of the Heart

(Developed) → Human Side ← → Divine Side ← (A Gift)

- Sensing Others' Love
- Realizing God's Love
- Feeling Secure
- Sensing God's Care
- Trusting People

- Trusting God's Promises
- Loving People
- Loving God

God's creation, the divine self is poured out into human form (see Philippians 2:6–11) and undergoes death on the cross. In identifying with the One who is God's undoing, you and I—not to mention the youth in our care—are undone and refashioned into new creations.[8]

Faith as an affair of the heart is a two-way exchange in several ways. Faith is an affair that both captures our heart and requires us to give of our heart. It is a relationship in which love and trust are both received and given. Faith is an affair with both a human side and a divine side (see fig. 8).

Consider first the human side. We know that a child who is loved and cared for develops faith in people. In feeling cared for when picked up, held, comforted, and fed, a child learns to love and trust people. A child's faith in a caregiver is based on his or her sensory and affective modes of knowing rather than on intellectual knowledge. The relationship established through being cared for and loved enables a child to trust people, believe in people, love people—all qualities inherent in being human.

Looking at the divine side, we recognize that faith in God is created similarly. "We love because he first loved us" (1 John 4:19, NRSV). Our awareness of God's love enables us to love God in return. God's faithfulness and steadfastness create faith within us just as a mother's faithfulness and steadfastness create trust in an infant. In his explanation to the Third Article of the Apostle's Creed, Martin Luther stated it this way:

> I believe I cannot by my own understanding or effort believe in Jesus Christ my Lord, or come to him. But the Holy Spirit has called me through the Gospel, enlightened me with his gifts, and sanctified and kept me in true faith."[9]

Such a faith is ". . . the assurance of things hoped for, the conviction of things not seen" (Hebrews 11:1, NRSV). This confidence is more than a feeling—it is an affection that bonds us to God. This dimension of faith is an affair of the heart.

And how is this love affair with God ignited? The ones best able to encourage this love affair are the human caregivers we have learned to trust—parents, grandparents, godparents, and others. Their conversations about God and their loving care make faith contagious in the home. Our research has made very evident the fact that a congregation's most potent force in promoting faith in God is encouraging and supporting discussions of faith in the home.

Faith: A Commitment of the Mind

Faith is more than an affair of the heart, however. Faith is also a commitment of the mind—the thinking, willing, and judging aspect of our lives. As a commitment of the mind, faith seeks to know and understand the God who loves us. It involves knowing biblical beliefs and the traditional truths the Christian Church holds and teaches about God. At the same time, faith, as a commitment of the mind, goes beyond equating belief of Church doctrine with the essence of faith—a tragic error committed by people who burned heretics for their beliefs.

Faith, as a commitment of the mind, is nurtured by what congregations teach in Sunday school or other religious instruction, namely, that God exists, that Christ died for us, and that Christ arose and lives with us today. Again facts like these, though important to learn, are not enough (see fig. 9). Martin Luther makes this very clear in his *Treatise on the Freedom of the Christian:*

Figure 9

A Vibrant Faith

Is an Affair of the Heart

and

A Commitment of the Mind

(Learned)

(A Gift)

Belief that . . .

Belief in . . .

- God Exists
- Christ Died for Us
- Christ Arose
- Christ Lives Today

- Christ As My Savior
- God's Promises
- God's Intervention
- Holy Spirit's Guidance

It is not enough, nor is it Christian to preach the life, works, and words of Christ as historical facts as if knowledge of these would suffice. Rather Christ ought to be preached to the end that He is Christ for you and me. Faith is produced by preaching why Christ came and what benefit it is to us to accept Him.[10]

In the German language of Martin Luther's time, the word *glaube* (belief) meant, "to hold dear," "to give allegiance," "to value highly." It identified believing with the volitional (willing) aspects of faith. The same thing is true for the Latin word *credo*. It literally means "I set my heart" or "I make a commitment." The commitment enables one to say "Christ is my Savior"; it enables one to claim his promise of salvation, presence, and power.

A parallel twofold aspect of faith is found in the Roman Catholic Church's *General Catechetical Directory:*

Faith, the maturing of which is to be promoted by catechesis, can be considered in two ways:

- as the total adherence given by man under the influence of Grace to God revealing himself (the faith by which one believes),
- or as the content of revelation and of the Christian message (the faith which one believes).

These two aspects of the faith assume progress of both together. The two can, however, be distinguished for reasons of methodology. [no. 36][11]

The revised Catholic directory, *General Directory for Catechesis*, upholds this distinction:

Who has encountered Christ desires to know him as much as possible, as well as to know the plan of the Father, which he revealed. Knowledge of the faith *(fides quae)* [the faith which one believes] is required by adherence to the faith *(fides qua)* [the faith by which one believes]. Even in the human order the love which one person has for another causes that person to wish to know the other all the more. [no. 85][12]

This difference between only cognitively believing in God and entering into a personal relationship with God was strikingly illustrated by Sharon Daloz Parks, at the Whidbey Institute in

Washington State. In her book *The Critical Years* she tells of sitting with a large university audience watching a film of Carl Jung, the famous psychologist. In the film Jung is asked, "Do you believe in God?" His immediate response is, "No." Many of the undergraduates broke out in laughter, assuming that Jung was too sophisticated to believe there is a God. But Jung continued by saying, "I don't have to believe in God—I know God." This time no one laughed.[13]

Faith: A Producer of Loving Actions

Our definition of faith is still not complete. We need one more element. Faith is an affair of the heart and a commitment of the mind that results in a flow of good actions. In one of his Wittenberg sermons, Martin Luther said:

> A faith without love is not enough—rather it is not faith but a counterfeit faith. Faith is a living, busy, active, mighty thing. It is

Figure 10

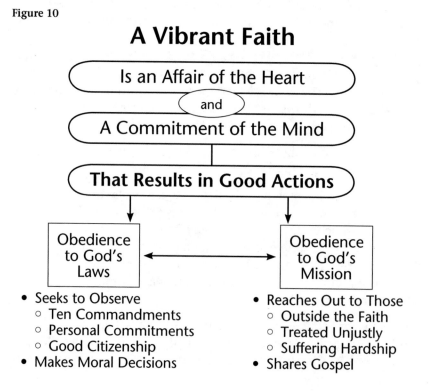

impossible for it not to do good works incessantly. Hence, a person is ready and glad to do good to everyone, to serve everyone, to suffer everything in love and praise of God.[14]

Clearly a vibrant faith is manifest in actions designed to serve God and others. An integral faith makes itself public in acts of decision, obedience, and service. People with such a faith take initiative and volunteer their services. Their actions represent a response of obedience to a deep sense of calling: "We are therefore Christ's ambassadors, as though God were making his appeal through us" (2 Corinthians 5:20, NIV).

A second result of an integral faith is obedience to God's moral laws. Why couple morality with faith? Because moral judgment and behavior are inextricably linked to a life of faith (see fig. 10). This conclusion shows up repeatedly in the research of Search Institute. This research consistently found a high correlation between people's identification with a personal God and their sense of moral responsibility. The two aspects of faith-life interrelate powerfully; they encourage each other.[15]

We can conclude that faith, as an affair of the heart and a commitment of the mind that results in service and moral behavior, is a close, personal relationship with God.

Faith Grows Through Dynamic Interaction

Faith creates a dynamic interaction between heart, mind, and action (see fig. 11); in turn, this dynamic interaction promotes greater faith. This interaction is seen in the way an affectional relationship with God increases people's interest in learning more about the God they have come to love and trust. Children who have a personal relationship with God learn far more readily in Sunday school than those lacking this relationship. In this case Christian education, in addressing faith as a commitment of the mind, serves to enhance the faith begun as an affair of the heart.

In like fashion, good actions tend to stimulate the response of heart and mind; for instance, adults who remember as a child going with their parents to help a neighbor in need show significantly higher faith scores than those who were never involved in service activities. Faithful actions solidify a person's sense of commitment and stimulate greater passion for one's Lord.

Figure 11

A Vibrant Faith

Involves the Total Person

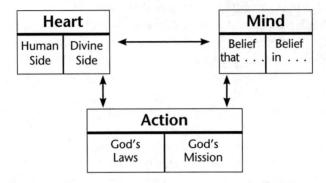

Christianity's outward reach, therefore, provides the ecstatic thrust that passion requires. Youth are quick to notice its absence in the Church, quick to recognize the inwardness and awelessness of self-preservation. Without passion, ministry has no thrust, no impulse to move beyond comfortable boundaries, no desire to share Jesus' self-giving love with those who suffer.[16]

Family Contributors to Faith

Having said all this, we can now ask: What can be done in the family to foster faith and, in doing so, foster close relationships with God within the family? Our answer is found in the following four family contributors to faith:

- becoming Gospel-oriented parents
- communicating moral values
- being involved in service activities
- sharing faith at home

Becoming Gospel-Oriented Parents

Gospel-Oriented Parents

What we mean by *Gospel-oriented parents* is best described by findings of *A Study of Generations*. The study gives descriptions of two types of church members, based on the qualities forming each family: Gospel-oriented church members and law-oriented members.

Gospel-oriented members
- value a spiritual dimension to life
- know a personal, caring God
- are relatively certain of their faith
- are biblically oriented
- consider their faith to be important
- take a positive attitude toward life and death and reject the idea of a salvation by works

Law-oriented church members form a very different profile. Law-oriented members
- cannot tolerate change
- have a need for religious absolutism
- tend to be prejudiced
- feel threatened by those different from themselves
- are self-seeking in their relation to religion
- believe in a salvation by works. They believe they gain favor with God by what they do.[17]

Though law-oriented church members may use the same religious language and quote the same Bible verses as do Gospel-oriented believers, theirs is a "consensual" or "extrinsic" religion. It might be classified as a "misbelief" religion. Such people lack a personal knowledge of the life-redeeming Gospel.

Though the study just mentioned is based on Lutherans, leaders in Catholic and Protestant denominations agreed in conversation with me (Merton Strommen) that these descriptions also describe the people of their congregations. These church leaders also find their members ranging along this theological continuum with a Gospel orientation at one end and a law orientation at the other end. A 1986 study entitled *Catholic High Schools: Their Impact on Low-Income Students* strongly supports this assessment.[18]

Two decades after *A Study of Generations*, another study, *Effective Christian Education*, demonstrated again that church members can be classified as either Gospel- or law-oriented. But the study found that the percentage of law-oriented adults had moved from 40 percent to close to 60 percent. Allowing for variation in statistics, one can conclude that roughly half the children in families of today's church are being introduced to a law-oriented concept of Christianity.[19]

Another way of identifying faith was developed for the *Effective Christian Education* study. Through interviews with theological scholars and denominational executives, an open-ended survey of several hundred adults from the six participating denominations, and reviews of the literature in psychology and religion, it was concluded that a person of faith integrates eight core dimensions of faith. These dimensions were assessed by means of thirty-eight items found to indicate the presence or absence of these dimensions. The items were called faith indicators to underscore that faith itself cannot be measured, only the indicators of faith.

By averaging each person's answers to the thirty-eight items, a score was determined that ranged from one (low) to seven (high). Those scoring from five to seven were judged to have reflected a mature faith. Those scoring from one to three were judged to have reflected an undeveloped faith. Subsequent validity studies showed that these measures did indeed identify people whose faith contrasted in these ways.

Those whose indicators of faith classified them in the top third of the responses were judged to have reflected a mature faith. Note the contrast between the scores of men and women:

Of women, 43 percent evidenced a mature faith.

Of men, 8 percent evidenced a mature faith.

Inasmuch as these adults included those with children, one might conclude that only one-fifth as many men as women are able to take spiritual leadership in their home.

When all adults in the Protestant Church are considered, using data from the *Effective Christian Education* study, we find the following:

Of women, 38 percent reflect a developed or mature faith.

Of men, 21 percent reflect a developed or mature faith.[20]

The measure used to assess indicators of a mature faith show that men have difficulty in relating to the vertical aspect of faith, namely their relationship with God. Lacking a vital relationship with Jesus Christ makes it difficult for men to foster a close relationship with God among members of their families.

What Margaret Krych says to teachers in *Teaching the Gospel Today* also can apply to fathers:

[Fathers], faith is a whole-person response. Children need to see your whole-person response to God's action in Christ; not only your words but also your attitudes, your behavior, your participation in worship, your enthusiasm in witnessing. Children quickly sense when there is a depth of quiet faith and the serenity that comes from a life of prayer and meditation on the scripture.[21]

The point is that parents must share their heart for, as well as their knowledge of, the Gospel. Faith goes from heart to lips, to ears, to action:

"The word is near you,
     on your lips and in your heart"
(that is, the word of faith we proclaim); because if you confess with your lips that Jesus is Lord and believe in your heart that God raised him from the dead, you will be saved. For one believes with the heart and so is justified, and one confesses with the mouth and so is saved. (Romans 10:8–10, NRSV)

Gospel-Oriented Parents Create Close Family Relationships with God

How do we know that being Gospel-oriented parents contributes to close relationships with God within a family? *A Study of Generations* answers this. Through this survey Search Institute came to know the values, beliefs, concerns, behaviors, and attitudes of Lutherans ages fifteen to sixty-five living in all parts of the country. Computer analysis using available sociological, psychological, and religious measures made it possible to produce precise comparisons.[22]

The study found that religious factors were far more influential in shaping the life of an individual than psychological or sociological factors. The study found that "the best indicator of what people will think and do is to know what they value and believe."[23]

The conclusion of the *Study of Generations* report was that religious commitments are the strongest determinants of how people live.

Children and youth tend to adopt the values and beliefs of their parents. If the parents embrace the beliefs and values of a Gospel-oriented faith, the children will adopt them. This conclusion is clear to adolescents themselves. When those involved in the

Effective Christian Education study were given a list of people and asked to identify the ones most influential in shaping their faith-life, the majority of youth singled out their parents. No other persons ranked close to parents, not even pastors or teachers.

Becoming Intentional About Being Gospel-Oriented Parents

In today's world parents need help forming, sustaining, and passing on a Gospel-oriented faith. In *Family Ministry*, Dolores Curran emphasizes the importance of this help. She says:

> We need to gather together the impressive data showing that the parent is the primary determinant of a person's faith, and present it over and over in every way possible until we convince parents of its validity. Until we do so, parents will continue to visualize themselves as adjuncts to the faith process. Adjuncts do not necessarily become responsible.[24]

Communicating Moral Values

Values are communicated most powerfully by parents. Though a child may be strongly influenced by his or her friends, the power of this peer group emerges as dominant only when the relationship of love with parents is vastly diminished. Caring parents are the primary influence in shaping the moral values of their children.

The values most parents wish to see in the lives of their children are traditional moral values, such as these:
- caring for your family
- doing good to others
- protecting the powerless
- showing generosity and mercy
- keeping promises
- postponing gratification

The motivations for living these values are the following:
- an ethic of responsible love
- concern for others
- personal faith

These traditional moral values are the ones idealized and encouraged in every civilization, ancient and modern. Because of their pervasiveness over the centuries, they could be called univer-

sal values. Traditional moral values can be found in every culture irrespective of country, period of time, or religion. These values find their highest expression in such Christian New Testament values as
- seeking first the Kingdom of God
- forgiving as God has forgiven
- loving others as God loves us
- living a life of service
- being transformed into Christ's likeness

In his book *The Abolition of Man,* C. S. Lewis concluded that the "human mind has no more power of inventing a new value than of imagining a new primary color, or indeed, of creating a new sun and a new sky for it to move on."[25]

Traditional values stand in sharp conflict with the current self-serving values being promoted every day through television, magazines, movies, and newspapers. These values tend to center in a preoccupation with oneself, a focus that fosters a dangerous individualism. A focus on oneself erodes commitments people make in marriage, in the workplace, in church, and in the community. Examples of self-serving values are these:
- looking out for yourself
- letting instincts be your guide
- not making commitments
- seeking material success
- seeking immediate gratification
- stressing self-expression rather than self-restraint
- defining morality as you choose

The motivation for living these values is self-enhancement and self-gratification

In contrast to such values, Christian parents want for their children the universal values expressed on page 90.

The conflict between traditional values and current social values is evident in the erosion of the traditional values of adolescents and the increase of at-risk behavior as they grow older. Figures 12 and 13 report data from the 1980s that show a steady decline in the percentage of adolescents identifying themselves with moral values such as being truthful to one's parents or refraining from sexual activity.[26] Recent research illumines a similar pattern. Data gathered

Figure 12

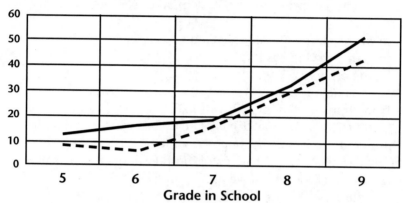

Percentage Attending Alcohol Parties

In the last year, how often have you been to a party where kids your age were drinking beer or liquor?

— Boys – – Girls

Figure 13

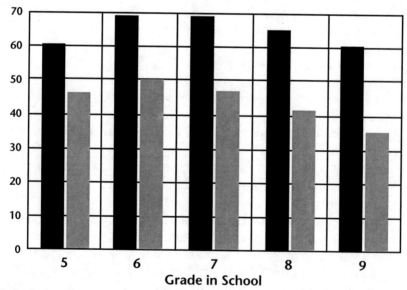

Percentage Opposed to Premarital Intercourse

"I don't think I will have sexual intercourse (make love, 'go all the way') with someone until I get married."

■ Girls ▒ Boys

by Search Institute in 2003, for example, show that the percentage of young people engaged in at-risk behavior rose each year between sixth and twelfth grade.[27]

How Values Are Communicated

Parents communicate values and internalize them in the lives of their children in six different ways:

- by congenial relationships
- by modeling
- by verbal sharing
- by the written word
- by induction
- by grace orientation

Congenial relationships. When a congenial relationship exists between parents and their children, the youth tend to adopt their parents' values even though they are never discussed directly. In other words, values can be communicated without being verbalized if there is a climate of love and genuine caring.

A study of counseling showed that when a congenial, warm relationship existed between therapist and client, the values of the client shifted in the direction of the values of the therapist, even though the values of the therapist were never mentioned; hence, the expression, "Values are not taught as much as they are caught."

When congeniality is missing, however, the adolescent is likely to reject the values of the parent and go in the opposite direction. This holds true for children raised by parents who exercise authoritarian control, using harsh words and cruel punishment.

The power of congenial relationships to transmit values is affirmed by *Youth Reaching Youth,* a project funded by the National Institute of Mental Health. The project was designed to train young people to reach out in friendship to alienated youth. Two hundred seventy-six high school students met weekly for seventeen months of training. Unexpectedly, at the end of the project a remarkable finding showed up in the measures of the religious interest and values of the 276 youth.

One group of youth was trained in a one-on-one approach by college-aged young adults under the guidance of a psychotherapist who was a Lutheran pastor. Another group was trained in an experiential group approach by college-aged young adults under the guidance of a leader who, at that time, was a nominal church member. The third group of youth was trained in a more cognitive group approach by college-aged young adults under the guidance of a leader who was an agnostic, a refugee from a fundamentalist church. All three professional trainers were gifted leaders, charismatic and congenial in their relationships with the youth. All three groups of college-aged young adults trained the high school youth in a similar congenial style. All knew they were not to use religious language in their friendship training because the project was government funded.

Except for weekend retreats, the high school youth were not in direct contact with the three professional leaders. The youth took a battery of tests three times—once at the beginning of the project, once in the middle, and again at the end of the seventeen months. The surprise came when we saw the results on measures of religious items following the third administration of tests:

- Youth trained under the leadership of the Christian psychotherapist had scores that showed an increase in religious interest and an increase in participation that could not be credited to chance.
- Youth trained under the leadership of the nominal church member had scores on religious items that remained the same over the three administrations.
- Youth trained under the leadership of the agnostic had scores on religious items that declined in a significant way that could not be credited to chance.

This empirical evidence attested to the power of congenial relationships with the youth. Once the trainers had established congenial relationships, their religious values were unconsciously adopted first by the college-aged young adults and then by a significant number of high school youth.[28]

This finding underscores the importance of close relationships in communicating values. Parents who establish warm, caring, congenial relationships with their children are communicating their own moral values without saying a word.

Modeling. A second method of communicating values occurs when parents model the values they hold. These values are reflected by their actions, their use of time, their conversation, and the commitments they make. These values-in-action of the parents are the ones children see and imitate. For this reason parents who intend to communicate traditional moral values to their children need to be conscious of how they, as parents, live, speak, and behave.

Elizabeth Dole related an illustration of communicating values. While president of the American Red Cross, she gave a banquet speech in Bloomington, Minnesota, that included the story of her spiritual journey. Her role model during this journey was her grandmother Cathy. Dole often spent Sunday afternoons enjoying not only her grandmother's hospitality (lemonade and cookies) but also her Bible games and stories. Her grandmother's Bible is now Elizabeth's prized possession.

In her speech Dole revealed several instances of how her grandmother witnessed her own values. When one of Cathy's sons was killed in a car accident, she used the insurance money to build a wing on a hospital in a church mission in Pakistan. At another time, when it became necessary for Cathy to enter a nursing home, she welcomed the opportunity saying, "Elizabeth, there might be some people there who don't know the Lord, and I can read the Bible to them."

Elizabeth added, "I love to find her notes in the margins of her Bible—notes that were written in the middle of the night when she couldn't sleep. I can't remember an unkind word or an ungracious deed marring her past. My grandmother was almost a perfect role model."[29]

Verbal sharing. A third method of communicating values is to share them verbally. Some parents, because they think they are forcing their own point of view on their children, hesitate to tell their children what they believe. It need not be that way; if parents explain why they feel deeply about a certain issue, their children will be nothing but appreciative. For instance, when family members hear and tell stories of a faithful God at Grandpa and Grandma's fiftieth wedding anniversary, the children, grandchildren, and great grandchildren present are all shaped by the lived values related in the stories. In a special way when laypeople—neighbors and friends—tell of how this gracious and almighty God has rescued, redeemed, healed, and changed their lives, people often respond with deep emotion.

Personal testimony can be more powerful than an average sermon. In fact, good Gospel preaching tells God's story, a story that is filled with personal testimony. Personal testimony invites the hearer into the story, to become part of the story. The four Gospels in the New Testament are filled with personal witness.

After I (Richard Hardel) had finished speaking to a congregation on the importance of sharing personal and family beliefs and values in the home, a mother came to me and said, "Dr. Hardel, you must hear what happened last week with my five-year-old son, Billy. While we were riding in our car, Billy was looking out the side window and seemed to be talking with someone. I asked him what he was doing. He responded, 'Oh, praying to God.' I was surprised at his response, and I asked him, 'Do you ever hear God answer your prayers?' He immediately responded, 'Oh, all the time.' And looking directly at me he asked, 'Don't you?' I was so surprised at the sincerity of his question that I honestly answered, 'I don't think I know how to listen to God.' Billy said, 'Let's do it right now! You must be very quiet when you listen to God.' So we continued driving, neither of us saying a word. We just listened carefully. Five minutes had quietly passed by when Billy turned to me and said, 'There, did you hear that? It's God!' I said, 'I don't think I have heard God.' I looked at the mother and asked her, 'Do you think God might sound just like Billy sometimes?'"

The Roman Catholic church in the United States brought over a form of personal witness from Spain by way of a spiritual renewal retreat called Cursillo. The Episcopal, Methodist, Presbyterian, Lutheran, and other denominations have similar spiritual retreats based on personal witness called by names such as Via de Cristo, Tres Dies, or Emmaus Walk.[30]

There are youth versions of these personal witness retreats called Teens Encounter Christ (TEC). A weekend TEC is filled with witness stories of lives changed by the Gospel of Jesus Christ. During the telling of these stories, the Holy Spirit draws participants into a new experience with God and frees them to share likewise what has happened to their lives.

The written word. Coupled with verbal sharing is the communication of values that occurs through the written word. History is filled with examples of people whose value orientation was changed by what they read. This includes reading the Bible stories and the stories of Christian heroes and heroines. These stories give examples of people who, often acting counterculturally, made the Kingdom of God their top priority.

Consequent to the *Effective Christian Education* study that showed fewer adults and youth reading the Bible, The Youth & Family Institute published a Bible reading program called *Good News Bearers* that acquaints children and parents with stories of the Bible. Every two weeks the children meet at the church to rehearse and dramatize one of the stories. High school students trained in peer ministry lead the program. They often become spiritual mentors to the children.[31]

Twice a year those who have completed the Bible reading program with their parents meet for a gala quiz event where teams from each grade compete in their ability to answer questions drawn from one of the stories. One of the questions used in the quiz game showed how well the stories of the Bible were being learned. The pastor asked: "Who was the husband of Queen Esther?" One of the teams answered: "Xerxes." When the pastor said: "Wrong, it is King Ahasuerus," they were puzzled. Later they came to him and said: "You were wrong. Xerxes and Ahasuerus are the same names in two different languages."

Induction. A fifth method of communication worthy of special note uses gentle reasoning to communicate values. Studies show that youth are more likely to internalize traditional values if an adult uses discussion to explain why certain moral laws are important and that breaking them can violate one's own inner needs, as well as bring unhappiness to someone else.

When adolescents whose parents use this method were singled out in the *Early Adolescent Study*, it became apparent that youth are more likely to live by the values embraced by their parents when reasoning is used. The opposite occurs for those adolescents whose parents do not use this method.

I (Richard Hardel) witnessed an example of value induction one Sunday while at a worship service with my family. When the ushers were walking to the front of the congregation with the offering plates, I leaned over to my son and said: "Kent, watch how many rows of pews the plates get past before anyone puts in money or an offering envelope." He watched intently and later responded: "Three rows and sometimes four." I then asked him: "What do you think children learn when they see what you see?" He quickly replied: "Offerings are optional for worshipers." Driving home from that worship service we discussed the importance of an offering and the modeling that is involved. The discussion ranged from God loving a cheerful giver to how the offering at a public worship can influence children's views of people's commitment to serve the Lord and support the mission and ministry of the congregation.

Kent and I concluded that each of us would always give an offering at each worship service even if we contributed monthly with a check. Now whenever we attend a worship service together we cheerfully ask one another: "You got your offering? Remember what the children see!"

Grace orientation. An important ingredient in all five ways of communicating values is a grace orientation. A consistent finding is that a parental focus on the love, the promise, and the presence of Jesus Christ inspires youth to internalize the values and lifestyles of a Christian. In contrast, overwhelming evidence shows that attempts to control youth by rules and regulations—a law orientation—incline youth to reject the values being forced on them.

The Morality of a Life Direction

In their efforts to shape adolescents' moral behavior, parents must keep in mind the difference between *sin* and *sins*. *Sin* is a state of being, an orientation to life that centers in oneself. *Sin* is making one's own interests a top priority. That is why pride is often called the primary sin from which all others are derived. *Sin* is placing oneself above God. *Sins,* on the other hand, are the immoral or unethical acts that result from the *sin* of self-interest or self-centeredness. When a sin is committed, a relationship is broken. Sin always separates. If parents focus on overcoming sin—that is, on forming a life direction of caring and concern for people—sins will decrease, and the desired positive behaviors will increasingly appear and relationships will grow.

The *Adolescent-Parent* study shows three behaviors of parents that are strongly associated with shaping adolescents' moral behavior:

- using demonstrative affection (hugs, "I love you's," and smiles)
- using democratic control (setting limits and explaining the reasons for them, giving clear consequences if the boundaries are broken, and holding the person accountable)

- using inductive discussion (encouraging adolescents to think about how their behavior affects both their relationships with others and their image of themselves)

When parents emphasize these three in their parenting, their youth will likely show self-esteem, have a desire to help others, and be willing to adopt traditional moral values.[32]

Being Involved in Service Activities

The issue of values and faith emerged in a striking way for Christ's disciples following three and one-half years of exposure to his ministry. According to the Gospels, the disciples' thinking was becoming more like that of the Pharisees, who loved prestige, honor, money, and the praise of men. This attitude showed itself in a number of incidents: in the argument Christ overheard while journeying to Jerusalem as to who was the greatest among them; when the mother of the sons of Zebedee came and asked Christ to command that her two sons sit, one at Christ's right hand and the other at his left; when Judas went to the chief priest to find out how much money he could get for betraying Jesus; in a dispute at the Passover meal as to which of them was to be regarded as the greatest; and when Peter denied Christ three times rather than risk being embarrassed or publicly harassed because of his relationship to Christ.

Something happened in the thinking and aspirations of these disciples to make them status conscious. Their thoughts had shifted to a preoccupation with themselves, their own advantage. And Christ noticed this. He used strong words when addressing them: "Get up and do not be afraid" (Matthew 17:7, NRSV).

Again, with a child in his lap, he asked, "Who is the greatest in the kingdom of God?" Turning to the disciples he said, "Truly I tell you, unless you change and become like children, you will never enter the kingdom of heaven" (Matthew 18:3, NRSV).

When the disciples began to dispute about greatness at the Passover meal, Jesus washed their feet and said, "Let the greatest among you become as the youngest, and the leader as one who serves. I am among you as one who serves."

Service Enhances Faith and Loyalty

If a preoccupation with status and position can destroy faith, humble service apparently can restore it. The giving of one's life in service to others, and ultimately to Christ, is faith enhancing. Dr. Harry Wendt, author of the Bible study program called Cross-ways, reflects on this action of Christ at the Passover meal: "A God who does feet wants a people who does feet."

Christ's antidote to a self-serving, would-be disciple is evident in Search Institute's findings based on a scale that assesses indicators of faith maturity. In this measurement, faith maturity is found to have two dimensions: (1) a life-transforming relationship with a loving God, and (2) a consistent devotion to serving others.

In a survey in the *Effective Christian Education* study, adults were asked to recall their experiences in church as children and youth. Those who remembered being involved in service projects as children or teenagers showed higher faith scores. Involvement in service proved to be a better predictor of faith maturity than participation in Sunday school, Bible study, or worship services.

The same correlation appeared for the youth. Those who participated in service projects showed higher faith scores. The respondents who reported growth in their faith during the previous two or three years were the ones most likely to have been involved in "helping people who are poor or hungry or helping people in town or city" or "spending time in helping projects through the church."

Service activities were found also to increase youth's bond to the church. Search Institute's analysis of data from the *Effective Christian Education* study gives convincing evidence of this. A chart listing the number of hours spent helping people shows that the more time youth give in service to the community through their congregation, the greater is their loyalty to the Church.[33]

Another benefit of service is noted in a study of forty-seven thousand adolescents drawn from hundreds of communities in the northwest area of the United States and reported in the book *The Troubled Journey*. This study shows that youth involved in service are half as likely to be involved in at-risk behaviors as nonservers. Note that those involved in this study are not church school youth but public school youth.[34]

Service activities clearly counter a self-centered piety and represent a way of reversing a well-documented trend of young people turning away from service professions and becoming concerned primarily with earning high salaries.

Learning Through Service

Peter Benson and Eugene Roehlkepartain make a convincing case for the importance of following service activities with reflection and discussion and making them learning experiences.[35] For example, service-learning can occur for a family when, having served soup in the homeless shelter, family members use the experience as a catalyst for rethinking family priorities and spending habits. If families develop service-learning habits, the probability of their adolescents reflecting the Ten Characteristics of Committed Youth by the time of high school graduation will increase.

In the past, service was not an important part of churches' Christian education programs. According to the *Effective Christian Education* study, only 29 percent of congregations were involving youth in service projects. More than half of Protestant young people had spent five hours or less doing projects to help other people.[36]

A stronger emphasis on service is found in Catholic parochial schools. The 1985 study of students entitled *The Catholic High School: A National Portrait* showed that 46 percent of the seniors were involved in some kind of service. This included not only service projects but also an introduction to conditions of need in the community.[37]

The importance of beginning service activity in the family is seen in what happens over time if service is not emphasized. Studies show that service interest and involvement declines dramatically across the adolescent years for both boys and girls. Clearly, this activity needs to be fostered in the home. If involved as a child in service projects, a person is likely to be involved as an adolescent and as an adult.

The importance of service for the welfare of society is being seen and encouraged also in public sectors. In 1984 the National Youth Leadership Council began a series of conferences with educators and policy makers to expand service opportunities for young people in Minnesota. This movement, praised by national experts as the most comprehensive state youth service program in the nation, has stimulated both state and federal legislation. In 1990 Congress passed the National and Community Service Act, modeled significantly on the Minnesota experience.

In June 1998 the state of Montana held the Governor's Conference on Youth in response to the President's Summit for America's Future. A major component of the conference was service projects. Highlighted were the service projects of Future Farmers of America, Future Homemakers of America, 4-H, Boy Scouts, Girl Scouts, and church congregations.

Sharing Faith at Home

There is a long-established tradition in Jewish and Christian homes of sharing the faith with one another:

> Hear, O Israel: The LORD your God, the LORD is one. Love the LORD your God with all your heart and with all your soul and with all your strength. These commandments that I give you today are to be upon your hearts. Impress them on your children. Talk about them when you sit at home and when you walk along the road, when you lie down and when you get up. Tie them as symbols on your hands and bind them on your foreheads. Write them on the doorframes of your houses and on your gates. (Deuteronomy 6:4–9, NIV)

These verses are recited every morning and evening by Orthodox Jews. Though Christian parents too have felt an obligation to pass the faith on to their children and their children's children, it has not been emphasized as a parental responsibility. When asked, only 7 percent of Christian education coordinators in the six major Protestant denominations said their church emphasized helping parents promote faith in their children.

Seven home faith-sharing dynamics are found to be directly related to mature faith in children and youth. The following lists the dynamics and the percentages of Protestant youth who currently experience them:[38]

- a mother who models the faith = 67 percent
- a father who models the faith = 43 percent
- a regular dialogue with mother on faith-life issues = 12 percent
- a servanthood event with a parent, an action of faith = 12 percent
- a regular reading of the Bible and devotions in the home = 9 percent

- a regular dialogue with father on faith-life issues = 5 percent
- a regular dialogue with an adult, not a parent, on faith-life issues = 4 percent

Four Keys for Nurturing Faith

Dr. David Anderson of The Youth & Family Institute has identified four keys that are essential for nurturing the faith, values, and character formation of children, youth, and adults:

1. **Caring Conversation.** Christian values and faith are passed on to the next generation through supportive conversation. Listening and responding to the daily concerns of the children in our lives makes it easier to have meaningful conversations regarding the love of God and are ways to express God's love to others.

2. **Devotions.** Adults need to learn the Christian message and the biblical story as their own story if they are to pass on their faith to their children and to other adults. Our Christian faith shapes the whole of our lives and involves a lifetime of study, reflection, and prayer. Faith is caught more than it is taught. Children learn as the family practices devotions at mealtimes, at bedtime, on family night, upon waking up, or at other family times.

3. **Rituals and Traditions.** Families identify themselves and tell their family stories through daily routines, celebrations, and rituals. Whether it's putting up a Christmas tree and hanging ornaments, preparing a meal for Thanksgiving Day, or preparing for opening day of fishing season, these activities speak volumes about what a family values, believes, and promotes and about how much the family values faith.

4. **Service.** Children, youth, and adults are most likely to be influenced by those who live out their faith in daily life and truly care for their neighbors. There are many opportunities for service: in the home, in the faith community of a parish, in the larger community, and in the world and all of creation. Whatever type of service is chosen, faith is shaped best when the service is done with family members or other intergenerational groups.[39]

The Power of Sharing Faith at Home

The power of a parent's sharing of faith became strikingly evident when four hundred youth (ages thirteen to eighteen) whose parents maintain the tradition of religious practices in their home were compared to four hundred youth whose parents, though members of a congregation, never talked about faith.[40]

Of special note for congregations is the finding that religious practices in the home virtually double the probability of a congregation's youth entering into the life and mission of Christ's church.

In making these comparisons, no attempt was made to cull parents who might have been ineffectual in the way they shared their faith. Though parents often acknowledge that their efforts to share their faith leave much to be desired, God's Spirit seems to work through the efforts themselves.

Another illustration of the power of sharing faith in the home is based on self-reports of adults in the *Early Adolescents and Their Parents* study. In this study 941 adults reported that when they were in high school, their parents never expressed their faith at home, while 798 adults reported that when in high school, their parents often did express their faith at home. A comparison of the two groups was then made based on a correlation with the Ten Characteristics of Committed Youth. Notice in figures 14 and 15 that when parents often talked about the faith, the number of people who evidenced some of the Ten Characteristics of Committed Youth more than doubled in most cases.

Figure 14

Involvement of Two Youth Groups

Youth Involvement	Youth Whose Parents Never Express Faith	Youth Whose Parents Often Express Faith
Participation in church	28%	46%
Commitment to faith	18%	37%
Service to others	12%	29%
Overall average	19%	37%

Figure 15

A Comparison Based on the Ten Characteristics of Committed Youth

Items Questioned About	Youth Whose Parents Never Express Faith	Youth Whose Parents Often Express Faith
Trusting in a personal Christ *Often or sometimes tried to bring the Gospel of Jesus to nonbelievers*	13%	50%
Understanding grace and living in grace *Often felt God's presence in your life*	15%	24%
Communing with God regularly *Often read the Bible or prayed when alone*	15%	42%
Demonstrating moral responsibility *Often or sometimes participated in local or national efforts to promote justice or peace*	8%	26%
Accepting responsibility in a congregation *Often participated in your church youth group; often attended church school, Sunday school, Bible studies, or other classes at church*	35%	78%
Accepting authority and being personally responsible *Often helped lead programs, classes, or events at church*	12%	44%
Having a hopeful and positive attitude *Are spiritually moved by the beauty of God's creation*	26%	54%
Engaging in mission and service *Often or sometimes participated in projects to help other people (e.g., hungry people, poor people, elderly people, handicapped people)*	34%	72%
Average percentage	22%	53%

The Holy Spirit shapes faith through personal, trusted relation-ships, often in our own homes. In Deuteronomy, chapter 6, we are reminded that the home is the primary place for shaping faith. Parents and other family members are to keep the commands of God, the words of God, and the stories of God first in their hearts. Because faith is caught more than taught, parents and other adults are to keep God at the center of their lives, and they are to teach the stories of God's faithfulness to their children and grandchil-dren. Parents are to talk to their children about God from within the messiness and ups and downs of family life.

> Keeping these words, loving God with all we are, and teaching the children are all part of the same fabric. The importance of remem-bering God in the Promised Land is emphasized. And the impor-tance of remembering God in our homes is underscored.[41]

What Can Congregations Do to Help Families Foster a Relationship with God?

The following is a sampling of resources and ideas that congrega-tions may find helpful in fostering a close relationship with God. For further sources of information, consult the Resource List.

- The Youth & Family Institute sponsors a two-day conference for congregational leadership teams called the Passing On Faith conference, which presents the model shared in this book. The Institute hosts many different seminars, workshops, and con-ferences, such as Parents of Promise. This one-day rally affirms mothers and fathers, uncles, aunts, grandparents, godparents, and other adult faith mentors as spiritual leaders. The rally is a fun celebration and reminder of the promise that parents and extended family make at the baptism or presentation of their child.
- The Center for Ministry Development (Roman Catholic) with Harcourt Religion Publishers has developed an intergeneration-al faith formation program called *People of Faith: Generations*

Learning Together. This includes a wonderful monthly magazine to help families nurture faith in the home.

- Kirk Weaver, executive director of Family Time Training, provides training and online resources to help parents nurture faith in the family.
- The Children and Family Institute in Menlo Park, California, run by two Roman Catholic nuns, offers a marvelous training workshop for families to learn how God is centered in every aspect of life. They have created a helpful resource, available through The Youth & Family Institute, titled *Faith-full Families: Family Celebrations through the Seasons.* Families learn how to create rituals and traditions to connect to God through the seasons of the year.
- Under the leadership of Pastor Brian Vander Ark, Ada Bible Church, in Ada, Michigan, has developed wonderful training and workbooks to help families practice faith through caring conversations, devotions, service, and traditions.
- In their book *HomeGrown Faith* (World Publishing, 2006), David and Kathy Lynn not only have produced helpful biblical foundations for connecting families to closer relationships with God but also share a plethora of practical actions for families to nurture and pass on faith.
- The Rev. Dr. Jerome Berryman, an Episcopal priest in Houston has developed a Bible story learning–and-faith-sharing program called *Godly Play* that uses Montessori methodology. Adults invite children into the story by using story objects on the floor. Children participate in the story and learn how to tell the story using the carefully crafted objects. A similar program in the Roman Catholic Church is titled *Catechesis of the Good Shepherd.*
- *The Way of the Child*, created by Wynn McGregor and published by Upper Room Books, helps children ages 6–11 develop an intimate, personal relationship with God through the experience and practice of spiritual disciplines that nurture that relationship for a lifetime. Through the child's spiritual growth, the family is brought closer to God.
- Zion Lutheran Church in Anoka, Minnesota, continues to help families foster a close relationship with God and with one another through a family small-group night. Families gather once a month for an intergenerational large-group time of worship

and other faith-formation activities. Then the families meet in small groups to discuss what is working in their faith formation at home.

- The Rev. Dr. Franklin Nelson, pastor of Woodbury Baptist Church in Woodbury, Minnesota, has developed a faith-building discussion tool called *TalkPoints*, which consists of one-on-one conversation starters on specific topics for husbands and wives and for parents with their children.

- *FaithLife in the Home Resource and Gift Guide* is designed by The Youth & Family Institute to help parents learn about the faith development of a child at specific milestones and ages. This helpful tool also connects godparents, uncles, aunts, grandparents, and parents to some of the best resources to nurture faith within the home at a specific milestone. Excellent resources like *FaithTalk*, *FaithTalk with Children*, *FaithTalk* Coasters, *Scripture Talk*, *Heart Ignite*, and *Milestones* Blessing Bowls are placed in the *FaithLife in the Home Resource and Gift Guide* at specific milestones in the child or young person's life. *FaithTalk* has 192 faith-share cards in a blue canvas holder that can be stored in the glove compartment of the family automobile, in a purse, on a table in the family room, or on the kitchen table. The 192 questions are divided into four areas, each with forty-eight cards: values, memories, etchings, and action. *FaithTalk* is designed for ages 11 and up. *FaithTalk with Children* is designed for adults to discuss faith with children ages 3–11. *FaithTalk* coasters are printed in Spanish and English and are designed to help young adults who have not had much connection with the ministries of a Christian congregation to wonder and share about God.

- Many denominations offer work-camp experiences that connect adults and youth in service-learning activities about faith. Group Publishing, in Loveland, Colorado, sponsors excellent work camps throughout the United States. Youthworks is another great organization that helps congregations connect youth and adults with God through service projects. Many congregations take families to help in areas hit by tornados, floods, hurricanes, and other disasters. Through service flowing from faith, with adults working side-by-side with youth, the Holy Spirit strengthens faith.[42]

- Lyman Coleman, working with the leadership of men's ministry in the Roman Catholic Church, has developed an excellent ministry, titled Men Marked with the Cross of Christ, to strengthen men as spiritual leaders in their homes and congregations.
- St. Edward's Catholic Church in Bloomington, Minnesota, connects parents to every aspect of faith formation. They host faith-formation training events for parents, godparents, and grandparents. They also bring in special speakers for intergenerational events.
- St. Peter's Church in Mesa, Arizona, has provided support for families through a Milestones Ministry that includes all ages, from infants to grandparents.
- First Presbyterian Church in Bend, Oregon, has developed a family ministry team to provide learning experiences to help uncles, aunts, baptismal sponsors, grandparents, and parents provide spiritual leadership in their home. They learn and practice the four key faith practices: caring conversation, devotions, rituals and traditions, and service. They also make the family ministry resource Web site of The Youth & Family Institute, *Ready, Click, Grow for Families,* available on their Web site for all families of the congregation.
- The seventh-grade Sunday school students in a congregation in Florida developed a newspaper for the congregations. The students were the reporters, each one interviewing three of the oldest members of the congregation, one parent, and two school-age youth about what it means to have saving faith. The students wrote a newspaper column about each person they interviewed. The stories were put on large pieces of newsprint and hung on the walls of the educational wing of the congregation for all to read. The youth were surprised to see how many adults were interested in reading their stories. The youth learned faith stories, but they also learned that telling their faith stories was valued by the adults.
- Bethlehem Congregation in Grand Marais, Minnesota, held a workshop for parents and children to formulate a family mission statement. During the workshop each family worked on developing a statement that would express what they wanted to see become a reality for them. When they completed their first

draft, a spokesperson for the family shared their statement with the other participants. On the Sunday following the mission statement workshop, the families assembled in the front of the chancel area and publicly pledged before God their intention to carry out their mission. One can imagine the significance this had for children as they participated with their parents in developing their family mission statement and then stood before the congregation to pledge their intention.

- Under the leadership of Doug Haugen, Lutheran Men in Mission has partnered with The Youth & Family Institute to develop a conference for men's ministry called Coming of Age and follow-up training to equip men to be mentors of faith. Lutheran Men in Mission, The Youth & Family Institute, and Lyman Coleman have formed a partnership to develop and sponsor men's retreats, titled Men of Heart, Soul, Mind, and Strength. The conference, retreat, and resources are meant to equip men ages 17–35 to be stronger mentors of faith in the home and community.
- Congregations can develop Milestones Ministry Visitation Teams, which serve as faith mentors or as an extra set of godparents who assist the family in tending the baptismal or faith journey.
- Families could give personal testimonies during public worship and other congregational gatherings to convey how important it truly is to share faith in the home.
- Bethlehem Lutheran Church in Aberdeen, South Dakota, has developed a wonderful Milestones Ministry. They also focus on the Four Keys for Nurturing Faith in the Home and Congregation.

Chapters 2 and 3 show the powerful effect families have on passing on a mature and committed faith. Chapter 4 will begin to look at the effect the congregation can have, in partnership with the family, in passing on faith.

Chapter 4

Faith-Focused
Christian Education

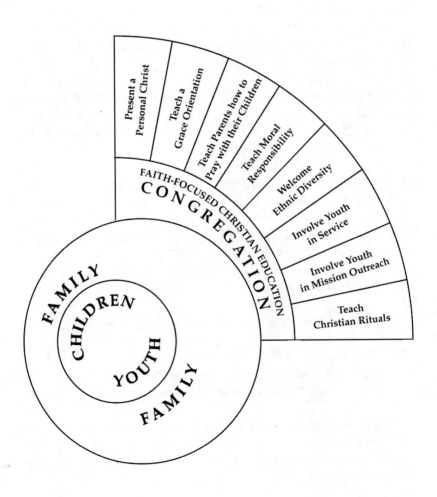

If we want Christian children, then we must have Christian adults. Faith is caught more than it is taught. The research by Christian Smith and others in the National Survey of Youth and Religion indicates that the modeling of parents in faith and values within their everyday lives is often more influential than the words the parents speak.

In sum, therefore, we think the best general rule of thumb parents might use to reckon their children's most likely religious outcomes is this: "We'll get what we are." By normal processes of socialization, and unless other significant forces intervene, most parents will likely end up getting out of their children religiously what they themselves are.[1]

Parents ignite faith in the lives of their children by making it an affair of the heart. They look to the congregation for help in making this faith a commitment of the mind. Through a congregation's program of Christian education, young people's minds are helped to understand what their hearts have come to know in the home—namely that Jesus loves them, cares for them, and is their savior and friend. In this book we advocate this kind of partnership between families and congregations.

A congregation's Christian education can find its direction by asking its members these questions: "What do you wish for your children and grandchildren when your congregation's Christian education program for them has ended? What are the outcomes you desire for your children?" Denominations are becoming more attentive to these questions. For example, the following three goals for adolescent faith formation in the Roman Catholic church are stated in *Renewing the Vision: A Framework for Catholic Youth Ministry:*

- To empower young people to live as disciples of Jesus Christ in our world today.
- To draw young people to responsible participation in the life, mission, and work of the Catholic faith community.
- To foster the total personal and spiritual growth of each young person.[2]

Christian education or faith formation includes more than going to Sunday school or other religious instruction classes. Viewed broadly, Christian education includes what Christian parents teach in their home; what the pastor presents from the pulpit; what is learned at youth meetings, Bible studies, and gatherings of men or women; and what is experienced in worship at home and within the congregation.

Christian educators must also do more than simply give religious information. Martin Luther made this very clear in his treatise on the *Freedom of the Christian* when he said: "It is not enough, nor is it Christian to preach the life, work, and words of Christ as if knowledge of these would suffice. Rather Christ ought to be preached to the end that *he* is Christ for you and me. Faith is produced by preaching *why* Christ came and what benefit it is to us to accept him."[3]

Christian Education: A Vital Congregational Emphasis

A congregational program of Christian education should have the same aim as a faith-forming family. In our model that aim is to help bring about the Ten Characteristics of Committed Youth identified in chapter 1.

1. Trusting in a personal Christ
2. Understanding grace and living in grace
3. Communing with God regularly
4. Demonstrating moral responsibility
5. Accepting responsibility in a congregation
6. Demonstrating unprejudiced and loving lives
7. Accepting authority and being personally responsible
8. Having a hopeful and positive attitude
9. Participating in the rituals of a Christian community
10. Engaging in mission and service

Protestant Christian Education Efforts: Sunday School

Since 1790 the Protestant Sunday school has had a history of being a vital agency for communicating the faith. Its primary goals were to bring young people to a conscious faith in Jesus Christ, to train lay leaders, and to meet the social needs of children. Evangelism was at the heart of the movement.

Two features characterized the early Sunday schools:

- They were completely lay-run and separate from the congregation.
- They were a significant spiritual force in the early days of our country.

Two hundred years of Sunday schools added such features as the following:

- Lay adults and parents were involved as much as children and youth.
- The Bible served as its basis of instruction.
- There was a concern for the moral and spiritual character of its members.
- There was an emphasis on motivating through awards.
- There was an emphasis on leadership by laypeople.
- There was an emphasis on children's work.[4]

As the Sunday school movement developed, it became less clear whether it was an agency concerned with social uplift (e.g., literacy, personal hygiene, personal morality), with the evangelization of the unsaved, or with the education of believers. Many Sunday schools persisted for years in doing a little bit of all three, but now most Sunday schools are emphasizing the education of believers.[5] The vitality with which these purposes have been maintained is reflected in the fact that the Sunday school remains today the longest-lasting and most intact religious movement in American Protestant history.

In the 1960s and 1970s, congregations' sense of urgency and importance for their educational programs began to decline. The decline was articulated in an issue of *Life* magazine that called Sunday school the most wasted hour in the week. At a consultation of Christian educators celebrating the two hundredth anniversary of the Sunday school, attention was drawn to the decline that had occurred between 1962 and 1979 in how parochial school youth of the Lutheran Church–Missouri Synod understood justification by faith and were involved in religious practices.[6]

The effects of the decline in the perceived importance of Sunday school were seen in a precipitous drop in church school enrollment between the years 1970 and 1980, when it plummeted from more than forty million students to thirty-one million students.

This decline became evident in a 1985 Search Institute feasibility study on Christian education for the Lilly Endowment. An initial step in the study was a visit to the national offices of six major Protestant denominations to determine whether top officials would actively respond to survey data resulting from a proposed study of Christian education in their denominations. These visits confirmed a significant change in the importance attributed to Christian education. One Presbyterian official said, "We used to assume that volunteers gave three years to teaching Sunday school. Now six to eight weeks is more likely the time of service." A United Methodist general secretary said, "It is quite common now for people to teach only three months, or even to teach two weeks on and two weeks off." He added, "Methodists today could be reaping the results of a past depreciation of Christian education."[7]

Though other factors contributed to this decline in a congregation's concern about nurturing the faith of their youth through Christian education, its results are evident: today's adolescents know less about the faith than did their parents at comparable ages.

Bruce Marshall, a college pastor, refers to this phenomenon in an article called "Recovering a Christian College":

> At the college where I teach, about 60 percent of the incoming students each year identify themselves as Lutherans, and many of that group have been in church virtually every Sunday of their lives. But only a few are aware that Moses appears in the Old Testament, and Jesus in the New. The number with a basic catechetical grasp of the biblical narrative, and what the narrative might be about, is remarkably small.
>
> These are bright students. But (except for the few who went to a Catholic high school) they are mostly ill equipped to consider Christian belief as a matter with which one might become intellectually engaged. Their cognitive grasp of the church's faith lags far behind what they know of mathematics or computers, and only the minority who become passionate about theology succeed in making up the difference. The church has failed to teach them the Christian faith, or even to suggest that it is something which one might have to learn if one wants to have a balanced Christian education.[8]

These observations describe what has happened in most congregations' Christian education programs, that is, a general lack of intentionality to achieve the goals defined by our Ten Characteristics of Committed Youth and Children. It reflects little awareness of the discrepancy between the *is* (the current spiritual characteristics of their children and youth) and the *ought* (the characteristics that could be true for their children and youth).

Rich Melheim, founder and chief creative officer of Faith Inkubators, drew high praise for his article "Conformation (Sic!) Is Dead." He states what many have observed about Confirmation instruction:

> The average adolescent "graduates" from Lutheran confirmation knowing very little and believing even less. . . . Blame whoever you want. Whatever the case, we are turning out a generation of biblically illiterate and spiritually immature youth who have never learned what we thought we taught them, and to whom God is about as relevant as wallpaper paste.[9]

Support for Melheim's strong judgment is found in the *Effective Christian Education* study. Almost two-thirds (63 percent) of the youth in Protestant mainline congregations show an undeveloped faith. Only one in ten (11 percent) evidence an integrated or mature faith.[10]

Richard R. Osmer, professor of Christian education at Princeton Theological Seminary, notes that for centuries after the Reformation, Luther's or Calvin's catechism was viewed as a classic text to be internalized through imitation and practice. Following successful mastery of the catechism, as part of a special service in which they were admitted to the Lord's Supper, children confessed for themselves the faith it represented.[11]

Osmer illustrates the theological vagueness that characterizes today's Christian education programs of mainline denominations by describing Paula, a university student, who had been raised in a Presbyterian church. Four years after her confirmation, she no longer believes that Christianity is the only way to God. As she puts it, "What you believe is a matter of what part of the world you happen to be born in and where your life journey takes you. I don't believe the same things I did when I was living at home, and I don't imagine I'll believe the things I do now in ten years."

Osmer notes that Paula's case is not an isolated one. At the turn of the twenty-first century, the market was filled with books expressing the effect of postmodernism or post postmodernism. According to Dean Hoge, Benton Johnson, and Donald Luidens in their book *Vanishing Boundaries: The Religion of Mainline Protestant Baby Boomers,* many young church members have departed from religion never to return. The authors studied five hundred confirmed Presbyterians between the ages of thirty-three and forty-two and found that nearly 50 percent of them had become religiously unaffiliated, they have established a permanent life structure in which their childhood faith and Confirmation vows are left far behind.[12]

In *U.S. Lifestyles and Mainline Churches,* Tex Sample expands on this point:

> The cultural left is made up of a group of about 33 million Americans, mostly baby boomers who seek self-fulfillment while being inner directed and marching to their own drum. . . . The people in our society who are least likely to attend church are those in the cultural left. . . . They are believers without belonging. . . . They, along with many cohorts in the cultural middle, are the basic reason for the decline of mainline churches.[13]

Roman Catholic Christian Education: Catholic Schools and CCD

The Catholic school mission, another significant force for Christian education, began during the mid-1850s, when Irish immigrants came in great numbers to the eastern seacoast cities of Boston and New York. The rapidly rising number of Irish Catholics in urban centers, combined with a growing conviction that public education—because of its Protestant flavor—was hostile to Catholicism, led to the establishment and growth of Catholic parochial schools in the northern and eastern United States.

Partly in response to another wave of Catholic immigrants in the 1880s, the Catholic school system expanded rapidly to total 1,700,000 students by 1920.[14] The mission of these schools was to obtain three goals with their students:

- academic excellence
- faith development
- sense of community

In 1966 Andrew Greeley carried out a major study of the religious effects of parochial education and introduced the concept of a multiplier effect. His view was that a devout family environment is necessary before the parochial school, as an agent of religious socialization, can have an effect on the child. Put negatively, for students whose childhoods were not spent in an environment of parental religiousness, these schools are unable to stimulate greater religiousness. The school therefore appears to act as a reinforcer; it is successful only if there is something to reinforce.[15]

The Roman Catholic Confraternity of Christian Doctrine (CCD) movement began in the United States in the 1920s and 1930s in parishes that did not have Catholic schools available. Its roots were the great missionary efforts of the Roman Catholic Church in the early 1900s. Consequently, the character of the CCD movement was more of an evangelizing one than a catechizing one. It depended heavily on volunteers and expected strong family involvement. Initial efforts were directed toward Catholic children in public schools in New York, minority children in Pittsburgh and Los Angeles, and children in rural areas like Oregon, Montana, and New Mexico. By 1935 a national office for the CCD programs was established in the Bishops' National Catholic Welfare Conference in Washington, D.C. By the early 1970s, nearly every Roman Catholic diocese in the United States had a diocesan office of religious education that looked after the religious education of youth not attending Catholic schools. Gradually the nomenclature changed from "CCD" to "parish religious education." Several voluntary conferences emerged to help give direction and support to this movement. The Diocesan Directors of Religious Education formed the National Conference of Diocesan Directors of Religious Education (NCDD) and the National Catholic Educational Association (NCEA) created a division for Catholic school administrators who were also responsible for parish religious education programs, the Diocesan Directors of Religious Education (NCDRE).

Like the recent Protestant experiences with the results of Christian education, Roman Catholics recently have become more and more concerned about their Christian education efforts. The universal Roman Catholic Church has issued numerous documents and exhortations. And the Roman Catholic bishops in the United States, along with the professional conferences of religious educators, are frequently reevaluating Christian education efforts in the face of great social and cultural changes.

Restoring Importance to Christian Education

Three compelling reasons give high priority to restoring Christian education in congregations:
- the current state of biblical knowledge
- the challenges of a pluralistic society
- the faith-enhancing potential of Christian education

The Current State of Biblical Knowledge

A national survey of American teenagers by the George Gallup Organization found the following to be true:
- Only 35 percent could name all four Gospels.
- Forty-four percent did not know how many disciples Jesus had.
- Twenty-nine percent did not know what religious event is celebrated at Easter.

In 1991 the Barna Research Group conducted a national telephone survey involving 1,005 randomly selected adults. One provocative finding shows that household income and age of respondents correlates negatively with the percentage of people who regard the Bible as "very important"[16] (see figs. 16 and 17).

Figure 16

Household Income and Importance of the Bible

Household Income	Bible Very Important
Under $20,000	70%
$20,000 to $39,000	57%
$40,000 to $59,000	50%
$60,000 or more	35%

Figure 17

Age and Importance of the Bible

Age	Bible Very Important
18–25	42%
26–44	53%
45–54	57%
55–64	60%
65 or older	76%

The Challenge of a Pluralistic Society

Martin Marty, retired professor of history of modern Christianity at the University of Chicago, notes that American Christians are woefully unprepared for being responsible agents of the faith: "They know too little of its story, its teaching, and its moral framework to exemplify and testify to their faith in a pluralistic society."[17]

Since World War II, mainstream Protestantism and Roman Catholicism have had to come to terms with pluralism. In today's mainstream society, non-Judeo and non-Christian groups such as Muslims, Zoroastrians, Hindus, and the like, are gaining prominence in every section of the country; diversity is a characteristic of today's religious scene.

The Christian education of children might be compared to a greenhouse where seedlings are protected and cared for until they are strong enough to be transplanted. In today's society this greenhouse has broken windows and unhinged doors, limiting the protection that can be given against secular beliefs and self-centered values. In other words, Christian education can no longer protect people from exposure to non-Christian beliefs and values. Instead, using the words of Marty, "It [Christian education] presents an opportunity for Christians to make sense of their surroundings for the sake of witness, citizenship, and their own sanity."[18] Christians have often lived in pluralistic societies. Christianity was born amid Jewish sects and Roman religions set within the context of a Greek culture; nevertheless, Christians flourished in these societies even though they were persecuted for their faith. In China churches were closed and the training of pastors was stopped, but house churches blossomed throughout the land with the result of an enormous increase in the number of Christians in that country.[19]

Jews have known from centuries of bitter experience that "if their children were going to grow up Jewish, they would have to help them develop that way through careful, intentional education and enculturation by the whole congregation, with the rabbi as their guide."[20] Likewise, intentional education and enculturation by the whole congregation is required for Christians in today's society. If we want our children to be Christians, we need to be far more intentional in grounding them firmly in the faith with a conceptual understanding of what is unique and redemptive about Christianity.

The Faith-Enhancing Potential of Christian Education

What in the life of the local church contributes most to nurturing a strong faith? This was a primary question to be answered by the *Effective Christian Education* study. Through sophisticated statistical analysis of its data, the research team identified six aspects of congregational life that contribute most directly to maturity of faith in adolescents and adults:

- faith-nurturing families
- formal Christian education
- quality of worship
- congregational sense of family
- service to others
- a thinking and caring environment

The effectiveness of a formal program of Christian education for adults and teenagers emerged second only to family in importance.

In spite of today's diminished attention to it, Christian education still outranks the four other faith-enhancing factors. This suggests that clergy who tend to place their emphasis only on the worship experience need to rediscover their role as teachers or rabbis.

William Willimon, professor of Christian ministry at Duke University, believes that Christian education has been based on an erroneous assumption that today's Christians live in a basically

Christian culture. He calls for a "renewed commitment to the adventurous task of creating and equipping Christians to live as mature representatives of Christ's kingdom within a world that neither knows Christ nor his kingdom."[21]

Restoring Content to Christian Education

The implications for the Christian church if its children and youth continue to enter adulthood as religious illiterates are similar to the implications of the cultural illiteracy that faces our nation in the civil sector.

Cultural Illiteracy

Professor E. D. Hirsch Jr., a specialist in language research, has drawn attention to a growing cultural illiteracy among students in today's public schools. In his book *Cultural Literacy*, a national best-seller, he credits a cafeteria-style education combined with an unwillingness of schools to place demands on students, as resulting in a steady dwindling of the amount of commonly shared information among generations.[22]

Because of this lack of commonly shared information, students have less of the background information that would enable them to grasp the meaning of words on a page. The explicit meanings of a piece of writing are only the tip of an iceberg of meaning. The larger part lies below the surface of the text and is seen in the light of the reader's own related knowledge.[23]

Hirsch credits the decline of cultural literacy to the educational theories of the past fifty years. These theories have stressed utility and the direct application of knowledge, assuming that many students are unable to assimilate the knowledge necessary for a literate society. The stance of theorists has been the following: Do not impose adult ideas before they can be truly understood. With this stance has come the devaluation of learning specific, historical information.

Hirsch calls for a different theory of education—one that stresses the importance of learning specific information in both early and late schooling. He deems it neither wrong nor unnatural to teach young children adult information before they can fully understand it.[24] He is convinced that our distaste for memorization is more pious than realistic. The absence of rote learning in formal education does not stop children from memorizing. Children are storing facts in their minds every day with astonishing voracity.

To prove his thesis, Hirsch has introduced a curriculum to inner-city schools that focuses on teaching information. He observed that a disadvantaged child often can decode and pronounce individual words, but frequently is unable to understand their meaning because of his or her lack of specific background information. The validity of Hirsch's emphasis on teaching specific information about our culture is seen in the high percentage of children who graduate from high schools that use his curriculum and go on to renowned universities such as Harvard.

Biblical Illiteracy

The parallel between the fields of public education and Christian education is striking. Christian educators, powerfully influenced by secular theorists, have minimized the mastery of biblical and doctrinal information lest they impose adult ideas before these ideas can be fully understood. Memorization of the catechism, formerly a requirement of confirmands, has been denigrated as rote learning; as a result, persons being confirmed today know far less about the Bible, creeds, commandments, or Church teachings than their counterparts in generations past.

With a limited background of biblical information, today's youth find it hard to understand what the words of the Scriptures connote or imply. Lacking historical background information about David, sacrifice, reconciliation, angels, sin, the Jordan River, Moses, Mary, Egyptian captivity, Mount of Transfiguration, justification, and the like, their understanding of the Christian faith is severely limited. Without such basic elements of biblical literacy, they are at a loss to describe the uniqueness of the Christian faith. Repelled by what they do not understand, they are prone to dismiss the Bible as boring.

We believe that a return should be made to grounding children and youth in the Scriptures—coming to know its stories, the saints of faith, its record of God's commands and promises, its accounts of divine intervention and description of the life to come. Early memorization of God's promises can indelibly imprint them in the minds of children to support their faith in times of need.

Appreciation for a Content-Oriented Education

Piaget's theories on the delaying of information have dominated the field of developmental psychology for the past fifty years. They are now being challenged by a new theory known as theory theory. This theory takes issue with the idea that as people age, the knowledge structures represented by connections in the brain turn on one by one.

It also contends that babies have more conceptual abilities than previously believed. In their book *Words, Thoughts, and Theories,* authors Meltzoff and Alison Gopnik of the University of Berkeley contend that infants form theories about how the world works, including ideas about the permanence of objects, the consequences of actions, and how other people think and feel. As they receive new information from the environment, babies modify their theories to better explain what they are seeing, hearing, and feeling.[25]

Katherine Kersten, commentator for National Public Radio's "All Things Considered," illustrates the effectiveness of a content-oriented education in her description of Trinity School in Bloomington, Minnesota, where her seventh-grade son is enrolled. Trinity is a school where the students are held to the highest expectations for all that they do. Trinity is one of the content-oriented schools, known as core knowledge schools, that have become part of the public school system in several city school districts. Trinity surrounds the students with examples of greatness and challenges their thinking with ideas found in great books. The school's reading list includes such authors as Aristotle, Rousseau, and Saint Augustine, and such writings as the Lincoln-Douglas debates.

Establishing such a tradition of excellence has even spilled over into sports. Trinity's 1994 student body of fifty-four students, grades ten through twelve, fielded a soccer team that defeated the defending state champion, Burnsville High (a large suburban high school).[26]

The secret of Trinity's success is as old as the ancient Greeks, the world's first great educators. The Greeks relied on examples found in the lives of great heroes and lawgivers to encourage, to illuminate, and to shape a pattern for life.

Core knowledge schools have demonstrated what can happen with children of low-income families and with minority students when there is a focus on facts. Their schools have been so successful that entire districts, such as Nashville, Tennessee, and Polk County, Florida, have switched to a core knowledge curriculum.[27]

The Christian Church has a tradition of catechetical instruction that remained relatively intact until the first two decades of the twentieth century. At that time the traditional method of preparing communicants began to be challenged by educators trained in public universities who viewed it as antichild and authoritarian. This marked the beginning of a steady decline in traditional catechetical instruction that has continued into the latter decades of the twentieth century. Less importance is given to asking youth to memorize key scriptural truths or to learn basic facts of the Christian faith.

Richard Osmer makes a case for a return to the use of the Presbyterian catechism. When referring to Paula, a college student, he says, "She stands in need of an intellectually challenging presentation of the Gospel that requires her to think about the faith in a rigorous manner."[28]

In *Rethinking Christian Education,* Osmer also calls for a shift to an understanding of Church in which congregations view themselves as cognitive minorities. They know they can no longer depend on other institutions to carry out their educational tasks. They must build their own alternative centers of education and no longer rely on what takes place during a single hour on Sunday.[29]

William Willimon agrees with making teaching a pastoral priority. He says: "The *Effective Christian Education* study highlights the great need, the intense hunger for effective Christian education in our churches. What we as pastors now need is a renewed commitment to the teaching task of the pastoral ministry, along with a new confidence in our ability to fulfill Jesus' mandate, 'You give them something to eat.'"[30]

The senior pastor of Emmanuel Baptist Church in San Jose, California, is one of those who sees his primary role in this way. His job title is preacher-teacher. All professional staff in his congregation of forty-five hundred members are responsible for initiating learning experiences in their areas of responsibility. They are to view Emmanuel as a teaching congregation intent on forming the faith of its members.

To enhance Emmanuel's effectiveness as a teaching congregation, most time in staff meetings is spent on evaluation. In the words of a staff person, "We evaluate everything, all the time. Every class, weekly workers meeting, and training session is evaluated and refined in order to improve our teaching ministries."

These accounts illustrate the role of a congregation in partnership with the family, which is to cultivate the faith germinated in the home. The congregation fulfills this role by teaching the beliefs that undergird the Christian faith and that help children develop a commitment of faith of the mind.

Christian Education As a Priority

A remarkable example of Christian education as a priority is found in the First Chinese Baptist Church of China Town, Los Angeles, where more than 70 percent of the congregation of two thousand members is involved each week in some form of Christian education. Here the focus is on well-trained leaders because it is believed they set the standards for the church. For them, to become a Christian and a member of this church is to be called into some form of service. To prepare for service, every member is encouraged to be trained, and in most cases trained as a leader.

To be trained in this congregation, a person must first take a year of classes on the Bible and theology. This is followed by a year of classes on teaching methods, educational psychology, and class preparation. During this second year, the trainee is teamed with a master teacher who can observe, correct, and instruct the person in good class procedure. Following a year of internship, the trainee can be given a class.

The 250 teachers in this congregation are trained both to teach Bible content and to use the teachable moment to pursue a relevant subject related to a student's expressed need. The teachers are trained to call on the students in their homes, to plan social activities with their classes, to pray for the welfare of their students, and to render spiritual care in many other ways.

While serving as teachers, these adults are committed to regular intercessory prayer, Wednesday prayer meetings, and monthly training meetings. At these monthly training meetings, teachers often will share lesson plans for the purpose of being critiqued by others.

One might expect that such high standards would discourage participation. On the contrary, a research team's visit to them in May 1997 showed that they have too many teachers. Teachers don't quit but tend to make it a career, most having served for more than twenty years. In fact, to gain teaching opportunities, some have connected with a branch church or have gone out as missionaries.

Few congregations can equal First Chinese Baptist's high level of dedication to Christian education, but many are not far behind. When visited by on-site researchers, thirty-eight of the forty-seven congregations viewed as exemplary in the *Effective Christian Education* study (because of their high faith scores) gave high importance to Christian education. In those thirty-eight congregations, five notable characteristics were usually singled out in the reports of the researchers making the visit:

- a high commitment among teachers
- an emphasis on adult education
- a caring, serving attitude
- an emphasis on the study of the Scriptures
- a strong prayer life

Commitment Among Teachers

Teachers at First Bilingual Baptist Church in Pico Rivera, California, regard teaching Sunday school as one of the most important aspects of their lives. A teacher in the adult department said, "My occupation is splicing telephone wires, but my real job is teaching Sunday school." He teaches two Sunday school classes on Sunday mornings as well as a group of Sunday school teachers on Sunday evenings. A similar commitment is evident for a teacher of fifth and sixth-grade children who teaches two Sunday school classes, regularly attends weekly workers meetings, and uses her vacation time to attend training seminars.

When the education director for one of the congregations was asked how his congregation was able to elicit such a high level of commitment, he replied: "We let them know that being a Sunday school teacher is a high calling. When we recruit we let them know the type of commitment we expect from them. They know what is expected and they respond."

Likewise, in the United Church of Christ (Iglesia Evangelica Unida de Puerto Rico), the research visitors noted the importance given the role of teacher. Once selected, trainees are asked to serve for at least a year as an assistant to a master teacher. This period of apprenticeship is called training in service.

The criteria for selecting teachers in this congregation are well defined. The teacher must have a good reputation in the community, must be faithful to the local church, must have knowledge of the Bible, and must be willing to teach. Interviews held with the teachers revealed a sense of pride and honor in being selected as a teacher. They view it as a ministry and not as a chore.

These two examples, along with the illustration of teacher commitment, underscore the importance of recruiting the right people for training in a valued ministry and the importance of supporting them with prayer and giving them the training they need.

An Emphasis on Adult Education

Another characteristic of congregations that give a high priority to Christian education is a strong focus on adult education. Although worship is viewed as being the engine of the church at First United Methodist Church in San Diego, California, a primary orientation of the congregation is training in discipleship; hence, Christian education, especially adult education, is second in importance. The adult education program that most members mentioned when interviewed was the San Diego Christian Studies program. The members of the group meet once a week for nine months, taking college-level courses during the three-hour sessions. The courses are taught by seminary and college professors, and upward of two hundred people typically enroll for individual courses.

Westwood United Methodist Church is another congregation that stresses adult education. It assumes that members come from a variety of backgrounds, therefore creating new classes to fit the specific needs. The strength of this adult education program is found in its staff of spiritually oriented teachers. For them spiritual formation is as important as learning the skills and strategies of good teaching. One teacher said when interviewed: "I think our teaching is only as good as our prayer life and our relationship with Christ. I share on Sunday morning what I gained at the Tuesday night Bible study and lived out during the week."

A Caring, Serving Attitude

Another striking feature of educationally oriented congregations is a strong emphasis on service to people in need—whether those in need are members of the church or not. One congregation in California explicitly views Christian education not only as learning but also as serving. These people combine Bible study and prayer with building projects in Mexico. They believe that through community projects, such as helping mentally challenged children learn to swim, people and the congregation are helped to grow spiritually.

A classic example of a serving attitude is found at Central Christian Church in Decatur, Illinois. This congregation's approach is reflected by a teacher of adults who spoke of the "excitement about learning when it deals with what happens in the lives of people." Faith is taught as something one lives in daily life. Hence, this congregation views service and involvement in social issues as a way to grow in faith. For them faith is caught as much as it is taught; one learns while doing.

True to this point of view is the congregation's service agency known as Disciples of Voluntary Effort (DOVE); since its founding the agency has found support in thirty-four Protestant and Roman Catholic churches. It offers a wide range of programs and services within a five-county area:

- a residential shelter from domestic violence
- a crisis hot line and legal assistance
- services for parents and children
- a treatment center for male abusers
- training and placement of more than 350 volunteers in more than fifty community agencies
- a mother-to-mother program that links suburban white mothers with welfare mothers, most of color, for friendship and support
- a preschool, a clothing room, and a community organization for low-income residents

Most of the staff and many of the volunteers in the program are members of Central Christian Church.

An Emphasis on the Study of the Scriptures

Another characteristic of congregations giving high priority to Christian education is their strong emphasis on the study of the Bible. This is especially true for Korean congregations. When visiting the Canaan Presbyterian Church in Chicago, I (Merton Strommen) watched 175 Korean high school youth participate in a worship service arranged solely for them. All youth came with Bibles that they used throughout the service, looking up the references the preacher made. I was impressed by their ability to locate the Bible references, whether in the Old or New Testament.

A Los Angeles Korean congregation of eight hundred members is divided into twelve sectors or areas. Members located in three of these sectors meet for Bible study and prayer on Mondays, members in three other sectors meet on Tuesdays, members in three other sectors meet on Wednesdays, and members in the last three sectors meet on Thursdays. Kai Cho Lee, an interpreter for our research visits to Korean congregations, told us that twenty to forty people attend her sector meeting on Thursdays. In addition to these sector meetings, a Friday night Bible study is open to the entire membership, regularly drawing two hundred or more people.

A good many congregations from a variety of denominations in the United States use Bible courses designed by Dr. Harry Wendt, a Lutheran theologian from Australia. One of his courses, Crossways, is a sixty-six-session exegetical journey through both the Old Testament and the New Testament. This course uses symbols on posters and overheads as a way to help people remember the themes and the main points of each book of the Bible. A second course, Divine Drama, is a shorter course of about thirty sessions that focuses on the themes of the Scriptures and how the promise of God is woven throughout the Scriptures. Participants have found these two resources to be excellent classes that are deep in both knowledge of the Scriptures and the connection between the Scriptures and life. One of the principles for passing on the faith embraced by The Youth & Family Institute is, "If we want Christian children and youth, we need Christian adults/parents."[31]

A Strong Prayer Life

A fifth characteristic research visitors noticed in congregations giving a high priority to Christian education was a strong prayer life.

Zion Lutheran Church, a congregation of nine hundred members in Puerto Rico, sets Friday evenings aside as family altar night. By prearrangement families gather in various homes for the purpose of praying and worshiping together.

Sinai Christian Church in Brooklyn, New York, with two hundred members, is another congregation that takes prayer seriously. On Monday evening the church has a prayer service or family prayer, which children and youth are invited to attend. About seventy-five persons attend this service. On Tuesday they have another prayer service from 10:00 a.m. to noon for those unable to attend the night before, such as the elderly, who cannot risk coming out at night.

Twenty-two reports made by research visitors as part of the *Effective Christian Education* study focused on those from nonwhite congregations giving a high priority to Christian education. Nineteen were found to emphasize prayer. This contrasts with Euro-American congregations where only ten out of twenty-five showed an emphasis on prayer.

Do Christians in nonwhite congregations feel a greater need for God's help? Such seems to be the attitude reflected in a statement by a member of First Lutheran Church, a rapidly growing African American congregation in Carson, California. He said: "We are a spiritual congregation. Every committee meeting starts with prayer. Church council meetings will sometimes pause for prayer to ask the Spirit for guidance."

Eight Essentials in a Faith-Focused Christian Education

The congregations described above foster an atmosphere that can bring reality to the ten objectives of a faith-focused Christian education. From these congregations and other studies, we can infer that a successful Christian educational program needs to accomplish eight essential tasks:

1. Present a personal Christ
2. Teach a grace orientation
3. Teach parents how to pray with their children
4. Teach moral responsibility
5. Welcome ethnic diversity
6. Involve youth in service
7. Involve youth in mission outreach
8. Teach Christian rituals

1. Present a Personal Christ

A clear purpose of Christian education is to help every person enter into a personal relationship with Jesus Christ. With respect to this objective, the Scriptures are direct and clear: "For God so loved the world that he gave his one and only Son, that whoever believes in him shall not perish but have eternal life" (John 3:16, NIV). "To all who received him, to those who believed in his name, he gave the right to become children of God" (John 1:12, NIV). For committed youth, Christianity is, first of all, a personal relationship.

Helping youth identify with a personal God goes beyond merely gaining assent to doctrinal statements. It involves something intensely personal—"I am convinced that God hears me, cares for me, forgives me; I have been in God's presence, I have the sense of being saved, I have been heard by God."

A Search Institute factor analysis of data from 7,050 high school youth drawn from ten different denominations identified five characteristics of youth who have a personal relationship with God:

• active with God's people
• motivated to grow and develop
• conscious of a strong sense of moral responsibility
• fueled by a desire to serve
• sustained by a hopeful, positive life perspective[32]

A similar analysis of younger adolescents, for whom a religious faith was central and important, revealed similar characteristics. They tend to

• be helping, serving adolescents
• have a healthy self-worth
• have a positive attitude toward church
• refrain from drug and alcohol use

- be less racially prejudiced
- be less involved in antisocial activities

Their value orientation tends to be one of service motivated by a concern for people.[33]

Coming to know Jesus as Savior and Lord clearly has a life-shaping effect on adolescents. What percent of church youth have such a personal relationship with Jesus Christ? The estimate in 1970 *(Five Cries of Youth)* was 30 percent. The estimate in 1990 *(Effective Christian Education* study) was 11 percent—a significant drop.

Whether the real percentages are 30 or 11 is not the main issue. Enough is known to say that most congregations are far from achieving this goal even with youth who have been part of the congregation since their baptism as an infant. Changes are needed if this central objective of the Christian church is to be realized.

What Can Congregations Do?

Secure teachers who have a personal relationship with Christ. An important place to start is with the recruitment of teachers. Sunday school is severely hindered in communicating a personal faith in Jesus if the teachers lack an integrated faith or teach with an undeveloped faith. And this is happening widely. According to the *Effective Christian Education* study, 61 percent of those teaching in a mainline Protestant congregation lack an integrated mature faith, and 29 percent evidence an undeveloped faith. It is fair to say that most of these teachers will not be able to ignite an enthusiasm for the person of Christ, because they lack this enthusiasm themselves.

Conscious of this, the director of Christian education at the previously mentioned Westwood United Methodist is selective when she recruits teachers. She says, "You can have all the programs in the world, but if the relationship is not there with Jesus Christ and with people, why bother to have them? Teachers should have some sense of who they are as people of God and be willing to share their faith with others." Careful recruitment procedures are gaining greater consideration for a variety of reasons. One reason is to reduce the risk of molestation. As a precaution, congregations are adopting a policy that all workers in the church, both paid and volunteer, submit to a screening program.

At a meeting of the research team for the *Effective Christian Education* study, an African American sociologist made an insightful observation regarding teachers in African American churches. He said: "You whites know the advantage of having teachers in your congregations who have a good education and superior materials. In our churches Sunday school is often little more than a grandmother with little education telling her pupils what Jesus means to her." The statement was interpreted by those of us in the room to mean that grandmother was nurturing faith in a way that is superior to the more cognitive emphasis found in white churches. This may be why the study found that faith scores, in terms of a personal relationship with God, were higher for African Americans than for whites.

Secure information on young people's spiritual journey. Discover from young people's self-reports where they are in their spiritual journey. This can be done in a variety of ways. The simplest is to invite them to draw on paper a faith-line that describes their pilgrimage. It can include symbols of growth, or the lack of it, and the dates when this growth occurred. In small groups, the youth can share their faith-lines.

A more precise assessment is gained from a survey containing specific items about faith to which youth can respond. One such survey, *Self-Portrait*, uses items from the book *Five Cries of Youth*. The survey yields group profiles that describe a group's concerns, values, and beliefs. It reported valuable information for adult mentors who were preparing to work with seventh-grade confirmands at Immanuel Lutheran Church in Minneapolis:

> Compared to church youth generally, the overall score of your confirmands is close to average on the scale entitled, "Awareness of God." Some youth acknowledge their awareness of God as Lord and Savior and others do not. This observation takes on more meaning when we look at individual items. Fifty percent of your confirmands say they "have a sense of being saved in Christ." The rest either say, "no" to this item or "not sure." Thirty-eight percent say they "have had a feeling of being in the presence of God." The rest say either "no" or "not sure." These percentages indicate that an important objective this year will be to help these confirmands into an experience of faith as an affair of the heart.[34]

Provide caring faith conversations with adults and youth.
An effective way to help individuals enter into a personal relationship with Jesus is through one-on-one conversations. And most helpful in facilitating such conversations is the *Self-Portrait* survey mentioned above.

Scales in the *Self-Portrait* instrument identify the degree to which an individual is concerned about an uncertain relationship with God and the degree to which the individual is aware of Christ as Savior. This kind of information facilitates conversation about a youth's relationship with God. Such a conversation is usually welcomed because it is a nagging problem for many youth. They find relief in discussing it but usually only in private.

Some young people have a relationship with God but don't know it. They need someone to realize this relationship for them. Others are troubled because they base their relationship with God on how they feel or on what they do. They need someone to show them that a relationship with God is based on what God has done and promises to do. Still others are plagued with doubts and inner rebellion and need someone to listen while they air their struggles. Again, such conversations are most possible when they are private, one-on-one conversations. *FaithTalk, FaithTalk with Children, Faith-Talk* Coasters, *Scripture Talk,* and *Milestones* Blessing Bowls are excellent resources, created by The Youth & Family Institute, for faith conversations.

2. Teach a Grace Orientation

A second desired outcome of a Christian education program is that youth and adults of a congregation understand and live a life oriented to grace. The importance of this objective calls to mind the two orientations to religion mentioned previously: (1) a law orientation where a person assumes that the way to be accepted by God is to live a good life, and (2) a Gospel or grace orientation where acceptance is based on believing what God has done and promises to do.

If a grace-oriented relationship with God is not modeled and taught in the home, the tendency of children and youth is to interpret Christianity as a religion of expectations, demands, or requirements; as a result, many grow into adulthood assuming that their efforts to live a good life qualify them as Christians. Their attention is on what they do and not on what God has done, is doing, and will do for them.

For people in an achievement-oriented culture, it is not natural to believe that acceptance into the family of God comes by simply believing God's promises. Even youth raised in a church that emphasizes being saved by grace often struggle to grasp this truth. They express agreement with statements such as the following:[35]

- The way to be accepted by God is to try sincerely to live a good life.
- The main emphasis of the Gospel is God's rules for right living.
- Although there are many religions in the world, most of them lead to the same God.
- God is satisfied if people live the best life they can.
- Salvation depends on being sincere in whatever you believe.
- If I say I believe in God and do right, I will go to heaven.

As is evident from the content of these items, youth agreeing to them see Christianity as basically something one does, a relationship with God that one achieves, a do-it-yourself religion.

High school youth oriented to such a religion reflect characteristics that differ markedly from the Ten Characteristics of Committed Youth. Though they may be strongly loyal to their church and committed to a moral code, these kids tend to be self-oriented in their values, prejudiced in their attitudes, lacking in a sense of mission, and living outside a personal relationship with Jesus Christ.[36] That is why it is so important to help children and youth into a grace orientation. By the time a congregation's youth graduate from high school, they should be able to distinguish between a Christianity that focuses on what a person does and a Christianity that focuses on God and his promises.

Though the concept of justification by faith is a cognitive truth to be taught as a biblical doctrine, a grace orientation is more than that. It is a spirit and attitude that youth catch. It is an orientation they sense in their teachers, in their parents, in their pastor. They catch it in their comments, attitudes of judgment, approaches to discipline, and even pulpit announcements. They sense it as an attitude of forgiveness and charity toward others and themselves.

What Can Congregations Do?

Teach the concept of grace. Few third graders will understand the word *grace*. But they would understand the translation given this word in the American Bible Society's Contemporary English Version titled *The Bible for Today's Families*. Here the word *grace (charis)* is translated, "treats us better than we deserve." This is something a third grader can understand.

The Seventh-day Adventist Church, seeking to move from a law orientation to a grace orientation, is writing a Sabbath day curriculum that places a focus on what God has done. To facilitate this objective, the John Hancock Youth and Family Center in La Sierra, California, has written more than five hundred biblical stories for use in the church.[37] In the story of David and Goliath, God is presented as the champion who wins the battle. Grace is taught as something God does. God is the Intervener, the Savior.

The emphasis on understanding grace continues in the Seventh-day Adventist Church, as noted by Stuart Tyner in his book *Searching for the God of Grace:* "[This book] is about how this treasure [grace] and this treasure alone can reorient our identity in our deepest reality."[38]

As a doctoral student at Princeton Seminary, Margaret Krych discovered a way of teaching a grace-oriented faith. Her approach, found in *Teaching the Gospel Today,* starts with the human predicaments of anxiety, conflict, and guilt—all realities in the lives of children, youth, and adults.[39] In her approach, she sees these realities as a result of sin. She defines sin as an inclination toward self-centeredness and making oneself the center of the universe. Sin and its results, described in these terms, are easily understood by children and youth, as well as adults.

Once the particular human predicament has been identified, the teacher can then draw attention to how reconciliation, forgiveness, and acceptance from God, made available through Jesus Christ, apply to the human predicament under discussion. The term *acceptance* is a good one because it can be used as a synonym for God's justification and forgiveness of sins. And the terms *forgiveness* and *reconciliation* are good words because they have contemporary meaning.

This method of correlating God's answer with questions real to children, youth, or adults is an adaptation of a method for communicating the Gospel made explicit by theologian Paul Tillich. For him the Gospel needs to be an engagement with the message in a way that grasps the very center of the student's existence. Tillich's point of view is well expressed in the following quotation from his book *Theology of Culture*:

> To communicate the Gospel means putting it before people so that they are able to decide for or against it. The Christian Gospel is a matter of decision. It is to be accepted or rejected. All that we, who communicate this Gospel, can do is to make possible a genuine decision. Such a decision is one based on understanding and on partial participation.[40]

Encourage and develop a spirit of openness. A grace orientation is characterized by an openness to people and to truth, a willingness to look at both sides of an issue and avoid a dogmatic rejection of a reasonable position.[41]

A youth survey administered at the end of the year to a high school Bible class shows how an atmosphere of openness encourages an understanding of justification by faith. This survey included a scale of items that assess youths' understanding of justification by faith. My (Merton Strommen's) surprise as the teacher was the remarkable advance in the understanding these Bible-class students had of justification by faith even though there had been no direct study of that belief. It appeared that the freedom they felt to express their doubts, concerns, and beliefs during the class had been conducive to capturing the spirit of grace and the meaning of acceptance by God.

Focus on Jesus Christ. Focusing on the enabling power of Jesus and using prayer as a way of seeking his guidance and help encourages a grace orientation. The important thing is that Jesus becomes the focus of attention, the one who is talked about, the one whose promises are claimed and memorized, and the person to whom prayer is directed.

Many are turned off by references to Jesus because they don't really know what he is like. Tony Campolo believes that the greatest barrier to confronting and loving the real Jesus may be the vision of Jesus we've created in our own image. In "Will the Real Jesus Please Stand Up?" he contends that many see a cultural Jesus through a cultural lens as a white, Anglo-Saxon, Protestant, Republican. Christians who follow this cultural Jesus seem to take the position that if we get enough power, if we get enough like-minded people in office, we can force America to be righteous.[42] A biblical Jesus, on the other hand, calls us to loving servanthood, to the giving of ourselves, to the mission to do what he did.

Another false characterization of Jesus is a law-oriented one. This is the Jesus that Phillip Yancey, a noted author and editor, came to know in the fundamentalist church and Bible college he attended. Later when he discovered the biblical Jesus, he wrote the book entitled *The Jesus I Never Knew*.[43]

Though Yancey appreciated the great theologians of the Church, the two thinkers who helped him most were Tolstoy and Dostoyevsky. Tolstoy, through his interpretation of the Sermon on the Mount as God's standards for us, showed Yancey how he always fell short of living up to the image of God. At the same time, Dostoyevsky, through his focus on forgiveness, showed Yancey how he, a sinner, could live in a state of forgiveness. The emphasis of these two writers brought Yancey into an awareness of the dialectic of being simultaneously a sinner and a saint. He came to see the biblical Jesus as one who graciously accepts him as he is. A congregation needs to present the biblical Jesus if its young people are to discover a grace orientation.

Encourage youth interest in the Bible. Creating an interest in the Bible among youth does not come easily. The Bible can be a threatening or puzzling book, especially for those who know only a few of its stories and little of its contents.

Years ago denominational youth offices promoted an aid to Bible reading called the Pocket Testament Movement. As members of this movement, young people signed cards pledging their intent to read a portion of the New Testament each day and carry a copy of it wherever possible. This encouragement to the reading of the Scriptures was followed by the distribution of a Bible reading guide. One such guide was called *The Uniting Word* because youth denomination-wide were reading the same passage each day and reflecting on the same verse.

Today, such national emphases on Bible reading are not a part of mainline denominational efforts, and fewer youth in these denominations read their Bibles with any degree of regularity. There is, however, a growing religious interest among today's young people that opens a door of opportunity for a new emphasis on Bible reading and study. For today's youth the Bible is not "old hat" because for most of them it is a new book. Few know its stories, important references, or key passages. Lacking these, youth have few fixed points for a faith—few promises to which they can cling.

Parents must encourage Bible reading for children at early stages—when children are infants, toddlers, preschoolers, and in the early grades of school. This is the time when religious interest is high and curiosity about adolescent issues begins to emerge. The desired outcome is that children become captured by an interest in reading their Bibles and in participating in discussions of the Scriptures. The Bible then becomes a point of entry for understanding and experiencing God.

Create adult interest in the Bible. Research clearly shows that one of the reasons youth have little interest in the Scriptures is that their parents and other primary caregivers are not reading the Scriptures. The reason many adults stay away from Bible studies is that they are afraid other people might discover how little they know about the Bible stories.

Knowing that most people are not familiar with the Bible, its history, its formation, as well as even its books, many congregations are using an intergenerational event called *Walk Thru the Bible*. The event involves a retreat in which a trained facilitator takes a group of participants on a fun journey through the books of the Old Testament. Six months later this group gathers again for a walk through the New Testament. By using visuals, symbols, rhyme, verse, and repetition, the families become familiar with the time in history of all the books of the Old Testament. The smiles and laughter of grandpas, grandmas, moms, dads, sons, and daughters that participate indicate that one need not be afraid of the Scriptures—one can have fun learning.[44]

Some congregations invite families to experience a *Walk Thru the Bible* event at the time a member of the family enters the Confirmation program. At this beginning of Confirmation, the congregation invites all of its members to make a covenant to read the Bible. Bible study offerings and worship services with thematic sermons can supplement these Bible reading efforts.

Milestones Ministry of The Youth & Family Institute is another example of an institution trying to encourage adults to read the Bible. This ministry includes three sessions to train uncles, aunts, grandparents, parents, godparents, and other faith mentors how to read the Bible stories to and with their children and how to discuss these great stories of a gracious God.

A further congregational ministry designed to stimulate an interest in adult Scripture reading, one that we have mentioned before, is the *Good News Bearers Ministry*. This Bible story learning program for third, fourth, fifth, and sixth graders includes a home Bible story reading program with parents. It also has a weekday program using the leadership of high school youth trained in peer ministry to teach Bible stories through creative drama and play. These same young people also perform biblical musicals for the whole congregation.[45]

In the last decade, many new Bible storybooks have been published, as well as new translations of the Bible. One of the best books to help adults and older youth learn more of the stories of the Bible is *The Book of God* (Zondervan Publishing House, 1996), by Walter Wangerin Jr. He presents the Bible as a novel. These new books make reading, learning, and telling Bible stories easier for young people and their families. However, the leadership of congregations, along with introducing these new resources to the people, also needs to train parents how to use them at home.

Capture the interest of high school students. A Bible study approach at First Lutheran Church in Duluth, Minnesota, has made the study of the Scriptures an exciting event for its high school students. Known as the X Factor, this program selects juniors and seniors with peer ministry training to serve as leaders. In a retreat setting, they learn how to warm up assembled youth with singing and games and how to conduct a Bible study using a prepared guide.

During the first year of the program, approximately thirty young people turned out each Thursday evening for X Factor. The next year there were sixty, and the following year there were between eighty and one hundred, many of whom came from unchurched homes in the community. For the junior and senior leaders, this event is a major ministry experience. One, an outstanding athlete and student, exclaimed, "Our Thursday evening studies are the highlight of my week."

Other churches have experienced the same enthusiastic growth when peer leaders are used. An interview of participants at Saint Luke's Lutheran Church in Bloomington, Minnesota, showed how much peer leaders are listened to and admired. According to several young people, these leaders wield a greater influence and power over them than their pastor or youth director. When on a retreat or trip, the word of the peer leader often carries more weight than the word of the adult.

Capture the interest of parents. The *Passing On Faith* model of The Youth & Family Institute emphasizes the role of parents and other adults in reading or telling Bible stories to their children each day. In this model the role of the congregation is not to teach the children but to teach the parents the skills, such as telling Bible stories, that will nurture the faith in the children God has placed in their hands.

There are many interesting and creative resources to help parents connect with their children through sharing the stories of the Scriptures. For example, the *Veggie Tales* are videos that can lead to wonderful discussions between parents and children about Scripture stories.

Another resource is *Godly Play,* created by Jerome Berryman, an Episcopal theologian and educator. *Godly Play* uses a Montessori method of education that invites the children into the story and equips them to tell the story. Parents sit on the floor with their children and use carved wooden figures on a piece of cloth to tell the story. The children then learn to tell the same story in their own words as they use the same objects the parents used. A similar method is used with young children in the Roman Catholic tradition called *Catechesis of the Good Shepherd.*[46]

3. Teach Parents How to Pray with Their Children

Every denomination has some wonderful prayer books for parents that even come with instructions for praying. But few congregations teach parents how to pray with each other and with their children. Children learn to pray best when they pray with their primary caregivers and experience firsthand that prayer is a valued spiritual discipline.

What Can Congregations Do?

Many congregations sponsor prayer vigils on Shrove Tuesday or Mardi Gras, the day before Lent begins, or at the beginning of each Church season. If children and parents go for fifteen minutes or an hour of prayer, they can all learn to pray together.

Still other congregations sponsor half-day and full-day seminars on learning a variety of ways and times to pray at home. In these seminars the whole family participates as a small group. The seminar has identified different times for prayer, different types of prayer, and different ways of prayer for families:

- mealtime
- travel time
- husband and wife time, or single-parent and best friend time
- sick time
- troubled time
- joyful time
- school and work time
- prayers for people in need
- prayers for friends and family
- prayers for grandparents, godparents, and mentors
- prayers of thanksgiving
- prayers of strengthening faith
- prayers of blessing one another
- prayers that can be sung
- prayers from the Scriptures
- prayers that are written or recited (in a home worship center, prayer towers, prayer boxes, prayer letters, prayer songs, prayer chains, prayer poems, breathing prayers, drawing prayers)

4. Teach Moral Responsibility

Developing morally responsible youth and adults is vital. Society's emphasis on self-enhancement and self-gratification has resulted in epidemic increases in life-denying behaviors. Parents and congregations need to become more intentional with respect to raising young people who are morally responsible.

How do parents and teachers create a sense of moral responsibility in children and youth who live in a time of conflicting moral standards? Research can be a great help. The *Harris Scholastic Research*, a 1989 national study of more than five thousand girls and boys between fourth and twelfth grades in public, private, and parochial schools across the nation, discovered that youth reflected five different orientations to ethical and moral issues. These orientations are called moral compasses. Each of these moral compasses encourages contrasting behaviors. Different percentages of the youth studied fit into different moral compasses.[47]

Civic Humanist (25 percent)
Youth of this orientation make moral judgments according to what is regarded as serving the common good of the neighborhood, town, or nation at large. Their motto: "Do what is best for everyone involved."

Conventionalist (20 percent)
Youth of this orientation make moral judgments according to what is generally accepted in the community and what they learn from such authority figures as parents and teachers. Their motto: "Follow the advice of an authority such as a parent, teacher, or youth leader."

Expressivist (18 percent)
Youth of this orientation make moral judgments according to the satisfaction of certain emotional feelings and psychological needs. Their motto: "Do what makes you happy."

Theist (16 percent)
Youth of this orientation make moral judgments according to a religious authority, such as the Scriptures, authoritative teaching, or the traditions of the religious community. Their motto: "Do what God or the Scriptures say is right."

Utilitarian (10 percent)
Youth of this orientation make moral judgments according to the practical advantages they afford the individual—that is, on the basis of how a particular decision would serve the person's self-interests. Their motto: "Do what will improve your situation or enable you to get ahead."

Note that only a minority (16 percent) of these American children operates with a moral compass formed on the basis of theistic assumptions and beliefs. An additional group (20 percent) reflects the orientation of their parents and teachers, an orientation that may be informed by religious assumptions and beliefs.

This research also shows the effect moral assumptions have on the decisions these children make. For instance, 65 percent of the high school students in the survey admit that when they have the opportunity, they will cheat. However, only 39 percent of those with a theistic moral compass would do so. Of those with an expressivist orientation, 54 percent say they would have sex if given the opportunity. Only 27 percent of those with a conventionalist orientation would do so. Of those with a civic humanist orientation, 39 percent agree that "homosexual relations are okay if that is a person's choice." Only 12 percent of the children influenced by theistic assumptions agree with this statement.

The power of these moral compasses to influence the behavior of children and youth is seen in the following moral dilemma:

If offered alcohol at a party, what percentage of youth from each orientation would refuse the offer?

Civic humanist—40 percent
Conventionalist—50 percent
Expressivist—34 percent
Theist—75 percent
Utilitarian—34 percent

These data demonstrate that the values and beliefs of children do matter. Values and beliefs shape children's attitudes and behaviors. In response to our question How does one create a sense of moral responsibility in children and youth who live in a time of conflicting moral standards? We can answer that Christian education can help youth develop moral responsibility by encouraging them to adopt values and beliefs that are biblically informed. Though younger children may depend on the guidance of their parents and teachers (a conventionalist compass), they will find guidance for their decisions in the written and incarnate Word as they gain independence.

What Can Congregations Do?

Teach the meaning of values. Although values are unconsciously absorbed from those loved and respected, values can also be taught and consciously claimed in creative and interesting ways. This is what Roland Larson, a consulting psychologist, and his wife, Doris, who is trained in social work, have done in their text called *Teaching Values*. Their purpose is threefold:

1. to help people understand personal, religious values
2. to explore methods of internalizing personal, religious values
3. to learn practical ways of helping to create a more vibrant faith

This book emerged from more than eight hundred educational workshops the Larsons have conducted for a wide variety of religious, educational, and community groups. First published as *Values and Faith*, their text has been recently revised for teaching values in schools, churches, and families. The book consists primarily of practical exercises with resources from the Bible that can be used with large or small groups in church, school, or family settings.[48]

Orient teachers to communicate values. Recruiting and orienting teachers who embody Christian values and beliefs is essential. A recruiting and orientation process should include having these influential adults reflect on their own moral compasses to determine whether they have a theistic orientation. Potential teachers need to be aware that their attitudes, side comments, and style of teaching all communicate a value orientation that children may sense and absorb.

Teach youth smart decision making. Thomas Everson, the former director of religious education at Boys Town, Nebraska, has developed a thoughtful curriculum for moral development and conscience formation titled *Pathways: Fostering Spiritual Growth Among At-Risk Youth*. Drawing from Kohlberg's justice-oriented theory of morality, from Gilligan's morality of caring, and from Charles Shelton's book *Morality and the Adolescent*, Everson presents a tested approach to moral development from a Christian perspective. An illustration of the guidance he gives in his manual is found in the six steps he gives to "Smart Decision-Making."

- **Me.** Start with yourself. Explore your options.
- **Adults.** Take time to talk with adults who care about you in order to get good directions.
- **God.** Find out what God has to say about your situation. Look in the Bible or talk with someone who can help you find out

what God has to say (e.g., a minister, priest, teacher, or youth leader).

- **Pray.** Always take time to pray.
- **Decide.** Make a decision and own the consequences. Be responsible for your own decisions. Do not blame your decisions on other people.
- **Evaluate.** How did your decision work out? Was it a good decision that you would like to make again? Or, was it a bad decision from which you can learn a valuable lesson?[49]

Support a theistic value orientation. In a culture of diverse moral compasses, children and youth who have adopted a theistic value orientation need support and encouragement. The need for this support became apparent to Richard Ross, youth director of the Tulip Grove Baptist Congregation in Nashville, Tennessee. At a weekend retreat, he heard several junior high girls say, "You don't know how stupid we feel being the only virgins in our age-group." As a response to these girls' dilemma, Ross developed the use of a commitment card for youth to pledge to remain sexually abstinent until marriage. Deciding whether to take the pledge caused youth to think through the values and behaviors they wanted for their lives. In making the pledge, the young women gained the support of all the others who had made the same pledge.

When Ross's program, known as *True Love Waits*, was introduced to his congregation, fifty-three youth signed the commitment card, pledging abstinence. They participated in a church service in which they made a formal commitment before their parents and received a ring to commemorate the event. Later these fifty-three youth stood before twelve hundred youth ministers of the Southern Baptist convention to tell of their promise and to express their conviction that others would want to do the same.

Almost immediately the youth ministers from thirty other denominations endorsed the program for use in their denomination and promoted its use. By the time a conference of Southern Baptists convened in Washington, D.C., in 1993, a total of twenty-five thousand pledge cards had been collected. These were spread out in the mall to demonstrate that an impressive number of young people value sexual purity.

The concept that true love indeed waits caught the interest and attention of the media. Soon such publications as *Time, Newsweek,*

Woman's Day, Vogue, Seventeen, New York Times, Washington Post,
and *USA Today* published articles about the movement. Ross and
some of his young people were interviewed about their approach to
sexual abstinence on programs such as *20/20, Today, Nightline with
Ted Koppel, Oprah Winfrey,* and *Donahue.* Remarkably this approach
to abstinence received little negative press and much admiration
and encouragement. By December 31, 1997, the program had se-
cured two hundred thousand signed pledges, including many from
countries around the world.[50]

5. Welcome Ethnic Diversity

By the year 2020, one out of two Americans will be from an ethnic
minority. From then on the minority group will be those who previously have been the white majority. Children, youth, and families need to anticipate this day by learning how to welcome into
their fellowship and friendship those who come from other cultures and ethnic groups.

Though usually less prejudiced than adults, young people still
tend to reflect the attitudes of their parents; hence, conscious efforts are needed to create the sensitivities that characterize a loving
and understanding attitude toward people different from oneself.

The *Effective Christian Education* study showed that little is
being done to create an understanding of how people from ethnic minority groups feel when they try to enter the life of a white
American culture. Extending a welcome to people from ethnic
groups requires more than a hearty hello and a warm handshake;
it requires an awareness of the inner battles that minorities fight
against discrimination, negative stereotyping, contrasting values,
and the meanings of words.

What Can Congregations Do?

Understand and welcome Asian American youth. The Asian
American group is the fastest-growing ethnic group in the United States. This population doubled in size during the 1970s and
1980s.[51] Donald Ng, a Chinese youth leader and Christian educator, identifies two major factors to consider when welcoming Asian
American youth: discrimination and culture. According to Ng, "It
is very difficult, if nearly impossible, for Asian American youth to

feel they are generally accepted. The reason for this is discrimination. Although desperately wanting to be included, they are often perceived as 'not American.'"[52]

The report "Civil Rights Issues Facing Asian Americans in the 1990s" profiles what many studies have indicated; that is, the discrimination Asian American students suffer in the distressing and hostile environments of the public schools. The majority of Asian American immigrant students believe that white Americans have negative and unwelcoming feelings toward them: "They [Americans] are afraid we are going to take over. . . . They think we are taking their jobs and money."[53]

Cultural differences must also be considered when welcoming Asian American youth. The Asian population includes Vietnamese, Samoans, Chinese, Indonesians, Japanese, Filipinos, and Koreans. Keep in mind that the cultural identities of different Asian groups in the United States are tremendously diverse; different groups speak different languages and come from different geographical traditions, and differences exist between foreign-born Asian Americans and American-born Asian Americans. Because of all these differences, welcoming Asian American youth requires listening to them and knowing who they really are; it means moving past any stereotypical images and welcoming them as people, not as a distortion or exaggeration.

A study of 1,215 Asian Pacific youth in the Seventh-day Adventist *Valuegenesis* study offers significant insights into this minority group. Though the sample is limited to this particular church body, it does give an indication of the Asian American situation and sensitivities.

The study found that education is a high value for Asians. Ninety-five percent of the Asian parents have graduated from high school, and almost half the fathers have at least a college degree. The securing of a good family income also is a high value. Seventy-seven percent of the Asian mothers are employed outside the home.

The primary tension for many Asian youth results from trying to adjust to two different sets of values and lifestyles: the immigrant parents' culture and the mainstream American culture. Some choose the American culture as their base of reference, some choose the Asian culture, and still others choose an integration of both cultures. Since just half the students (48 percent) speak an Asian language at home, parents and youth find it difficult to communicate on sensitive and conflicting issues. Their degree of happiness with family life decreases steadily from 75 percent for ninth graders to 66 percent for twelfth graders.

In spite of their educational prowess, more than half of Asian youth fight self-doubt. Ninety-one percent report times of sadness and depression, and 70 percent reveal a high degree of anxiety over their relationships with friends.[54]

Understand and welcome Latino youth. The second fastest-growing minority group in the United States is Hispanics. This population increased 70 percent between 1980 and 1990 and is quickly becoming the largest minority in the United States. Los Angeles has become the second largest Latino-populated city in the world. Overall, the Latino population is young, with a median age of twenty-four.

María-Elena Cardena, a Latina, writes about the challenge of fostering spiritual growth among at-risk Latino youth. She feels that one of the biggest obstacles is overcoming the negative image of Latinos that the media have created over the past two decades.

It is important to understand that for many Latinos, the family is first before all other commitments or responsibilities. Building relationships with the Latino youth and their families is more important than involving them in a program. Latinos tend to personalize relationships. Welcoming them means cultivating a friendship with them. They find Euro-Americans to be resistant to such relationships and consequently to be cold and unfriendly. The Latino connection with the feeling level of relationships has attracted them to charismatic and Pentecostal styles of spirituality.

Points of special contact with Latino youth are the following:

Drama. Their love for drama is built into their history.

Signs, symbols, and icons. Icons are not only a source of spiritual inspiration but also teaching tools.

Ritual. Ritual gives them a sense of permanence amid a life that is often chaotic.

An effective welcome for Latinos would include inviting them to work for the betterment of the community. Latino youth, according to Cardena, have a spirit of generosity toward the disadvantaged. Because of their feelings of solidarity with people who have little, they are likely to respond to a service project.[55]

Understand and welcome African American youth. According to the *Effective Christian Education* study, African Americans are more receptive to matters of faith than are Euro-Americans. The maturity of faith scores of African American church members are significantly higher than those of white church members. The African American ability to understand the Gospel and respond to it in remarkable ways has a history. Buster Soaries, an African American author, describes this ability in the context of slavery:

> Slaves were able to hear the authentic biblical story and identify with the redemptive, liberating nature of God in spite of the oppressive vessels through which the story was being delivered. The irony of the African American Christian heritage is that black slaves were able to accept belief in and acceptance of a loving God whose messengers were practicing hate and a saving Jesus whose disciples were practicing destruction.[56]

In extending welcome to African Americans, Euro-Americans need to recognize the discrimination and racism that is ever present in white culture, subtly operating in ways that subvert a warm welcome and discourage interaction.

Soaries is convinced the African American community needs to reestablish a moral consensus that centers on spiritual growth, academic excellence, economic empowerment, and political representation. An effective welcome to these people is one that supports their efforts to move ahead in these areas and to take responsibility for their future.

Soaries illustrates the kind of welcome that might be given African Americans by telling of an experience he had while conducting a workshop in Detroit for youth leaders from African American parishes. He noted that a group of Russian youth was visiting America, and he asked the youth leaders if they could arrange a visit to an African American church on Sunday morning, knowing that the Russian youth spoke no English and had never been exposed to the African American community. He then asked the youth leaders to identify the kind of preparations they would make to ensure that the Russian students would have a worthwhile experience. Their answers were profound. The list went on and on as they proceeded to describe all the ways they could accommodate a group of foreign students.

Soaries then asked the youth leaders to identify from the list which things they currently were doing for the African American youth of their own churches and communities. The answer turned out to be a resounding "none" They were more prepared to be flexible and creative to meet the needs of foreign kids than they were for their own kids.[57]

Understand and welcome American Indians. Though American Indians constitute only one-half of 1 percent of the American population, they are a vital part of the history of the United States. Reaves Nawhooks, pastor of Lincoln and Omaha Indians, says, "There appears to be no attempt to understand how we can respond to them and coexist with them in this society and at this time."[58]

Nearly three hundred tribes live in this country, each with its own language, history, customs, traditions, and often food and dress. A few characteristics, however, apply to all tribal people, according to Nawhooks:

Because they do not speak the same languages, American Indians often do not understand one another. The word *family* does not mean the same thing to them as it does to Anglo-Americans. Family for them includes not only immediate family but also aunts, uncles, cousins, and even close friends. The word *wealth* also has a different meaning for them than it has for most Americans. Tribal people consider wealth to be a large family; a person who has no family is considered to have died poor, even though she or he may have had an abundance of money, land, and material possessions.

In contrast with the Western way of taking and saving, tribal people live by giving and sharing. Contributing to others is deemed the ideal—not competing and trying to get ahead. The dilemma for the American Indians is to decide which way of thinking (contributing or competing) to adopt. This dilemma needs to be understood and appreciated.

Examples of congregations that welcome minorities. Two congregations, Bethany Covenant and Bloomington Covenant in Minneapolis, Minnesota, responded to an invitation from the mayor of Richfield to help minority peoples feel more a part of the community. In 1997 the two congregations adopted a five-year plan of outreach to the people of an apartment complex whose population is primarily Latino, Asian American, and African American. Realizing that the adults (mostly single moms on welfare) are threatened by a church building, the congregations rent one of the apartments in the complex for the activities they offer. These activities include one-on-one tutoring for kids, women's support groups, and a Bible study program. Volunteers from the two congregations conduct these activities.

Because the congregations have established a relationship with the residents of this apartment complex, a number of children have begun attending Sunday school at the congregations' churches. Just one year after the start of the program, sixteen of the twenty-one youth enrolled for confirmation instruction were children from families living in the apartment complex.

6. Involve Youth in Service

Developing a service orientation in faith-focused Christian education is important for several reasons. First, service was a central theme in Christ's ministry, finding its clarion call the night he instituted the Lord's Supper and washed the feet of his disciples. Earlier when James and John were seeking power in Christ's Kingdom, Christ said, "Whoever wishes to be great among you must be your servant" (Matthew 20:26, NRSV).

The service emphasis of the Christian faith stands in contrast to the mind-set of today's culture. Over the past several decades, there has been a discernible shift from serving others to "looking out for number one." This shift in values, well documented by Alexander Astin over the past twenty-five years, evidences itself in fewer young people choosing to enter service professions such as ministry, teaching, and social work.[59] This shift is reflected in shortages of pastors and teachers.

Reversing this shift requires introducing service early in children's lives. Benson and Roehlkepartain report from the *Effective Christian Education* study that "only 29 percent of Protestant young people in the study had spent eleven hours or more in a congregation-sponsored service project in their lifetime."[60] Furthermore, only 29 percent of the Protestant congregations have emphasized the involvement of young people in service projects. As a result, more than half the young people in the study have spent five or fewer hours in their lifetime "doing projects to help people in their town or city." Similar percentages of teenagers say they have spent five hours or less in their lifetime "learning about or doing something about people who are poor or hungry."[61]

When congregations neglect a service dimension in their ministry, they miss an important ingredient in youth work—one that educator and youth leader Dean Feldman notes: "The goal is to help young people begin to see themselves not as consumers of religion but as practitioners of the faith."[62]

An unexpected gain from involvement in service activities is an increase in church members' loyalty and affection for their congregation. This became apparent when three thousand churchgoing youth, grades seven through twelve, were asked to agree or disagree with the statement "The church I attend matters a great deal to me." Of those who strongly agreed with the statement, 20 percent had spent no time in service through their congregations, but 43 percent had spent forty hours or more in service in their lifetime through their congregations.[63] Service projects and service-learning not only bond the youth with their congregation and enhance their understanding of mission but also enhance youths' sense of worth and significance.

Today's youth leaders sense the importance of involving youth in service activities. A survey of one hundred denominational youth ministry executives and experts conducted by Group Publishing found that "developing youth as servants" ranks as one of their five top concerns. Eight out of ten of the respondents indicated that this emphasis ranks high or very high in their mind as a youth issue for the twenty-first century.[64]

Training young people for congregational leadership was, at one time, an important objective of denominational youth leaders. They equipped youth for leadership through weeklong training programs on how to lead meetings, how to plan and present programs, how to grow spiritually through personal disciplines, and how to participate in the life of the congregation. The youth appreciated the training because it demonstrated that they were valued as coworkers in the Kingdom of God. The effects of the training were seen in the way the youth later emerged into positions of leadership within their congregations.

Today leadership training is largely neglected; moreover, a close identification with the congregation is often discouraged by the way Sunday morning worship services are arranged, especially in larger congregations. Children and youth often attend Sunday school during the time their parents attend worship services. This separation conditions them to not attend worship services with adults and to not identify with the ongoing work of the church.

What Can Congregations Do?

Develop service projects and service-learning activities. Benson and Roehlkepartain sound an important note in their publication *Beyond Leaf Raking: Learning to Serve/Serving to Learn.* They observe that service activities should be followed by a time when participants reflect on the activity, arrive at generalizations regarding broader issues, and apply what they learned to new situations. David Kolb, a specialist in learning styles, developed the following Service-Learning Cycle:

1. *Concrete experience and observation.* (Plan and do service with others. For example, serve in a downtown soup kitchen.)
2. *Considered reflection.* (Reflect on the service experience. For example, what kind of people came for food? How did the youth feel as they served?)
3. *Synthesis and abstract conceptualization.* (Synthesize information and feelings from the service experience and generalize them to broader issues. For example, explore the causes of hunger in the United States)
4. *Testing of concepts in new situations.* (Apply the new understandings to life experiences. For example, plant gardens with low-income families to help provide healthier diets at lower cost.)[65]

Service learning as described in the Service-Learning Cycle can occur in a variety of service situations: it can take place after a week of rebuilding homes in Appalachia; it can take place while rethinking family priorities and spending habits after serving soup in a homeless shelter; or it can take place while reflecting on the elements of Christian worship after leading a worship service in a nursing home.

The connection between learning and serving is seen as contributing to the spiritual growth of members of the First Bilingual Baptist Church in Pico Rivera, California. This congregation was singled out for special study because of its members' high faith scores in the *Effective Christian Education* study. One of its members summed up the connection they make between learning and serving by saying, "We want to help people live the Christian life, not just study it." The mission projects of this congregation's young people combine Bible study and prayer with building projects in Mexico. "When we go across the border," said one young man, "and we see the poverty in which many people live, we thank the Lord for the blessings he has given us." Community projects, such as helping children with a disability learn to swim, are viewed as ways by which the congregation's young people will grow spiritually.

Another congregation singled out for special study because of its high faith scores was Ray of Hope, a Black Disciples church located in Decatur, Georgia. Two of the pastor's goals have been "to make content live and practical and to ask members to participate in their own learning." Under her leadership the congregation is engaged in such ministries as providing food for homeless shelters, participating in Meals on Wheels, and visiting people in prison. Members who are involved in such social services bring their concerns into the life of the congregation.

New members are received and nurtured with care. Each one becomes a part of the congregation's prayer concern, and each is assigned a shepherd-sponsor from the congregation to support and guide his or her involvement in the life of the congregation.

7. Involve Youth in Mission Outreach

Another essential in faith-focused Christian education is to involve youth and adults together in mission outreach. This means communicating a concern that others may come to believe in Jesus Christ. When this ingredient is missing, youth surmise that such a faith is not important and that believing in Jesus is not of eternal significance. When it is present, the dedication of youth to mission can have impressive results.[66] Because the desired outcome is faith formation, it is important for adults and youth to engage in service side by side.

A dedication to mission revitalized a previously "dead" congregation of longtime members in rural Alabama. The church, Liberty Baptist, located a mile from a small town with only one thriving business, was singled out for a visit because its youth, adults, and leaders are all unanimous in their praise of the youth program. A strong sense of mission motivates the young people. Many of them come to the church at seven o'clock on Monday mornings for a prayer breakfast. On Thursday evenings they have their regular meeting, which once a month is dedicated to evangelistic visitation. The youth, who have been trained in how to share their faith, go out in pairs to visit friends who are not involved in church or who have been absent from church for a few weeks. The adults who work with the youth are allowed only to drive the youth to the homes they visit. Adults stay in the car while the youth go inside to visit their friends. The ardency of these youth is seen also in their attending the state youth evangelism conference each year and going on summer mission trips. The range and sheer number of their activities has invigorated the congregation's entire membership.

What Can Congregations Do?

In *Fostering Spiritual Growth Among At-Risk Youth,* Tom Everson summarizes what he learned through visits to twenty-eight different sites where efforts were being made to connect at-risk youth with the Christian faith. As part of this Lilly Endowment–funded project, Everson queried the youth themselves as to which factors helped facilitate their spiritual journeys. He found that their answers were divided into three basic categories: people, programs, and strategies.[67] The people, programs, and strategies he found that nurtured the spiritual journey of at-risk youth might well be the same ones that move a congregation's youth and adults to mission outreach.

People. The people who facilitated at-risk youths' spiritual journeys had a number of qualities that made their facilitations effective:
- They unconditionally accept at-risk youth as lovable persons even when the youth behave badly.
- They themselves are growing in their spiritual lives—they walk the talk.

- They are direct in presenting spiritual messages; they don't mince words or try to water down the messages.
- They set clear boundaries and have low tolerance for negative behaviors.
- They are committed to walking with and challenging youth to change behaviors and lifestyles over an extended period of time.
- They are good, active listeners. They respond by challenging youth to take responsibility for their behaviors.
- They go out of their way to build relationships.
- They foster a sense of belonging by inviting at-risk youth to events such as retreats, choir concerts, Scripture studies, or service programs.
- They make liberal use of effective praise, taking the time to affirm giftedness, potential, and progress.
- They do not give up easily when they encounter rough times with the youth they serve.

Programs. The following are programs that the at-risk youth in Everson's survey identified as helpful:
- Twelve-Step programs, especially those associated with Alcoholics Anonymous and other substance abuse programs
- Scripture studies and prayer meetings that provided key environments for sharing and receiving the Good News
- service programs that enable them to recognize their gifts and abilities and share them with others in positive ways
- retreats that represent the format for being positively influenced by spiritual values
- worship that inspires them when they are allowed to participate
- religious education programs that address the issues they face and teach them faith skills
- outdoor camping programs that get them out of their everyday surroundings to experience the world in a new way

Strategies. Youth involved in Everson's survey identified the following involvement strategies as helpful to their spiritual journey:
- music, particularly popular Christian music, that is viewed as a positive alternative to secular music
- movies and TV shows with themes that relate to scriptural values
- journaling that enables them to express thoughts and feelings

- drama and role-playing that helps them put spiritual principles into practice in their lives
- concrete symbols of faith, such as a rock, a key, or a cross, that help because of youths' great need to touch, feel, and see such objects
- singing that enhances youths' sense of God's presence for those who have the talent
- stories, including personal narratives and Scripture stories, that stick with youth long after having been heard
- faith skills such as how to pray, how to use the Bible, and how to worship
- art that provides youth a way to express themselves and to describe their images of God

8. Teach Christian Rituals

In partnership with the home, a Christian education program should provide training for adults in the rituals and traditions of the Christian community and should teach them how to create family symbols and traditions of faith for the home.

In fall 1998 the Southeastern Minnesota Synod of the Evangelical Lutheran Church in America held an intergenerational, half-day training event to help families learn how to connect the rituals and traditions of the Christian community to their everyday lives together in their homes. The conference leaders, hoping about eighty parents and children would attend, were surprised when more than four hundred people, including grandparents, registered for the event.

Symbols and practices of the Christian faith have always been important for relating the Christian stories in Christian congregations and homes. In Deuteronomy 6:7 we learn that when our children ask us what is the meaning of the decrees and rituals, we are to tell them our stories. "When your children ask you in time to come, What is the meaning of the stipulations, decrees and laws the LORD our God has commanded you? you shall say to them, We were slaves of Pharaoh in Egypt, but the LORD brought us out of Egypt with a mighty hand" (Deuteronomy 6:20–21, NIV).

Family traditions such as daily routines, celebrations, and family stories speak clearly about what the family believes, values, and promotes. Family greetings, a table grace, bedtime prayers, the blessing of the Christmas tree, a birthday or baptismal anniversary celebration, or a Thanksgiving Day meal all can communicate the Good News of Jesus Christ. As Grandpa tells a story of God's faithfulness in his life to his grandchild, the story becomes a family story and the grandchild finds identity in this story. Grandpa's God story becomes the grandchild's story too. This God who loves Grandpa also loves the grandchild.

In "Understanding the Human Being: The Importance of the First Three Years of Life," Dr. Silvanna Quattrocchi Montanaro, a medical doctor, writes that pregnancy begins a child's faith formation, and from that time on everything parents do with that child is education. Simple, everyday tasks like feeding the child, washing the child, taking the child for a walk in the sunshine, are rituals that can be used to talk about God's presence and grace.[68]

From birth to age three, a child develops needs for order, movement, language, and steps toward independence. From three to six years of age, a child perfects the abilities she or he has already developed and expands the knowledge and experience gained from mother, father, other caregivers, the environment, and his or her own knowledge. The rituals, traditions, and patterned behaviors of the family are essential in the faith formation of a child.[69]

Christian congregations that are steeped in tradition and have a liturgical worship life understand the drama of family life that focuses on the word of God, the sacraments, and other holy moments with God. One of the most prominent people in the Roman Catholic tradition, Sofia Cavalletti, describes this wonderfully in two of her books: *The Religious Potential of the Child* and *Living Liturgy: Elementary Reflections*.[70]

Fewer homes in our present culture in the United States have symbols of the Christian faith than did homes twenty-five years ago. As we have pointed out earlier in this book, fewer parents know and tell biblical stories to their children. Fewer people can tell the stories depicted in the stained-glass windows of their church, the stations of the cross, the chrismons hanging on the Christmas tree, the carvings in the altar or lectern, the paintings, the murals, or the banners.

What Can Congregations Do?

An effective Christian education ministry that is beginning to appear in congregations is known as *The Catechesis of the Good Shepherd in a Parish Setting*. The author of this book, Tina Lillig, describes the approach:

> The approach does not use a series of catechetical books or take place in a classroom. Rather, a room is prepared for the children in which every object is a help to knowing God. Everything in this room, known as the atrium, is intended to be appropriate to the ages and sizes of the children who gather there. The atrium allows the children to come into contact with scripture, the liturgy of the church and, for the older ones, the whole of sacred story.[71]

Liturgy Training Publications has published a resource entitled *The Good Shepherd and the Child: A Joyful Journey* that offers parents and educators a gentle way to enter into and honor the spiritual life of the child. Caring adults who listen, pray, and journey with them in the faith nurture children's natural openness to and wonder of God's presence. The mysteries of life are presented to the children in the parables of the Kingdom. Baptism is shared as the gift of life. In the Eucharist children and adults meet Jesus, the Good Shepherd, and all of life is celebrated in the tradition of the Church year.[72]

At Saint John Luthern Church in Winter Park, Florida, one of the pastors designed a family night that was a liturgical scavenger hunt. He borrowed mannequins from local department stores and dressed them in robes and vestments from a variety of Christian traditions. On each vestment was a descriptive information sign like, "Hi, I am a chasuble. It means 'little house.' Don't you think there should be a door and window on me?" The altar was properly dressed with paraments and Eucharistic vessels of a variety of traditions, and each parament and vessel had a card of information. Even the areas of the worship center were identified by carefully designed, informative signs (narthex, nave, chancel, sanctuary, sacristy, etc.). There was even a room filled with candles and explanations and descriptions of how candles are used in the congregation and in the home during specific seasons of the Church year.

Each family received a worship center information sheet that contained the names of everything marked in the worship center. After a short opening devotion, each family was told they had twenty-two minutes to discover as many of the things listed on the worship center information sheet as possible. The sound of a bell noted the end of the time for the family information search, and the families then gathered in the fellowship room to discuss the new things they discovered and to talk about other symbols of the Christian community. In an evaluation of the experience, the families noted how much fun they had together and how much they learned in such a short time.

At Holy Trinity Episcopal Church in Menlo Park, California, six to eight families join together once a month to share dinner and create family rituals through child-related activities. The program is called *Faith-Full Families*. A person trained by the Child and Family Institute facilitates the classes. Each family continues in its own home the rituals learned in the class.[73]

In Omaha, Nebraska, at Rejoice Church, a family blessing class is taught by Cheryl Gries, the director of youth and family ministry. Families learn to develop short blessings for each season of the Church year that they will use as they greet and leave one another during a particular season. For example, families use greetings like these: "Go with God, seek peace, and pursue it," "We share the same Christmas gift—Jesus," "May the light of Jesus shine brightly in you as you help others shine," "Stay near the cross," "He's risen! He's risen indeed!" "Remember, you are splashed with promise!" or "Keep growing in Christ, laugh after laugh!"

In his book *Pilgrimage As Rite of Passage: A Guidebook for Youth Ministry*, Robert J. Brancatelli outlines a process for helping young people ages fourteen to eighteen make the often difficult transition into adulthood. The process involves both ritual and catechesis, providing a learning experience that engages the senses, the imagination, and the intellect. The process consists of three catechetical sessions on the themes of challenges, gifts, and belonging; a ritual interaction between males and females; an overnight pilgrimage; and a mystagogy session.[74]

Congregation leaders can learn more about celebrating rituals and traditions in the home and the congregation at specific milestones from the *Milestones Ministry Manual* of The Youth & Family Institute. *Frogs Without Legs Can't Hear*, by David W. Anderson and Paul Hill (Augsburg Fortress, 2003), has an entire chapter on rituals and tradition as essential for faith formation in the home and the congregation. Another great resource is *For Everything a Season: 75 Blessings for Daily Life,* by the Nilsen Family (Zion Publishing, 1999).

Chapter 5

Congregations As Family

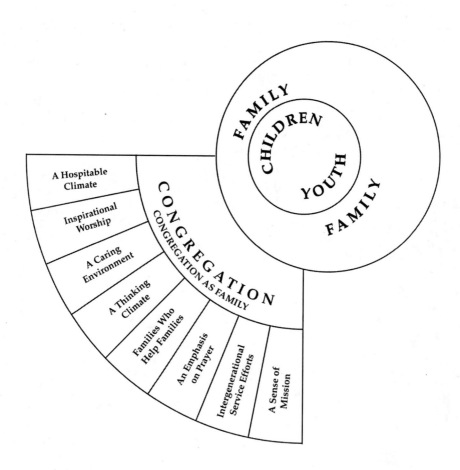

The Need for Congregations to Be Family

As important as it is for a parish to strengthen families in order to become a domestic church, it is equally important for a congregation to become like a family. The need for a supportive community beyond blood family was true for Jesus. Many members of his blood family did not support his work. The Gospels record that when the Jewish Feast of Tabernacles was near, Jesus' brothers, not believing him, said: "You ought to leave here and go to Judea, so that your disciples may see the miracles you do. No one who wants to become a public figure acts in secret. Since you are doing these things, show yourself to the world" (John 7:2–5, NIV).

The family from which Jesus drew much of his support consisted of the believers who surrounded him. He made this most obvious in comments that Matthew recorded:

> While Jesus was still talking to the crowd, his mother and brothers stood outside, wanting to speak to him. Someone told him, "Your mother and brothers are standing outside, wanting to speak to you."
>
> He replied to him, "Who is my mother, and who are my brothers?" Pointing to his disciples, he said, "Here are my mother and my brothers. For whoever does the will of my Father in heaven is my brother and sister and mother." (Matthew 12:46–50, NIV)

In a congregation in the Bronx, New York, I (Merton Strommen) discovered the kind of faith family Jesus had. The church building was located in a dismal, decaying part of the city. Yet it was freshly painted, and people of several nationalities were inside painting biblical murals on the wall, building kitchen facilities, or preparing food. When I was introduced to a woman from the West Indies, now a member of the congregation, her first remark was dramatic. With a wave of her arm that included all the people who were there she said: "This is my family. These are my people." Her congregation had become her family.

Luke's description of the Church following Pentecost likens it to a family:

All the believers were together and had everything in common. Selling their possessions and goods, they gave to anyone as he had need. Every day they continued to meet together in the temple courts. They broke bread in their homes and ate together with glad and sincere hearts, praising God and enjoying the favor of all the people. (Acts 2:44–47, NIV)

Congregations are blessed when they have members who invite others into their homes, who serve as mentors to youth, or who become surrogate families to lonely people or dysfunctional families. Such people create a congregational tone that conveys a sense of family—a quality Paul especially singled out when writing to the congregation of Colossae. "We always thank God, the Father of our Lord Jesus Christ, when we pray for you, because we have heard of your faith in Christ Jesus and of the love you have for all the saints" (Colossians 1:3–4, NIV).

We live in a time when many families are disintegrating. There will continue to be hurting people, more psychologically scarred youth, more fragmented families in the future of every congregation. Fewer youth will know close family life and the security of being loved and cared for. For them a congregation can provide the experience of being part of a close family by providing them with extra adult faith mentors from the congregation.

Like no other institution, a congregation can become family to its members. Through intergenerational activities a congregation can create opportunities for members to become surrogate faith-parents, uncles, aunts, brothers, or sisters to one another. A congregation is the only institution in a community that is open to all ages and is equipped in its program and message to provide a family experience.

The Effect of Congregations As Family

The unique potential of a congregation to act as a surrogate family became apparent in the *Effective Christian Education* study described earlier. Recall that the purpose of this study was to discover what in the life of a congregation, family, or community is most effective in encouraging faith and loyalty in youth and adults. When the study was completed, Search Institute used its measures of faith and loyalty to single out thirty congregations (five from each denomination) whose youth and adults measured highest in faith and loyalty. In addition, twenty-two minority congregations also were singled out using other criteria for establishing effectiveness. These fifty-two congregations were then visited by two trained observers, who discovered the characteristics that account for the congregations' effectiveness in promoting faith and loyalty.

What these on-site researchers identified most often as a notable characteristic of the congregations they visited was the sense of family. Thirty-nine of the forty-seven reports (those available from the fifty-two visits) made special mention of this quality. The reports referred to members' enjoyment in being together, their consciousness of a close fellowship, and their bonding through a common allegiance to Jesus Christ.[1]

Factors That Make a Congregation Family

Figure 18 lists the factors that enhance a congregation's sense of family:

Figure 18

Eight Factors That Make a Congregation Family

1. A Hospitable Climate
2. Inspirational Worship
3. A Caring Environment
4. A Thinking Climate
5. Families Who Help Families
6. An Emphasis on Prayer
7. Intergenerational Service Efforts
8. A Sense of Mission

A Hospitable Environment

The *Effective Christian Education* study found that a strong contributor to a congregational sense of family is the welcome a congregation gives strangers.[2] This finding shows that when people visit a congregation for the first time, they will make up their minds within twenty minutes of leaving their cars in the parking lot and entering the church building whether they will revisit the congregation. This means having parking spaces marked "For Our Visitors," having information readily available, and having people greet and direct visitors where to go. These actions are interpreted as signs of a warm, welcoming congregation.

Congregations with a hospitable environment acknowledge the presence and gifts of their children and youth. When visiting a congregation, families with children usually ask two questions: "Where are the bathrooms?" and "Are children welcome in the worship service?" An important question congregation members can ask themselves is, Upon entering our church building, how do families know their children are welcome?

When the Lutheran Church–Missouri Synod carried out a study of its people in 1995, it was curious to know if its youth and adults sensed a friendly atmosphere in their local congregations. Figure 19 shows how the people of this synod responded to items assessing this dimension.[3]

Figure 19

Percentages of Adults and Youth Agreeing with Statements Characterizing Their Congregation's Atmosphere

Statement	Adults	Youth
It feels warm here.	61%	55%
It accepts people who are different.	60%	59%
It is friendly.	68%	72%
People here care about me.	58%	63%
People here take time to get to know me.	40%	43%
Average percentage	51%	52%

These results are similar to findings from other studies, showing that people can sense the friendliness of a congregation with a high degree of accuracy. However, one can hardly be satisfied to find that only half of one's membership says their congregation has a warm and welcoming spirit.

When leaders of the Seventh-day Adventist Church did a study of twelve thousand of its youth, it found even more sobering percentages. When sixth graders were asked if their congregations feel warm, 61 percent said yes. But when the leaders asked their twelfth graders the same question, only 38 percent answered yes. This finding prompted a series of actions to establish more friendly congregational atmospheres.

A stereotype of congregations as being unfriendly is apparently held by many young adults known as Busters or Generation X (people born between 1964 and 1981). Many of these young people are reluctant to identify with the organized Church. In response, two pastors, Dieter Zander and Tim Celek, made them the special focus of their ministries. In 1984 Zander founded New Song Church in Covina, California, for those too young for a mainstream church and too old for youth groups. Within ten years, weekend attendance at this church reached twelve hundred people, with an average age of twenty-six.

In 1988 Celek founded Calvary Church Newport Mesa in Costa Mesa, California. By 1996 fourteen hundred young people were attending each weekend.

The two pastors have since authored a book called *Inside the Soul of a New Generation*. They are convinced that the Generation X population is not resistant to spiritual matters or to the concept of God. Rather, these young people resist the Christian Church (as they stereotype it). They see it as separatist, institutional, judgmental, irrelevant, and controlling.

Zander and Celek identify four Rs as necessary for communicating with this generation:
1. communication that is Real
2. communication that is Rousing
3. communication that is Relevant
4. communication that is Relational
Of the four Rs, they consider the relational aspect of communication as most important. They predict that more and more evangelism, especially of the young, will happen through relationships,

and that the Gospel will be communicated more incarnationally than propositionally or cognitively.

Clearly the friendliness and warmth of a congregation is important. A warm climate not only disarms preconceptions but also generates faith.

The power of this kind of welcoming atmosphere gained empirical evidence in a complex computer analysis conducted by Search Institute to determine what would most likely cause youth to leave a congregation. The most powerful predictor turned out to be "not being made to feel welcome." This predictor outdistanced the other thirty-eight predictors, all of which were strong competitors. The analysis showed that the youth most likely to stay with their congregations are those who know there is a group at church that misses them and will be there to welcome them when they return.[4]

I (Merton Strommen) had the privilege of attending a large African American congregation in the Bronx, New York. Being the only white person in an audience of more than a thousand, I was easily identified as a stranger. Before and after the service at least thirty people welcomed me. The depth of their welcoming attitude toward strangers was such that even a twelve-year-old boy had assimilated it. He was the last one to greet me before I left. He said, "Glad to have you with us mister. Hope you come again."

Creating a Hospitable Environment

The following are ideas and practical examples of how a congregation can create a hospitable environment:

- Train intergenerational teams of ushers who not only hand out worship bulletins but seat visitors next to members and introduce them to one another before worship begins and assist people who arrive after worship has begun.
- Train parking assistants who not only assist with parking but direct people to the worship and education areas.
- Welcome children to the worship service. Lois Brokering, an early childhood educator and member of Saint Stephen Lutheran Church in Bloomington, Minnesota, created Rainbow Bags to welcome children to the worship service. Outside the doors to the worship center, a large wooden rainbow with pegs holds double-handled cloth bags that have the symbol of the rainbow on them. Inside each bag are materials the children can use

during worship—materials such as soft toys, puppets of biblical characters, crayons and Bible story pictures to be colored, a children's bulletin, plain paper, and a couple of pencils. The Rainbow Bags make it clear to both children and parents that children are welcome at the worship service.

- Have a team of people survey the facilities to see if everything is accessible to children and youth. Can children reach door handles? Can children drink from the water fountains without the assistance of an adult? Can children reach the water basins to turn the water on and off as they wash their hands? If they are with their parents at worship, can children see what is happening in front? Does the church nursery have trained staff members? Is the furniture and other equipment in the nursery suitable and safe for children? Are all the rooms kept clean? Do the congregation's facilities use symbols to direct people to them? If so, can children see these symbols?

- Make the church inviting and accessible to visitors. Are outside signs large enough and placed so that motorists can see them easily when driving by? Are efforts made to inform and invite people of the community? Is the narthex or gathering room large enough for people to have caring conversations before and after worship? Will visitors know which door to enter when they arrive at the church? Establish a task force of people who have the gift of hospitality. Their task is to think of many ways the congregation can warmly welcome people in everything the congregation does.

Inspirational Worship

Researchers who visited the fifty-two exemplary congregations for the *Effective Christian Education* study found that worship services that all ages enjoy and find meaningful help create a sense of family. The services in these congregations were celebrative and inspirational and emphasized music. Through the computer analysis Search Institute did to determine why youth might leave a congregation, the researchers found that the second most common reason is "failing to be inspired at the worship service."[5] This reason is being noticed with increasing concern by congregational leaders. Many of today's generation do not respond to the high culture represented in traditional liturgies, in the classical, educational hymns, or in the formal approach of many services.

Without question the Christian faith has, in the past, been strongly identified with high culture. The Church has been the fount and inspiration of much of the classical art and music that graces art museums and concert halls today. But the more our Church culture is linked with a specialized vocabulary, music, art, and decorum, the more it will be seen as the religion of the elite.

To minimize this culture conflict, efforts are being made to present the faith in the language of popular culture, while seeking to preserve basic and distinctive truths of the faith. Doing so, however, has caused worship wars in many congregations.

In his book *The Other Story: Lutherans in Worship,* David Luecke, pastor and former seminary professor, identifies five characteristics of the contemporary worship found in many churches:

- features contemporary music
- is typically visitor friendly
- emphasizes informality for the sake of good communication
- usually features revitalized preaching
- tends to feature many different leaders in addition to the pastor, who stand in front and face the congregation

This shift in emphasis by many congregations involves more than substituting contemporary music for traditional music. Luecke says, "It brings a shift in the way a number of functions of leadership in worship are done."[6] This shift represents an attempt to look through the eyes of visitors at all actions and functions of the congregation during worship.

The congregations making this shift hope it will reverse the numerical decline of the great majority of mainline denominational congregations. The shift is an attempt to do what Muhlenberg, a trained organist, theologian, and missionary, who served over 250 years ago, decided was necessary to reach American Indians: "Learn the Indian melodies and tones and propagate the Law and Gospel with these tones so it would make an impression and then, with God's blessing, help await the fruitage."[7]

The fastest-growing congregations today are those that have established at least one of their services as contemporary with a special emphasis on contemporary music. On the other hand, almost every denomination has congregations that are exceptions to this trend and continue to grow rapidly, using traditional music and a traditional worship style. The common denominator in regard to music seems to be the quality of the music.

In 1994 the magazine *Your Church* conducted a survey of randomly selected American churches of all denominations. The survey showed that half the churches in America view their music as traditional, one-fourth as moderately traditional, and the other fourth as nontraditional. The survey also showed that congregations with nontraditional music reported significantly higher attendance in proportion to their membership (85 percent) than churches with traditional music (58 percent). With respect to membership gains, only 38 percent of traditional churches grew more than 1 percent, whereas 54 percent of the less traditional churches grew 1 percent or more.[8]

Numbers cannot be the sole basis for validating this shift from traditional high culture worship toward a more contemporary one, however. Marva Dawn, church musician and theologian, signals a growing concern in the title of her book *Reaching Out Without Dumbing Down*. Dawn is concerned about what people will know or understand about the faith five or ten years from now. She states in her book:

> Many churches who want desperately to attract people to Christ miss the mark by offering worship so shallow that not enough of Christ is proclaimed to engender lasting belief. If worship is only fun, how will those attracted to such worship have enough commitment to work on the conflicts that inevitably develop?[9]

What is needed, she insists, is a dialectical tension in the Church's worship services between the demands of truth and the demands of love. The pole of truth is essential to keep the Church alive with theological content and depth. The pole of love is necessary to minister effectively to those who need that truth.

Os Guinness, in his concern about the megachurch movement, says this about the issue:

> "It is perfectly legitimate to convey the Gospel in cartoons to a nonliterary generation incapable of rising above MTV. But five years later, if the new disciples are truly won to Christ, will they be reading and understanding Paul's Letter to Romans?"[10]

When the great reformer Martin Luther encouraged pastors to use the language of the people, he also stressed the need to help those weak in faith grow deeper in faith.[11] Likewise, Neil Postman's words in *Amusing Ourselves to Death* are worthy of note: "Christianity is a demanding and serious religion. When it is delivered as easy and amusing, it is another kind of religion altogether."[12] As noted in chapter 1, Christian Smith, in the book *Soul Searching*, affirms Neil Postman's words and stresses the need for spiritual leadership in the home and the congregation to take children and youth much deeper into the passion of God in Christ.

Sociologists Benton Johnson, Dean Hoge, and Donald Luidens have found that decisive "orthodox Christian belief" is necessary to impel people to commit their time and other resources to a distinctively Christian witness and obedience.[13] Recognizing the pitfalls inherent in both the traditional and contemporary approaches to worship, tension needs to be maintained between these two polarities.

Dawn believes that the object of worship must always be God. She insists that many of the antagonists in the war between traditional and contemporary worship miss this real issue:

> Both can easily become idolatrous. Many defenders of traditional worship pridefully insist that the historic liturgy of the Church is the only way to do it right, while their counterparts advocating contemporary worship styles often try to control God and convert people by their own efforts. Both prevent God from being the subject and object of our worship.[14]

Her position is this:

> Instead of throwing away the past, we can update, renew, reform, revive it. We can use new melodies, fresh instruction, thorough education, gentle reminders of what we are doing and why. Couldn't we teach in Sunday school the biblical roots of the liturgy? Then children, when participating in the Salutation, will know it comes from the story of Ruth and Boaz. They will know the Agnus Dei comes from John the Baptist, the Sanctus from Isaiah, the Magnificat from Mary, and the Nunc Dimittis from Simeon. What a rich web of witnesses we call to mind when we enact the liturgy.[15]

Dawn's comment corresponds to the argument presented in chapter 4 on the need for religious literacy. Just as students in school are showing a decline in academic achievement because of their decline in cultural literacy, so we face a similar decline in religious literacy. A worship service ought not only inspire but also help nurture a deeper understanding of the faith.

As mentioned previously, an important aspect of contemporary worship is its music. When David Luecke tried to establish a working definition of contemporary church music, he ranged from rock to country-western to modern classical. His working definition is based on what is currently popular in contemporary music.[16]

Christian Copyright and Licensing, an organization that supplies copyright permissions, describes a contemporary praise and worship song as music that usually incorporates contemporary harmonies and rhythms. Its lyrics usually use a first-person expression of praise to God, and the melody supports the lyrics by its emotionally expressive contour and design. The top twenty-five songs reported by churches applying for copyright permissions are usually more syncopated than the straight beat of traditional hymns. The songs' pronounced beat lends them to hand clapping. The songs are usually easy to learn and remember. Many have only one verse, and if there are more verses, only a word or two may change. The songs can be correctly called choruses that focus mainly on expressions of feeling and sentiment.

Authors Celek and Zander are convinced that music of this type is more important to today's young generation than it is to any other generation. Songs that touch them most are those that speak to their pain, their isolation, their experience.[17] Celek and Zander maintain that if a secular song is used in a worship service, it is placed in a Christian context. Their point is that these songs are already a part of the young people's experience. The songs have already touched them. Now it is possible to look at what meanings the young people can derive from them in light of God's truth. The authors claim a precedent for using secular music in worship in the way Martin Luther and Charles Wesley adapted tavern songs to convey Christian messages.

This approach, however, probably places a worship service in the category of evangelization. If so, it should be viewed for what it is, namely, an effort to reach those who will probably not respond to a traditional worship service.

I (Merton Strommen) was impressed by the two-hour service of an Episcopalian congregation in the little town of Buena Vista, Colorado. The service there maintained the structure and hymns of a traditional service but used choruses during the opening service and during an extended time of prayer. Words for the praise and worship choruses appeared on a screen, while a band of musicians led the singing with the assistance of a cantor. The tone of a personalized faith was evident, and depth in meaning came through the presence of traditional liturgy and strong, expository preaching. This congregation, once a mission outpost numbering as few as ten people, has become a self-supporting congregation with a membership of 220.

Marva Dawn describes how her home congregation in an African American community of Portland, Oregon, blends musical styles every week:

> One Sunday we began with a black spiritual, then sang "We Are Marching in the Light" from South Africa, and ended the opening devotional songs with a chorus from the Taize community in France. Other worship music in that service included three different traditions—a Lutheran chorale, an evangelical hymn, and a soulfully sung solo.[18]

Calvary Lutheran Church in Golden Valley, Minnesota, introduced a contemporary service that featured an instrumental group, a song leader, and songs contributed by members of the congregation. The service, first conducted in a small chapel, was soon drawing more people than the chapel could accommodate. It soon took over one of the services in the large auditorium that seats two thousand people. The church leaders found that songs that address the heart and are singable are attractive and meaningful to many people.

In light of biblical illiteracy and its effect on the Church's future, one must again ask: What will the youth who have been fed a constant diet of choruses know ten or twenty years from now? What will they who do not know the great hymns of the faith have lost? Often musical choruses are lines straight from the Scriptures that reflect an emotion much like that expressed in the Psalms, but a worship service is also a time for expanding the spiritual understanding of youth and adults. Therefore choruses that are immediately appealing need to be balanced with songs that enrich one's understanding and appreciation of the faith.

Creating Inspirational Worship

The following are examples and suggestions for creating inspirational worship:

- Have a worship action team plan themes for worship throughout the year. Some of the themes can connect to the Church year and others to local or family events within the congregation.
- Lyle Shaller of Yokefellow Institute, as well as numerous other consultants, has indicated that congregations should add an alternative worship service targeting Busters or Generation X people.
- Sally Mancini, former director of family ministry at Trinity Episcopal Church in Menlo Park, California, has developed an alternative worship service focused on families and led by families. This service and a traditional service take place simultaneously. The worship center is set up to be children and family friendly. Rugs are put down in front along with small chairs so children know they are invited to sit in the front. This family-friendly worship connects teaching with worship and uses the family as a natural small group.
- The Youth & Family Institute has developed a new worship resource called *Milestones Ministry Manual.* This resource is part of the *Passing On Faith* conceptual model and introduces complete children-, youth-, and family-friendly worship services designed around family milestones. This resource strengthens the congregation's partnership with the home in nurturing faith. For example, the focus on the Sunday of the Church year that emphasizes the baptism of Jesus expands to focus on all the baptized people of God celebrating their baptismal birthdays together. All the members of the congregation bring their baptismal candles or pick one up in the narthex. During the worship service, the people renounce the devil and all his empty promises, renewing their baptismal promises to follow Christ. They light their baptismal candles while they sing songs of faithful commitment to Christ. Each baptized person also receives a home devotion to be used on the anniversary of his or her Baptism.
- Saint Timothy Catholic Church in Mesa, Arizona, continues a youth ministry program called *Life Teen,* which focuses on reaching teenagers, bringing them into the presence of Christ, and transforming their lives through quality worship. The worship is a balance of tradition, ritual, and contemporary music.

The *Life Teen* leaders know the youth cultures and are passionate about transforming youth to be committed to Christ. The *Life Teen* model has been very successful. In fact, Saint Timothy Catholic Church's worship service for teens at six o'clock on Sunday evenings is so popular that to get a seat, one must arrive by a quarter after five.

The *Life Teen* model reaches teens on four levels: emotional, intellectual, spiritual, and relational. When teens arrive at worship, they are greeted with a sense of hospitality and a sense of belonging. Before the Mass, teens engage in faith conversation and a music warm-up. The priest knows what is going on in the lives of the teens and helps them transform from individualistic people to members of a community. Talented young people lead the worship, using quality contemporary and liturgical music. Then the pastor delivers a message, and the teens begin their focused prayers.

At the worship, everything is focused around the Eucharist. During the Eucharist, all the youth come forward and encircle the altar. The teens take Communion first, followed by the other adults who attend. This celebration of the Eucharist is a powerfully moving experience that targets the audience, moving the teens into the presence of God.

Life Teen is about transformation. The goal of this liturgy is to create an environment for transformation. Teens should meet Jesus and fall so deeply in love with God that they ask God to change their lives and then make a lifelong commitment to follow Jesus.

A Caring Environment

Search Institute's *Innovation and Change* study, a six-year study on factors that facilitate or hinder an institution's ability to move ahead, shows that a congregation's environment wields considerable influence. Youth quickly sense a congregation's atmosphere. Tensions caused by divisive feelings and power struggles repel them, but an atmosphere of warmth, cohesiveness, and exuberance draws them in. An operational style that is open-minded and offers freedom and warmth contributes greatly to a caring climate, while preference for status quo and self-protection convey carelessness.[19]

In one of its findings, the *Valuegenesis* study revealed the faith-generating power of familylike caring environments. The study identified the youth who saw their families, parochial schools, and congregations as caring environments. It also assessed the number giving evidence of a mature faith (see fig. 20).[20]

Figure 20

Environmental Influence on Youths' Maturity of Faith

Categories of Youth	Youth with Mature Faith
Youth lacking a caring environment	5%
Youth with one caring environment	17%
Youth with two caring environments	30%
Youth with three caring environments	53%

This evidence is dramatic; it demonstrates the importance of Christ's words when he said, "Love one another as I have loved you," and the significance of the early Christians about whom it was said, "Behold how they love one another." Recall here *A Study of Generations,* mentioned in previous chapters, that identified two orientations among the members of a congregation: a law orientation and a grace orientation.

Congregations that are predominantly grace oriented see God as personal and caring, and they live in a gracious, caring way. Those congregations that are predominantly law oriented tend to see salvation as something to be earned, and they tend to be concerned about how people live.[21]

When oral reports were being given by people who had made their first visits to exemplary congregations (ones ranking highest in scores on measures of mature faith), one of the visitors said:

> I came to this church and found them puzzled as to why they were singled out as an exemplary congregation. They said, "We don't have an unusual program of Christian education." But after being there three days, I saw how they loved each other and cared for each other, as well as for people in the community. Being with them was like being at a revival.

In a visit to the First Christian Church in Pine Bluff, Arkansas (another exemplary congregation ranking high in faith scores), this same visitor asked people to describe their congregation. The ministers, teachers, adults, youth, and children who were interviewed all spoke of their congregation as a family. "This is a caring community. . . . Everybody cares, everybody shares. . . . People care about me. . . . You can go to anyone for help. . . . Everybody is together, there is a closeness. . . . Everybody knows what is going on." Where there is a caring congregation, there tend to be people who evidence a mature faith. No doubt caring and mature faith interact to better increase each other.

Creating a Caring Environment

The following are examples and suggestions for creating a caring environment:

- Provide caregiving ministry training.
- Train youth to be caregivers.
- Make sure the ministries of the congregation are reaching out to nonmembers in the community as well as members.
- Make sure the community is always informed of the ministries provided through the congregation.
- Ask members of the community how the congregation can better respond to the specific needs of the community.
- Develop a strong ministry of prayer. Prayer teams should be intergenerational. Give clear information as to how people should request prayer, how the prayer request should be acted upon, and what kind of follow-up there will be to the person requesting the prayers. Welcome prayer requests for celebrating as well as for healing troubled relationships and curing physical diseases.
- The Youth & Family Institute provides peer ministry training as designed by Dr. Barbara Varenhorst, a school psychologist. Adults are equipped to train youth to work as peer ministers in the congregation and community. Peer ministry training provides the youth with a strong biblical and theological foundation and helps them develop listening and communication skills that equip them for a ministry of compassion and caregiving.[22]
- A number of churches have congregations involved in a caregiving ministry called Stephen Ministry. Stephen Ministry training was developed by Kenneth C. Haugk, a pastor and psychologist

who is based in Saint Louis, Missouri. In this ministry adults are trained to be caregivers in their communities. The training is excellent, long, and thorough. The training manual lists more than one hundred needs or opportunities for caregiving. Congregations that are involved in Stephen Ministry have developed a warm, caring climate.[23]

A Thinking Atmosphere

A multivariate computer analysis was made of the data from the *Effective Christian Education* study by Search Institute to see what congregational factors contribute to a sense of family. It showed that an environment that encourages people to think is very important. This finding was surprising because many people have assumed that faith is encouraged by a dogmatic approach, that is, every person thinking in the exact same way and having the same opinions.

However, discussing both sides of an issue and being stimulated to think deeply about religious issues actually enhances community. It not only respects individuals' insights but promotes the discovery of deeper truth. A small Korean congregation in Chicago that goes by the name Chicago Christian Church illustrates a thinking atmosphere. Its pastor fosters an intellectually stimulating atmosphere through an approach to preaching and teaching that stimulates thought, encourages questions, and provokes inquiry. During the researchers' visit to this exemplary congregation, it became clear that the congregation valued learning, grappling with issues, and dealing with the complexities of the Scriptures.

When researchers interviewed church members, the members spoke highly of the open teaching style of the pastor, his Bible-centered and nonemotional approach. One of the Sunday school teachers contrasted the open-mindedness of the pastor with the black-and-white, dogmatic theology he had known in his past. At the same time, he appreciated the seriousness with which the pastor dealt with theological issues and interpreted the Scriptures.

The educational director in this church also supported a thinking climate. His goal was to help students learn how to use the Bible to relate faith to questions of real life. He wanted to equip students to discern aspects of society that conflict with the values and faith of a Christian. This small congregation of 132 members reports between two and ten adult Baptisms each year.

Saint John Lutheran Church in Winter Park, Florida, emphasizes intellectual wellness. It features a congregation-based wellness ministry called Living Well in Christ. Through conferences, Christian education classes, seminars, and workshops, this ministry challenges people of the congregation to use the creative talents and resources God has given them to resolve family and community problems.

Creating a Thinking Environment

The following are examples and suggestions for creating a thinking climate in a congregation:

- Develop a lay school of theology that offers a variety of classes that take people deeper into their understanding of the Christian faith and the Christian church. Use the skills of the members of the congregation whenever possible and meet in the homes of members.
- Invite special guests to present certain issues of the world, and wonder together how a community of faith should respond. The guest could be a Jewish rabbi who shares, for example, his experience at a Nazi concentration camp, or perhaps a Palestinian Christian or a missionary from a very troubled area of the world could share her or his experiences. In small groups discuss how a faith community might respond.
- Invite such people as the mayor, school superintendent and principals, law and justice officials, members of the hospital and health communities, leaders of social-services organizations, members of the chamber of commerce, or county officials to develop strategies for making the community a safe and healthy place for children and families to grow.
- Provide training in vision, mission, and strategy for leadership people.
- Offer classes in planning and organizational skills.
- Provide classes in reading and creative problem solving.
- Have youth and adults with computer skills create software programs for nurturing faith in the home, for use in Christian education classes, and for use in the business and accounting aspects of the congregation.
- Invite artists from the congregation to participate in an art festi-

val around specific themes of the Church year.

- Invite members of the congregation and the community with skills such as singing or playing an instrument, writing plays, and creating poetry to create theater, concert, and recital events for the congregation.
- Develop action teams that use skills and creativity to develop solutions to current problems. For example, choose six people, all of whom are in their thirties and who have skills in financial planning. Form them into a creative ministry think tank to brainstorm ways of raising money for new ministries whose costs are beyond the budget.

Families Who Help Families

A congregational sense of family is fostered when families reach out as a support group to other families who are struggling with terminal illness, the loss of a loved one, a pending divorce, a case of drug addiction, poverty, or other similar problems.

The effect this concern and care among families has on a congregation may not be immediately discernible. For example, it may seem of little consequence that friends, grandparents, godparents, or noncustodial fathers or mothers visit single-parent homes. Yet when psychological measures are taken in schools of the children whose homes are visited regularly, significant improvements are seen in contrast to children whose homes are seldom or never visited.

Awareness among mental health professionals of the power and significance of support groups has increased in recent years. Two social scientists, M. Pilisuk and C. Froland, tell us that "to lack a support group is serious."[24] Their studies have found that persons who have lost their circle of intimate relationships through geographic mobility become substantially more prone to illness in all forms.

Research regularly finds that social relationships have a beneficial effect on health. Social involvement, for instance, is closely linked to survival of cancer. But a study conducted by psychologist H. Peters-Golden of one hundred persons with cancer showed that one in three felt they had no one to turn to. Once their illness was diagnosed as cancer, 72 percent of these people noticed a change in how their friends treated them. When Peters-Golden interviewed one hundred cancer-free individuals, she found that the majority (61 percent) admitted they would likely avoid contact with someone they knew who had cancer. Consequently many cancer patients see their networks of support disappearing.[25] At the same time, J. R. Bloom concludes that social support is the strongest predictor of coping response, one of the most important factors in a person's defeat of cancer.[26] These realities show the importance of congregations having families that support other families.

Support groups in a congregation can give more than emotional and material support. They also can provide spiritual support that nurtures life-sustaining faith for those in need.

To aid or supplement support for struggling families, some congregations in the United States have established a wellness ministry within the congregation. Some congregations even staff this ministry with a parish nurse. For example, Saint John Lutheran Church in Mound, Minnesota, has a parish nurse who not only directs seminars and workshops on personal and family well-being but also connects families in crisis with other families who have experienced and grown from a similar crisis.

This parish nurse ministry was developed by Dr. Granger E. Westburg. Now church colleges like Concordia College in Moorhead, Minnesota, have developed a parish nurse training program that connects faith with lifestyle choices and behavior and makes prayer a vital part of ministry.[27]

Creating Helping Families

The following are examples and suggestions for creating helping families:

- Train families (children, youth, and adults) who have experienced and grown from family struggles to minister to other families experiencing difficulties. Connect the families in need to the families trained as caregivers.
- Develop classes on such topics as grief and loss of love so participants can become support groups after completion of the class.
- Develop a ministry action team to do family needs assessments and to make specific needs and specific families known to families or individuals who are willing to give support.
- Provide Christian parenting classes and support groups for parents with preschool children.
- Research of Search Institute's Asset Development shows that to

be healthy and able to succeed, each child (and each family) needs a significant relationship with at least three adults besides his or her parents. Consequently, a congregation could provide information classes and training for senior citizens willing to offer such relationships.

An Emphasis on Prayer

Another characteristic of congregations with a good sense of family is a strong emphasis on prayer. For such congregations, the importance of prayer is reflected in meetings of prayer groups, in publishing prayer lists, and in offering public prayers.

A strong emphasis on prayer is a response to the Scriptures that remind us "our struggle is not against flesh and blood, but against the rulers, against the authorities, against the powers of this dark world and against the spiritual forces of evil in the heavenly realms" (Ephesians 6:12, NIV).

Prayer creates a form of fellowship that is fundamental to a community of believers. For example, when youth hear that their activities have been made a focus of prayer, then they have reason to believe their spiritual growth is indeed important to adults in the congregation.

Prayer brings together a consciousness of the presence of God, of who we are as the people of God, and of specific needs in the community. This consciousness was evoked in a congregation that I (Dick Hardel) observed. The consciousness was evoked when I (Dick Hardel) led the prayers in the liturgy one Sunday at Our Savior Lutheran Church in Saint Petersburg, Florida. The congregation became totally silent as I prayed:

> Gracious God, we ask your blessing on our junior high and senior high youth and their families, and the teachers in our community schools. For this is final exam week at our schools. We know that 67 percent of all junior high and senior high students cheat on tests. These are our youth. Strengthen them when tempted to cheat, help them to be honest and to respond the best they can.
>
> Lord, give them the ability to study hard and well this week and know they are loved by you and us, not because of their grades, but because we are the family of God.
>
> Pour out your grace upon the teachers and the parents who

work with these students. Support them with the knowledge of your love and guidance. Amen.

Similarly, the congregation at Rejoice Lutheran Church in Omaha, Nebraska, became silent when the pastor began the prayers of the people with this line: "Lord, we pray this morning for the Pizza Hut that burned down last night." Some youth of the congregation had worked there, many families of the congregations had eaten there, and some members knew the owners.

When visitors interviewed members of Sinai Christian Church (mentioned in chapter 4), in Brooklyn, New York, the church that holds Monday evening and Tuesday morning prayer services, they were impressed by how everybody viewed the congregation as a family. The visitors' report contained these words: "They care for each other and pray when somebody is in difficulty. The unity in the congregation is shared not only by the adults and youth but by the children as well."

Larry Dossey, a medical doctor and graduate of Harvard Medical School, was surprised when he discovered scientific evidence of the healing power of prayer. Unsettled by what he found, he embarked on ten years of research, probing the relationship between prayer and healing. Convinced by what he found, he wrote a book on prayer and the practice of medicine called *Healing Words*. He recommends that prayer for a patient become part of a doctor's routine treatment of illness; in fact, on the basis of his research, he believes that ignoring the healing power of prayer could be identified as malpractice.[28]

Thomas A. Droege, head of the Interfaith Health Program at the Carter Center in Atlanta, makes a similar point in his book *The Faith Factor in Healing*. He says, "If one's faith is grounded only in medicine and what it can do, it is idolatrous."[29]

This factor of what faith can do for the human psyche is gaining public and scholarly consideration. Harold G. Koenig, director of Duke University's Center for the Study of Religion, Spirituality, and Health, presents groundbreaking scientific evidence for the healing power of faith. He shows how a practicing faith is associated with longevity, health, resilience, and mental vitality.[30]

Creating an Emphasis on Prayer

The following are examples and suggestions for creating an emphasis on prayer:

- Offer classes on types of prayer, such as speaking prayers, writing prayers, breathing prayers, singing prayers, contemplating, and meditating.
- Train individuals to lead prayers in homes as well as in public worship.
- Provide workshops and seminars for families to learn the basics of prayer and the skills of praying.
- Begin each new season of the Church year with a prayer vigil for the congregation, and encourage people to keep this prayer vigil in their homes.
- Ask an extended family member to write the prayer for a Sunday worship service, and invite him or her to read the prayer at the service.
- Collect prayer requests from individuals, and then incorporate the requests into the prayers at a Sunday worship service.
- Invite the children to the altar during a worship service and ask them for any prayer requests they have for that day or weekend. Then say a prayer for each child as requested.
- Hold regular prayer and healing services for the people of the community.

Intergenerational Service Efforts

Another factor that creates a congregational sense of family is individual involvement in service and outreach ministry. This is substantiated by some thirty Minneapolis and Saint Paul congregations that participated in a visioning process to identify what they would like to see happening three years later. A vision that surfaced for most of these congregations was one of youth and adults working together on a project of meaningful service. People saw that such an activity would have two positive outcomes: it would enhance people's identification with their congregation, and it would encourage greater faith in both youth and adults.

Evidence supporting the first outcome is found in the *Effective Christian Education* study.[31] Three thousand churchgoing youth (seventh to twelfth graders) were asked if they agreed with the statement "The church I attend means a great deal to me." Their responses differed on the basis of their involvement in service through their congregation. Of those who had given no time in service through their congregation, 20 percent agreed with the statement. Of those youth who had spent forty hours or more in their lifetime in service through their congregation, 43 percent agreed with the statement.

This increased identification with the Church when there is greater service involvement is matched by the second outcome—a greater evidence of faith. It is impossible to determine which is the cause and which is the effect. It may be that greater faith is the reason for greater involvement in service activities; however, as mentioned previously, we know that adults who remember having been involved in church service projects as children or youth show significantly higher faith scores than those who carry no such memory. In fact, their memories of involvement in service are better predictors of their faith maturity as adults than are their memories of participation in Sunday school, Bible study, or worship services.[32]

A third outcome of intergenerational service projects—one not foreseen by the congregations involved in the visioning process—is the special fellowship that takes place between the adults and the youth who participate. The value of such an outcome is supported by the previously mentioned finding that youth who have a relationship with several adults besides those in their immediate family show an increased maturity of faith as they get older.

In the book *Common Fire*, authors Laurent A. Parks Daloz, Cheryl H. Keen, James P. Keen, and Sharon Daloz Parks share their experiences of interviewing more than one hundred people who had sustained long-term commitments to work on behalf of the common good, even in the face of global complexity, diversity, and ambiguity. The authors wanted to know what these people were like, how they became that way, what keeps them going in spite of discouragement, and what can be done to encourage this kind of citizenship in others. They found that a predominant characteristic of these committed people is the way they feel connected with the world. As one interviewee said: "I feel identified with the reality of service. It's become internalized. I'm not interested in the world because somebody said I should be. I really have no choice. It's become a part of me. It's what I care about."[33]

The authors also observed that commitment is not limited to an individual's own circle. Rather, it includes being committed to "a transformative process in society and the world, where one feels connected to a global network of concerned professionals and connected to a wider work."[34]

For these committed people there is a deep gladness that permeates the pain and hard work of seeking the larger good, and a commitment that remains over the years because they feel the real suffering of real people. These committed people have experienced an interdependence that has led them to place a high value on mutually nurturing relationships with others. As a public interest lawyer said, "You don't make it on your own. In my experience, people who tried it on their own were the people who lost their commitments."[35]

Creating Intergenerational Service Efforts

The following are examples and suggestions for creating intergenerational service efforts:

- A classic example of creating service efforts is found in the congregation at Our Savior's Lutheran Church in Minneapolis, Minnesota. This historic congregation, dating back to 1869, grew to sixteen hundred members under the leadership of a distinguished roster of pastors. As a missionary church, it established innovative ministries as well as eight new congregations in the city of Minneapolis. But as its inner city neighborhood declined, members began moving out to the suburbs. However, a core group remained, convinced that God's mission for them was to be Christ's presence in their area, known as the Phillips Neighborhood. Among the neighborhood's many minority populations were six thousand American Indians, the largest number found in any city in the United States. The median income in the neighborhood was seven thousand dollars a year, and the area also had a high crime rate.

    With just 250 active members, the congregation had developed an amazing ministry. It provided housing in the church gymnasium for forty homeless men each night and transitional housing for several families. It established an English learning center for refugees and immigrants, where as many as 125 people attended classes four evenings a week. In one year six hundred people were taught by volunteers who were trained as tutors by the Minnesota Literacy Council. The congregation also had a children's after-school program. On vacation days the program was all day long. During summer the congregation provided eight weeks of children's activities to help working parents. Needless to say, this ministry, with its 250 members and several hundred volunteers, was using all the space in the church building seven days a week. All this was in addition to the regular church program of Bible studies, Sunday school, choir, and a youth program.

Then in 1995, the Friday before Christmas, a fire destroyed all the facilities. In the year that followed, the church council, serving as a task force, convened members through retreats and workshops to create a vision for the future of the congregation. Providentially, insurance on the destroyed church provided a legacy of $3.4 million that began drawing interest while the new vision was being shaped. Members led the visioning process with questions such as these: What does God have in mind for us? What should be our ministry in the future? What partnerships might we establish with other congregations, social-service agencies, schools, and community organizations?

- Congregations can also be involved in service on a national level. In April 1997 a conference, the President's Summit for America's Future, was convened by the president of the United States and two former presidents under the chairmanship of General Colin Powell. Its goal was to mobilize voluntary, charitable organizations across the nation to meet the needs of America's children and youth. Of particular interest were children from low-income households, single-parent families, and neighborhoods where violence, drugs, and crowded schools make it difficult for children to learn.

As part of this national effort, a Seventh-day Adventist church represented by José Rojas offered to mobilize volunteers throughout his denomination using a program that had already proven effective in a number of inner-city settings. José, a former gang member in Los Angeles and now a pastor, had demonstrated success in working with such youth. He pledged to mobilize three thousand volunteer tutors, activate one hundred tutoring sites, and reach ten thousand children and youth between 1997 and 1998.

The Adventist program was opened to volunteers, regardless of race, color, language, gender, or religious affiliation. This program's success is a good example of how congregations can be activist partners in meeting national priorities that address the needs of children and youth in our nation.

A Sense of Mission

Nothing can create a greater sense of family in a congregation than for all children, youth, and adults to be motivated by a strong sense of mission outreach. When members feel like they are a part of something bigger than themselves, they tend to bond and unite with the congregation.

Evidence of the power of a shared mission surfaced in a major study conducted by Search Institute and reported in *The Innovative Church*.[36] The study found that the most accurate predictor that congregations will move ahead in purposeful and innovative ways is a strong sense of mission that all members understand and desire. A sense of mission outranked nineteen other factors that make for an innovative, progressive congregation.

At his training seminar on organizational development, E. Steven Sonnenberg, then a senior consultant with University Associates in San Diego, California, explained that in organizational development, three initial factors are essential: vision, mission, and belief system.[37]

For a Christian congregation, mission centers on Jesus' command to the Apostles to make disciples of all nations. Such a mission means being concerned that all come to know Jesus as Lord and Savior. This sense of mission has motivated people to go out into mission fields. It unites people in common cause and in common prayer.

George Barna, founder and president of Barna Research Group, equates vision with mission in his book *Turning Vision into Action*. In speaking about visionary Christians, he refers to those who have learned that the Bible is serious when it teaches that time is precious. Not knowing when the end will come and when Jesus will return for his followers, we have a task. Jesus is counting on us "to be his arms, and legs, his hands and feet, his eyes, ears and mouth to a world that desperately needs his presence."[38]

Visionary believers, according to Barna, can be discerned in four ways:

• They behave differently.
• They interact with other people differently.
• They produce results differently.
• They relate to God differently.

Their sense of mission causes them to set priorities and use their time in ways that are notably different from the usual.

Creating a Sense of Mission

The following are examples and suggestions for creating a sense of mission:

• A sense of mission that centers on proclaiming Jesus Christ is illustrated in the annual presentation of the Passion story by members of North Heights Lutheran Church. Thirteen thousand tickets for eighteen presentations are quickly sold. Seven hundred fifty members participate in the presentation as performers, parking guides, ushers, and support staff. These people not only come for each performance but also attend on other evenings to rehearse, prepare costumes, work through logistics, and pray. When the former pastor, Morris Vaagenes, was asked how this enormous contribution of time and effort was possible from people busy with work and home responsibilities, his answer related to their sense of mission: "I believe they are willing to do this because they know people are being reached for Christ."

In an article describing the play, Darlene Pfister of the *Minneapolis Star Tribune* told an inspiring story about Ginny Zimmerman, one of the participants.[39] Ginny wanted to participate in the production even though she suffered from a host of physical ailments, including multiple sclerosis, lupus, and chronic fatigue syndrome. Ginny made it through the rehearsals and up to the final dress rehearsal on Maundy Thursday. By then she felt too weak to continue. That night four cast members took her up to the cross and prayed for her. She woke the next day symptom free. She not only finished all the performances but was still symptom free three years later.

• Clara Olson, children's pastor at New Hope Community, Portland, Oregon, is an example of a person with a sense of mission. Under her leadership two types of children's groups have been established in her congregation: Tender Loving Care groups and Kids Clubs.

The Tender Loving Care groups are for children ages six to twelve whose parents are working through such crises as divorce, grief, alcohol or chemical dependency, and the like. The children meet while their parents attend a support group related to their crisis. In the safe environment of the church, a healing process for children is introduced through audio, visual, and kinesthetic educational experiences. The leaders, known as positive action leaders, are trained to help children develop coping skills that will enable them to build healthy self-esteem, learn to express their feelings openly, work though various family crisis issues, establish healthy boundaries, learn assertiveness, develop a growing relationship with God, discover how to become a Christian, and apply the Scriptures to life. Although the issues of dysfunctional families are directly addressed, attention is always directed to learning how a family can be made more nurturing.

The Kids Clubs serve primarily as an outreach to children who do not have a church connection. The clubs provide an alternative to traditional Sunday school or church-based programming. The children meet once a week in homes across the city. For an hour, they learn Bible stories, make crafts, complete projects, play games, sing, role-play, develop new friends, and pray. Most clubs meet after school and are independent of any adult group.

What is significant about this children's ministry is the dedication of the leaders. After initial screening they are trained to become mentors to the ten to twelve children in their groups. They then are required to give weekly reports regarding their personal devotional life and the contacts they have made with members of their groups.

Despite the weekly requirements of such leadership, the number of teachers and groups has grown from the one in 1997 to more than sixty now providing leadership for more than one hundred children's groups.

When a sense of mission is present in a congregation, it helps create a sense of family. It enables a congregation to affect the lives of its own people and all those who come in contact with them.

When most or many of the factors that make a congregation a family are present, the congregation will have a sense of
family. Congregations with a sense of family, in partnership with
families that are close to one another and close to God, will raise
young people who have a committed faith in God.

Chapter 6

Creating a Christian Youth Subculture

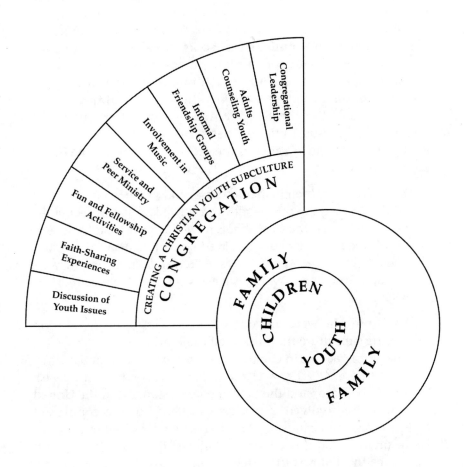

The labels in the figure read:

Congregational Leadership

Adults Counseling Youth

Informal Friendship Groups

Involvement in Music

Service and Peer Ministry

Fun and Fellowship Activities

Faith-Sharing Experiences

Discussion of Youth Issues

CREATING A CHRISTIAN YOUTH SUBCULTURE

CONGREGATION

FAMILY

CHILDREN

YOUTH

FAMILY

The Need

For youth to grow in faith maturity and a commitment to living a life that reflects the Gospel, a Christian youth subculture is very important. When the culture of the nation no longer supports the Christian faith, a Christian youth subculture becomes a safe place for youth to discuss their questions and concerns about faith, to develop leadership skills, and to form relationships with other youth and caring adults.

Hence, an imperative in congregational life is creating a Christian youth subculture. It makes a major contribution to the development of youth committed to Jesus Christ. It represents a necessary ingredient in a ministry that seeks to make the Ten Characteristics of Committed Youth a reality in our congregations.

Creating a Christian youth subculture is important today because North American youth are growing up in a culture like the one described by the Apostle Paul in his letters to the churches of Corinth and Ephesus. In these cities sexual immorality was a part of religion, and idol worship was the order of the day. To the Christian people living in these cultures Paul writes:

> You were dead through the trespasses and sins in which you once lived, following the course of this world, following the ruler of the power of the air, the spirit that is now at work among those who are disobedient. All of us once lived among them in the passions of our flesh, following the desires of flesh and senses, and we were by nature children of wrath, like everyone else. (Ephesians 2:1–3, NRSV)

For those who were converted to Christianity, a congregation became the subculture that sustained their faith.

The young people in congregations today are in a similar situation. In his book *All Kids Are Our Kids,* Peter Benson lists nine at-risk patterns of behavior and the percentages of students in the United States who are involved in this type of behavior.[1] To counteract the insidious and vicious pressure to become involved in these at-risk behaviors, youth need a close fellowship group. Some youth experience this fellowship in their family, but many do not. Many youth need a support group like the one Christ established with his disciples. By living together, going on retreats together, worshiping together, Christ's unlearned disciples were empowered to sustain faith in Jesus and to continue his ministry after his Ascension.

Christian support groups are important not only because of children's exposure to the negative aspects of our culture but also because of Christ's call for unconditional commitment. Christ calls us to a loyalty that transcends even family:

> If anyone comes to me and does not hate his father and mother, his wife and children, his brothers and sisters—yes, even his own life—he cannot be my disciple. And anyone who does not carry his cross and follow me cannot be my disciple. (Luke 14:26–27, NIV)

Yet, paradoxically, what Christ asks his followers to give up, he gives back with interest:

> "I tell you the truth," Jesus replied, "no one who has left home or brothers or sisters or mother or father or children or fields for me and the gospel will fail to receive a hundred times as much in this present age (homes, brothers, sisters, mothers, children and fields—and with them, persecutions) and in the age to come, eternal life." (Mark 10:29–30, NIV)

To maintain this level of loyalty to Christ while living in a society with conflicting systems of value, our youth need the kind of support Paul gave the Christians in Thessalonica to whom he wrote: "You know how we lived among you for your sake. You became imitators of us and of the Lord; in spite of severe suffering, you welcomed the message with the joy given by the Holy Spirit" (1 Thessalonians 1:5–6, NIV).

A Brief History of Youth Support Ministry

The need for Christian support groups has been recognized for generations because Christianity has always been a counter culture. Its ethical stance and value system have always run against the social norms of American life. As early as 1724, Cotton Mather wrote about societies that were formed to sustain the faith of young people. Though (according to Mather) these societies "proved to be strong engines to uphold the power of godliness, they were frowned on by the Puritan fathers, who viewed them as a dangerous innovation."[2]

Societies for youth and young adults continued to emerge during subsequent years. Among the well-known organizations, the oldest was the Young Men's Christian Association (YMCA) founded in Boston in 1851. The Young Women's Christian Association (YWCA) first appeared in New York in 1855. The Young Men's and Women's Hebrews Associations (YMHA, YWHA) followed soon after.

In 1860 a great laymen's revival was fostered by the YMCA. Large weekly prayer meetings of young men were held in YMCA settings. In his book *The Development of the Young People's Movement*, Frank Erb says, "The success of the YMCA on a purely religious basis led to the organization of young people in individual churches."[3]

An outcome of these prayer meetings was the creation of the Young People's Association in 1867. Its stated purpose was "the conversion of souls, the development of Christian character, and the training of converts in religious work."

But, according to Charles Courtoy, youth director for the United Methodist Church, it was not until the 1880s that the model adopted by all the mainline denominations emerged. The model, according to Courtoy's "Historical Analysis of the Three Eras of Mainline Protestant Youth Work," was the Christian Endeavor Society. The creator of this model, Dr. Francis E. Clark, pastor of the Williton Congregational Church in Portland, Maine, identified the need for its creation:

> In the winter of 1880–1881, in connection with some Sunday school prayer meetings, quite a large number of boys and girls of my congregation seemed hopefully converted. Their ages ranged from ten to eighteen, most of whom being over fourteen years old. The question became serious. How should this band be trained, how shall they be set to work, how shall they be fitted for church membership? Is it safe with only the present agencies at work to admit them for church membership?[4]

Along with becoming an auxiliary organization for the Church to train converted youth in the work of the Church, the Christian Endeavor Society provided a desperately needed social function of a safe and acceptable arena for the sexes to meet for recreation.

Three Eras of Youth Support Groups

Courtoy identified three eras of youth work in the mainline Protestant denominations: the Era of Societies and Leagues, the Era of Sunday Evening Fellowships, and the Era of Youth Ministry. Each of these eras has been conditioned by the nature of Christian education during that period.

The Era of Societies and Leagues (1888–1930s)

The kind of youth work during the Era of Societies and Leagues was dominated by the auxiliary youth societies. These societies were organized because the Sunday school's focus on evangelism did not accommodate the broader needs of the fast expanding youth populace.[5]

The reaction to Frances Clark's imaginative and innovative peer-oriented group came quickly. Within five years most of the mainline denominations had established their own youth organizations, patterning them after Clark's Christian Endeavor model and calling them a league (for example, the Epworth League, the Walther League, and the Luther League) or a society. Many used the name Christian Endeavor Society without adopting its principles—such as prayer meetings, pledges, consecration meetings, dual membership, and outreach committees. Clark considered these principles an integral part of the Christian Endeavor Society.

The following is the pledge that was required of every member of an original Christian Endeavor Society:

> Trusting in the Lord Jesus Christ for strength, I promise Him that I will strive to do whatever He would like to have me do; that I will make it the rule of my life to pray and to read the Bible every day, and to support my church in every way, especially by attending all her regular Sunday and midweek services, unless prevented by some reason which I can conscientiously give to my Savior, and that, just as far as I know how, throughout my whole life, I will endeavor to live a Christian life.
>
> As an active member, I promise to be true to all my du-

ties, to be present at, and take some part, aside from singing, in every Christian Endeavor prayer meeting, unless hindered by some reason which I can conscientiously give to my Lord and Master. If obliged to be absent from the monthly consecration meeting of the society, I will, if possible, send at least a verse of Scripture to be read in response to my name at the roll call."[6]

One cannot imagine such a pledge being taken by most youth raised in today's mainline denominations. However, some evangelical Christian groups today are challenging their youth to commit themselves publicly to living a Christlike lifestyle. For example, some groups support the "Meet You at the Pole" prayer rallies and the WWJD (What Would Jesus Do?) bracelets, T-shirts, and buttons that have become popular among many young people.

The popularity of Christian Endeavor Societies and the other denominational youth societies is seen in the attendance at youth conventions. In 1895 fifty-six thousand people assembled in Boston for a Christian Endeavor convention.

Adding to the rapid growth of these societies was the YMCA's Student Volunteer Movement that began through the influence of Dwight L. Moody. Thousands of students were recruited through this movement and sent to mission fields.[7]

In his book *The Youth Movement*, which describes the origins of Lutheran youth organizations, Gerald Jenny credits the emergence of Luther Leagues to the strong movement occurring in other Protestant denominations.[8] Between 1910 and 1920, Luther Leagues became established as national Lutheran organizations. Their purpose was to keep young people in the Church, to preserve them from evil influences, and to bridge the period from Confirmation to adult membership. But the history of the young people's movement in the Lutheran church is a record of an uphill struggle for recognition and acceptance. According to Jenny, "the majority of clergy were hostile to the innovation"[9] even though its purpose was to preserve young people's life of faith.

F. G. Cressey describes the efforts in 1907 to establish fellowship groups for young men living in cities that threatened their moral and spiritual lives. The purpose of his book *The Church and Young Men* was to help those "who are engaged in promoting the spiritual welfare of young men."[10] He notes that during a single decade, between 1910 and 1919, the following groups were founded:

Boy Scouts, Camp Fire Girls, Girl Scouts, 4-H Clubs, Junior Red Cross, Junior Achievement, the Pioneers of the YMCA, and the Girl Reserves of the YWCA. The focus of all these groups was on the development of good character in the lives of those migrating to cities.

Cressey notes that the percentage of young men in young people's societies of his day was only 36 percent, the same percentage of males (37 percent) found in the entire Church membership. Therefore, he pleaded that, for the sake of the young men, some means be adopted for making a service in which

> "by prayer and praise and brotherly interchange of experience, the souls of young men shall be built up in likeness to Christ, and in whose atmosphere of faith and love and fellowship some may be born into the kingdom of God."[11]

According to Courtoy, it was during the first quarter of the twentieth century that more and more of these youth societies fell under the control of liberal Christian educators. It was because of their influence that a second era in youth work emerged.

The Era of Sunday Evening Fellowships (1936–1950s)

This second era was characterized by a unified approach to youth work based on the philosophy and theory of Christian education. When the Congregational Christian Church set up Pilgrim Fellowships, the rest of the member denominations in the International Council of Religious Education followed suit. They changed the name of their youth programs to such names as the Methodist Youth Fellowship, the Westminster Youth Fellowship, the Reformed Church Youth Fellowship, the Christian Youth Fellowship, and the Baptist Youth Fellowship.

The concept of fellowship that dominated this era reflected the vision Christian educators had for Christian nurture—the concept of growing in fellowship with an immanent God. The aim of the fellowship was to help youth grow as Jesus had—"filled with wisdom; and [with] the favor of God . . . upon him" (Luke 2:40, NRSV).

Rather than operating as an auxiliary youth league or society outside the control of a local congregation, the youth program now was under the congregation's control. In most cases its fellowship activities were directly under the supervision of a local church committee on Christian education.[12] The general pattern of operation was Sunday school on Sunday mornings and youth fellowship on Sunday evenings.

In many ways the Sunday evening youth fellowship functioned as a youth club. Designated officers were elected: president, vice president, secretary, treasurer, and five program area chairpersons. The five program areas were Christian faith, Christian witness, Christian outreach, Christian citizenship, and Christian fellowship. These program areas were adopted in the thirty-nine denominations and provided the organizing principle for the development of curriculum and program resources for local congregations. Program and business at Sunday evening fellowships centered on one of these five program areas.

Even though they were influenced by what was being done in the thirty-nine denominations, not all denominations shifted to this approach to youth work. Lutheran youth organizations maintained their autonomy and auxiliary status. The Walther League, for instance, remained separate from the Lutheran Church–Missouri Synod, growing into a well-funded and strong organization. In the 1960s the Walther League built a three-story castle-like building to house a team of highly skilled professional writers, youth, and group leaders. The team marketed its publications, materials, and services, and in doing so, gave rise to an impressive number of youth activities in local congregations—activities such as Bible studies, worship, talent quests, choral unions, camping trips, and athletic and recreational events.

The Baptist Young People's Union (1896–1934) of the Southern Baptist Convention also did not adopt the fellowship model. Rather, its leaders chose the name Baptist Training Union and subsumed its activities under the Baptist Sunday School Board. Its youth program came to be seen as an essential part of the Christian educational program of every Baptist church of the Southern Baptist Convention.[13]

The Roman Catholic Church took a different course and established the Youth Department in 1940 to serve as the official agency of the hierarchy in the field of youth work. This department supervised the National Catholic Youth Council, a federation of local youth groups. The council's purpose was to promote four types of activities among Catholic youth: religious activities, cultural activities, social activities, and athletic activities. The council relied on diocesan youth leaders to train volunteer youth leaders in local parishes to carry out the program.[14] But due to a strong emphasis on parochial schools, youth work in local congregations was slow in being developed.

The demise of the Era of Sunday Evening Fellowships began during the 1950s, when older youth began dropping out of fellowship groups. Many felt that the most important activities of youth work were too focused on debate, discussion, and the general deepening of intellectual abilities. A study team established by the National Council of Churches came up with findings that called into question much of the current Christian education enterprise. Because the approach was based on the theory of Christian nurture, it did not address the reemerging question of how a person becomes a Christian. During the Era of Societies and Leagues, the answer to this question had been unequivocal: young people become Christians through conversion as a result of the Sunday school program.[15]

The Era of Youth Ministry (1960s–1980s)

This third era of youth support groups emerged as a result of two factors: the general disillusionment with youth work that was built on an educational base and the growing demand for youth to be given more of a voice in the institutions that affect their lives. Hence, the Era of Youth Ministry developed with an emphasis on empowering youth for ministry in the present as part of the ongoing ministry of their Church.[16]

But the transition from the Era of Sunday Evening Fellowships to the Era of Youth Ministry did not come easily. Polarization occurred between many youth staffs and denominational boards of education who employed them. One source of conflict centered on declaring that youth were full laity while not making clear how they became full laity. Little attention was given to evangelizing the non-Christian youth population, which was much larger than the Christian population.[17]

A second source of conflict was a shift from an educational approach to an approach that included missions, stewardship, evangelism, social concerns, and worship. During this period many denominations made deliberate efforts to shift youth work out of the control of denominational Christian education officials.

In contrast to the Era of Societies and Leagues and the Era of Sunday Evening Fellowship, the Era of Youth Ministry had no uniform plan of organizing youth work that clearly reflected this kind of emphasis. This could have been because there was a great deal of confusion and ambiguity as to the purpose of a youth ministry and how it was to be established and implemented.[18]

Five basic affirmations did emerge, however, that served as guidelines to local churches attempting to carry out a ministry with youth during this era:

- Youth are full laity and should be treated accordingly.
- A youth ministry should be designed locally and should reflect its unique situation and needs.
- A youth ministry should be person-centered rather than program-centered.
- Youth and adults are partners who share leadership responsibilities in youth ministry.
- Youth live in a world with persons who need ministry.[19]

The phrase "youth ministry" was chosen because it conveys the idea of youth actively involved in the real work of God. Since this ministry is dynamic, it was assumed that it could not be planned at a national headquarters. Instead, each local group had to be open to God's activity and determine what it should do.

Imbued with this kind of thinking, denominational staffs began to dismantle youth fellowship structures and to stop the publication of manuals and handbooks as well as program resources, membership cards, and jewelry designed to implement the fellowship. The loose structure associated with a youth ministry meant that only a few youth and adult leadership positions were needed; therefore the training emphasis shifted from training in congregational leadership to a person-centered training in personal growth and human relations skills.

Because the youth ministry emphasis lacked a clear and compelling theology, no effort was made to address the basic spiritual needs of persons. With emphasis on youth being full laity who did not need an organization of their own, denominational youth organizations such as the United Methodist Youth Fellowship, the Presbyterian Youth Fellowship, the Walther League, and the Luther League of America were dismantled. This resulted in the loss of some remarkable youth organizations that had been successful in sustaining youth in the faith and developing in them a love for their church.

One of the important goals in youth work prior to the Era of Youth Ministry was training in congregational leadership. Functioning leagues elected officers (president, vice president, secretary, treasurer, and pocket testament secretaries) who provided the necessary leadership. To assist them in assuming their responsibilities, weeklong leadership training events were provided by the denominations for both the officers and the adults who served as sponsors.

The training that took place in the Era of Societies and Leagues and the Era of Sunday Evening Fellowships was extensive. It included training in how to lead a meeting, how to conduct a program, and how to handle finances, as well as training in tithing through the use of a tithing box and in Bible reading through the use of a pocket testament pledge and a Bible reading guide called *The Uniting Word*. Training in the memorization of the Scriptures using cards containing God's promises was also provided. These card packets were called the Grow Series.

Youth in these two eras gained a strong sense of identification with their churches and valuable skills for assuming leadership within their congregations. Years later many of the people involved in these groups as youth assumed positions of congregational leadership and responsibility. Without question this past emphasis on equipping youth for congregational leadership is providing benefits to the Church today.

During the Era of Youth Ministry, when youth organizations were being disbanded, it was assumed that youth would volunteer for church boards and committees and participate in meaningful ways without training. This did not happen in most congregations. The experiment that was attempted during this period of history proved to be a dismal failure. Youth were not being equipped for leadership in either their youth organizations or their congregations.

As a result of this abortive experiment, a precipitous decline occurred in the number of youth participating in the youth activities of most mainline denominations. Taking up the slack created during the Era of Youth Ministry were the flourishing activities of a number of parachurch youth organizations such as Young Life, Youth for Christ, and Youth in Mission.[20] These organizations grew rapidly as large numbers of church youth left their Protestant congregational youth programs and became involved in the para-church organization programs.

In the Roman Catholic Church, there was a growing awareness of the limitations of a parish ministry with early adolescents that was dominated by a schooling approach. The schooling approach centered on courses designed around a textbook series with weekly one-hour sessions held in classrooms; a young person's experience of church was mainly another experience of school.

In his book *Early Adolescent Ministry*, John Roberto presents a new vision of youth ministry that emphasizes three goals:

1. Youth ministry works to foster the total personal and spiritual growth of each young person.
2. Youth ministry seeks to draw young people to responsible participation in the life, mission, and work of the faith community.
3. Youth ministry empowers young people to transform the world as disciples of Jesus Christ by living and working for justice and peace.[21]

For Roberto, youth ministry is not limited to the programs and activities sponsored within the church community. It is also directed outward to the needs, concerns, and issues of youth in society.[22]

Needed Today:
A New Era of Youth Support Ministry

The 1980s and 1990s have seen a steady decline in youths' participation in the life of the church. This is documented in studies of all the major denominations conducted by Search Institute and the Carnegie Council on Adolescent Development. The results draw one major conclusion: we are losing our youth from the Church and the faith to a life of at-risk behaviors. Clearly an effort is needed to revitalize this important ministry in the life of congregations.

Donald Ratcliff and James A. Davies, authors of the book *Handbook of Youth Ministry*, point out that an effective youth ministry is vital to the future of the Church. They quote from a study by the American Institute for Church Growth that found that a ministry to youth was the second most important reason people give for joining a congregation. (Preaching was identified as number one.)[23]

The same finding emerged from a survey of 553 families conducted by Group Publishing, a nondenominational publisher of youth ministry resources in Loveland, Colorado. Their researchers interviewed people in twenty rapidly growing churches as to what attracts them to a church. For these people, preaching ranked first in importance and youth ministry ranked second.[24]

What is needed to revitalize today's youth ministry? What new directions should be taken? What obstacles to faith do young people face? What obstacles do youth ministers face? These are the kinds of questions being asked today.

To gain answers to these kinds of questions, seventy-five hundred youth ministers at a gathering in Atlanta, Georgia, in February 1996 were asked to reflect on the joys, struggles, likes, and dislikes they experience in their work. The respondents, 2,121 professionals, answered a number of sentence-completion questions. They wrote whatever came to their minds when completing sentence starters such as these:

• What I like least about youth ministry is . . .
• I wish I had more training in . . .
• It pleases me in youth ministry when . . .
• My biggest concern in youth ministry today is . . .

Mark Lamport, professor at Huntington College and director of this research project, processed the written material as preparation for developing a questionnaire. He found that a top-ranking concern had to do with focus—there was a tendency for youth work to be activity oriented instead of being focused on making disciples of Jesus Christ. A second high-ranking concern centered on what youth ministers see happening to their teens—their involvement in at-risk behaviors, their backsliding, or their dysfunctional families. Other troublesome issues for the youth ministers included lack of parental cooperation with youth, youth's congregational disinterest, and the minister's feelings of personal inadequacy.

These same youth ministers expressed a strong need for training in various areas, such as counseling youth, preparing adults for mentoring, training parents for parenting, and assisting youth in becoming peer ministers. Their growing awareness of a need to work with parents and families signals the need for a new era in youth support ministry.

The failed experiment of the Era of Youth Ministry illustrated what can happen when congregations do not maintain strong youth groups. Young people need to be part of a subculture that supports them in their decision to live for Christ. They need a place where they can feel free to explore the issues they face as Christians. They need to develop strong friendships rooted in faith. They need to feel supported in their efforts to be part of the mission of Jesus Christ. A Christian youth support group is an aspect of congregational life that youth need.

In August 2005, an ecumenical and qualitative study of exemplary congregations in youth ministry, involving several different denominations (Assembly of God, Evangelical Covenant, Lutheran, Presbyterian [USA], Roman Catholic, Southern Baptist, and United Methodist), affirmed the need for the development of a spirit and culture of youth ministry.

> When all the relationships, practices, characteristics, and dimensions of these youth ministries have been identified, one still does not have the full picture of what makes these congregations' youth ministries so influential in the lives of young people. The genius of these places seems best described as a "culture," with a pervasive and distinct spirit and atmosphere that is larger and more powerful than its individual parts. It's this combination and interaction of core values, expectations, relationships, practices, and so on, that generate a culture of youth ministry.[25]

Creating a Christian Youth Subculture

What makes up a viable and effective Christian youth subculture? The answer lies in the eight components shown in figure 21 and described in the following section.

Figure 21

Eight Essential Components for a Christian Youth Subculture

1. Discussion of Youth Issues
2. Faith-Sharing Experiences
3. Fun and Fellowship Activities
4. Service and Peer Ministry
5. Involvement in Music
6. Informal Friendship Groups
7. Adults Counseling Youth
8. Congregational Leadership

Eight Components of a Christian Youth Subculture

Discussion of Youth Issues

Pressured on all sides to adopt a secular view of life, youth need a time and a place to feel free to examine another perspective—one that centers on God and God's word. Close fellowship is generated when there is a frank exchange of views, when efforts are made to discover what God says about an issue, and when time is taken for praying together for guidance and strength. These discussions can be led by an adult or by older peers.

After a two-hour Christian education event, Andy, an eighth grader in a family loosely connected to Our Savior Lutheran Church in Saint Petersburg, Florida, said to the youth pastor, "You know, Pastor Dick, you are a good guy, and I like being with you, but I don't know if I believe this stuff about God." The youth pastor responded, "What stuff?"

"Oh, about creation and God as the Creator of the universe," answered Andy. "In school I have been taught the big bang theory and how it all happened by chance. This God stuff seems pretty far out."

"But you believe the big bang theory?" asked the youth pastor.

"I guess so," replied Andy. "I really don't know! I want to keep talking to you and the other kids."

Years later Andy became the youth minister at an Episcopal Church in Saint Petersburg. The existing Christian subculture in the congregation and the opportunity for discussion of issues it offered enabled him to wonder about God and to ask his questions, and it continued to affirm his membership in the Body of Christ even when he wasn't sure of his beliefs. An effective Christian youth subculture allows youth to explore and express doubts of faith as well as certainty of faith, much like the disciple Thomas in the post-Resurrection story in John, chapter 20.

The following are examples of discussion opportunities that nurture a Christian subculture.

Bible-centered discussion groups led by adults. I (Merton Strommen) conducted Bible-centered discussions with groups of youth in my home over a period of thirty years. Before retiring, I invited some of these youth, now adults, to spend an evening reminiscing about what they remembered from those Wednesday night sessions. I discovered that they could not remember specific content but instead had vivid memories of the freedom they experienced to explore their doubts and certainties, to sense the caring and warmth of a fellowship group. One member of the group who had been dabbling with Rosacrucianism (a religious philosophy purporting to have secret wisdom) as a youth said to the others assembled in our home, "I would not be a Christian today if I had not felt your willingness to let me express heretical views and your willingness to speak up and express your own faith in Jesus Christ."

Establishing such opportunities for youth to discuss their real-life issues is important and cannot be left to chance. Attention needs to be given to preparation and procedures. Below is a summary of what I found helpful in making gatherings of twelve to fifteen young people meaningful and life changing:

- Create a warm, congenial atmosphere. Involve the group in identifying characteristics they desire for the group, followed by a weekly evaluation of how well these characteristics are being realized.
- Adopt the stance of an eager learner. Avoid being seen as a teacher who asks questions the youth are required to answer; rather, engage the group in an exploration of what God might be saying to us through the stories of the Scriptures.

- Prepare your mind and spirit for each meeting. This involves reading up on the issue to be discussed, locating Bible verses related to the subject, and supporting yourself and the evening with prayer.
- Conduct each session with a format in mind. For example, pose a question or issue that the youth have raised and invite the group to study several references germane to the issue, while looking for an answer to this question: What is God saying to us regarding this issue?
- Give members responsibility for class progress. To encourage this, periodically evaluate the group's progress toward the characteristics they want to see in their group. Acquaint them with the roles that build a group and facilitate progress.

The groups I met with varied in the degree to which they were life changing for the youth. One group that was especially spirited continued to meet annually after they graduated from high school.

Bible-centered discussion groups led by youth. First Lutheran Church in Duluth, Minnesota, has shifted from adult-led Bible discussion groups for youth to youth-led discussion groups for youth. I (Merton Strommen) sat in on a Sunday morning session while fifteen young members of a leadership team met with the youth director to go over the guide he had prepared for the next youth gathering. The guide posed the issues to be discussed, the questions to be asked, and the Scripture readings to be considered. The youth leaders went through the lesson in the same manner they would conduct their group the following evening.

What impressed me was the dedication of these youth. Though deeply involved in the activities of their high schools, their responsibility as church youth leaders came first. Impressive too was the power and influence these youth had with their peers and those younger than them. According to the adult youth leaders, when on retreats or trips, the word of a young youth leader is more influential to a child or youth than that of an adult youth leader.

Six years after inaugurating this approach, this congregation began experiencing an overabundance of youth applying for membership on the leadership team. In response to the interest, two additional teams were established—one to mentor seventh through twelfth graders on Sunday mornings in a gathering known as the

Club House and one to mentor fourth through sixth graders in Sunday school. These teams, trained through peer ministry and a preparatory retreat, also assist with lock-ins, summer camp, and special events.

The selection process for membership on a leadership team is intensive. First, a letter is sent to those young people who are regarded as good candidates, inviting them to apply for membership. Applicants are then interviewed by five or six seniors and their youth director.

A selection is made based on the evaluations of these seniors and the youth director. Those who are selected, and it is viewed as an honor, are then asked to read and sign a covenant form.

This approach of youth-led Bible discussion gatherings has increased attendance from fifteen attending meetings on Sunday mornings to a group of eighty to one hundred meeting not just for forty-five minutes, but for two hours every Thursday evening when school is in session. Half of those attending are not members of the congregation.

The story of the founding of Willow Creek Community Church in South Barrington, Illinois, illustrates what can result when youth come to see the relevance of the Scriptures to their lives. The church began when a group of young people met for Bible discussions under the leadership of Bill Hybel, their youth pastor. Bill's approach was to have the kids come to the meeting to discuss Bible verses on a particular subject (for example, confidence, prayer, confession of sin, friendship, or obedience). Together they would read each verse and then try to apply it to their life.

As the group grew, Bill and the kids began to talk about having an evening gathering to which they would invite their unchurched friends. They adapted the content of the meeting in light of how they thought their friends might react; for example, one member of the group suggested acting out a short drama on the subject of the evening, and another asked for a media presentation related to it. A key suggestion came from one of the youth who asked Bill: "Instead of long walks through the sticky pages of the Bible where you hit six or seven topics at a time, why don't you just narrow it down? Make a point that is biblical but relevant to kids' lives, tell some good stories to illustrate it, and keep it down to about twenty-five minutes. I'm not asking you to compromise the Bible, but just give it to us in manageable doses."[26]

This conversation pointed Bill in a new direction. He not only began using drama and media presentations in his approach to unchurched people, but he also focused on issues and topics relevant to young people's lives. His key question became this: How does this passage, this biblical truth, this doctrine, relate to daily life?

This new approach, encouraged by the young people, became stunningly successful during Bill's years as youth director at South Park Church. Soon twelve hundred youth were coming to his meetings each week. It was then that he decided to start a church for the unchurched, now known as Willow Creek Community Church. He called on many of his young people to staff the new church and form the core of the congregation. Because of the dedication and struggle of this young pastor and his youth, Willow Creek Community Church has become a pacesetter for other congregations, drawing hundreds of unchurched people into a living faith; preaching to as many as twenty thousand people on a given weekend; and, by 1995, involving seventy-five hundred people in one thousand small groups.

Faith-Sharing Experiences

To become partners in the mission of the church, youth need to learn how to verbalize their faith, to put into words what they think and feel. Once feelings and concerns about their relationship with God have been conceptualized into words, they are able to deal with matters of faith rationally. They can begin forming a theology of their own.

But putting into words what they believe and treasure is not easy. Youth often fumble for the right words and feel awkward trying to describe some aspects of religious experience. For that reason they listen with a special eagerness when others share, hoping to hear words that describe how they feel or think about some faith issue. These words, which they can then use for themselves, expand their faith-oriented vocabulary.

Groups that share and discuss matters of faith provide security and support of like-minded youth. In hearing one another talk about their faith, youth provide models for one another—something many young people lack.

The following are examples of faith-sharing topics that nurture a Christian youth subculture:

Being committed to Christ as Savior. Not all youth who have been baptized know Jesus Christ as their savior. Some are uncertain of their relationship with God and are troubled by this. In *A Study of Generations,* two out of three Lutheran youth were found to be troubled to some degree about an uncertain relationship with God. Some were uncertain about their relationship with God because they fail to live up to the standards of being a Christian. Others assume that being a Christian is a joyous experience, and lacking these feelings, they doubt that Christ is their Savior. Others have wandered away from their Lord like sheep and need to be brought back. They have allowed their relationship with God to become a low priority in their life and have become focused on advancing their own interests and satisfying their own desires. Significantly, 58 percent of the youth in six Protestant denominations, all participants in the *Effective Christian Education* study, were involved during one year in three or more at-risk behaviors, the kind that can sabotage their future.

Even more significant is the finding from the same study that less than one in ten youth possesses a mature faith. Granted, maturity of faith usually isn't developed fully until adulthood, but the characteristics of committed youth that emerged from the study reported in *Five Cries of Youth* create a sense of hope for our young people. In this study, six characteristics indicated church youth who were committed:

- being aware of a personal God
- being active with God's people
- feeling a sense of moral responsibility
- evidencing a desire to grow in Christian life
- expressing a desire to serve
- possessing a hopeful outlook on life

Faith-sharing experiences need to include times when an appeal is made for youth to return to the Creator of life and times when youth are helped to see the basis for believing they are children of God.

The Roman Catholic Church offers a faith-sharing experience in a youth version of Cursillo, a course in Christianity that seeks to deepen the young people's understanding of faith in Christ, encourages discussions with peers about faith, and strengthens their commitment to live a life of faith in Christ. This weekend spiritual renewal retreat is often held at a Roman Catholic high school. Other denominations have also adopted this course, sometimes calling it TEC, Chrysalis, or Tirosh (Hebrew word for new wine).[27]

The Episcopal Diocese of Central Florida has developed a unique weekend for junior high youth called New Beginnings that responds to the issues, concerns, and needs of this age-group. It is designed to help participants grow in their love of themselves, of others, and of the Lord Jesus Christ. The weekend is filled with skits, songs, prayers, and times to receive what the Lord has done for each person.

Clarifying beliefs. Faith sharing also includes times when matters of faith can be examined and questioned. This feature is especially important for youth who live in what Stephen Carter calls a culture of disbelief. In his book *The Culture of Disbelief*, Carter argues that our culture rejects religion as a valid source for public discourse, making matters of faith seem like private matters only. For that reason he considered as a title for this book the phrase he uses as a chapter heading: "God As a Hobby."[28]

Public schools offer little opportunity to study religion as a significant force in the lives of people. When Paul Vitz conducted an empirical study of how public school textbooks treat religion and traditional values, he found few if any references to religious activity in contemporary American life. A systematic review of United States history textbooks for grades eleven and twelve showed that none of the texts identified religion as significant to American history.[29] This ignoring of religion as a viable force worthy of inclusion in history textbooks raises questions for youth regarding the importance of their faith. While schools hesitate to discuss religion, interest in religious matters is growing in other sectors of our society. Major newspapers have added a weekly Faith and Values section that gives inspiring accounts of how faith has bettered the lives of people, and *Time* magazine featured "Faith and Healing" on the front cover of its June 24, 1997, issue. This topic is one that youth should be able to discuss in school, but because this often is not possible, such discussion needs to be part of a congregation's youth ministry.

Sharing faith in a variety of ways. When a congregation focuses on faith sharing for youth, it finds that many opportunities for doing so already exist with its various ministries. Youth-led worship experiences, singing groups, witness groups, visitation teams, drama groups, clown ministry, retreats, Christian music concerts, leadership training, and musicals all can be occasions for sharing faith.

Youth Encounter in Minneapolis, Minnesota, trains college-aged people to work on a music and witness team for a year or more. They travel throughout the United States, assisting youth in sharing and celebrating their faith in Christ. Through music, skits, community-building activities, and worship, they train and invite youth to share their faith with one another.

First Presbyterian Church in Maitland, Florida, under the leadership of Bev Richardson, developed a clown troupe that welcomes and trains disabled youth. Each rehearsal and performance is filled with faith-sharing moments.

Fun and Fellowship Activities

Events that challenge youth with a sense of adventure and establish a warm fellowship are important for creating a strong youth subculture. These events go beyond local discussion or faith-sharing meetings to include such experiences as trips, camps, retreats, concerts, conventions, service projects, and exchange programs. These events have special value because they provide new experiences and strengthen friendships formed during the event. The Boy Scouts and Explorers have several high-adventure camps that church youth ministry groups often can use.

Fun and fellowship activities, however, can fall into the trap of becoming only entertainment. For that reason these activities need to contribute purposely to a strengthening of the youths' relationship with Jesus Christ. For example, a youth ministry skiing outing must be more than going to a mountain to ski. The stories retold to family and friends upon returning should not only describe the experience of skiing an expert trail for the first time but should also describe the morning worship service that was held on top of the mountain. Likewise, a youth ministry event at the beach should be more than sand, sun, and water. The stories retold should include the sunrise worship service or sunset worship service. A wonder walk in a national forest should be connected to the eighth Psalm or the first article of the Apostle's Creed.

Wise leaders know how to use travel time in vans, cars, or buses as an opportunity for faith growth and relationship building. Many youth leaders design travel journals for youth that include faith discussion, Bible studies, prompt creative expression, interviews, and fun activities.

I (Dick Hardel) once took a small group of youth and adults to the circus on Epiphany. They were to note all the connections of the Epiphany story to worship at church and to events at the circus.

Mark Devries, a youth and family minister of First Presbyterian Church in Nashville, Tennessee, uses a banquet to combine fun and fellowship for graduating seniors, their parents, and other adults who have been significant in their lives. During the festive evening, each senior is given a three-ringed notebook that features on its front cover a picture of themselves in some youth activity. Inside the notebook the young people find letters from adults who have come to know and love them—people such as their Sunday school teachers, youth leaders, relatives, and, of course, parents. These letters, in a variety of ways, tell the young people how proud their loved ones are of what they have done. The young people's loved ones also pledge to pray for them as they move on to college or work. Before the banquet ends the adults stand behind their graduating senior and give that person a blessing.

At Trinity Lutheran Church in Town and Country, Missouri, under the direction of Rob Rose and Nancy Going, the high school youth designed and staffed a weekend coffee house for youth. The coffee house is called The Fifth Quarter. After football games and basketball games, the place is crowded with youth. It provides a safe place for them to meet with their friends, discuss important issues, develop new relationships, and just hang out.

Service and Peer Ministry

Service. Involvement in service activities is a powerful faith-generating activity. For many youth, being involved in projects of ministering with poor, less advantaged, or suffering people can be life-changing experiences. Here is what some of the youth at Zion Lutheran Church in Anoka, Minnesota, wrote in their journals after a trip in January 1995 to Nicaragua.

Despair is going to school for an education to become an impoverished widow of eight.

Luxury is running water.

Despair is the man looking day after day for a job to feed a starving family.

Luxury is a meal today.

Despair is the woman with no identity trying to please the man who beats her.

Luxury is a pair of shoes.

Despair is the one-room shack of tin and scrap garbage that is home to a family of ten.

Luxury is a dollar made today.

Despair is the innocent eyes of the children with no future to look forward to.

Luxury is a future.

—Molly Youngquist, age 18

I want to stay and commit myself to God and these people. I feel that there is something within me that breaks every time I see a small child and know I can't help them all.

—Jenni Nilsen, age 17

The lessons I have learned here will forever teach me. I will always strive to find new ways to walk with my brothers and sisters no matter where they may be. I am blessed. This is something I needed to do. I have no regrets. God, please be with me as I go back. Help me to be a stronger person than I used to be. Life is very precious, and I have learned that by what you have shown me. I only hope I can continue to see the world through your eyes. I have felt your presence, and I have never been moved so deeply or so powerfully.

—Jason Durst, age 17

It is clear from what these youth say about their two-week stay in Nicaragua that their lives were changed. They saw how self-centered and materialistic their values were, how loving and generous were the poor people they visited, and how important it is that they dedicate their own lives to serving the less privileged people of the world.

Peer ministry: youth helping youth. In their book *Friend to Friend,* J. David Stone and Larry Keefauver share a simple step-by-step process that youth can use to help a friend through a struggle with grief, guilt, depression, worry, anger, or indifference. The authors don't suggest that youth act as counselors to their friends but rather as friends who guide and refer. Among their many helpful suggestions, Stone and Keefauver offer these questions to help guide a friend:

- What do you want for yourself?
- What are you feeling?
- What are you doing to get what you want?
- What do you need to do?

Then they add four follow-up questions:

- Will you do it?
- When will you do it?
- How will you do it?
- Will you let me know how it goes?[30]

Another form of peer ministry is peer helping. Dr. Barbara Varenhorst developed such a program in March 1970 in the school district of Palo Alto, California. She developed the program because she repeatedly heard from students that when they needed help with their personal problems, they went to their friends. Occasionally students would say, "But I don't know how to help my friends when they come to me for help."

Varenhorst realized that adolescents represent a vast resource that was not being used. Though youth have the desire and credibility to help their peers, most of them lack the skills. So Varenhorst developed a program that would teach them.

This highly successful program, improved over the years, has an added theological dimension. Varenhorst's process does three things:

- It provides task-oriented training that equips youth for a ministry with their peers.
- It helps youth develop caring skills that nurture the social, emotional, and spiritual life of participants.
- It introduces a way of carrying out a service to others that is related to specific or general needs.

Basic to this ministry is the training component that equips participants not only to perform certain service tasks but also to cope with interpersonal issues in their own daily lives. The program actually introduces a way of life, the habitual practice of "doing unto the least of these." Youth follow the example of Christ, who spent his life ministering to others—healing the sick, comforting the grief-stricken, providing food to the hungry, calming the fears of the anxious, and welcoming the outcasts of society.[31]

At Saint Paul's Lutheran Church in Grand Island, Nebraska, Cheryl Gries, director of youth and family ministry from 1990 to 1993, trained youth in peer ministry. They became such wonderful caregivers that the public school system asked Cheryl if her peer ministers would assist grade-schoolers in an after-school remedial reading course. The peer ministers agreed to help these children, and everyone involved noticed that it was not only the remedial reading that helped the grade-school children, but it was also the relationships they developed with the high school youth who cared for them.

Because it is often difficult for congregations to find volunteer adults to lead vacation Bible school, congregations are training youth for such leadership. Some will take their vacation Bible school skills on the road to other congregations that cannot find teachers within their own congregation.

Some Christian Bible camps employ youth to serve as camp counselors. The model of young adult leaders serving as camp counselors for younger children attending summer Bible camp is an excellent model for a congregation. The key is to train youth to serve and to lead other youth.

The potential of a peer ministry program for reaching out to lonely, alienated youth was tested by a major research project of Search Institute that was funded by the National Institute of Mental Health. Researchers had one question in mind: Can young people be trained to help others of their age-group who seem headed for lives of unhappiness, delinquency, and general tragedy?

In search of an answer to this question, researchers developed three different methods of training:

- a one-to-one method based on a tutoring or counseling approach
- a group skills method aimed at initiating and maintaining relationships over time
- a peer group method geared to teach communication skills using positive reinforcement

From January to March 1971, under the leadership of thirty-four young adults who had been trained by professionals in one of the three methods, 124 high school juniors participated in weekly training sessions. The project attracted youth whose overwhelming characteristic was a value orientation toward helping others.

These youth, once trained, trained a group of 143 juniors during April and June of the same year, using the training methods they had experienced. The youth doing the training were as effective in training their peers as were the young adults who had trained them.

During the following fall and winter, each of these 267 junior volunteers was asked to seek out at least two alienated youth and show them friendship. They were also asked to discover what battles, hopes, dreams, and aspirations these youth had. Using this information they were then to determine what kinds of changes would be best for them.

Because of this group's outreach activities, 493 lonely youth were reached. As a result of the friendships that were established, 92 percent of the preachers reported seeing positive changes in the lives of the "reached." Of these, 45 percent became members of a group, and 10 percent accepted adult assistance. When a random sample of the reached youth was interviewed using a scale known as Progress from Relationships, all showed improvement, and 22 percent showed a marked improvement in their attitudes and behavior.

The project demonstrated that high school youth indeed can be trained to reach out in friendship to lonely, alienated youth. Even more important, it demonstrated the power of friendship to make an observable change in the lives of such youth.[32]

Involvement in Music

By the time young people reach their teens, they have learned a second native language called rock music. Donald Posterski and Reginald Bibby, in *Teen Trends: A Nation in Motion,* report that music is one of the few ways by which adults can enter the world of young people. Music is an avenue by which congregations that are serious about engaging youth in an active ministry can reach them.[33]

Music is so powerful it can even connect people unchurched with the Gospel. A restaurant–night club chain called House of

222   Passing On the Faith

Blues now offers a Sunday Gospel brunch. Recently, the House of Blues in Chicago featured the Soul Children of Chicago, an African American youth Gospel choir. The club was packed for Sunday brunch, and the audience's hearts and souls resounded with the marvelous music of faith that the youth choir provided.

In the early days of our country, organized choirs were a rallying point for immigrant youth, and singing was an important ingredient in the youth organizations. Some congregations today maintain this emphasis. One of these is Prince of Peace Lutheran Church in Burnsville, Minnesota, which has a youth choir of several hundred voices. Choir rehearsals begin with a Bible study and a time for sharing the faith. This choir does not attempt to imitate college choirs by pressing for excellence in a rendition of traditional choral anthems. Rather it sings contemporary songs that the youth can enjoy while enhancing their sense of fellowship.

A church that makes full use of music is the Liberty Chapel United Church of Christ, an African American rural church in Monncure, North Carolina. This church of 224 members, singled out as an exemplary church in the *Effective Christian Education* study, was visited by two people to discover what accounted for its high faith scores. The visitors found that music was central to the congregation's worship and educational program. Eight choirs had been formed from its membership: a senior choir, a young adult choir, a junior choir, an Angelettes choir, the Relative Gospel Singers, the Starlight Wonders, the Goldenaires, and the Bright Stars. Almost every evening of the week at least one of the choirs rehearses. As a result of its emphasis on music, the church has attracted a number of musicians, some of whom are quite young. A twelve-year-old boy who played drums at one of the services said, "What I like best about this church is that I can play the drums during the service." An educational innovation in this congregation is music instruction.

At Grace Lutheran Church in Evansville, Indiana, almost every member sings in a choir. One of the choirs, Sounds of Grace, has traveled annually to different areas of the United States to sing in congregations of every denomination. This ministry was not only a powerful witness of the faith of these young people to the audiences but also the basis of the audiences' discussions and personal growth in faith.

Informal Friendship Groups

In *Teen Trends: A Nation in Motion,* Posterski and Bibby state that two doors open for congregations to reach youth are music and friendships. In their survey of youth in Canada, friendships proved to be one of their highest values.[34] This suggests that activities developed for youth of a congregation should be of the kind that encourage long-lasting, caring friendships.

In the *Effective Christian Education* study, little correlation was found between youths' faith and church loyalty scores and their attendance at youth group meetings. But a significant correlation was found between youths' faith and church loyalty scores and the religiousness of their friends. The study shows that informal friendships can be a significant contributor to the Ten Characteristics of Committed Youth.

A congregation's youth group will at best reach only a portion of youth raised in the congregation, but all members are usually connected to small groups of friends. Therefore, for a congregation to train its youth to be leaders in the informal groups with which youth are already connected is most effective.

A program known as Logos has proved successful in generating friendships. The Logos program consists of four parts. One is a shared meal on Wednesday evenings, when six youth sit with two table-parents. This eating together and later playing together has proven effective in establishing friendships as well as enabling youth to relate to another generation. Other parts of the evening include study time, playtime, and a closing worship period the youth lead. These four parts of the program allow youth to participate in activities not possible on Sunday mornings.

A characteristic of congregations that use Logos is a high percentage of attendance and retention of youth who are members of the congregation. These Wednesday evening get-togethers bond the entire congregation, forming a growing community of faith. In congregations where this program is used, 70 to 90 percent of the congregations' youth population has taken membership.

Placentia Presbyterian Church in Los Angeles is one of the four thousand churches using the Logos program. Over a number of years the church has been remarkably effective in maintaining the interest and participation of their youth throughout the high school years. The program has helped establish a very strong core of youth, some of whom have become active in outreach mission programs.

Adults Counseling Youth

Congregations willing to become a wellness center for those who need healing can anticipate an increasing number of youth who need counseling from adults. The following are levels of counseling that can be made available:

Level 1: Caring by adults. A Christian youth subculture is encouraged by adults who serve as models, mentors, and guides to their youth. The asset-building research of Search Institute indicates that every child needs a significant relationship with at least three adults other than a parent to be healthy. Also, the *Effective Christian Education* study found a high correlation between caring adults and mature faith, growth in faith, congregational loyalty, and denominational loyalty among youth. One can assume that the value of caring adults rivals the value of friendships youth form among themselves.

Caring volunteer adults who work with youth should be equipped with listening and caregiving skills. Peer ministry and Stephen Ministry training are two of the best training models for doing this. A prior consideration, however, is the careful recruiting of these volunteers. J. David Stone, a popular Methodist youth leader and author, has, at many workshops and seminars, stated three essential qualifications of adults who are to be trained for working with youth:

- They love the Lord.
- They love the church.
- They love to be with youth.

Anything else can be taught and learned.

Doing the work to find adults who care for young people is important. *Kids These Days: What Americans Think About the Next Generation,* a 1997 national study conducted by a public policy research organization, found that only 37 percent of adults believe today's youngsters will eventually make this country a better place. The study, also referred to in chapter 1, found that adults have a stunning level of antagonism not only toward teenagers but also toward young children.

A positive approach to altering adult attitudes toward youth and encouraging caring attitudes and behaviors in young people was introduced in 1989 by Roland Larson and his wife Doris, members of Westwood Lutheran Church in Minneapolis. They established an annual Caring Youth Award, given to a young person who demonstrates uncommon caring. The award has nothing to do with achievement in scholastics, athletics, or other accomplishments; rather, its purpose is to encourage and reward both a day-to-day lifestyle of caring concern for others and unselfish volunteerism. By presenting the award, the congregation seeks to elevate the level and awareness of caring among young people.

This idea caught on in the suburb of Saint Louis Park, Minnesota. Beginning in 1990, a number of organizations in this community decided to celebrate a Caring Youth Day also. The event was announced by the mayor who, by proclamation, declared that a Youth Development Committee would host a communitywide event to recognize the youth who have demonstrated through behavior and lifestyle that they care about others. By 1997 seventeen community organizations were participating in this event. The event has won applause and commendation by first ladies Barbara Bush and Hillary Rodham Clinton.

Wheat Ridge Ministries in Itasca, Illinois, a foundation that plants seeds of hope and new ministries, is employing the same idea. This organization gives youth servant awards each year. Youth are honored for their creativity and leadership in the church.

How can volunteer adults be equipped to serve today's youth in caring and thoughtful ways? Mark Holmen, former director of youth and family ministry at Calvary Lutheran in Minneapolis, draws on twenty years of experience preparing college students to work with youth in Bible camp settings and shares what he has learned.

He begins with a look at today's youth by addressing these questions: Who are they? What are their needs, abilities, and minor emotional disturbances? What serious handicaps trouble some?

To provide a safe and secure environment, he presents an essential policy of screening all adults who volunteer to work with children and youth. This policy lowers the legal risk for the church and ensures parents that every precaution is being taken to provide rightly motivated adults.

Holmen quotes Bonaro Overstreet, a noted psychologist, who said, "We are not only our brother's keeper: in countless large and small ways we are our brother's maker."[35] He stresses the power of praise and gentle words of encouragement in his training of lay adults.

The purpose of Holmen's program, Faith Trainers, is to train adults to help youth move through several levels of commitment to become disciples of Christ. The first level involves activities for youth who have no sense of commitment to the church's youth program. The second level is a "come and see" level that invites youth to events where they can meet friends. A third level is a "follow me" category where those who are regular participants become involved in one or more service projects. The desired outcome is a commitment to Jesus Christ followed by a desire to discover God's role in their lives.[36]

Level 2: Mentoring by adults. Another way adults can make a positive difference in the lives of young people is through a mentoring program. Of the many programs found in the United States, probably the oldest and best known mentoring program is the Big Brothers and Big Sisters program. In 1997 it made seventy-five thousand matches between volunteer adults and youngsters.

Most local Big Brothers and Big Sisters programs recruit and carefully screen volunteer applicants for one-on-one matches. They also screen youth, who usually come from single-parent households and who, along with their parents, must be willing to be a part of the program. On the average the adult-youth pairs meet for three to four hours, three times a month, for at least a year.

A carefully conducted evaluation of the program's value, using randomly selected matches and a control group, showed that the program yields a wide range of tangible benefits. The most notable results are the deterrent effect on initiation of drug and alcohol use and the overall positive effects on academic performance. Noteworthy, however, is that the wise standards and strong support system of the Big Brothers and Big Sisters programs are critical in making the relationships work.[37]

The significance of adults mentoring youth is highlighted by three major studies carried out by Search Institute—one involving eleven thousand junior and senior high youth in Minnesota, another involving eight thousand randomly selected fifth through ninth graders from thirteen denominations, and a third involving three thousand seventh and eighth graders. The question being pursued was, When kids need help, where do they go?

Contrary to the popular stereotype that adolescents abandon adults and turn to peers for affirmation and advice, these studies provided overwhelming evidence that students in every grade level between grades five and twelve prefer adult support. The preference for adults in comparison to peers is less dramatic in the late high school years than in the fifth to eighth grade years, but the preference still exists. These findings are based on youth's responses to questions about major life issues. It is reasonable to suppose that the results would have been different if the questions were about gaining advice on such things as appearances, clothing style, dating choice, and the like.[38] In *Soul Searching*, Christian Smith notes that

> much existing research has suggested the crucial importance in adolescents' lives of meaningful relational ties to parents and non-parent adults—grown-up friends, teachers, mentors, coaches, and other parents—who can help watch over, care for, and provide resources to teens.[39]

First Presbyterian Church in Nashville, Tennessee, made an interesting adaptation of a mentoring program. Finding that some adults dropped out as mentors because they were terrified by the responsibility of trying to talk with teenagers, church leaders established a prayer partner program to take its place. Adults were recruited to pray daily for a given youth. Interestingly, more adult-youth relationships resulted from the prayer program than from the original mentoring program.

In the prayer partner program, the youth, who know they are being prayed for each day, meet their prayer partner at an annual banquet. At that time they exchange cards that identify topics for which they would appreciate prayers. In subsequent months, each partner prays for the other.

Level 3: Counseling by youth staff. Counseling teenagers ranks high as an essential part of a youth minister's responsibility. This has become a crucial need as an increasing number of youth are becoming involved in at-risk behaviors that often lead to tragedies such as an unmarried fifteen-year-old giving birth to a stillborn child, a teenager becoming addicted to drugs, or a youth suffering sexual abuse at home. These have become everyday situations that confront youth leaders. Counseling as a dimension of youth ministry is necessary and unavoidable.

Most youth leaders are not trained counselors and should not attempt to do what clinicians do. But a youth leader can become involved in a listening ministry that has four objectives:

1. *Understand.* A youth leader needs to try to see life from the perspective of the troubled young person. This requires listening not only to the words but also to the feelings of ambivalence, the dissatisfaction with self, the cry of the soul. A youth leader needs to be a listener to know the inner life of a person, to know what to say.

2. *Establish a sense of partnership.* The youth leader and the troubled youth determine together how best to handle a situation. In this approach a youth leader seeks to help the troubled youth clarify his or her thinking, to put bewildering feelings into words, and to consider several alternative courses of action. Reaching this objective usually involves a conversation in which both parties recognize the pressure of sin and the power of evil and explore together how best the issue can be faced.

3. *Foster a sense of hope.* Having a deep conviction that there is not a single person for whom Christ did not die will help create a sense of hope in the heart and life of the young person. There is hope for everyone, regardless of his or her situation. This conviction and faith enables the responses and demeanor of the youth leader to convey that there is Good News for this person. God, who has changed people in the past and is changing them now, is ready to enter into another situation.

4. *Make a referral to a professional counselor.* This should be a person whom the youth leader knows is able to provide the help the troubled youth needs.

Counseling that seeks these four objectives is well within the prerogative and responsibility of a youth and family minister.

Level 4: Counseling by trained counselors. Les Parrott III, an associate professor of clinical psychology and director of the Center for Relationship Development at Seattle Pacific University, has written a counseling guide for professional counselors called *Helping the Struggling Adolescent*. The guide identifies common pitfalls in counseling adolescents, the legal and ethical issues that are related to counseling, and forty rapid assessment tools with user instructions. The guide addresses thirty common problems for counselors and youth workers.

Parrott quotes the American Psychological Association, a national professional organization of psychologists, which requires professionals to "provide services and only use techniques for which they are qualified by training and experience." He notes that a responsible therapist will only accept clients who can benefit from the training and skill that the therapist has acquired. Research has shown that inexpert counseling can indeed be worse than no treatment at all.[40]

Failure to practice at a reasonable level of competence, Parrott notes, may result in one's being sued for damage due to malpractice. Generally, malpractice is defined as a failure to meet prevailing, professionally accepted standards of practice. Detailed ethical guidelines for counselors are available from the American Psychological Association and the American Counseling Association.

Congregational Leadership

A Christian youth subculture is enhanced when youth become involved in the life of a congregation. The percentages listed in figure 22 responses of 7,050 church youth of nine major church bodies who participated in the national study described in the book *Five Cries of Youth*, give dramatic evidence of the strong relationship that exists between frequent church attendance and an indication of a commendable lifestyle.

Though most of the high school youth who frequently attend church are probably from families that nurture faith and have a well-established lifestyle, the youths' church attendance reinforces what some parents seek to inculcate. And for the many youth who do not come from Christian homes, the congregation becomes a second family, where the adults they come to know shape their lives in significant ways. For these youth, frequent attendance is crucial in shaping their lives.

Figure 22

Relationship Between Youth's Church Attendance and Lifestyle

Statements to Which Youth Responded	Frequency of Youth Attending Church (size of sample questioned) and Percentage of Youth Agreeing with Statement						
	Never (320)	Rarely (532)	Once a Month (419)	Every Other Week (818)	Every Week (3772)	Several Times a Week (1032)
As long as you love the other person, sexual inter-course before marriage is okay.	58%	53%	43%	36%	27%	21%
I sometimes get "high" on alcoholic beverages.	51%	50%	46%	37%	27%	18%
During the past six months I have not read the Bible at all.	63%	52%	42%	41%	41%	17%
From the money I get, I give nothing to charity, church, or temple.	70%	55%	43%	35%	31%	19%
All in all, I feel happy about my church.	20%	31%	35%	48%	59%	73%
I have spent time in a program of service to others.	39%	50%	55%	56%	59%	67%

Training through a task-force approach. Training youth in congregational leadership requires more than a staff worker or a family can give; hence, other lay adults must provide training, modeling, and assistance. One way this can be done is through a task-force approach. Out of sheer necessity, youth pastor Richard Ross of Tulip Grove Baptist Church arrived at the idea of training with a task-force approach. His youth program was attracting an increasing number of youth, and he was developing new, creative ways to minister to his youth. The problem was that he was becoming an event manager, always preparing for the next big thing. He was finding less and less time for counseling and ministering to youth, which he was trained to do, and he had less and less time to spend with his family and to work on his own well-being. Complicating his schedule were his duties as youth minister consultant at the Sunday School Board for the entire Southern Baptist Convention. A concerned lay youth adviser drew him aside and said he had to find another way to carry out his youth ministry. In response to this counsel, Ross developed a plan that uses task forces, or lead teams. These teams of youth and adults, ranging in number from ten to fifteen, are trained to assume full responsibility for activities that formerly were the pastor's responsibility.

In one year, fifteen events were taken over by fifteen different task forces or lead teams. They met for whatever number of months members felt necessary to prepare for their youth event. Key to the success of these teams was the chairperson, who was chosen with considerable care.

One team of six adults and four youth planned an eight-day mission trip. The team's purpose was to prepare forty to fifty youth to conduct a vacation Bible school for minority children in an inner city. The chairperson of the team followed a well-developed agenda that included a detailed budget, a list of team assignments, and a grid showing the sequence of classes for each day of vacation Bible school, Monday through Friday.

The preparation schedule requested that each Wednesday evening, May 7 through July 9, the forty to fifty youth attend preparation sessions. At these sessions the youth were given assignments, instruction in teaching methods, craft ideas, experience in leading songs, help in presenting object lessons, guidance in how to witness to children, and a general orientation to the trip. To go on the mission trip, each participant was asked to attend at least seven of the ten meetings offered and pass a test related to their assignments.

The task-force approach to youth ministry is now being adopted by hundreds of youth ministers. Therefore, in his 1997 book, *Planning Youth Ministry: From Boot-up to Exit*, Richard Ross gives specific instruction on how to gain a congregation's approval and support for a task-force strategy.

Training Leaders. In his book *Effective Youth Ministry: A Congregational Approach*, Dr. Roland D. Martinson notes that to be effective, a congregation's youth ministry must seek out people with specific leadership skills—people such as visitors, musicians, journalists, photographers, teachers, cooks, backpackers, bikers, dancers, and actors. The pastor and members of the youth ministry committee can be considered the congregation's talent scouts. In seeking these people, the needs of every youth must be considered. The training of these people should focus on helping leaders develop skills in the following areas:
- faith formation
- congregational ministry with youth
- effective communication
- group leadership and cooperative work
- planning and problem solving
- advocacy for youth
- their specific responsibility in youth ministry[41]

Some Christian Bible camp leaders use a formal training curriculum called *Counselors in Training* (CIT) to provide training for older high school youth. The high school youth develop skills for leading Bible studies, facilitating small groups, organizing outdoor recreational activities, and using games and active-learning designs for teaching the faith. While most of the training relates to camping ministry, it can easily be adapted for training in congregational ministry.

Yvonne Steindal, former director of youth and family ministry at First Lutheran Church in Beaver Dam, Wisconsin, and Richard Hardel, former executive director of The Youth & Family Institute, developed a weeklong training event for high school youth. Their primary purpose was to equip the youth with skills for assuming leadership within their own congregations. Training was extensive—beginning on a Sunday evening and continuing through the following Saturday afternoon, approximately eight hours per day. Using an unpublished training manual entitled *Youth Connection, Building Leaders for Our Church,* Steindal and Hardel conducted training sessions on the following topics:

- Lo and Behold: Vision
- Blueprints: Planning Process
- It's About God: Personal Spirituality
- Holy Togetherness: Community Building
- Is Anybody Listening? Communication
- Connection: Group Dynamics
- Take Charge: Leadership Development
- From Apathy to Activity: Learning the Faith
- Could This Be Fun? Games and Recreation
- Stepping Back to Move Forward: Retreats
- Lifting Up Holy Hands: Worship
- Go in Peace, Serve the Lord: Servanthood
- Side by Side: Working with Adults
- PR Power: Making Youth Visible
- When You Get in Over Your Head: HELP!

Congregational initiative in recruiting and training youth and adults for leadership is an essential component in a lasting and effective Christian youth subculture. In turn, creating an effective Christian youth subculture is critical for an effective youth and family ministry.

At the Spirit of Youth Ministry National Conference in August 2005, the project team for the *Study of Exemplary Youth Ministry in Congregations* shared forty-four faith assets that support youth in growing in faith. There are four categories of assets in each of two areas: Congregational Assets and Youth Ministry Assets.

Congregational Assets

Theological Character
1. **God's living presence:** possesses a sense of God's living presence in community, at worship, through study, and in service
2. **Centrality of faith:** recognizes and participates in God's sustaining and transforming life and work

3. **Emphasizes prayer:** practices the presence of God as individuals and community through prayer and worship
4. **Focus on discipleship:** committed to know and follow Jesus Christ
5. **Emphasizes the Scriptures:** values the authority of the Scriptures in its life and mission
6. **Centrality of mission:** consistently witnesses, serves, and promotes more responsibility and seeks justice

Pastoral Leadership

7. **Spiritual influence:** knows and models the transforming presence of God in life and ministry
8. **Interpersonal competence:** builds a sense of community and relates well with adults and youth
9. **Supports youth ministry:** understands, guides, and advocates for youth ministry
10. **Supports leaders:** affirms and mentors youth and adults leading youth ministry

Congregational Qualities

11. **Supports youth ministry:** youth and ministry with young people are high priorities
12. **Demonstrates hospitality:** values and welcomes all people, especially youth
13. **Strives for excellence:** sets high standards, evaluates, and engages in continuous improvement
14. **Encourages thinking:** welcomes questions and reflection on faith and life
15. **Creates community:** reflects high quality personal and group relationships
16. **Encourages support groups:** engages members in study, in conversation about faith and daily life, and in prayer
17. **Promotes worship:** expands and renews spirit-filled, uplifting worship through the congregation's life
18. **Fosters ethical responsibility:** encourages individual and social-moral responsibility
19. **Promotes service:** sponsors outreach, service projects, and cultural immersions both locally and globally
20. **Demonstrates effective practices:** engages in a wide variety of ministry practices

Youth Involvement

21. **Participates in the congregation:** youth are engaged in a wide spectrum of congregational relationships and practices
22. **Assumes ministry leadership:** youth are invited, equipped, and affirmed for leadership in congregational activities

Youth Ministry Assets

Youth Minister

23. **Provides competent leadership:** reflects superior theological, theoretical, and practical knowledge and skill in leadership
24. **Models faith:** is a role model reflecting a living faith for youth and adults
25. **Mentors faith life:** assists adult leaders and youth in their faith life both one-on-one and in groups
26. **Develops teams:** reflects clear vision and attracts gifted youth and adults into leadership
27. **Knows youth:** knows youth and changes in youth culture and uses these understandings in ministry
28. **Establishes effective relationships:** enjoys effective relationships with youth, parents, volunteers, and staff

Youth and Adult Leadership

29. **Equip for peer ministry:** youth practice friendship, caregiving, and outreach supported by training and caring adults
30. **Establish adult-youth mentoring:** adults engage youth in faith and life supported in informed leadership
31. **Participate in training:** evaluate and equip youth and adults for ministry in an atmosphere of high expectations
32. **Possess vibrant faith:** youth and adult leaders possess and practice a vital and informed faith
33. **Engage competent adult volunteers:** foster authentic relationships and effective practices with youth within a clear vision strengthened by training and support

Youth Ministry Effectiveness

34. **Establishes a caring environment:** provides multiple nurturing relationships and activities resulting in a welcoming atmosphere of respect, growth, and belonging

35. **Develops quality relationships:** develops authentic relationships among youth and adults establishing an environment of presence and life engagement

36. **Focuses on Jesus Christ:** the life and ministry of Jesus inspires the ministry's mission, practices, and relationships

37. **Considers life issues:** the full range of young people's lives is valued and addressed

38. **Uses many approaches:** intentionally, creatively employs multiple activities appropriate to the ministry's mission and context

39. **Organizes well:** engages participants and leaders in long-range planning, implementation, evaluation, and innovation in an atmosphere of high expectations

Family Involvement

40. **Possesses strong parental faith:** parents possess and practice a vital and informed faith

41. **Promotes family faith practices:** parents engage youth and family in conversations, prayer, Bible reading, and service that nurture faith and life

42. **Reflects family harmony:** expressions of respect and love create an atmosphere promoting faith

43. **Equips parents:** offers instruction and guidance that nurture parental faith and equip parents for nurturing faith at home

44. **Fosters parent-youth relationships:** offers parent-youth activities that strengthen parent-youth relationships[42]

Chapter 7

Healthy Communities,
Healthy Children

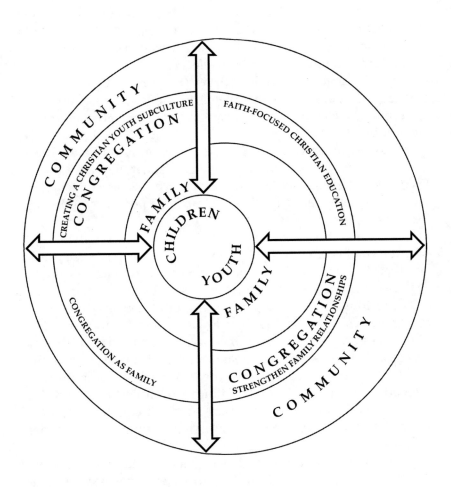

COMMUNITY

CONGREGATION

CREATING A CHRISTIAN YOUTH SUBCULTURE

FAITH-FOCUSED CHRISTIAN EDUCATION

FAMILY

CHILDREN

YOUTH

FAMILY

CONGREGATION AS FAMILY

CONGREGATION

STRENGTHEN FAMILY RELATIONSHIPS

COMMUNITY

Though family and congregation are the most powerful and influential factors in shaping the lives of children and youth, the communities in which they are found can either hinder or enhance their effect. It takes more than effective families and strong congregations to raise healthy kids.

A study of 112 communities revealed the community's formative power. This study used developmental assets to identify how much communities vary both in the way they protect youth from at-risk behaviors and the ways they provide nurturing environments. Developmental assets, to be described later, are experiences that enhance the life of an adolescent.

The least healthy communities are those in which youth have the fewest developmental assets. The most healthy communities are those in which youth have the most developmental assets. The reason for a community's powerful effect on youth lies in the community's influence on people with restricted mobility such as the ill, the elderly, and children and youth, who must make do with their immediate communities, whether or not those communities are healthy.[1]

Families, congregations, and communities must do more than love their youth. They must also demonstrate that they value them. Every young person should gain the confidence, character, competence, and connections needed to contribute positively to her or his church and to society.

Congregations are in a good position to serve as catalysts to rally the whole community in developing positive assets for youth and their families. Congregations not only are in touch with such agencies as businesses, health services, social services, educational institutions, and civic organizations, but they also can have a strong influence on shaping these agencies' policies and attitudes. The effect of the involvement of congregations is seen in the fact that religious involvement is greatest in the most healthy communities (70 percent) and lowest in the least healthy communities. Similarly, a majority of the youth in the healthiest communities are involved in structured activities, such as a congregation provides, but only 39 percent from the least healthy communities are involved.[2]

Community institutions such as schools, churches, youth organizations, hospitals and health services, law and justice organizations, social services, and businesses have a responsibility for the health of their communities because they are the most powerful and influential forces in shaping it. They each can contribute to the health of the community by seeking to increase the number of developmental assets found among its youth.

What Is Happening
to American Communities?

In his book *All Kids Are Our Kids,* Peter Benson, president of Search Institute, presents a description of what is happening in American communities.[3] He identifies signs of a crumbling infrastructure that creates the dilemma reflected in a report from the American Medical Association:

> For the first time in the history of this country, young people are less healthy and less prepared to take their places in society than were their parents. And this is happening at a time when our society is more complex, more challenging, and more competitive than ever before.[4]

Benson refers to the following signs of deterioration:
- the sharp increase in at-risk behaviors over previous decades— such as sexual activity, drinking, smoking, and drug use
- our nation's top rating, among comparable nations, in high-risk behaviors, in lower academic achievement, in homicides, and in poverty among youth
- minimum participation of youth in serving others and the community
- a decline in psychological support from family
- the rupture in community support for young people
- overemphasis on individual gain at the expense of the community

In his search for a solution to the decline of healthy communities, Benson identifies the limitations of the deficit-reduction or problem-focused paradigm in which problems are attacked one at a time. One limitation of the paradigm is its assumption that absence of symptoms represents good health. Still another is the paradigm's tendency to encourage reliance on professionals and discourage the involvement of ordinary citizens. A third limitation is the paradigm's tendency to be costly even though it may do little to get to the roots of the problem.

A New Paradigm: Community Asset Building

In light of what is happening in communities in the United States, Benson calls for a new and different paradigm—an asset-building paradigm that centers on nurturing the positive building blocks of development that all young people need. This paradigm does not require a choice between being reactive or proactive about community health. Rather, it welcomes a balance in which efforts to reduce the number of problems are matched in intensity with efforts to increase a community's number of assets.

Benson assumes that as communities become asset-building places, the health and well-being of youth will improve. His assumption is based on convincing evidence from scientific literature and from his studies of more than one hundred thousand middle and high school youth in 312 towns and cities throughout the United States.[5]

The developmental assets Benson identifies fall into two major categories—those that are external to youth and those that are internal to youth.

External Assets

Support. The support assets are those experiences that communicate love, affirmation, and acceptance.

Empowerment. The empowerment assets are those experiences that make youth feel valued and valuable. Empowerment assets help children and youth grow up respected, conscious of their strengths, and aware that they can make a difference in the world. Benson believes that the support and empowerment assets need to be balanced with boundaries and boundary reinforcement.

Boundaries and expectations. These assets involve giving clear signals about what is expected, what is approved and celebrated, and what deserves censure.

Constructive use of time. Constructive use of time assets are provided through organizations and programs. These require settings and opportunities that connect youth to caring adults who nurture youths' skills and capacities through group activities, lessons, relationships, and supervision.[6]

Internal Assets

Commitment to learning. Learning assets are personal qualities and behaviors that are conducive to intellectual growth.

Positive values. Positive values assets are foundational because they form youths' personal character, shape their choices, and enable them to practice moral restraint.

Social competency. Social competency assets are often emphasized in alcohol and drug prevention programs. The peaceful conflict resolution asset is one that is often taught in schools.

Positive identity. Positive identity assets are those that keep young people from becoming powerless victims without a sense of initiative, direction, and purpose.[7]

The forty assets Benson identifies in figure 23 fall within this framework of eight major assets and represent a common core of developmental assets that matter for all youth regardless of socioeconomic circumstances. As more of these assets are found in a community, fewer youth become involved in at-risk behaviors, more youth engage in positive behaviors, feeling compassion for others, acting as leaders, succeeding in school, and developing a healthy lifestyle, and more youth show the resiliency needed to rebound in the face of adversity.

It may be that the most important contribution of this framework has less to do with the forty individual assets and more to do with the big picture of healthy development. Hence attention needs to center more on the larger framework with its eight categories and less on the forty individual assets.

Figure 23

Forty Developmental Assets

Search Institute has identified the following building blocks of healthy development that help young people grow up healthy, caring, and responsible.

EXTERNAL ASSETS

Category	Asset Name and Definition
Support	1. **Family support**—Family life provides high levels of love and support.
	2. **Positive family communication**—Young person and her or his parent(s) communicate positively, and young person is willing to seek advice and counsel from parent(s).
	3. **Other adult relationships**—Young person receives support from three or more nonparent adults.
	4. **Caring neighborhood**—Young person experiences caring neighbors.
	5. **Caring school climate**—School provides a caring, encouraging environment.
	6. **Parent involvement in schooling**—Parent(s) are actively involved in helping young person succeed in school.
Empowerment	7. **Community values youth**—Young person perceives that adults in the community value youth.
	8. **Youth as resources**—Young people are given useful roles in the community.
	9. **Service to others**—Young person serves in the community one hour or more per week.
	10. **Safety**—Young person feels safe at home, at school, and in the neighborhood.
Boundaries and	11. **Family boundaries**—Family has clear rules and consequences and monitors the young person's whereabouts.
Expectations	12. **School boundaries**—School provides clear rules and consequences.
	13. **Neighborhood boundaries**—Neighbors take responsibility for monitoring young people's behavior.
	14. **Adult role models**—Parent(s) and other adults model positive, responsible behavior.
	15. **Positive peer influence**—Young person's best friends model responsible behavior.
	16. **High expectations**—Both parent(s) and teachers encourage the young person to do well.
Constructive	17. **Creative activities**—Young person spends three or more hours per week in lessons or practice in music, theater, or other arts.
	18. **Youth programs**—Young person spends three or more hours per week in sports, clubs, or organizations at school and/or in the community.

Category	Asset Name and Definition
Constructive (continued)	19. **Religious community**—Young person spends one or more hours per week in activities in a religious institution. 20. **Time at home**—Young person is out with friends "with nothing special to do" two or fewer nights per week.

Internal Assets

Commitment to Learning	21. **Achievement motivation**—Young person is motivated to do well in school. 22. **School engagement**—Young person is actively engaged in learning. 23. **Homework**—Young person reports doing at least one hour of homework every school day. 24. **Bonding to school**—Young person cares about her or his school. 25. **Reading for pleasure**—Young person reads for pleasure three or more hours per week.
Positive Values	26. **Caring**—Young person places high value on helping other people. 27. **Equality and social justice**—Young person places high value on promoting equality and reducing hunger and poverty. 28. **Integrity**—Young person acts on convictions and stands up for her or his beliefs. 29. **Honesty**—Young person "tells the truth even when it is not easy." 30. **Responsibility**—Young person accepts and takes personal responsibility. 31. **Restraint**—Young person believes it is important not to be sexually active or to use alcohol or other drugs.
Social Competencies	32. **Planning and decision making**—Young person knows how to plan ahead and make choices. 33. **Interpersonal competence**—Young person has empathy, sensitivity, and friendship skills. 34. **Cultural competence**—Young person has knowledge of and comfort with people of different cultural, racial, or ethnic backgrounds. 35. **Resistance skills**—Young person can resist negative peer pressure and dangerous situations. 36. **Peaceful conflict resolution**—Young person seeks to resolve conflict nonviolently.
Positive Identity	37. **Personal power**—Young person feels he or she has control over "things that happen to me." 38. **Self-esteem**—Young person reports having a high self-esteem. 39. **Sense of purpose**—Young person reports that "my life has a purpose." 40. **Positive view of personal future**—Young person is optimistic about her or his personal future.

The strength of this paradigm is its focus on health and a language that everyone in a community can understand and use. This paradigm enables a congregation to join hands with other congregations, with the schools, and with other civic organizations in addressing the disturbing breakdown of community life. The paradigm calls for a multitude of small acts that have minimal costs and are within the capacity of every person, young and old.

Power of Developmental Assets

Developmental assets are powerful predictors of behavior. They serve as protective factors because they inhibit behaviors such as alcohol and drug abuse, violence, premarital sex, and school failure. Figure 24 shows how the percentages of young people involved in at-risk behaviors varies dramatically according to the number of assets that are a part of their life.

Developmental assets also serve as enhancement factors, as they promote positive developmental outcomes; thus, they can be called indicators of thriving. Figure 25 shows how a young person's success in school mounts as the number of assets being experienced increases.[8]

In addition, developmental assets serve as resiliency factors, assets that enable youth to bounce back from adverse situations, helping them to weather adversity. Resiliency literature shows that youth who rebound from divorce, sexual or physical abuse, or parental addictions are markedly different from those who do not.[9]

Figure 26 shows that 76 percent of the sixth- to twelfth-grade youth attending school in 312 towns and cities throughout the United States know only twenty or fewer of these assets.[10]

The remarkable power of the developmental asset of achievement motivation is illustrated by the widely publicized actions of Eugene Lang. While addressing a sixth-grade commencement exercise at a Harlem school he attended as a boy, he suddenly departed from his prepared remarks. He began talking about the importance of having and fulfilling dreams in life. Then, in a surge of inspiration, he stunned the sixty-one underprivileged children by offering to pay for their college educations if they would remain in school and work toward that goal.

Figure 24

The Protective Consequences of Developmental Assets for Nine High-Risk Patterns of Behavior

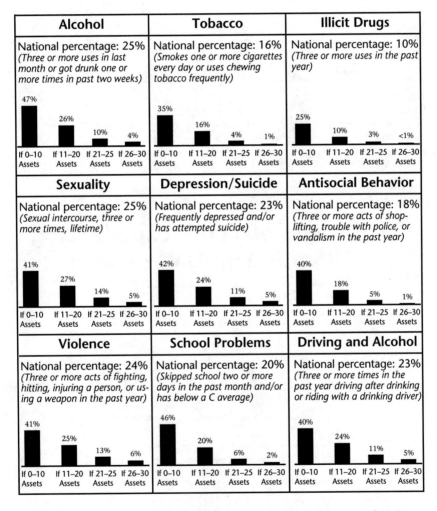

Alcohol	Tobacco	Illicit Drugs
National percentage: 25% *(Three or more uses in last month or got drunk one or more times in past two weeks)*	National percentage: 16% *(Smokes one or more cigarettes every day or uses chewing tobacco frequently)*	National percentage: 10% *(Three or more uses in the past year)*
47% · 26% · 10% · 4%	35% · 16% · 4% · 1%	25% · 10% · 3% · <1%
If 0–10 Assets · If 11–20 Assets · If 21–25 Assets · If 26–30 Assets	If 0–10 Assets · If 11–20 Assets · If 21–25 Assets · If 26–30 Assets	If 0–10 Assets · If 11–20 Assets · If 21–25 Assets · If 26–30 Assets

Sexuality	Depression/Suicide	Antisocial Behavior
National percentage: 25% *(Sexual intercourse, three or more times, lifetime)*	National percentage: 23% *(Frequently depressed and/or has attempted suicide)*	National percentage: 18% *(Three or more acts of shoplifting, trouble with police, or vandalism in the past year)*
41% · 27% · 14% · 5%	42% · 24% · 11% · 5%	40% · 18% · 5% · 1%
If 0–10 Assets · If 11–20 Assets · If 21–25 Assets · If 26–30 Assets	If 0–10 Assets · If 11–20 Assets · If 21–25 Assets · If 26–30 Assets	If 0–10 Assets · If 11–20 Assets · If 21–25 Assets · If 26–30 Assets

Violence	School Problems	Driving and Alcohol
National percentage: 24% *(Three or more acts of fighting, hitting, injuring a person, or using a weapon in the past year)*	National percentage: 20% *(Skipped school two or more days in the past month and/or has below a C average)*	National percentage: 23% *(Three or more times in the past year driving after drinking or riding with a drinking driver)*
41% · 25% · 13% · 6%	46% · 20% · 6% · 2%	40% · 24% · 11% · 5%
If 0–10 Assets · If 11–20 Assets · If 21–25 Assets · If 26–30 Assets	If 0–10 Assets · If 11–20 Assets · If 21–25 Assets · If 26–30 Assets	If 0–10 Assets · If 11–20 Assets · If 21–25 Assets · If 26–30 Assets

Note: Based on total national sample of 254,464 students, grades six to twelve. Percentages indicate how many youth engage in each pattern based on the level of the original thirty assets they experience.

Figure 25

Assets and Thriving

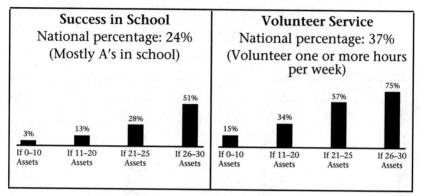

Success in School
National percentage: 24%
(Mostly A's in school)

3% — If 0–10 Assets
13% — If 11–20 Assets
28% — If 21–25 Assets
51% — If 26–30 Assets

Volunteer Service
National percentage: 37%
(Volunteer one or more hours per week)

15% — If 0–10 Assets
34% — If 11–20 Assets
57% — If 21–25 Assets
75% — If 26–30 Assets

Note: Based on the original framework of thirty assets.

Figure 26

Percentages of Youth Experiencing Different Levels of Assets

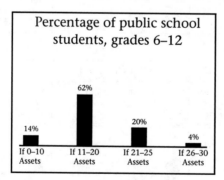

Percentage of public school
students, grades 6–12

14% — If 0–10 Assets
62% — If 11–20 Assets
20% — If 21–25 Assets
4% — If 26–30 Assets

Note: Based on the original framework of thirty assets.

Though these students were soon scattered throughout nineteen different high schools, Lang kept in touch with his adopted class by means of tutors, trips to colleges, an open door to his office, and above all, his energetic encouragement. Six years later, forty-eight of the fifty-one who had stayed in Harlem graduated from high school. Twenty-five were accepted at colleges that ranged from Swarthmore in Pennsylvania to La Guardia Community College in Queens.

Lang's approach, known as "I Have a Dream," inspired philanthropists in other cities to sponsor sixth-grade classes in their communities. To coordinate their efforts Lang established a national foundation. His conviction is that helping children identify their dream of the kind of career they want to follow has an effect. In wanting to be somebody, students gain ambition, motivation, and self-respect.[11]

Communities Can Become Caring

The importance of the social context in which youth are raised is well illustrated by recent efforts of schools to enhance students' social development. This began in the early 1980s when the concept of schools becoming caring communities emerged from extensive pioneer studies. During the 1990s, careful efforts have been made to evaluate the effect that caring schools have on students.

Though researchers' definition of *community* has varied between "a sense of belonging," to "member participation," to "community values," they have agreed that the word *community* refers to a quality that meets students' psychological needs of membership, autonomy, and competence. These needs, they believe, are met when students participate in a cohesive, caring group with a shared purpose—a caring community.[12]

In schools where students experience a caring community, a large number of positive outcomes have occurred. These outcomes include personal and social qualities and school-related qualities such as general social competence, conflict resolution skills, commitment to democratic values, empathy, self-esteem, a positive attitude toward school, an achievement motivation, an intrinsic motivation for learning, and reading comprehension.[13]

A large study involved an extensive examination of the caring community concept in twenty-four elementary schools throughout the United States. Both students and faculty were assessed for their perception of the school as a caring community. Researchers administered an extensive battery of tests that encompassed contextual and socio-demographic characteristics, such as classroom practices, classroom climate, teachers' attitudes, teachers' beliefs, teachers' behaviors, students' attitudes, students' motives, students' behaviors, and students' performance.

The study revealed four major characteristics of caring community schools:

- Schools differ greatly in the extent to which they can be called a caring community.
- Caring communities tend to produce a large number of desirable outcomes.
- The qualities that determine a caring community are established by the activities and practices of both teachers and students.
- Where teachers and students make efforts to establish a caring community, significant increases occur in their perception of the school as such a community.

This research gives striking evidence of the value of efforts to make schools places where children and youth are cared for, where their welfare is considered of highest value. It also gives direction for parents and community leaders who are concerned about what they see happening to youth.

The Hastings, Minnesota, community is one of hundreds in the United States adopting the asset-building approach. During its initial sessions, the planning committee wondered which values should be emphasized in the process of building a healthier community. To determine these values, the steering committee submitted a list of eighteen values to be ranked by people in schools, churches, and community organizations. Though the group of 819 people who responded was not a representative sample, it provided an approximation of what the community as a whole valued. Honesty was ranked number one (687 votes), responsibility was ranked number two (665 votes), and compassion and caring were ranked number three (495 votes).

The *Kids These Days* study found that six in ten adults are troubled over their youngsters' failure to reflect positive values.[14] These parents singled out especially the virtues of honesty, respect, and responsibility as lacking. It is precisely in promoting such values that the church can assist.

Such assistance is believed possible by the bishops of the Roman Catholic church. The possibility of parishes helping change our social culture through a focus on the forty developmental assets caught their attention. In the 1997 publication *Renewing the Vision: A Framework for Catholic Youth Ministry*, the bishops adopt Search Institute's five basic considerations regarding asset building, all pertinent to church ministry:

- Asset development begins at birth and needs to be sustained throughout childhood and adolescence.
- Asset building depends on building positive relationships with children and adolescents and requires a highly consistent community in which children and adolescents are exposed to clear messages about what is important.
- Families can and should be the most powerful generators of developmental assets.
- Assets are more likely to blossom if they are nurtured simultaneously by families, schools, youth organizations, neighborhoods, religious institutions, and health care providers and in informal settings.
- Everyone in a community has a role to play.[15]

Congregational Outreach into a Community

Over the years a key factor in establishing a sense of community has been the presence of religious institutions. David Bodenhammer, the director of a project on religion and urban culture, emphasizes this point when he says, "Of all the facets of modern society, religion may be the most place-based institution of all, serving more than any other organization as a neighborhood anchor."[16]

In addition to being place-based, the congregation deals directly with values and morals, a primary concern of the American public. For the American public, values and character explain why things are going wrong or right. "Most Americans believe that values are the vaccine: if you inoculate teens with them they will be able to resist the world's many traps."[17]

Since most congregations find themselves in communities where the average number of assets experienced by their youth is only eighteen of the forty assets, they need to consider how they can become a catalyst for increasing this number. A congregation could, for example, introduce asset-building programs that other community organizations can use, or focus on helping youth discover a personal faith, knowing that a personal faith builds assets.

Congregations As Catalysts

Joan Wynn and her colleagues at the University of Chicago formulated a framework for assessing the importance a community places on its youth. They identified four key areas:

- opportunities for youth to participate in community life
- avenues for youth to contribute to the welfare of others
- opportunities for youth to connect with peers and adults in the community
- adequate access to community facilities and events[18]

Congregations can contribute to these aspects of a caring community simply be providing programs and facilities. Congregations can also inform and motivate their people to participate actively in community efforts to make these elements available for youth.

The strategic importance of early congregational involvement in a community effort to build assets was underscored by Lynn Borud, a key player in Nampa, Idaho's, Healthy Youth Initiative. Writing in 1996 when the concept of asset building was new, she made these observations:

> Thinking back now, I would have built stronger bridges at the beginning with all the religious congregations in Nampa.
>
> Congregations are a powerful community group, and it makes sense that communities work hand-in-hand with them. We had some religious leaders involved, but in Nampa, as in many other places, there's not a great deal of unity among all the ministerial associations.
>
> When we were about to release the results of Search Institute's *Attitudes and Behaviors* survey of young people, ministers who had not been involved expressed some concern. The survey told us that our community needed to do a better job of helping our young people avoid problems like sexual activity, drug use,

and suicidal thoughts. But some of the pastors asked, "Why are we focusing on the bottom of the barrel in terms of community news?"

Another concern was that we were trying to impose a shape on the congregations' youth ministry programs, when actually we were just trying to bring data, information, ideas, and partnering prospects to the table.

We've since worked to build understanding across the religious communities, but in retrospect, I wish I had had one-to-one visits with many churches at the very beginning.[19]

An obvious need for getting broad involvement is to develop a mutual understanding of what is needed and how best these needs can be met. One way to bring about such an understanding is to agree on a vision-mission statement. This is not an easy undertaking. Elaine Zuzek, cochair of YouthFirst, a healthy communities initiative in Hastings, Minnesota, told of how hard it was for her to gain agreement on a clear statement of mission. However, after forty people representing different parts of the community had wrestled with the question for four months, they finally did arrive at a statement that has held up over the years: "Our mission is to build a healthy community by engaging all community members to develop, support, and nurture positive assets in our youth."[20]

Seattle and Bellevue, twin cities in the state of Washington, have also launched community initiatives. Their mission statement might be inferred from their jointly adopted theme: "It's About Time . . . for Kids: Real Assets, Real Results." Their first step involved more than one hundred community dialogues to establish the word *asset* in the minds of their general public.

Meanwhile, in the small town of Monroe, Washington, thirty miles east of Seattle, Pastor Paul Sundberg of Morning Star Lutheran Church, organizer for an asset-building initiative in his town, had a different strategy. His goals were to build better bridges among congregations, and to achieve more individual rather than organizational commitment. His slogan was "Shared Language + Shared Purpose = Shared Community." As this slogan suggests, his initial intent was to lay a good foundation for ongoing community education, with congregations playing a significant role.[21]

Congregation Programs Replicable for Communities

Congregations are in a good position to initiate and introduce asset-building programs to a community. Examples of such programs are those Joy G. Dryfoos found most effective when she reviewed programs that are used in schools and communities to address some aspect of at-risk behavior. Among the programs she identified were the following:

- senior high youth leading junior high or younger youth
- nonparent adults giving individualized attention (mentoring) to at-risk youth
- parents and youth learning to communicate with one another on ethical issues[22]

Peer Helping Programs

An example of a peer helping program is the one at Saint Andrew Lutheran Church and Eden Prairie High School in Eden Prairie, Minnesota. Here church and school trained twenty-two peer helpers who provided critical services during the aftermath of the abduction of Grant Hussey, a soccer player and popular student at the high school and a member of Saint Andrew Lutheran Church. The incident drew considerable media attention and caused much alarm among students and parents. Days after the abduction, two bodies were found in a car that had been driven into a wooded area, hidden from public view. The boy had been shot, and his abductor had committed suicide.

This abduction and murder-suicide was a traumatic experience for students at the high school who knew and loved the young man. Their common emotion was anger, followed by the question Why did it have to happen to him? Though the school provided professional counseling, the persons sought out most by the students were the twenty-two peer helpers. Some of the helpers met with students in a drop-in group room, others stood near the offices of the professional staff to help those waiting to get in, and still other helpers served as floaters, searching out individuals or small groups that were having a difficult time.

The effectiveness of these peer helpers was singled out for special mention by the *Minneapolis Star Tribune,* who featured Julie Neitzel from Saint Andrew Lutheran Church, and by the evening news of WCCO television. The high school principal of Eden Prairie said of the peer helpers, "Without their help we probably would not have been able to manage."

Training in peer helping is available through a course called Peer Ministry Training, developed by Dr. Barbara Varenhorst. The course equips youth to reach out to peers in caring ways and has the added benefit of helping trainees to greater self-understanding of coping with adolescence.[23] Originally designed to train young people in schools and community organizations, the course is now available with a theological component for use in congregations. Varenhorst's program addresses twenty-five of the forty developmental assets. She lists eleven assets that are most directly addressed in this course:

Social Competencies
- planning and decision making
- interpersonal competence
- resistance skills
- nonviolent conflict resolution

Positive Identity
- personal control
- self-esteem
- sense of purpose
- positive view of personal future

Values
- prosocial: helping others
- prosocial: equality and justice
- personal responsibility

Terri Ulschmid serves in Nativity of Mary Catholic Church, Minneapolis, Minnesota, and facilitates a peer ministry group of seventh and eighth graders at the church's grade school. Story after story tells of how the youth's peer ministry training has made a difference. One boy relates how he spent a number of months befriending a third grader who needed help in learning friendship skills and appropriate behavior. He helped by eating lunch with him daily and spending additional time with him as a friend. Another boy said, "Peer ministry has been a ministry to myself. I needed to get my own life straightened out." Prone to tease other kids, he came to realize the negative effects he was having on others. Ulschmid noted that as her youth took their ministry seriously, their own values changed: "As I teach them I am amazed at how their value system is affected. After helping a younger person who is picked on because he is socially awkward, the peer minister discovers that his or her own desire to put down other classmates soon disappears."

Mentoring Programs

The redemptive power of mentoring is illustrated in the story of David Wanstall, an American Indian youth from the Eastern Shosone and Northern Arapahoe nations' Wind River Reservation in Wyoming. The eldest son of an alcoholic father, David lost, in close succession, a grandfather, an uncle, a great-aunt, and his father—all from excessive drinking. Wanstall soon lost his focus and began skipping school, spending most of his time watching television at a nearby hospital.[24]

According to Arapahoe tradition, the oldest brother in a family is to bond with a special nephew. Sun Rhodes, president of Amer-Indian Architectural Firm in St. Paul, Minnesota, decided to adopt David, who by this time was failing all of his classes, as his nephew. Sun brought David home to live with him in St. Paul. One of the requirements he placed on his nephew was that he spend at least two hours each night in his private learning altar. At least once a week he gave him a "you've got to do well in school" lecture.

By the end of his freshman year, David's grades had improved drastically, and he was no longer a truant. By the time he was a junior and a senior, he was winning scholarships and earning accolades. As a senior he planned to become a lawyer specializing in psychological issues.

The power of a mentoring relationship gained a research base through a major national study conducted between 1992 and 1993. The study involved six agencies of Big Brothers and Big Sisters. Through a comprehensive and scientifically valid research effort, an evaluation was made of the outcomes of Big Brother and Big Sister mentoring of approximately one thousand ten- to sixteen-year-olds. Seventy percent of the participants were African American, almost all living with a single parent.[25]

The randomly selected experimental and control groups were compared after a period of eighteen months to see if mentoring resulted in less use of drugs and alcohol, less violence, improved school attendance, improved attitudes toward schoolwork, and improved peer and family relationships.

The results were highly positive. Seventy percent of minority little brothers and little sisters were less likely to begin using drugs than were those in the control group. The little brothers and sisters skipped half as many days of school as did the control group, they felt more competent about doing schoolwork, and they showed modest improvements in their grade point averages. The study concluded that a mentoring relationship is most successful when an adult spends time with the young person at least three times a month, four hours each meeting, for at least one year.

Gary Walker, president of Public/Private Ventures, says this of the study:

> The Big Brothers and Big Sisters findings provide evidence that here is something that works. It works by engineering the hardest of all things to engineer, namely, a human relationship. The study shows that positive youth development means having an adult friend.[26]

Dwight Hobbes, a columnist for *Insight News,* an African American weekly newspaper, became concerned over results of achievement tests in Twin City schools. In the 1997 Minnesota basic skills tests, only 172 of the 1,169 African American eighth graders passed the mathematics test. Of the 1,183 who took the reading test, only 178 passed. Only 15 percent of the African American youth passed their basic tests. Hobbes made an appeal in the *St. Paul Pioneer Press* for African American adults to reach out and mentor failing students:

> The 85 percent of blacks who flunked have a snowball's chance in hell of improving their skills by graduation, of going on to decent jobs (never mind college), and of being able to afford housing outside ghetto zones.
>
> One-to-one mentoring, because of its immediacy, can get through to kids. Sustained contact with someone of character can nullify the influence of idiots. This individual can be there when the parent, usually a single mother, is too busy trying to make ends meet and does not have the time to drum a sense of right and wrong into a hard, young head.

Only when we stop shaking our heads, get off our behinds, and involve ourselves in young lives, can we help them value education and pursue worthwhile futures.[27]

A review of the literature on mentoring by Rebecca Saito and Dale Blyth of Search Institute, identified four other types of mentoring:

- long-term tutoring programs for underachieving students, which seek to build skills and promote academic progress
- short-term, school-based tutoring programs that use volunteer students as teachers
- team mentoring in which two or more mentors work with a young person for two to four hours once a week for several years
- mentoring in which one adult volunteer works with a small group of young people. The Girl Scouts, for example, view their volunteer troop leaders and assistants as mentors. Here the mentor makes a long-term commitment to meet regularly with the group as a leader or coleader. The effect tends to be stronger than that of the individual mentor.[28]

The McKnight Foundation funded an evaluative study of the mentoring, tutoring, and friendship programs for children and youth in Minneapolis. The study focused on a consortium of agencies known as the Buddy System. The study found that regardless of the type of mentoring program, mentoring is a win-win situation. In the five programs being evaluated, more than one thousand volunteers were working with more than eighteen hundred young people who were being reached in significant, beneficial, and cost-effective relationships.[29]

Abe Bergen, former director for youth education of the General Conference Mennonite Church, in Winnipeg, Canada, served a church that pioneered the mentoring ministry. His denomination has published two books that incorporate what congregations have learned about mentoring over the years: *A Mentoring Guide for Congregational Youth Ministry* and *One on One: Making the Most of Your Mentoring Relationship.*[30]

Mennonite congregations, with a tradition of mentoring, are uniquely equipped to assist their communities in establishing mentoring programs.

The June 1995 newsletter of the Canadian Mentor Strategy National Training Leaders Organization reports that more than twenty-two hundred people had been trained by an initial core of thirty national mentor leaders. These newly trained mentors then were paired with one hundred thirty thousand students. What these thirty initial mentor leaders were able to accomplish in Canada can also happen, proportionately, in communities where only a few people are trained in mentoring.

Computer information on mentoring is now readily available on the World Wide Web. According to the March 1995 newsletter of the Canadian Mentor Strategy National Training Leaders Organization, a Web search found 661 documents associated with mentoring. Many of these were bibliographies dealing with mentoring. Resources for mentoring are now available to people no matter how distant their community might be from resource centers.

Intergenerational Programs

The Catholic Church's *General Directory for Catechesis* emphasizes that catechesis is for all ages and generations. "It should not be overlooked that the recipient of catechesis is the whole Christian community and every person in it."[31] John Roberto, creator of the *Generations of Faith* program, highlights the following benefits of intergenerational learning:

- builds community and meaningful relationships across all the generations in a parish
- provides a setting for each generation to share and learn from the other generations
- provides an environment where new ways of living one's faith can be practiced
- provides adult role models for children and youth
- promotes understanding of shared values and a common faith, as well as respect for individuals in all stage and ages of life
- helps to overcome the age-segregated nature of our society and Church programs[32]

Mount Calvary congregation in Phoenix, Arizona, is intentional about helping individuals, families, and communities make positive connections between generations. Its program is premised on the fact that each age—infant, toddler, preschooler, elementary schooler, junior high schooler, high schooler, young adult, midlife adult, young senior, and senior—brings to the others distinctive needs and resources; hence, activities are planned for every generation.

When committees are formed, one person from each generation is selected to consider such issues as keeping the campus looking good or improving their outreach efforts to people in the community.

The pastor, Rev. Donald D. Smidt, has established an organization called Connecting Generations, of which he is president. Through this consulting practice he offers his intergenerational experience and expertise:

> I am a change consultant with the goal of helping people of every age, or generation, recognize and utilize their unique gifts for others. Better still, if I train and empower church leaders to do this for their people of all ages together, that will be enough.[33]

Pastor Smidt emphasizes moments in the life of young and old that are so vital to change that he calls them the "critical edge." Critical edge moments may center on a book, a flower, a card, a toy, a movie, a day of fishing, a basketball game, a counseling session, or a day away.

The outcomes of this intergenerational program include the following:

- More are using the language and reflecting a consciousness of other generations instead of thinking only of their age-group.
- One generation is now serving another.
- An environment has been established where all ages feel welcome, from the six-year-old to the ninety-six-year-old.

The popularity of intergenerational programs is evident in the variety of community efforts being made to bring generations together in meaningful ways. The following are examples of activities that members of a congregation can encourage for their community:

- An integrated arts program in Ann Arbor, Michigan, called Grand Persons brings children together with older persons. In matched pairs they work together on such things as poetry, writing, woodworking, drawing, sewing, and dancing.
- In Pittsburgh, Pennsylvania, a program called Generations Together uses volunteer senior citizens to help youth acquire such basic skills as reading, writing, math, science, and such cultural enrichment as music, poetry, drama, weaving, quilting, painting, and oral history.

- At Oregon State University in Corvallis, Oregon, journalism students help produce newsletters for residents in nursing homes and senior citizen centers, designing brochures for the Area Agency on Aging, and writing feature articles for publication on topics like patient rights and concerns for the aging population.
- In Toronto, Ontario, Canada, secondary students assist in providing home support services for the elderly and handicapped, both during school hours as part of their courses and after school hours as volunteers or paid employees. Senior citizens come to the school as teaching volunteers to participate with the youth in discussing the service experiences. A vocational school program allows students to provide seniors with such services as hairdressing, appliance and carpentry repairs, dry cleaning, printing, small engine repair, and furniture refinishing.
- In Santa Cruz and San Francisco, California, intergenerational child care centers have been established. These preschools are based on the concept of integrating elders and children in a child care setting.
- In Saint Louis Park, Minnesota, seniors volunteer to wait for the school bus with children in the morning and to meet them on the corner when the school bus returns after school. These volunteer seniors not only solve a safety problem because parents are often going to work, but they also develop wonderful, trusting relationships with the children.
- Pastor Lee Hovel of Trinity Lutheran Church in Mission, Kansas, has designed worship services that focus on the leadership and gifts of the generations of the family as they celebrate family milestones and moments of change.

These illustrations identify the many ways members of a congregation can develop intergenerational events in the community to promote meaningful interaction among children, youth, and adults.

Wellness Programs

Wellness programs are powerful creators of assets in communities. In Omaha, Nebraska, the Nebraska Synod of the Evangelical Lutheran Church in America partnered with Immanuel Medical Center (now Alegent Health), a large teaching hospital, to develop a congregation-based wellness ministry in the community. This innovative ministry, called Project L.I.F.E! (Lifestyle Improvement for Excellence), was piloted in eleven congregations in the greater Omaha area. With an initial grant from Lutheran Brotherhood (now called Thrivent) and money provided by the hospital, Project L.I.F.E! hired a person to serve as project coordinator and formed a project team of leaders from the synod and the hospital. The intent of this new ministry was to move from a model of illness-based ministries to a model of wellness-based ministries—from ministry in hospitals to congregations reaching out into the community. Project L.I.F.E! focuses on prevention rather than rehabilitation.

Each of the eleven pilot congregations had local project teams that were oriented in the ministry of wellness as a ministry of helping people live a balanced life with God centered in each of seven areas of well-being—environmental, social, spiritual, occupational, physical, emotional, and intellectual. The congregations' project teams were also equipped with skills for recruiting other people in their congregation to carry out the ministry.

The following vision and mission statement of Project L.I.F.E! clearly shows how a congregation can, by way of its ministry, connect all generations of people and make a difference in their lives.

Vision. Project L.I.F.E! is a process of developing all the ministries of a faith community with a focus on the quality and longevity of the lives of the people in the surrounding community.

Project L.I.F.E! looks from the cross to the community and raises the question What difference does our ministry to these people make?

Mission. Project L.I.F.E! is a wellness ministry developed by the Nebraska Synod of the Evangelical Lutheran Church in America in partnership with Immanuel Medical Center to promote healthy lifestyle practices among people of all ages. The two primary foci of Project L.I.F.E! are the following:
- to educate individuals and communities about the direct relationship between personal lifestyle, spirituality, quality of life, and health
- to motivate individuals and communities to strive for balanced levels of emotional, physical, social, intellectual, spiritual, occupational, and environmental well-being[34]

As part of its wellness ministry to the community, Saint John Lutheran Church in Winter Park, Florida, not only has a director of wellness ministry on staff but also has developed a clown ministry troupe. This Life in Christ Circus brings the Gospel of Jesus Christ and the healing power of laughter and play to children of all ages in the community. Over a period of time, these Christ Clowns averaged more than one hundred appearances a year, participating in such volunteer activities as meals-on-wheels and visiting such places as community hospitals; homes for autistic children; the House of Hope, a national home for runaway teenage girls; Friendly Village, a care center for people with severe mental and physical disabilities; nursing homes throughout the community; retirement centers; Christian congregations; and inner-city schools. The troupe also did benefits to raise money for community social services.

Through Christ Clown College, the congregation also recruits and trains other people in the history and art of clown ministry. The leadership of this clown ministry began Christian Clown Connection, a training event for advanced skills in clown ministry. For fourteen years now, this annual weekend training event has been bringing some of the best theologians and clowns together as a faculty for clown ministry training.

Music Programs

As mentioned in other places in this book, music is a great avenue for entering young people's lives and, in doing so, creating assets for them. Since 1992 CitySongs, a project introduced by Dr. Helen Kivnick, professor in the school of social work at the University of Minnesota, has met twice a week to use choir and music performances to help young people develop individual strengths and reinforce skills learned at home, school, and church. Participants are eight to fourteen years old and come primarily from inner-city areas. CitySong choirs are led by Sam Davis, a musician who helps the group members write their own songs.

During a half hour period, the children discuss an issue they face. If the topic is violence, for instance, Davis or one of the volunteers asks the group to describe what to do or what not to do when threatened by violence. Davis then helps group members formulate verses for a song using their own words. A song they sang for the First Annual Conference on Asset Building of Search Institute had the following lyrics:

Don't put nobody down, boss nobody around,
We all must appreciate before we terminate.
We respect O.P.P. [Other People's Property]
Don't steal from nobody,
Forget the drugs,
And just think about the hugs.

Their singing for the closing session of the conference won a standing ovation. Afterward a delegate at the conference met one of the singers, a young African American boy about ten years old. The boy thanked her for coming. When the delegate responded with appreciation for his singing, he paused and then asked: "Would you like my autograph?" Here was a boy who might have become a nobody but who now was feeling like a very important person. The CitySongs program was building assets for him.

The secret of this program's success goes beyond the music, however, to the staff and volunteers who interact with the youth twice a week. Two musicians, a social worker with interns, and eight volunteers (some of whom are high school students) provide ample opportunity for the forty to fifty young people to rub shoulders with positive role models.

Robert Coles, a psychiatrist and a Harvard professor, emphasizes an important point when he says, "We grow morally as a consequence of learning how to be with others, how to behave in this world, a learning prompted by taking to heart what we have seen and heard."[35]

Coles quotes Anna Freud as saying, "For elementary students, this is the age a child's conscience is built—or isn't; it is the time a child's character is built and consolidated—or isn't."

North Heights Lutheran Church in St. Paul, Minnesota, uses music, drama, and intergenerational participation of children, youth, and adults to present the Gospel story to a wide community of people. During the month of April, there are eighteen presentations to sell-out audiences of fourteen hundred people each evening.

Congregations and Youths' Personal Faith

Congregations' ultimate mission is to nurture faith in Jesus, the Christ. Achieving the forty developmental assets, though an important goal for congregations, is not their ultimate goal. Limiting a youth ministry to building assets could result in nice kids who have no faith.

The assets paradigm, enormously useful in addressing the issue of unhealthy communities in the secular arena, must be limited to a language all groups in a community can use. Because of our pluralistic society, the paradigm cannot include in its list the most powerful asset of all: faith in Jesus Christ; hence, a congregational ministry must be seen as having two objectives:

- to build these assets in the lives of both its own youth and families and those of the community
- to bring the youth and adults it serves into a conscious commitment to Jesus Christ as Lord and Savior

These two objectives are not opposed to each other but are complementary. A number of Search Institute research studies, noted also in other sections of this book, reveal that personal faith increases the likelihood that almost half of the forty developmental assets will be found in young people.

Search Institute conducted a major study of more than seven thousand high school youth from ten denominations, resulting in the book *Five Cries of Youth*. The study's highly reliable measure of youths' sense of a personal God showed strong correlations with the following assets:

- moral restraint
- service to others (prosocial behavior)
- religious community (involvement)
- positive view of the future
- achievement motivation[36]

Search Institute's *Adolescent-Parent* study of more than eight thousand young adolescents and ten thousand parents randomly drawn from eleven major Protestant and Catholic denominations identified youth who experience religion as a liberating force in their lives. Significantly these youth were found to have the following assets in greater degree than those lacking this faith:

- self-esteem
- moral restraint (less likely to be involved in at-risk behaviors)
- family boundaries (acceptance of parental standards)
- achievement motivation
- religious community

- service to others
- cultural competence (not racially prejudiced)[37]

A third study by Search Institute, *A Study of Generations*, analyzed the answers to 740 items given to almost five thousand Lutherans. An analysis of the faith component showed that it is the most powerful predictor of people's attitudes and behavior—stronger than psychological, sociological, and personal factors such as age, occupation, level of education, or financial status. People of faith tend to reflect the following assets:

- caring (compassionate caring)
- equality and social justice (involvement in social issues)
- religious community
- service to others
- caring neighborhood (supporting others in crisis)
- adult role models (neighborliness)
- family boundaries (acceptance of authority)
- sense of purpose (life purpose)
- family support (family caring life)
- positive family communication (identification with parents)
- neighborhood boundaries (acceptance of community norms)
- positive view of personal future (attitudes toward life)[38]

The complementary nature of the two objectives of a congregational ministry is shown graphically in the strong correlation between the importance youth accord religion and service involvement. Among those who view religion as not important, only 29 percent are involved in a service activity. On the other hand, of those who deem religion very important, 60 percent are involved in a service activity.[39] The importance of the service-to-others asset is seen in the fact that about 40 percent of an adolescent's hours are discretionary; hence, it is important for communities to provide opportunities for adolescents to spend their free time in constructive, stimulating activities.

A congregation cannot address all forty developmental assets at one time while giving priority to the faith issue. Nor need one focus only on the missing assets. The wisest approach in a congregational ministry is to single out for attention those assets that hold the greatest promise of having an initial effect. High on the list should be those assets that are most effective in deterring youth from at-risk behaviors:

External Assets
- family support (love and interest)
- parental standards (determining appropriate conduct)
- time at home (four nights a week or more)
- church, school, and community activities (structured use of time)
- parental faith (shared when together as a family)

Internal Assets
- achievement motivation (to do well in something)
- internalized moral values (sex, drug, and alcohol restraint)
- educational aspiration (wants future education)
- service orientation (values helping people)
- personal faith (considers it important)

A focus on these assets does not mean ignoring the others.[40] Many of these are built through incidental contacts with young people—the times when an adult displays special interest in a young person, praising something he or she has done. These are the "molecules of time" that Benson speaks of in his book *All Kids Are Our Kids* that do not cost a thing yet build assets.

A National Effort for Healthy Communities, Healthy Kids

A President's Summit for America's Future, held in Philadelphia in April 1997 brought General Colin Powell, President Clinton, and several former presidents together with corporate executives and community and volunteer leaders. Their goal was to boost volunteering substantially within three years, emphasizing helping youth.

The report commissioned for the summit, called *America's Promise: The Alliance for Youth,* begins by declaring that "every child and adolescent in America should have the confidence, competence, and connections needed to live a healthy, fulfilling life and contribute positively to society."[41] The report then identifies five fundamental resources that, if consistently provided, not only will contribute to youth development but also will significantly reduce problems facing America's youth. The resources, similar to the developmental assets described earlier, are the following:

- ongoing relationships with caring adults
- safe places and structured activities
- a healthy start for a healthy future
- marketable skills through effective education
- opportunities to serve

The intent of *America's Promise* is to connect two million additional young people, from birth to age twenty, to all five fundamental resources. These connections will occur primarily through the natural support systems in neighborhoods and communities—families, neighbors, associations, youth organizations, human service agencies, religious institutions, schools, businesses, and youth themselves.[42]

In an interview six months after the summit meeting, Colin Powell reflected on why he sees this battle as one of extreme urgency. He sees *America's Promise* to be an organization seeking to rescue youngsters from "a farm system for jails." The "lost children," he says, "show up at school without structure, without discipline, without self-esteem, without language skills, without having been taught right or wrong at age six." The reason is that "there is nobody, no adult in their family" who teaches them about guilt or shame. So the streets take over.[43]

For Powell, the goal of *America's Promise* is to re-create the kind of nurturing environment he knew as a boy when he lived in the Bronx. Then the communities were together. Families and parents were together. There was a church that was an important presence. "I sometimes compare it to a pinball machine. You had flippers which constantly kept the kid in place."[44]

The interviewers, Cokie and Steven Roberts, summarized their conversation with Colin Powell by saying, "Six months after the historic summit, Powell is pushing people to keep their promises even as he tries to fulfill his."[45]

The summit report concludes by stressing the importance of mobilizing communities to provide the five resources described earlier, using the following principles as guides for community action and planning:

- The five resources build on one another. It's the integration of the five resources that offers real promise.

- Developmental resources are too fragile for most American youth. Too many young people lack consistent, ongoing access to the five resources.
- Young people need ongoing exposure to each resource throughout the first two decades of life. All five resources gain power when they are experienced multiple times in multiple settings.
- All residents and organizations can provide these resources. The success of *America's Promise* depends on residents recognizing and tapping into their own capacity to make a difference in young people's lives.

As mentioned earlier, congregations and other communities of faith play a critical role in asset development within a community. They are often the only regular weekly gathering of intergenerational groups of people remaining in a community where people can rally to the cause of healthy communities and offer a faith system that supports it.

Chapter 8 will explore how our culture of individualism has created conditions where people do not know one another in neighborhoods, in congregations, and sadly, even within families. Yet every Sunday a remnant of people from three or four generations gathers in faith communities to worship. A congregation's ministry needs to support its members in their faith and in their efforts to sustain healthy lifestyles. But congregations must learn to develop ministries together outside the walls of the churches and expand them into the communities. From a faith base, congregations can make a difference in the quality and longevity of the lives of not only the people in the congregations but also of many people in the larger civil community.

Chapter 8

Transforming Today's Culture

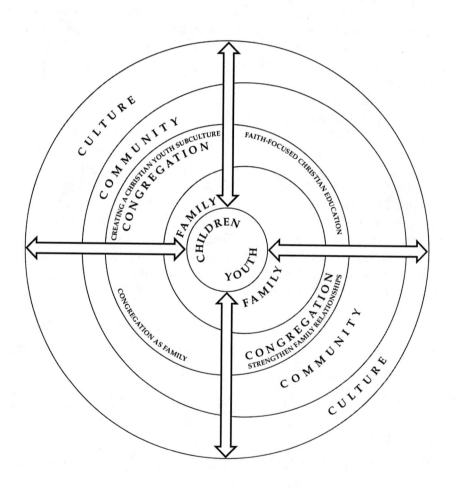

The purpose of this book is to present a model of youth and family ministry that will increase the probability that the Ten Characteristics of Committed Youth become a reality. Our chapters have shown how this probability can be increased by attention to families, congregations, and communities as powerful factors in the faith development of young people. Of these three factors, family was emphasized the most because it is the life shaper of young minds and hearts. We noted that parents play a vital role in how family relationships are established and how a family relates to God.

Next in importance as a shaper of young lives is the congregation. When its program of education is faith focused and it has a strong sense of family, it not only complements the family in passing on the faith but also partially fills the void where faith is lacking. Further, when a congregation values youth by training them to minister to their peers, youth gain assets for a healthy life. And when a youth group provides a much-needed Christian subculture, young people can be sustained in their commitment to Jesus Christ.

Less influential, but a significant contributor in the development of children and youth, is the community in which they live. People of faith act as role models, affecting many youth, and other congregations help enliven the spiritual tone of a community. When the community is healthy, more of its children and youth reflect evidence of health. When a community is unhealthy, it erodes the positive effect of home and church.

As indicated by our conceptual model, there is another significant factor in the faith development of children and youth. This factor is today's culture, an ever-present phenomenon we breathe in like air.

How do we define culture? It is a way of living that has become normative for a group of human beings. Culture includes music, art, media, and intellectual stimuli that contain and communicate norms and values. But a culture whose basic norms and values are life enriching and are a source of enjoyment and blessing can be misrepresented and eroded by the media that communicate them. Media that encourage self-gratification, individualism, antiauthoritarianism, and the like are powerful shapers of the attitudes and values not only of young people but also of families, communities, and the culture itself.

Culture As a Shaping Influence

Every national and religious group has its distinctive culture (Scandinavian, Muslim, Indian, etc.). But such cultures are not the focus of this chapter. Rather, the focus of this chapter is the shaping influence of the culture in the United States as communicated by the mass media.

Robert N. Bellah, professor of sociology at the University of California, focused his research and conclusions in *Habits of the Heart*[1] on the shaping influence of the American culture. He identified people's moral and intellectual dispositions—their notions, opinions, and ideas—contending that they shape people's mental responses to become what he calls "habits of the heart."

Bellah's diagnosis is that one habit of the American heart that dominates the American culture is individualism. For those occupied with this habit of the heart, goals in life revolve around personal choice. For them, "meaning in life is to become one's own person, almost to the point of giving birth to oneself."[2] Such people find it difficult to commit themselves to a marriage, a family, a congregation, an organization, or a workforce.

When individualism guides a person, the following transformation takes place: Being good becomes being good at things, and being right shifts from being ethical to having the right answers. When individualism becomes a habit of the heart, utility replaces duty, self-expression unseats authority.

In an article published ten years after *Habits of the Heart*, Bellah and his associates note that the consequences of radical individualism are strikingly evident today.[3] Diminished civic commitment is matched by a diminished involvement in groups, resulting in a declining social capital.

Those in the upper class are withdrawing into gated, guarded communities. The middle class is tending not to join groups. They belong to only one or two organizations, the likeliest being a church. They are increasingly suspicious of politics, and as a result their participation in it is steadily declining. People in the lower class feel they have nothing to lose and consequently are much less cooperative with efforts at social control.

In a nationwide best-seller, *The Culture of Narcissism: American Life in an Age of Diminishing Expectations,* Christopher Lasch points out how society's emphasis on individualism has led the American culture into narcissism. The narcissist has no interest in the future because he or she has little interest in the past; thus, the culture loses its sense of succession of generations and its motivation to effectively pass on the faith to the next generation and prepare youth to take their place in church and in society. Lasch says, "The contemporary climate is therapeutic, not religious. People today hunger not for personal salvation, let alone for the restoration of an earlier golden age, but for the feeling, the momentary illusion of personal well-being, health, and psychic security."[4] Lasch's conclusion is supported by the research that Christian Smith reports on in *Soul Searching*. Smith's data indicates that the Christian faith has been colonized into a feel-good, therapeutic religion he calls Moralistic Therapeutic Deism.[5]

Steven Carter identifies another aspect of today's culture in his book *The Culture of Disbelief*. He says, "We have created a political and legal culture that presses the religiously faithful to be other than themselves, to act publicly, and sometimes privately as well, as though their faith does not matter to them."[6] Our culture tends to relegate religion to the ranks of being nothing more important than another hobby, something private and something trivial.

In the Rockford Institute's December *Religion and Society Report*, Harold O. J. Brown gives an example of how faith is becoming so private:

> Employees at a telemarketing firm are forbidden to say "Merry Christmas" to a caller, even if the caller says "Merry Christmas" to them. "Happy Hanukkah" is also prohibited as a sign of discrimination although "Happy Holidays" is permitted.
>
> What we see here reveals two things: first, that there is growing prejudice in the United States against the majority religious tradition, which also affects the important minority tradition as well; and second, that the majority population has been browbeaten and intimidated to the point where it supinely accepts thought control and censureship, whether it comes from government or commerce.[7]

This culture of disbelief reflects the attitude that religion is not really a fit activity for intelligent, public-spirited adults. Allan Bloom notes this attitude in *Closing the American Mind*. He writes that a teacher in the university who "takes Scripture at its word, would be accused of scientific incompetence or lack of sophistication."[8]

This cultural opposition to a particularistic faith is something that George A. Lindbeck, a theologian at Yale Divinity, addresses in *The Nature of Doctrine: Religion and Theology in a Post-Liberal Age:*

> The viability of a unified world of the future may well depend on counteracting the acids of modernity. It may depend on communal enclaves that socialize their members into a highly particular outlook supportive of concern for others rather than for individual rights and entitlements, and of a sense of responsibility for the wider society rather than for personal fulfillment.[9]

In *U.S. Lifestyles and Mainline Churches*, Tex Sample, a professor of Church and society at the Saint Paul School of Theology in Kansas City, Missouri, describes how the American culture's focus on individualism has developed a self-fulfillment ethic in direct contrast to the self-denial ethic of the Christian Church. Representative of the self-fulfillment ethic are the post–World War II baby boomers who have developed a psychology of affluence with three basic assumptions:

• An individual is entitled to affluence.
• The economy can and will continue to provide the cornucopia of goods and services to guarantee an individual's right to affluence.
• Fulfillment of self is a basic, lifelong project.

When asked what they want, boomers respond, "More!" Sample concludes that the more people hold to an ethic of self-fulfillment, the less likely they are to belong to a church.[10]

This cultural preoccupation with the self manifests itself in behaviors that make the headlines of today's newspapers. News accounts often feature outcomes of unbridled sexual freedom, gross materialism, unrelenting greed, and an insatiable desire for power. Newspaper articles feature people unwilling to make or honor their commitments to others.

The sobering effect of this cultural phenomenon on families, children, and youth is identified by Peter Benson in *All Kids Are Our Kids:*

Compared with other technologically advanced nations, the United States has the dubious distinction of being a leader in several problem areas, including teenage pregnancy, adolescent alcohol and drug use, and school dropouts. This country fares poorly in rankings on international comparisons of student achievement.[11]

Poor children in the United States are worse off economically than poor children in other affluent nations. Adolescents in the United States are much more likely than adolescents in other countries to be victims of homicide or accidents. Indeed, adolescents in the United States are ten to fifteen times more likely to die from a homicide than adolescents in any European country.

Something in the culture of the United States is fostering a lifestyle that destroys futures. Those most affected by the negative aspects of the American culture are the most vulnerable, namely those having the least support from family, congregation, or community.

The Bible's Attitude Toward Culture

The conviction of biblical writers regarding the negative effect of the world's culture on the life of a believer is clearly stated. For the writers of the Bible, the world is everything in the present order of things that is an object of desire apart from and in rivalry to God. The Bible links this world of influence to the devil and a kingdom of darkness; hence, all moral evil to be found in the world is to be ascribed to the devil.

The Apostle James minced no words when he said, "Don't you know that friendship with the world is hatred toward God? Anyone who chooses to be a friend of the world becomes an enemy of God" (James 4:4, NIV).

The psalmist warns us in Psalm 20:7 (NRSV):

Some take pride in chariots, and some in horses, but our pride is in the name of the LORD, our God.
They will collapse and fall, but we shall rise and stand upright.

The Apostle John is no less pointed in his epistle:

> Do not love the world or anything in the world. If anyone loves the world, the love of the Father is not in him. For everything in the world—the cravings of sinful man, the lust of his eyes and the boasting of what he has and does—comes not from the Father but from the world. The world and its desires pass away, but the man who does the will of God lives forever. (1 John 2:15–17, NIV)

Christ, similarly disposed toward the culture of his day and its effect on the lives of people, reflects his concern as he prays on the night of his betrayal:

> I have given [my disciples] your word and the world has hated them, for they are not of the world any more than I am of the world. My prayer is not that you take them out of the world but that you protect them from the evil one. (John 17:14–15, NIV)

These uncompromising statements regarding the conflict between the world's culture and a life of faith, however, have been interpreted in various ways by Christians through the centuries.

Christian Stances Toward Culture

In *Christ and Culture,* H. Richard Niebuhr identifies five different ways Christians have related to their culture:
- Christ against culture—separation from the world
- Christ of culture—accommodation to culture
- Christ above culture—a synthesis of Christ and culture
- Christ and culture in paradox—theology of dualism
- Christ, the transformer of culture—conversion of culture

Having reviewed these five approaches and evaluated their strengths and weaknesses, Niebuhr admits in his concluding postscript that the problem of relating culture is not settled. He himself is unable to say this is the Christian answer. Though he finds something commendable in several of the approaches, he yet finds something to critique.[12]

Anthony Campolo, a sociologist at Eastern College, views Niebuhr's categories as contexts for understanding different approaches to youth ministry. He sees them as describing how in different ways various youth ministries attempt to relate to the culture of our day.

Christ Against Culture

The Christ against culture stance views contemporary culture as completely contrary to Christianity. For people with this stance, the world is a totally secular society, dominated by "the desire of the flesh, the desire of the eyes, and pride in riches" (1 John 2:16, NRSV). They often refer to 2 Corinthians 6:17: "Therefore come out from them, and be separate from them, says the Lord" (NRSV).

As noted by Campolo, this view dominates many conservative and fundamentalist circles. Because these groups view their faith as antithetical to culture, they frequently issue diatribes against some aspect of culture. They emphasize that personal guilt and piety are central to religious faith. This approach amounts to a retreat from active involvement in today's culture.[13]

The Amish are an extreme example of a group that is withdrawn from the world and is committed to separating itself from the dictates of the world. Obedient to the viewpoint established by Jacob Amman, the Amish people willingly submit to highly specific rules regarding talking, dressing, walking, working, and traveling. They accept these rules, believing they will help in keeping their group separate from the outside world. They are committed to the notion that they need man-made laws to follow God's word.

To a lesser degree, some Christian denominations have established similar man-made rules to shelter and protect their youth from a sinful world—rules like those against dancing, drinking, using drugs, or going to movies. One denomination, the Seventh-day Adventist, has tried to enforce sixteen standards, or rules, all designed to minimize worldly temptations, promote health, and keep persons in the faith.

The merit in establishing boundaries within which the faith is best lived is seen in figure 27, which compares behaviors of twelfth graders of the Seventh-day Adventist Church to behaviors of a national sample of other American twelfth graders.[14]

Figure 27

Seventh-day Adventist Twelfth Graders' and American Twelfth Graders' Involvement in At-Risk Behaviors

Item	Seventh-day Adventist Twelfth Graders	American Twelfth Graders
Alcohol use six or more times in one year	15%	54%
Marijuana use one or more times in the last year	11%	20%
Sexual intercourse one or more times in your lifetime	27%	63%

It is obvious from this comparison that establishing boundaries for youth in relationship to the faith does reduce the number of young people involved in alcohol and drug abuse and premarital sex. Other studies show that in denominations where abstinence from alcohol, drugs, and sexual activity and the like are advocated, fewer youth are involved in at-risk behaviors.

However, a negative side to an overemphasis on rules and regulations for Christian living is a resulting law orientation that squelches the concept of grace. When boundaries and rules become the primary standards for evaluating young people, youth may think their salvation is determined by how well they observe the boundaries and rules.

A law orientation is seen in the strong percentages of Seventh-day Adventist twelfth graders who agree with the following items:
• I know that to be saved, I have to live by God's rules. (83%)
• The more I follow Adventist standards and practices, the more likely it is I will be saved. (47%)

If a law orientation can be avoided, and if youth can internalize the boundaries instead, the boundaries can provide a needed moral structure for a life of faith.

The experience of five Orthodox Jewish students at Yale University illustrates the act of separating from the culture to remain faithful to religious norms. Repulsed by the dorm life at Yale, they asked to be excused from the university's requirement that undergraduates live on the campus their first two years. These five students pointed to the standards of their faith and tradition, arguing that modesty, privacy, and sexual abstinence before marriage are required of them in their religion. They claimed that the atmosphere in their dorm was a sort of Sodom and Gomorrah free-for-all. But their concept of obedience to tradition and faithfulness to God did not fit Yale's worldview; hence, their request was refused.

Convinced of their position and moral stance, they brought suit against the university. Other Jewish students at Yale did not support these five students. For the other Jewish students, being Jewish means remaining faithful to Jewish norms within the dominant culture, not being a sect outside it.

Sheltering children and youth from the dark side of the culture does have benefits. Studies on violence show that exposure to violence in movies and on television encourages violence in children. Though these findings have been presented to producers of mass media, the media continue to air violent movies and TV programs. In 1997 a study of national TV violence, a project costing $3.3 million, covered programming on twenty-three channels, seven days a week from 6 a.m. to 11 p.m. The findings, published in March 1997, showed that the overall prevalence of violence and the way violence is treated has generally remained the same. According to the study, 58 percent of TV programs contained violence, 73 percent of programs contained violence with no remorse, criticism, or penalty for the violence; 58 percent of programs had repeated behavioral violence; and 40 percent of violent incidents on TV were initiated by characters portrayed as attractive role models or heroes for children.[15]

Many parents concerned over behaviors and attitudes that are becoming prevalent in public schools have chosen home schooling. They believe that a home school improves children's relations with adults and shelters children from a peer culture that leads to violence, premarital sex, drugs, alcohol, and laziness. Furthermore, these parents welcome the opportunity to provide the religious and moral teaching lacking in the public school.

Home schools, officially sanctioned in the 1980s, are anything but a passing fancy. From just a handful of home schools in 1966, the number reached three hundred thousand by 1990 and accelerated to nine hundred thousand by the end of 1996. Continued growth is likely because the research is showing that home-educated children do as well academically as their school-educated peers. On standardized tests such as the Iowa Test of Basic Skills, home-schooled children score on average in the seventy-seventh percentile, considerably above national averages.

Shielding children and youth from base attitudes, substance abuse, and violence in the culture by way of home schooling has its critics. Some contend that home schooling fails to prepare young people for their eventual encounter with these elements in today's culture. Others fear it may impede a child's ability to relate to a variety of people and situations, an ability that is important for a Christian's participation in the larger community. Efforts are being made by those involved with home schools to counter these possible disadvantages.

Many evangelical high schools that provide shelter from today's culture now stress academics. As a result, a high percentage of their graduates go on to college. Steve Stecklow, writing for the *Wall Street Journal*, tells of a school near Nanuet, New York, where 127 of the 135 pupils are African American. In 1994 the twelve five-year-old kindergartners from this school all scored in the ninety-ninth percentile on the Stanford Achievement Test (SAT), third graders learn to write resumes, eighth graders study organic chemistry, and the stated goal is to get every child into Harvard University.[16]

Christ of Culture

Another way by which Christians have related to their culture is to acquiesce to its moral and ethical values. According to H. Richard Niebuhr, "There are those who feel no great tension between the church and the world, the social norms and the Gospel, the workings of divine grace and human effort, the ethics of salvation and the ethics of social progress."[17] Niebuhr identifies this kind of thinking with cultural Protestantism. Much like Gnosticism, it retains the religion, but drops the ethics of Christian living.[18]

Youth ministers and pastors who reflect this stance toward culture show it in their youth programs. Tony Campolo characterizes them this way: "Instead of developing personal piety or social concern, entertainment such as special singing groups, hayrides, and other recreational activities are the principal and often the only functions."[19] It is often the goal of youth ministers and pastors of this stance to do whatever attracts the largest numbers of young people rather than to bring young people into a living relationship with Jesus Christ and to develop a strong sense of discipleship. Campolo says, "The Christ of culture approach typifies churches where there is little concern about the specific content of the faith. Being a good Christian is equated with being a good American or a good moral person."[20] When asked if youth ministers today have a theological agenda for the next decade, Campolo realized how detached theology has become from young people's concerns, that youth's view of sexuality has become disengaged from the theological premise that our bodies are temples of the Holy Spirit. Many people feel that the sexual attitudes of young people are basically the same today as in the past, when in fact there has been a dramatic change of behavior. Our culture as a whole has become much more sexually engaged.[21]

The Christ of culture stance tends to modify religious beliefs. This is evident in the efforts to identify a homosexual or lesbian orientation as a God-given alternative lifestyle. This reinterpretation of the Scriptures has divided most Protestant denominations. Contributing to denominational conflict is our culture's resistance to allow an opposing point of view to be heard.

An opening sentence in the *Monitor*, a monthly newspaper of the American Psychological Association, reflects this resistance when it says, "A small but persistent group of therapists refuses to believe the data that show homosexuality is a normal path of development." The *Monitor* then proceeds to critique the reparative therapy movement and the work of psychologists actively helping homosexuals who want to become heterosexual.

Reparative therapy has a success rate comparable to any form of psychotherapy (one-third success, one-third partial success, and one-third unsuccessful). Yet it is usually not given a hearing. Joseph Nicolosi, a clinical psychologist in Encino, California, and the author of *Healing Homosexuality*, contends that this is because of the strong political and cultural ideology that has risen around a same-sex orientation. Nicolosi is the therapy's chief proponent. He heads up an organization of nine hundred mental health professionals, educators, and public health officials who hold to his position. He insists that political correctness has begun to interfere with honest scientific discourse.

Those wishing to present homosexuality as abnormal often have difficulty. "Don't Forsake Homosexuals Who Want Help," an article in the *Wall Street Journal* written by three psychiatrists and two psychologists, all heads of university clinics, insists that "young men and their parents have the right to know, contrary to media propaganda, there is no proven biological basis for homosexuality." The authors report that "it has been our clinical experience that as men become more comfortable and confident with their manhood, same-sex attractions decrease significantly. Eventually many find the freedom they are seeking and are able to have normal relationships with women."[22]

These highly trained clinicians are trying to counteract a point of view they believe the culture has come to believe is politically correct. They are doing what Carter calls for in his book *The Culture of Disbelief,* namely, trying to establish an openness to liberal dialogue. Carter insists that "religions should not be forced to disguise or remake themselves before they can be involved in secular political argument."[23]

The issue of Christian standards acquiescing to the American culture is a pressing one for authors Wade Roof and William McKinney. In their report *American Mainline Religion: Its Changing Shape and Future,* they call for a countering of the secular drift that has had a disproportionate impact on mainline Protestants. They note that liberal Protestantism's "competition" is not the conservatives it has spurned but the secularists it has spawned. They call for a more responsible individualism in a communal framework.[24]

The move of some seminaries toward a cultural Christianity is noted in a report based on a three-year study of two theological seminaries—one an evangelical school and the other a mainline school. Authors Carroll Jackson, Barbara Wheeler, Daniel Aleshire, and Penny Long give a revealing report of the study in *Being There: Culture and Formation in Two Theological Schools.* The study found that the teaching, thought, life, and practices in the mainline school they studied were heavily influenced by today's culture. The authors see the Gospel of Jesus Christ in this mainline school being reduced to political correctness.

An illustration is given of how a policy on inclusive language, held firmly by many students, was used at this seminary. A veteran faculty member who was retiring and for whom a farewell service was planned requested that a hymn he wrote—probably during the days of protest against the Vietnam war—be sung at the service. The problem was that the hymn included the words *Lord, Father,* and *Almighty God*—words that are now taboo according to some people at this seminary. A great struggle ensued. In the end the hymn was included in the service, but students who objected pinned a protest message to their clothing. There was apparently no thought that in a Christian community, celebrating a faithful, dedicated professor might be more honorable than fighting yet another skirmish in the great gender war.[25]

Christ Above Culture

Niebuhr describes the majority of Christians as refusing to take either the position of the anticultural radical or that of the accommodator of Christ to the culture. He calls this majority Christians of the center. Christians of the center support the primacy of grace and the necessity of works of obedience that flow from faith.[26] Such Christians are aware that there are laws other than those from Christ that also are valid and are from God. This Christ above culture position differs from the other two positions in that neither radical faith nor cultural Christianity take Christ or culture seriously enough, but rather emphasize an enormous gulf between the two.[27]

The Christ above culture stance sees culture as the work of God-given reason in God-given nature. But opposed to this law is the divine law revealed through both the prophets and Jesus Christ, which rational people discover. His command to "Sell all and give to the poor" is found in divine law only. The task of bringing Christ and culture, God's work and human beings' law and grace, into one system of thought involves shifting the infinite to the finite.

The gulf is established because people with the Christ above culture position believe what this culture deems impossible. They believe that Jesus was begotten of God and born of a virgin, and that during his ministry he walked on water, healed the blind, and raised people from the dead. They believe Jesus was physically raised from the dead himself to establish for them the promise of eternal life.

Responding to a higher calling, they are willing to accept treatment as cruel as that described in Hebrews 11:35–38 (NIV):

Women received back their dead, raised to life again. Others were tortured and refused to be released, so that they might gain a better resurrection. Some faced jeers and flogging, while still others were chained and put in prison. They were stoned; they were sawed in two; they were put to death by the sword. They went about in sheepskins and goatskins, destitute, persecuted and mistreated—the world was not worthy of them.

Those of the Christ above culture view hold that God's call supersedes the dictates of this life and this culture. For them, another life awaits that is far better than this earthly one. They believe in miracles, in God's intervening to do what seems impossible. Although these believers are present in all denominations, they are found mainly in the fastest-growing churches, the Charismatic and Pentecostal congregations, whose theology and worship revolves around signs and wonders.

An article in *Time* magazine identifies the wide gulf that currently exists between those who believe in miracles (69 percent) and those who do not. The article includes a story of how God causes the impossible to happen for a grieving family.

Betsy and Leonard Jernigan noticed strange signs in their otherwise healthy four-month-old, Elizabeth. The baby's grandfather, Isaac Manly, a Harvard-trained surgeon, noticed the signs too and was worried. Subsequent tests showed that the symptoms were caused by a brain tumor.

For five days the parents prayed for their daughter "with a passion uncommon for both of us."[28] But exploratory surgery revealed the worst. Their child was suffering from an extremely rare malignant meningioma that promised certain death. Elizabeth's prognosis was continued growth of the aggressive tumor and grievous paralysis before death.

Elizabeth's grandmother had been thinking about the Bible's instructions for healing.

Are any among you sick? They should call for the elders of the church and have them pray over them, anointing them with oil in the name of the Lord. The prayer of faith will save the sick, and the Lord will raise them up. (James 5:14–15, NRSV)

The grandparents then asked an Episcopal priest, a friend of the family, if he would lead an anointing. He did, and he left the consecrated oil used in the anointing for use again before the surgery. The family continued to pray.

The night before the scheduled shunt surgery, a doctor found so much thick, infected fluid on Elizabeth's brain that he asked to postpone the operation for a few days. But twelve hours later, when he returned to do another tap, he found hardly any fluid. He went ahead with the surgery, but was able to remove only part of the tumor.

A month after the surgery, when the same surgeon made a last-ditch effort to remove the rest of the tumor, he and his associates could no longer find the lesion. When the brain tissue was examined, the pathologist could find no cancer. The medical community called it a spontaneous remission. The family called it a miracle.

In the article, the father said this of his daughter, now thirteen years old:

> In the years ahead, if you happen to see a young girl walking down the street with her right eye permanently closed, please don't think some tragedy has befallen her. Instead, have cheerful thoughts, knowing that the Holy Spirit dwells in her, and our God is powerful, benevolent, and magnificent.[29]

Christ and Culture in Paradox

Another way of relating to culture is to observe the Christ and culture in paradox stance that Niebuhr identifies as another centralist position. This position views Christ and culture as "both-and." He calls people who hold this view dualists. Like the Christ against culture radicals, those of the Christ and culture in paradox stance pronounce the whole of human culture to be godless and sick unto death. But they differ in knowing they belong to this culture and cannot get out of it. Hence they look to God to sustain them.[30]

The dualist view comes from the Apostle Paul, who defines the ethics of the Christian culture as differing radically from the ethics of unbelievers. Dualists see Christians living within a world culture, but at the same time they see the culture in which Christians live out their faith as a distinct otherworld culture. They make injunctions against the sexual immorality, theft, idleness, drunkenness, and other common vices that take place in the world culture, and within their own culture they regulate marriage and divorce and the relations of husbands and wives and parents and children. They give directions on how to conduct religious meetings and how to provide financial support for needy Christian communities.

Contrary to the radical Christ against culture people, dualists do not see the world culture as completely evil. Dualists are regenerated and enlightened by the Spirit, seeing the natural wisdom of humans as the work of God. What the wisdom of this world's culture offers through education in language, arts, history, and the sciences represent special opportunities for the free Christian person.

The dualist holds that Christ gives people the knowledge and the freedom to do faithfully and lovingly whatever is consistent with the wisdom of the culture. Life in culture represents a sphere in which Christ can be followed; the rules to be followed in this cultural life are independent of Christian or church law.[31]

Dualists, however, are basically cultural conservatives. They do not seek to transform society but rather to live out their Christian life as people who are content with world culture institutions.

A striking example of dualists' efforts to help youth live as Christians in a corrupt and dangerous culture comes from Melanie Spears, an Episcopal priest who is serving All Saints' mission to American Indians in southern Minneapolis. Overwhelmed by the number of funerals she has had to conduct for young people in her parish killed by gang members (in one year twenty of her youth had been shot or stabbed to death), she looked for an answer.

The neighborhood her parish's young people lived in was controlled by gangs. The people were below the poverty level, and there was much drug dealing, prostitution, and violence. Young people joined gangs for protection, identification, and acceptance. For those raised in dysfunctional families, a gang becomes their family. As many girls join gangs as boys, but the girls' role is to serve the males.

Spears, herself an American Indian, met with her American Indian group to devise a way to combat gang membership. With the help of her group, she devised the Bear Clan, a Gospel-oriented youth group with gang features that uses traditional symbols of American Indian cultures.

Like other gangs, her group devised an initiation ritual, rules, membership requirements, a name, and symbols. They chose the name Bear Clan, because for many American Indians, a bear symbolizes courage and strength. The group developed a logo that featured in its design a cross, a bear, and the name Makwah or Mato. This logo, prominently displayed on a cap given to each initiate, is proudly worn by members to identify their membership. Members cannot join another gang or wear other gang colors.

The original group, which began with twelve youth, more than doubled in size during its first two years. The group meets once a week for two hours. After an opening ritual and a review of their rules, they eat a meal together. Then following a presentation by Spears on Bear Clan rules and lifestyles, the youth assemble in small groups under the leadership of a mentor to discuss the presentation and decide how they might live in response to it.

The following are the rules of the Bear Clan:
• Take care of yourself and live a healthy lifestyle.
• Watch out for your neighbor with care and love.
• Serve the community in unselfish acts.
• Know your cultural heritage.
• Learn and practice a spiritual path.

At the end of one year, a certificate is given to each participant who has followed the five Bear Clan rules and has attended the weekly sessions.

Significant traditions of their American Indian cultures are a part of each meeting. These include meeting in a circle, using the smoke of sagebrush during prayer times, singing the song composed for the Dakota and Ojibwa Indians, and giving gifts. At one of their meetings they learned that the father of a member had been shot and killed. During this session each member gave a gift (called a tobacco tie) to the grieving member and offered a personal prayer.

The significance of such rituals is something that Emile Durkheim noted some years ago in *The Elemental Forms of the Religious Life*. He noted that ritual performs four functions: it creates social solidarity, it enhances commitment, it educates so that participants will not forget, and it creates psychological peace and well-being.[32]

Since the Bear Clan came into existence two years ago, Spears has not had to conduct a single funeral for these youth who have learned to love and trust one another. None of the youth have joined other gangs but rather have felt a loyalty and appreciation for the gang they have formed. Their involvement has launched them on a spiritual journey, as they have learned to accept responsibility for their own future.

The Bear Clan now is a joint project of Mazakute Memorial Church, All Saints Episcopal Church, and the Catholic Office of Indian Ministry.

Another illustration of the Christ and culture in paradox approach is the way the La Canada Presbyterian Church, La Canada, California, draws on secular wisdom in its ministry to parents. In 1972 two of its members, faculty in a nearby junior college, faced the likelihood that their courses in parenting would be eliminated by a cut in public funds. After a month of prayer, the congregation decided to make these two courses available to the community by way of their congregation.

The courses in child development run for thirty-four weeks, September to June, and involve weekly classes of two or two and one-half hours in length. Parents register for these courses as a college student would, paying tuition of $265. Parents know the classes are taught in an atmosphere of Christian support and nurture.

By 1997 the number of courses offered by the La Canada congregation had increased from two to nineteen, all taught by professionally trained teachers with degrees in early childhood education. Of the eight hundred parents participating in these classes, close to 80 percent were nonmembers of the congregation. The community's interest in these parenting courses can be seen in the long line of parents waiting to sign up on registration day in May. Some come as early as four in the morning to be sure they can register for their desired course before it fills up.

Christ, the Transformer of Culture

The proponents of Niebuhr's fifth Christian stance toward culture believe that culture is under God's sovereign rule and that they as Christians must carry on cultural work in obedience to their Lord.

This stance's positive and hopeful attitude toward culture distinguishes it from the Christ and culture as paradox stance. Its affirmative stand toward culture emerges from three theological convictions: a positive regard for creation and a sense of responsibility for God's created order; a view of culture as redeemable, as subject to conversion; and a belief that all things are possible in a history that is fundamentally more than a course of human events.[33]

People of this stance believe Christians should be doing what they see the Son doing, namely the works of his Father. Calvin, more than Luther, looked for the permeation of all life by the Gospel. According to Calvin, the Gospel promises the transformation of mankind in all its nature and culture.

The clearest exposition of this way of relating to culture comes from the English theologian F. D. Maurice. For him the conversion of humanity from self-centeredness to Christ-centeredness was the universal and present possibility that included all phases of culture—its social customs, political systems, languages, and economic organizations. In his view there is no phase of human culture over which Christ does not rule, and no human work that is not subject to Christ's transforming power.[34]

Campolo resonates with this fifth way of Niebuhr's and identifies it as most compatible with the notion of Christian praxis (living out the Christian life). He admits, though, that praxis is possible to a limited extent with the other stances. His contention is that culture is redeemable, that Christians can significantly and positively influence social conditions. The transformation of society, in his opinion, is the central task of the Church.[35]

Campolo describes methods of activism consistent with this view, methods such as political activism where youth become involved in letter writing and local politics as well as in social activism, which includes crosscultural experiences and service activities. His son, Bart, for instance, coordinates a program in the inner city of Philadelphia that involves more than one hundred church youth who give their time without pay, sleeping in church basements and storefront buildings, to minister to children on the streets.

Campolo contends that

> not only should young people be prepared culturally for ministry, but also spiritually prepared. It is most difficult to give unless one has first received. Yet, consistent with the concept of praxis, many young people who become involved in inner city work report that they grow spiritually while involved in their ministry.[36]

Campolo's perspective on the biblical concept of the Kingdom of God is that people committed to Christ are called to do more than to improve a good America. Rather, God is calling them to transform the current social order. Accordingly, the consumption of unrenewable mineral resources, the pollution of the environment, and the military spending and support of oppressive political regimes that our economic system thrives on are evils that must be challenged and ended.

Campolo believes that a critical mass of committed Christians is needed to transform the social order. In his book *Growing Up in America,* Campolo concludes that if the current generation of teenagers isn't present to the Church and is swallowed up by culture, it won't be because leaders in the churches demanded too much from them but because they demanded too little.[37]

An illustration of how one committed Christian can touch the lives of millions of Americans is found in an article by Howard Rosenberg of the *Los Angeles Times.* He writes about the impact made by the popular CBS drama *Touched by an Angel.* This production, created by Martha Williamson, a self-defined committed Christian, achieved the improbable by making God fashionable in prime time. According to Rosenberg, *Touched by an Angel,* after its opening run in the fall of 1994, it proved to skeptical network programmers that a series of positive presentations that are unapologetic about God could attract a wide following in prime time. The show's message was simple: No matter how bleak things may seem, we all are loved by God. God has a plan for each of us. God, who will always meet us where we are, is totally capable of leading us to what we should do.

Williamson, who as a little girl asked God to help her find something important to do with her life, received letters from people who told her how the program had changed their lives. One person wrote, "After I saw your show, I called my estranged brother and asked him to come home."[38]

The evidence of what can happen when people in a community join hands to address a common problem is found in Grand Forks, North Dakota. This city was hit by the worst floods in its history, and a fire gutted its downtown business section. The flood inundated 90 percent of the city and damaged three-fourths of its homes. City leaders feared the city would experience devastating population loss, an irretrievable flight of business, and irreparable harm to its educational and religious programs.

But a remarkable transformation took place, brought about through the concerted efforts of twenty thousand volunteers and the joint efforts of the religious community. About forty area churches set aside religious differences to form VICTORY (Valley Interfaith Coalition to Recovery). Mainline Protestant, Evangelical, and Roman Catholic churches and the B'nai Israel Synagogue began working together to provide furniture, clothing, and other assistance to citizens in need. The group also helped the Christian Reformed World Relief Committee rebuild homes the flood damaged.

Even more important than the relief, however, was the transformation of spirit and attitude. Residents are convinced the city has been irrevocably changed. "We are not the same people we were last year," said Mayor Pat Owens. "But we're better, because we've learned what we need to value. We've learned what matters." Robin Silverman, president of the board of directors of the synagogue said, "What we learned from this is how much we mean to each other, and how little different we are from each other."

To solve the problem of too few rooms for teaching Confirmation classes, the Lutheran pastors and lay leaders of the community worked together. Instead of holding separate classes, they combined all classes and mentors, developing a process that brought the whole Lutheran community together. Each Wednesday evening approximately eight hundred students and their mentors would gather at the local college auditorium for a Confirmation event. A variety of local contemporary Christian bands performed at these weekly events, engaging teenagers in faith talk through a language familiar to them—the language of rock music. Through a grant from Thrivent (formerly Lutheran Brotherhood), the group leaders were able to bring the best theologians and pastors to speak and facilitate the Confirmation event. Concordia College allowed the group to use its best media equipment and gave the group use of the college's technicians. Each event was scripted and directed. The confirmands felt valued by the community because even in its worst time, the community of faith cared enough about the faith life of youth to sacrifice for them and give them the best.

The transformation of society also includes spiritual renewal. This can occur in some of the most unlikely places. Robert Benne, a professor of religion at Roanoke College, spent three of his sabbaticals in Cambridge, England, a city dominated by its great secular university and its high-tech industries. Cambridge might be regarded as a poor candidate for spiritual transformation, but Benne reports that the city has at least a dozen flourishing evangelical and charismatic congregations. Each one attracts students from Cambridge University, so that literally thousands of students worship at these churches during the academic year.

The churches feature expository preaching of thirty- to forty-minute sermons, music that appeals to young and old alike, outlets for service, and evangelism for outreach to students and unchurched members of the community. The city of Cambridge has become a stronghold for evangelical renewal and is linked with a growing evangelical movement in Britain.

Yet another example of an effort to transform society is the mission statement of Search Institute, which is explicitly geared to the transformation of society. Search Institute's five-year strategic plan is to become a primary resource for community mobilization efforts at asset building. The goal is to help create healthy communities on a national level and in turn to help create healthy youth. By the spring of 1998, more than 450 communities had adopted this objective.

The president's summit that resulted in the *Alliance for Youth* is also intent on social transformation. General Colin Powell has dedicated himself to bringing about a transformation in the inner cities so that adults take seriously the responsibility of raising healthy children.

Moving into the Twenty-first Century

In 1990 Royal Dutch Shell, a company known for its success in scenario planning, hired Joseph Jaworski to assemble a team and prepare a picture of the future. Jaworski's first step was to gather leading thinkers from around the world—thinkers in such disciplines as politics, science, energy, education, business, economics, technology, religion, and the arts. Members of this team spread out all over the world to do on-the-ground research, first in emerging countries, then in newly industrializing countries, and finally in industrialized countries.

In his book *Synchronicity: The Inner Path of Leadership,* Jaworski says, "We came away from this experience with a profoundly different view of the world than we had going into it. We saw that our work over the next eight months was to tell two compelling stories of the future that formed in our minds."[39] The stories are "Scenario A—The Story of Barricades" and "Scenario B—The New Frontiers Story."

"Scenario A—The Story of Barricades" is a story in which the fissure between the rich and the poor countries of the world widens as the rich find ways to exclude the poor through immigration controls and restrictive tariffs. After the turn of the century, growth among the economically isolated rich countries stagnates.

By the end of the first decade of the twenty-first century, the self-reinforcing problems of overpopulation, resource depletion, disease, and increasing lawlessness cause a tidal flow of migrants beating against the golden curtains of the rich. By the beginning of the third decade, the scale of problems in the world of barricades is overwhelming.

"Scenario B—The New Frontiers Story" is a story of a world in which the center of gravity of the world economy shifts from the rich to the poor. The most striking feature is a dramatic economic growth in poor countries. With this economic shift comes a power shift as poor countries become more involved in decision making. Regionalism, a first step toward globalism, begins to flourish.

By the end of the scenario period, 2020, the world is a very different place. In many developing countries improved education has resulted in lower birth rates, economic growth has led to environmental reform, and greater economic liberalization has supported a drive toward democracy.[40]

Leadership for the Twenty-first Century

When Jaworski's group's scenarios were presented to world leaders in government and business in 1993, Jaworski recognized that people in important places from all parts of the world wished to make

"Scenario B—The New Frontiers Story" a reality. He became convinced that with collective effort and support, such a future can be created. However, this would require a high quality of leadership.

For Jaworski true leadership involves creating a domain in which we continually learn and become more capable of participating in our unfolding future.[41] True leadership involves collectively listening to what is wanting and waiting to emerge in the world and then courageously doing what is necessary to allow it to happen. True leadership for the twenty-first century requires three fundamental shifts of mind:

- a fundamental shift in worldview—shifting from a view of the universe as fixed and determined to a view of the universe as open, dynamic, interconnected, and full of living qualities
- a fundamental shift in understanding relationships—accepting one another as legitimate human beings who see one another in an I-Thou (close, intimate) relationship
- a fundamental shift in the nature of commitment—shifting toward commitment that begins with a willingness to listen to the inner voice that helps guide us as our journey unfolds, but also toward a commitment that places us in a state of surrender, forcing us to see ourselves as an essential part of the unfolding of the universe

Jaworski made this commitment himself by leaving a lucrative law practice to start a leadership forum dedicated to the transformation of communities. He demonstrates that leadership can bring forth predictable miracles if it is more about *being* than *doing*.

Laurent A. Parks Daloz, Sharon Daloz Parks, Cheryl H. Keen, and James P. Keen studied the quality of leadership needed by communities of the twenty-first century. Their approach, funded by the Lilly Endowment, involved selecting and interviewing more than one hundred people who had sustained long-term commitments to work on behalf of the common good. They used the following criteria to select these community leaders:

- commitment to the common good: people with strong convictions, clear focus, inclusive vision, and working on behalf of the good of the whole
- perseverance and resilience: people who have sustained more than twenty years of work on behalf of a more just and humane world

- ethical congruence between life and work: people for whom there is integrity between what they profess and how they live
- engagement with diversity and complexity: people who seek to understand the systemic implications of their work and have a critical perspective of their own culture

These hundred-plus people were interviewed over a period of several years to provide answers, in terms of themselves, to these primary questions:

- What are such people like?
- How do they become that way?
- What keeps them going in spite of inevitable discouragement?
- What can be done to encourage this kind of citizenship to meet the challenges of the twenty-first century?

Their findings, presented in *Common Fire: Lives of Commitment in a Complex World,* are manifold.[42] We refer only to those findings germane to the purpose of this book. The group of researchers found that human growth requires a healthy mixture of the familiar and the unfamiliar, the reliable and the unexpected. "A good home provides the protection of sturdy walls and a sheltering roof, but windows and doors are also essential" is a good metaphor for human growth. Slightly more than half of those interviewed described at least one parent who was publicly active in a manner that conveyed concern and care for the wider community.

Two types of experiences, when present in combination, increase the likelihood of forming citizens needed in the twenty-first century: trustworthy and transformational relationships with threshold people, and hospitable spaces within which those relationships might develop and new forms of agency might be practiced.

Threshold people include loving parents who care for the wider world; welcoming and diverse neighbors, teachers, and other children; peers and adults who nourish loyalty and positive purpose in the adolescent years; mentors who challenge, support, and inspire young adults; spouses, partners, and other family members who share common commitments; children and grandchildren who embody the promise and responsibilities of the future; and professional colleagues and other kindred spirits who provide good company and invigorate vision.

Hospitable and safe spaces include a home where trust and service are nourished, hospitality is practiced, and the wider world is present; a neighborhood where it is safe to explore and discover different people and places; a community both within and beyond the neighborhood where physical, emotional, and intellectual safety is protected; intensive learning environments; institutional environments that sponsor positive forms of belonging and learning; and places that provide for reflection and renewal in adult life.

Citizen leadership is the result of the intertwining effects of many factors. No one item can be singled out as determinative. However, the authors do report that "in the majority of the people we studied, religion played an important role in the formation of commitment, a finding similar to those of other studies."[43] Here the authors refer to religion not in its narrow ideological sense, but rather in the broader sense conveyed by the word *faith*.

With respect to children, youth, and adults, the authors note that the household constitutes the minicommons in which they learn the essential features of committed citizenship. Hence, the authors give the following suggestions:

- Strengthen the family household as the ground of commitment. This involves providing a safe environment, at least one trustworthy adult, opportunities to learn, and time and space to express and heal the hurts of life.
- Recognize that home extends beyond the domicile. Cultivate connections with individuals and institutions that strengthen and enlarge the family circle.
- Welcome the world into the home. The practice of hospitality has a powerful function in the formation of commitment. Reading enriches one's awareness of the world beyond the home. (Most participants in the study were avid readers.)
- Encourage an ethic of family service. Family lore can teach that commitments to the common good are part of family heritage and identity.[44]

Campolo notes in his conclusion of *Growing Up in America* that true Christianity requires youth and adults to embrace a lifestyle that will set them in opposition to the accepted patterns of the American middle-class social system. Youth and family ministry can equip people to stand against the value orientation and goals prescribed by the dominant community:

America is not Christendom. Cultural religion is a subtle imitation of Christianity. The future of civilization, then, may well be determined by the extent to which the Christian church makes youth ministry to the American urban and to the two-thirds nations' poor, a priority of its missionary program.[45]

As is evident, the transformation of culture to the point that it will contribute to the probability that the Ten Characteristics of Committed Youth become a reality is a huge task. Nevertheless it is a task that needs to be undertaken. The efforts and initiatives that we have recorded here are hopeful signs that humans are not alone in taking on the challenge, but that the Spirit of God promised by Jesus is at work transforming people who in turn transform the culture.

The next chapter will complete the vision of a radical model for passing on the faith. In the final chapter we will move from the *vision* of the model to the *action* of the model.

Chapter 9

The Circle of Creation

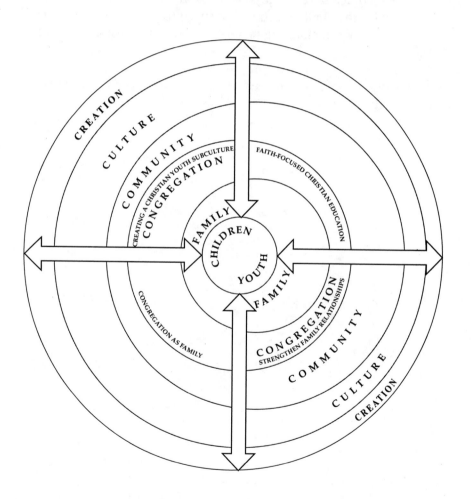

Several years ago while I (Dick Hardel) was traveling in Canberra, Australia, a friend drove me up Black Mountain, which overlooks the city. It was night and the city was beautiful. When I looked up, however, I saw something more stunning: the majesty of the heavens and millions of stars. When my friend pointed out the constellation of the Southern Cross, tears began to flow from my eyes and down my cheeks. They may have even splashed to the ground! Seeing that cross gave me new insight into our magnificent Creator. From my heart to my lips to my ears, I began to recite from Psalm 8:

> When I look at your heavens, the work of your fingers, the moon and the stars that you have established; what are human beings that you are mindful of them, mortals that you care for them? (3–4, NRSV)

The Southern Cross gave me a new vision of God. I saw the glory and splendor of God in the millions of stars, the beauty of the mountain, and the glow of the city below. I experienced God's love for me and for all creation, despite the mess of my sin and the mess that sin has made on Earth. My experience was more than seeing God's glory in the majestic heavens. It was sensing that God's power is seen in mercy, God's deep love for me and all creation. It is the love of God for all people and all creation that is at the heart of the radical model for youth and family ministry.

Theology of the Cross

The radical model for youth and family ministry is rooted in a theology of the cross—a theology of faith and revelation. Faith is necessary in order to see God's hidden revelation. Through faith, human beings are able to recognize God everywhere, including in the Incarnation, in creation, in humility, in the shame of the cross, in suffering, in the empty cross and empty tomb, in Resurrection, and in those who are poor and in need. Only through faith can people see God's love and marvelous saving acts in Christ.

The cross of Jesus Christ is given not simply to look back at and remember what God has done in the past but also to look through and recognize God's action today. The cross of Christ changes how

we see God's action in everyday life and in all the circles of relationships. The cross of Jesus Christ invites us to see that suffering,
despair, and even death give way to hope and new life. The cross
calls people of faith to live in relationship with God and with all
creation, so that others can see the grace of God even in the midst
of struggle and suffering.

We must think theologically so that our focus doesn't shift
from God being the center to humans being the center. Without a
theology of the cross, God's way of working in the world remains
hidden and people blame God if life doesn't go their way. When
people do not see the reality of sin and its effects, they assume God
is wrathful, and God's mercy and love remain hidden.

The hidden message of God, who desires to be close to all creation, is revealed in the cross. A theology of the cross focuses not
on the works of humankind but on the work of God. The cross
reveals the mysterious passage from life, through death, to the new
life that God makes possible. There is a dialectical relationship between law and gospel, sin and grace, suffering and healing, and
death and resurrection. Each pair appears to be two things in opposition and conflict, yet the cross shows us that God works through
the former to bring about the latter.

God sets up a law for all creation to battle the forces of chaos
and in giving life to the world (see Psalm 148:5,6). In the Old Testament, one cannot separate justice (or law) and covenant. To love
God and neighbor is the law of creation in human existence. Sin
and rebellion against God happens when humans try to live outside God's law and thus promote their own wants at the expense
of the neighbor. Human beings end up making God in their image
rather than reflecting the image of God.

If there were only a law of creation, then the proclamation is of
a hidden God. Our Creator is very near and wants to live near, right
next to and in relationship with, creation. But our relationship to
the Creator and God's purpose of blessing and life remains hidden
in the law of creation. If only the law of creation is proclaimed,
then sinful human beings are led to despair in their relationship
with the Creator.

But because the cross of Jesus Christ is at the center of creation,
redemption and creation are connected. Looking at creation through
the cross transforms the fulfilling of the law from demand to gift.

Despair is turned to contrition and repentance. The Incarnation and atonement of Jesus Christ are the heart of this transformation.

Jesus, the Christ, reframes the picture of God, oneself, one's neighbor, Earth, and all creation. Now there is thanksgiving to God at every turn because through the cross, the person sees that "every generous act of giving, with every perfect gift, is from above, coming down from the Father of lights" (James 1:17, NRSV).

Creation Reveals the Hidden God

God existed before creation, is above all creation, and remains wholly other than creation. Out of love God created the universe. God's very nature is relational in nature, as the Scriptures reveal. God is One being in three persons: Creator, Redeemer, Sustainer (Father, Son, Holy Spirit). God is intimately involved with all creation. God is transcendent, while lovingly sustaining each creature, desiring harmony and communion with all creation.

In Genesis, God declares that all creation is "very good" (Genesis 1:31, NRSV). God established a covenant with human beings and with all creation (see Genesis 9:9 and following). Through the cross of Jesus Christ, God reconciles all creation and makes peace (see Colossians 1:20).

In the Old Testament Book of Job, we are reminded that creation expresses the relationship of God with human beings and with all creation:

> But ask the animals, and they will teach you;
> the birds of the air, and they will tell you;
> ask the plants of the earth, and they will teach you;
> and the fish of the sea will declare to you.
> Who among all these does not know that
> the hand of the Lord has done this?
> In his hand is the life of every living thing
> and the breath of every human being.

(12:7–10, NRSV)

The Old Testament and New Testament words for salvation, or to save, mean to make whole or to make safe. The gracious, saving act of God in Jesus Christ was to make broken relationships whole. Throughout creation, we can see sin, brokenness, death, and suffering giving way to grace, wholeness, healing, and resurrection.

Lightning struck a tree in Yellowstone National Park, and a fire destroyed thousands of acres. The nation mourned the destruction, yet surprisingly, a short time later new life sprang forth. The forest was not destroyed, but rather by the power of God, redeemed. Suffering and death were followed by healing and resurrection.

A hurricane with more destructive power than anyone imagined hit the Gulf Coast. Chaos and fear rent public systems of care and protection. Governmental systems failed to protect the land and the people, especially the poor. More than a thousand people died. Many more lost everything they owned. Yet throughout the nation, the people of God opened their hearts to heal the brokenness, and to this very day, continue to work in rebuilding homes and lives. Sin, death, and suffering are giving way to grace, healing, and renewal.

Humanity's Relationship to Creation

In 1972 the *Apollo 17* astronauts took an awe-inspiring photograph of the planet Earth from space. It was a beautiful vision of a blue jewel placed in a specific space in the universe. During some newscasts, when the photo was first shared with the public, parts of the biblical creation story were read. Earth was given a nickname—the blue marble. The view from space still evokes awe, not simply because it is beautiful but because it conveys the sense that Earth and all its inhabitants are one.

Earth is a sacred place in God's universe. It is the holy place of the Incarnation and atonement. My friend and former professor, Dr. Norman Habel, calls Earth a sanctuary, "a planet chosen by God as the locus of life in all its majesty and mystery. . . . [We] are summoned to revere the Earth and to work with Christ to restore its full fruitfulness and flourishing."[1]

God created human beings and the rest of creation to be interdependent. This relationship must be viewed in the context of God's relationship with creation, all of which was created good.

Human beings were created in the image of God and, in the words of Genesis, were given "dominion over . . . every living thing" (1:28, NRSV). That does not mean humans are meant to lord it over creation. Rather, using an image from Genesis, we are to "till" and "keep" the garden of Eden (2:15, NRSV). Humans are to be stewards of God's creation so the mercy and glory of God are seen throughout the universe.

Reconcilation with God, one another, and all creation begins when Christians recognize sin and brokenness. The message that we must also be reconciled to Earth and to all creation doesn't get as much attention. We must remember that we don't exist apart from Earth. When Earth's resources are taken for granted or, worse, hoarded, degraded, or polluted, Earth's creatures, including humans, are affected. Too many of us are blind to the full effect our lifestyles have on Earth and its inhabitants, though we can sense that when nature is out of balance, we are out of balance. When we are not living in balance, we become disoriented and cannot find our home, our sacred place. Earth is our home, and we are part of the household of creation. The call to love God and our neighbor is also a call to care for Earth.

God's loving presence made visible in creation makes all of life sacramental. God is present with us always, and there are signs of this reality all around us. Even seemingly ordinary elements such as water, bread, and wine give us glimpses of the presence of God. David Rhoads, professor of New Testament at the Lutheran School of Theology in Chicago, highlights the sacramentality of nature's elements:

> What difference does it make to our view of the daily food we eat and the daily drinks we drink knowing that bread and wine are sacramental? What difference does it make to our experience of water and soil and air, knowing that water is sacramental? The Eucharist is meant not only to lead us to experience the particularity of its symbolic meaning in the communion meal. It also leads us to think differently about all common elements of life—in such a way that our common experiences of them also become sacramental. That is, all elements of nature may convey for us the grace of God. . . . As Martin Luther wrote, "God writes the Gospel, not in the Bible alone, but also on trees and in the flowers and clouds and stars."[2]

Earth is our home, a place where we live in relationship with God and one another. This explains the centrality of the two great commandments: to love God and to love our neighbor. Our love for one another and for God obligates us to take care of Earth. We must strive for an ecology—a system or pattern of relationships with our environment—that reflects the sacredness of God's creation. Over the last several decades, the blue marble image of Earth has served to remind many people of this challenge.

The cross of Jesus Christ unveils the power of God hidden as mercy and gives us a new picture of God and of Earth. The vision of the new picture gives us a new and fresh way to read the Scriptures. Scripture scholars have also reminded us of the challenge to be faithful stewards of God's creation. Some scholars are at work on the Earth Bible series, which presents an interesting new look at reading the Scriptures based on six ecojustice principles. One of the principles, for example, is the principle of mutual custodianship: "Earth is a balanced and diverse domain where responsible custodians can function as partners with, rather than rulers over, Earth to sustain its balance and a diverse Earth community."[3]

Creation Harmed by Humanity's Sin

The rebellious nature of humanity against the will of God can tend to obscure God's mercy from sight. When human beings try to create God in their own image, the picture of God is distorted. Instead of recognizing the presence of a loving God of all creation, we mistakenly think God is wrathful.

Sin and separation from God cause brokenness in all creation. In Genesis, God explains to Adam the effect of sin on creation:

> Cursed is the ground because of you; in toil you shall eat of it all the days of your life; thorns and thistles it shall bring forth for you; and you shall eat the plants of the field. By the sweat of your face you shall eat bread until you return to the ground, for out of it you were taken; you are dust, and to dust you shall return. (3:17–19, NRSV)

The prophet Hosea proclaims to the nation of Israel that the conduct of the people of Israel should reflect the nature of God. Hosea interprets God's judgment upon sin and unfaithfulness not as arbitrary acts, but as consequences of sin. The break of the covenant relationship with God changes the picture. The mercy of God is hidden, and Israel's sin affects creation (see Hosea 4:1–3; also see Isaiah 24:5–6 and Revelation 11:18).

Today prophets from all over the world are telling us that something is out of balance with humankind's relationship with the rest of creation and thus with God. The movie *An Inconvenient Truth* is not simply a soapbox for a politician. The cartoon movie *Happy Feet* is not simply a nice children's movie. Both paint pictures that should bring more than concern. We should recognize the brokenness in humanity's relationship with God and with creation and respond with contrition, repentance, and reconciliation.

I am writing this chapter on Holy Saturday in 2007. The front page headline of today's Minneapolis newspaper, the *Star Tribune,* reads as follows: "A Vision of Earth in Crisis: Widespread Hunger, Drought, Floods, Death." The article is a toned-down version of a report on global warming issued by the United Nations the day before. The newspaper article reports on the U.N.'s vision of the Earth's future as a result of global warming:

North America: more floods in the western mountains; more fires and disturbances to forests from pests and diseases; more heat waves.

Latin America: gradual decrease of tropical forest and replacement by savanna in eastern Amazonia; more farmlands will become deserts; glaciers will disappear and make drinking water more scarce.

Africa: a scarcity of water for 75 million to 250 million people by 2020; a reduced amount of farmland; shorter growing seasons and smaller yields; a decrease in the number of freshwater fish.

Asia: more floods and avalanches; less water flowing through the rivers in the Himalayas; less water available in central, south, east, and southeast regions.

Australia and New Zealand: gradual decrease in water availability by 2030 in south and east Australia; a reduction in the diversity of plants and animals at the Great Barrier Reef and Queensland Wet Tropics by 2020.

Polar Regions: smaller and thinning glaciers and ice sheets; forced changes in people's ways of life.[4]

Prophetic voices are crying out from all areas of Earth, liberals and conservatives, Democrats and Republicans. Are we forgetting that we are called to be stewards of creation and that we live in a covenant relationship with God, with one another, and with all creation? The air we breathe is continually being polluted and our water quality degraded. Our burning of fossil fuels creates sulfur and nitrogen oxides, which, when combined with water, produce acid deposition; the release of mercury oxides from a methyl mercury, a toxin that will cause nervous system damage and birth defects in the fetus of pregnant women; a loss of tundra vegetation; and the list goes on and on. The circle of creation cries out for people to image God to all creation, to reconcile, to renew, and to restore Earth so people can see the power of God in mercy rather than judgment.

The Relationship Between the Environmental Crisis and Love of Christians

Most of the major environmental problems, such as air pollution, water pollution, loss of habitat and green space due to urban sprawl, and the effects of global warming, hurt Earth and its inhabitants. The research warns that the people who will be hurt the most are the people who are poor, young, and elderly. The Scriptures implore us to be reconciled to God and to join with Christ in reconciling the world to God—to take care of the poor and the least among us.

> All this is from God, who reconciled us to himself through Christ and gave us the ministry of reconciliation; that is, in Christ, God was reconciling the world to himself—not counting its trespasses against it—and entrusting the message of reconciliation to us (see 2 Corinthians 5:18–21, NRSV).

Dr. Edward J. P. Hauser, an environmentalist on the Bishop's Task Force for Caring for Creation, in North Carolina, suggests that there are six R's that guide Christians as they attempt to mend the broken relationships we have with God, Earth, and our neighbors:

1. Reconciliation. Through the reconciling act of God in Christ Jesus, God calls the people of God to participate in the healing within all creation. Unless we are reconciled to our Creator God, we cannot hope to heal the brokenness of creation.

2. Repentance. The degradation of creation tells us we are in desperate need of repentance. This repentance is about the way humans interact with the whole of creation.

3. Restoration. Christians must become active in restoring the whole creation, beginning with small steps, for example: reducing the burning of fossil fuel, insisting on new automobile technology that improves mileage per gallon consumption and uses other sources of energy, studying ecojustice issues, and supporting programs that provide for food, shelter, and jobs for those in need.

4. Reducing. The United States contains less than 5 percent of the world's population and yet consumes more than 25 percent of all the resources in the world. We must reduce our consumption and change our lifestyles to allow for renewable resources.

5. Reusing. One example is treating wastewater so the water can be reused. Christians can actively encourage our government representatives to support bills that provide clean air and water.

6. Recycling. Recycling is now a part of our lifestyles. Most communities have special recycling places for toxic chemicals in thermometers, computers, batteries, televisions, paints, and so on.[5]

Most of the mainline Christian Churches have issued official statements calling for action. For example:

- In 2002, in the "Declaration on the Environment," signed by Pope John Paul II and Patriarch Bartholomew, a call was issued to First World people to turn away from unjust and destructive consumer culture. Pope John Paul II's General Audience Address on January 17, 2001, was a call to sustain an ecological conversion. Both the declaration and the address can be found on the Web site of the Catholic Conservation Center.
- The significance of the integrated concern of creation, family, and God became inseparable in the Episcopal Church. "The Statement on the Environment" can be found on the Web site of the Episcopal Church.

There are many more examples. One can find the unique emphasis the different denominations have focused on in the area of stewardship of creation by checking the denominations' Web sites.

Concern with the stewardship of creation has been expressed by not only mainline denominations in the United States. The evangelical denominations have also focused on social action in response to environmental concerns. This is part of a growing movement to help Christians understand that caring for creation is essential for passing on the faith. A fellowship of Christians called "The Evangelical Environmental Network" publishes *Creation Care* magazine, develops curricula, engages in advocacy, and creates other resources for laypeople and clergy. The network has developed a wonderful statement of faith titled An Evangelical Declaration on the Care of Creation. I encourage readers from mainline Christian denominations to read it.

Connecting with God Through Nature and Passing On Faith

The research of Drs. David Anderson, Paul Hill, and Roland Martinson in their book *Coming of Age* (Augsburg, 2006) shows that in most congregations, a large group of people between 17 and 35 years of age, mostly men, are missing from the faith community. The research indicates that a majority have a love for the outdoors and high adventure. They are missing from the faith communities because they do not find the communities accepting of their passion for climbing mountains, college and professional sports, fishing, hunting, NASCAR, kayaking, white-water rafting, skiing, surfing, sailing, snowboarding, hiking, and so on. These activities often happen over the weekend. Many don't think the communities of faith value their lifestyle choices and even that these communities judge them as being not fit for relationship with the congregation. These people do not find the congregations to be safe places for them to be who they are. Might the circle of creation be another door to evangelism and discipleship to help men and women with a passion for high adventure connect to the Creator God of mercy and majesty? Could congregations find a way to bless these people whose lives are filled with milestones of quests and adventure and encircle them with God's grace?

The circle of creation brings such blessing to a person's spiritual life. It is not just jogging, bicycling, or workouts but also nature that provides personal and humbling spiritual experiences, encounters with God. For some it is a burning bush in the wilderness, a vision of the openness of the plains, or a majestic view from the top of a mountain. Some feel the breath of God as the wind rustles the leaves on the trees as they walk through the woods. Others feel the presence of the Creator as they work in the garden in their backyard.

I remember watching my father-in-law, a farmer in Illinois, kneel down in the field, scoop up soil with both hands, smell it, and look to the heavens. It was his spring planting time. He was of the earth, and being close to the earth, he was close to the Creator. Sometimes his John Deere tractor took him on a tour of a cathedral of God. Some people saw only a cornfield or a soybean field. My father-in-law saw God and experienced a close relationship with God.

When I was in my late twenties, my father and I climbed a mountain while deer hunting in Montana. When we reached the top of the mountain, my father said to me, "Let's not worry about deer hunting." He never said another word. We just listened to God in the wind, in the streams, and in the earth. It was a cathedral.

Engaging in outdoor activities is not leisure time. It is an investment in our health and the well-being of our children. In his book *Last Child in the Woods*, Richard Louv says that if we considered time spent on outdoor activities as an investment in health rather than as leisure time, more adults would take their children on hikes, and both adults and children would have more fun.[6]

When adults, children, and youth spend time in nature, faith and values are passed on. Faith and values are caught more than they are taught. Relationships with adults[7] and contact with nature are necessary for healthy child development. Nature informs our years. It lifts us and carries us. Nature inspires creativity in a child by demanding visualization and the full use of the senses. It raises questions of wonder and of God. "It is a good thing to learn more about nature in order to share this knowledge with children; it's even better if the adult and child learn about nature together. And it's a lot more fun."[8]

Louv stresses, in *Last Child in the Woods*, that we must save our children from Nature-Deficit Disorder. Young people today are aware of global threats to the environment. But the problem is they have had very little physical contact and intimacy with nature. Louv explains how society is teaching young people to avoid direct experience in nature. We are afraid to let our children play outside. It does not seem safe to let a child climb a tree and wonder from the heights. We have gotten to the point that "organized sports on manicured playing fields is the only officially sanctioned form of outdoor recreation."[9]

"The most important protection we can give [children] is our love and our time," says Louv.[10] As we walk with our children through the woods, along the ocean or lakeshore, or along a creek, we need to teach our children how to pay attention to nature. As we canoe in the boundary waters, adults should help children look for signs in nature of changes in the weather and of how to respond to the signs so every moment is enjoyed and a child is not filled with fear.

The effects of Nature-Deficit Disorder can be seen in individuals, families, congregations, and communities. The human cost of adults and children not spending time together in nature can be seen in a diminished use of the senses, apathy toward care of creation, feelings of isolation and containment, a lack of response for those treated unjustly and for the poor, and obesity in our children.

The positive effects of adults and youth spending time together in nature can also be seen. Nature introduces children and adults to the idea that they are not alone in this world. There are realities and relationships that exist alongside their own. Nature gives new angles to see life, to see oneself, to see Earth, and to see God. It raises questions about the relationship and responsibility to each. After spending time together in nature, creative thinkers have renewed energy and an impulse to create. Some are filled with details of what they have experienced and others are filled with stories of what was seen or remained unseen. Slowly these experiences bring a living sense of kinship with the Earth in the lives of children. Some children and adults even develop a special place to continue to renew and reflect on life. They go back to that place often.

I know many people are totally against raising animals, showing animals, or going hunting and fishing. Being in nature can be so messy. The image of killing a fish or an animal or selling one's 4-H bull or lamb, which may become someone else's steak or lamb chop meal, is distasteful. Some avoid organizations like Boy Scouts, Girl Scouts, and 4-H because they focus on the outdoors, survival, raising livestock and crops, and being out in nature. To protect their children, they keep them indoors. The children learn to play things that can be plugged into electric sockets or are run by batteries. No one teaches the children life skills. The fact is that life is messy. Being a family is messy. It is only dangerous when no one has taught children how to pay careful attention to nature and to respect the creatures of Earth.

Parents alone cannot heal the broken bond of children to nature. They need the assistance of extended family—godparents, uncles, aunts, neighbors, friends, and other caring adults to walk alongside the children. Louv shares some helpful hints:

- "Spend more time with your children; educate them about the human dangers, but in the context of building self-confidence, sensory awareness, and knowledge of the many people they can trust."
- "Know your neighbors" and "encourage your children to know trustworthy adults in their neighborhoods."
- "If your child is going beyond your visual contact, encourage him or her to play with a group of peers rather than alone."
- "Employ technology. Tracking bracelets may be overdoing it, but a cell phone can be a life preserver."
- "To increase your child's safety, encourage more time outdoors, in nature. Natural play strengthens children's self-confidence and arouses their senses."[11]

Connecting with God in Creation

Love of God and neighbor demands care for creation. Paul Gorman, founder and director of the National Religious Partnership for the Environment, emphasizes that when we separate children from creation, we separate them from God our Creator. Gorman sees this separation as sinful.[12]

The ministry of Bible camps has been tremendous, providing experiences with God that move young people into full-time ministry as pastors, religious educators, and directors of youth and family ministry. Even though some parents do not understand the focus of outdoor ministry, the Holy Spirit is at work. Children and youth are not in the midst of nature simply because it is pretty. Through the plants, animals, millions of stars in the sky, rain, lightning, wind, sunshine, canoeing, fishing, horseback riding, and hiking, they are introduced to transcendence, a sense there is something bigger than the person. God is at work in all of creation, as well as in the hearts of the youth. Bible camps provide trained and caring counselors to walk alongside the children as they wonder about God. In their conversations, devotions, service, and rituals and traditions of Bible camps, God is at work shaping faith through all the circles of relationships. Parents soon learn that it is not about the curriculum. It is about awakening to creation and seeing the Creator.

In *Last Child in the Woods,* Louv tells what he learned about the connection of God and creation from a time when one of his sons and he went fishing off the coast of California with Robert F. Kennedy Jr., the son of Robert F. and Ethel Kennedy and the nephew of former President John F. Kennedy.

Robert shared how his experience with nature when he was a child has shaped his fathering. Every afternoon he played in the woods when he was growing up. Fishing, sailing, hiking, and observing in the woods filled his life with wonder and adventure. He felt a connection with creation and with the Creator God. During this time with Louv, Robert expressed, "We shouldn't be worshiping nature as God, but nature is the way that God communicates to us most forcefully." Robert shared further how God communicates to us through one another, through organized religion, through great books, and through music and art. But through creation God communicates the details of mercy, grace, and joy. When people do not care for the environment and contribute to its brokenness, Kennedy says, "it's the moral equivalent of tearing the last pages out of the last Bible on Earth." God connects us with one another through creation, not the Internet. Connected to God, we must care for one another and for Earth.[13]

Environmental Wellness for Spiritual Leadership (Clergy)

Jeff Hawkins, a pastor and an associate of The Youth & Family Institute, has developed a new ministry for clergy wellness by using his family's ninety-nine acre farm in Wabash County, Indiana. The

Latin root of the word *pastor* is the same as for the word *pasture*. The ministry Hawkins has developed is Hands-On Pastoral Education using Clergy Sustaining Agriculture (HOPE CSA). Through this ministry Hawkins offers a course of experiential learning and academic study to assist pastors to become healthier and more effective leaders. HOPE CSA teaches what Hawkins calls "holy health." Holy health embraces a wide vision of wellness that includes spiritual, emotional, intellectual, physical, relational, environmental, and vocational wellness.

Each group of about a dozen clergy spend one full day on the farm each month. Half their day is spent engaging in nature's processes by way of light farmwork, such as gardening or tending animals. At noon the clergy share a hearty meal of farm-grown food. The other half-day is spent in prayer, reflection, study, and discussion based on what they observed and experienced in nature. This becomes the basis for new thinking and innovation in the parish ministry. This resource for spiritual leadership encourages health for family and congregation.

It is Hawkins's contention that the farther we are removed from creation, the more we risk being removed from critical insights about God, the Church, and ourselves. A small farm is a great place for clergy to learn more about being stewards of the congregational household while gaining skills for working in nature.[14]

Circle of Creation As a Door to Connect to Men on the Fringe of Faith

With the aid of Lyman Coleman and others, the Roman Catholic Church has developed a retreat process called Men Marked with the Cross of Christ. It aims to reach men who are on the fringe, barely or not at all connected to a faith community. The desired outcome of the retreat and follow-up small-group process is to create a safe space for men to be themselves, to go deep into the cross of Jesus Christ and discover the healing power of Christ, who is in the hidden wounds of so many men. The men experience the healing power of the Gospel to become spiritual leaders in the home, the congregation, and the community. More information can be found on their Web site. The following is one of the many responses of men who have encountered God, the Burning Bush, in the wilderness of their lives:

> Before knowing about this ministry or weekend, my prayer (was)
> I want more of God, less of me; I had no idea. I needed to empty
> myself and be filled!! Praise God. I can finally say my prayers are
> answered because this is a new day and more to come. This is
> life changing, transformation, the healing power of God. Encoun-
> ter God touching the void in your life. Awesome, healing God
> touched me and I know I'll be okay!

Coleman is working with The Youth & Family Institute to share
this ministry with Protestant congregations. It is presently called
Fire on the Mountain or One Day to Live.

Greening Our Worship in Home and Congregation

A great concept from Diana Garland, in her research for her book
Family Ministry (InterVarsity Press, 1999), is that if we want people
to practice faith formation and greening in their worship at home,
we must model it in the congregation's worship services. We need
to connect to God as the healer of all brokenness in creation in Jesus Christ and as the power who renews Earth in the Holy Spirit.

Many theologians from a variety of denominations join Dr.
David Rhoads and Dr. Norman Habel in expressing a need to connect with Earth as sanctuary, as a spiritual home, as a sacred space
where God chooses to become one with us through the Incarnation
and the sacraments. Through the cross of Jesus Christ, we need to
listen to God's voice speaking to us in all creation. We will hear
words of law and gospel, sin and grace, confession and forgiveness,
lament and praise, solidarity and resistance, death and new life.
Habel explains his view:

> We need to expand our expression of worship to include celebrat-
> ing with Earth, with Earth community, and with all creation. We
> need to expand our worship to include listening to God's voice
> speaking to us through God's word—words of affirmation and
> caution—and through the voices of those who are being op-
> pressed and abused, who cry out against what human beings do
> to each other and to other members of the Earth community we
> share.[15]

The Church year provides us with a cycle for celebrating God's mercy and love. Beginning with Advent and ending with Christ the King Sunday, the Church year lifts up the major events of God's faithfulness and love. These events are described beautifully and clearly in the Apostles' Creed and the Nicene Creed. The second article of the creeds, which focuses on the Incarnation, atonement, passion, death, Resurrection, proclaiming the victory to the dead, Ascension, and second coming of Christ, are covered well in the seasons of Advent, Christmas, Epiphany, Lent, and Easter. The emphases of the third article of the creeds on the outpouring of the Holy Spirit and the growth of the Church are covered well in the celebration of Pentecost and the season of Pentecost.

What seems to be missing in the Church year is the emphasis on the first article of the creeds—on creation. There are some special days, such as rogation days to celebrate spring planting and fall harvest; Saint Francis of Assisi's feast day for the blessing of animals; and national festival days like Thanksgiving, Earth Day, and Day of Care of Creation, that are good places to start paying more attention to creation, but few congregations are picking up on them. One would think that because of the mainline Christian denominations' sacramental theology of the means of grace in water and word and in bread and wine that there would be a Season of Creation.

The Catholic Church's *General Norms for the Liturgical Year and the Calendar* suggest that local Churches designate rogation and ember days and plan celebrations at which people "offer prayers to the Lord for the needs of all people, especially for the productivity of the earth and for human labor" (n. 45). Theologian Kevin Irwin has expressed disappointment that the Catholic Church in the United States has not, for the most part, followed this suggestion.[16]

Habel suggests that one possible time in the Church year to focus on a five-week Season of Creation would begin on the first Sunday in September and culminate in the festival of Saint Francis of Assisi in early October. He also suggests a name for each week: sanctuary, earth, sky, waters, and healing.[17]

As I sat in worship on Easter Sunday at a congregation that I coach in this radical model of youth and family ministry, I noticed they did not use an organ, band, or choir for the prelude. They had designed the chancel area and the nave to look as if we were sitting in a garden. It was filled with beautiful potted plants and spring flowers. The prelude was the beautiful voices of a variety of birds singing praises to God. The message of God's redemption of the world was proclaimed, and not a word had been spoken yet. I began to think that perhaps a congregation could develop a Green Team or an Environmental Ministry Team to connect all the ministries of the congregation with caring for creation, including worship throughout the year. They might try the following:

- Do an energy audit of the congregation's buildings.
- Make recycling receptacles visible and convenient.
- Provide healthy food and fair-trade coffee from reusable mugs.
- Discuss movies such as *An Inconvenient Truth* (2006, 95 minutes, rated PG) on the effects of global warming or *Affluenza* (1997, 56 minutes, not rated) on our consumer culture.
- Do an environmental audit of the property and suggest changes.
- Encourage the composting of biodegradable waste.
- Bring nature indoors (e.g., rocks, water, light, animals, trees, plants).
- Create banners to remind people that "The Earth is full of God's glory!"
- Encourage artistic expression by sponsoring art shows and fairs.
- Use potted flowering plants instead of cut flowers.
- Use beeswax candles instead of oil-based candles.
- Use trees with root balls for Christmas and plant them after the holiday.
- Bake organic, whole-grain Communion bread.
- Use local wine that does not require shipping.
- Discuss the issues of justice and advocacy and plans for caring for creation.
- Consider worshiping outdoors.
- Consider using energy that is gathered from the sun or wind.

Many more excellent suggestions can be found on the Web sites of the following organizations: Web of Creation, Earth Ministry, Evangelical Environment Network, Eco-Justice Working Group of the National Council of the Churches of Christ, Congregations Caring for Creation.

Conclusion

The circle of creation opens the doors of the congregation to see the sacred space of Earth as God's cathedral, the place where God has chosen to dwell with us. This circle of relationship is an opportunity to love the Lord our God with all our hearts, souls, and strength and to love our neighbors as ourselves. It provides the Christian Church with opportunities to connect to people who have been left outside the faith communities, because it reminds us that caring for all of creation is a spiritual act. It partners home, congregation, and community to care for God's cathedral. Faith formation is about God's grace and love. We do not create God in our image, but we are called to reflect the image of God in everything we do on Earth, to Earth, and with Earth. Isaiah describes a new creation where the wolf will live with the lamb and a little child will lead them. It is a walk in the woods with our children, fishing and hunting together, planting a garden, eating together, and sharing food with those who are hungry. These are the moments of the world being made whole. In the circle of creation are the green pastures and still waters. Share them with your children and your children's children.

Chapter 10

From Vision to Action

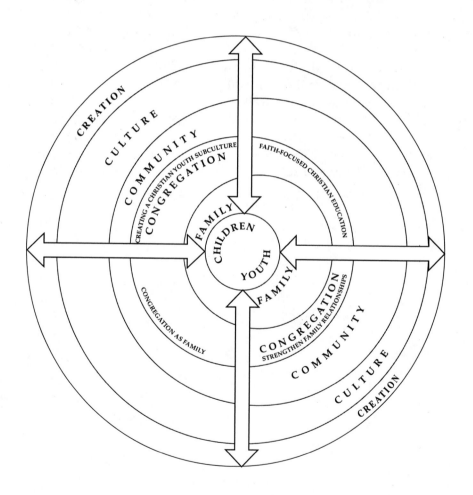

This book has presented a vision of what we, the authors, believe is possible—namely, that young people can incarnate the Ten Characteristics of Committed Youth. In holding this vision, we perhaps differ from those who have a low expectation of the faith possible for youth. The research shows that this vision can best be accomplished when home and congregation partner to nurture faith, live well in Christ, and pass on faith.

Our vision is based on our conviction that God is transforming lives today as God did in the days of the Apostles. Like the Apostles, those of us who minister in the twenty-first century need to enter fully into the life of the Holy Spirit. For us this means giving greater attention to the life-generating factors in families, congregations, and communities that make for spiritual health—factors that we have advocated in the previous chapters:

- closer family relationships
- closer relationships with God
- a faith-focused Christian education
- a congregational sense of family
- Christian youth subcultures
- healthier communities
- the transformation of culture
- stewardship of creation

People in the Old and New Testaments were energized by a vision of what God can do. They lived a faith-directed life based on a compelling vision of the future, a vision rooted in the promises of God. This vision was a sustaining force for them during difficult times, as well as a motivator of action and a prompter of prayers.

Isaiah is a good example of a person with a vision based on and sustained by faith in God. In his vision Isaiah is so caught up with standing before the Holy One that when God asks whom he should send to speak his Word, Isaiah quickly and boldly volunteers: "Here am I; send me!" (Isaiah 6:8, NRSV). From the cauterized and cleansed lips of Isaiah come words of faith, hope, purpose, and meaning for the people of God who are in the world but not of the world.

The Book of Isaiah is filled with expressions of similar faith-based vision:

> The people who walked in darkness have seen a great light; those who lived in a land of deep darkness—on them light has shined. (Isaiah 9:2, NRSV)

For a child has been born for us, a son given to us; authority rests upon his shoulders; and he is named Wonderful Counselor, Mighty God, Everlasting Father, Prince of Peace. (Isaiah 9:6, NRSV)

But he was wounded for our transgressions, crushed for our iniquities; upon him was the punishment that made us whole, and by his bruises we are healed. (Isaiah 53:5, NRSV)

Arise, shine; for your light has come, and the glory of the LORD has risen upon you. (Isaiah 60:1, NRSV)

The Spirit of the Lord GOD is upon me, because the LORD has anointed me; he has sent me to bring good news to the oppressed, to bind up the brokenhearted, to proclaim liberty to the captives, and release to the prisoners. (Isaiah 61:1, NRSV)

Vision motivates when it is based on faith in God and when people of faith realize that the vision is about doing the will of God. Far too often faith communities get stuck in their mission and ministry because there is little of the presence and power of God in their vision. Their energy is directed toward sustaining a budget, maintaining the present level of ministry, or giving reasons for not growing and developing disciples. For a congregation to move from vision to action, the leaders must stand before God and listen to God's word of direction. The vision to action process must be rooted in the presence of God and supported with prayer and meditation.

In his book *Without Vision, the People Perish,* George Barna challenges the church, the people of God:

Unless God's people have a clear understanding of where they're headed, the probability of a successful journey is severely limited, at best. Unless you attend to His call upon your life and ministry, you are likely to experience confusion, dissipation, and lack of impact.[1]

On the cover of *FaithQuakes,* Leonard I. Sweet, a historian, writes this dedication:

For Christians with the shakes, who know that the church is the last hope for saving our families, our cities, our businesses, and the earth.[2]

Sweet is saying that it is time for the faith communities to move from vision to action.

We recognize that to alter family routines, redirect congregational activities, join hands for establishing a healthier community, shape culture, and be faithful stewards of creation, we must embrace a vision of a preferable future—a vision based on faith.

A Faith-Based Vision

In a previous chapter we gave examples of parishes' vision statements and the process for developing them. Here we offer Saint John the Evangelist Church as a congregation that exemplifies a faith-based vision. Saint John, located in Rochester, New York, is a Roman Catholic parish with thirteen hundred members. Its vision is stated as follows:

> To be a eucharistic faith community that ministers to the spiritual, emotional, and physical needs of its members and the needs of the larger community to which we belong, to spread the Gospel of Jesus Christ by word and by action.

Saint John Parish views the family as the domestic church (church of the home) and the congregation as a family system (church as a family).

The Domestic Church

As a domestic church, Saint John encourages families to make faith sharing a part of weekly home life. The parish's religious education program is family centered and mostly intergenerational. It is guided by a curriculum outline that encourages families to consider six different aspects of faith each month:

- Sharing the word: Passages of Scripture are given with a commentary and thought questions for families to use.
- Ritual: Rituals such as celebration of family saints, Advent wreaths, and Lenten place mats are suggested for different times of the year.

- Prayer of the month: Prayers such as the Saint Francis of Assisi peace prayer, the litany of saints, Psalm 42, Psalm 23, and Glory to God are selected for each month.
- Charity and justice: Suggestions are given for activities appropriate to different times of the year, such as food banks, Thanksgiving baskets, Lenten cans, clothing collections, and picnics with neighbors.
- Doctrine: Suggestions are made for reading and discussing an aspect of Christian truth, such as morality, forgiveness, prayer, social justice, church, the sacraments, and Bible epistles.
- Saint of the month: A different saint is highlighted each month so that members become familiar with great Christians of the Christian faith, such as Saint John the Evangelist, Saint Francis of Assisi, Saint Elizabeth, and Mary, the mother of God.

The Parish As Family

The vision of the parish as a family at Saint John is fourfold. First of all, the parish strives to be a welcoming, inclusive faith community, reaching out to embrace all people. The congregation makes an effort to welcome those who have not had a faith background, as well as those who wish to continue their journey of faith within a Catholic community.

Second, the parish seeks to be a prayerful parish, offering worship services that inspire, uplift, and revitalize all who participate. The services include a traditional, a contemporary, an anticipatory, and a quieter Mass. One of the worship services provides a unique time to be with families of all ages.

A third aspect of this congregation's vision is a desire to be a hope-filled and caring parish where members reach out in nurturing, supportive ways to one another and to people in the larger community. Hence, parishioners are involved in a range of ministries from the House of Mercy to the Francis House, from a jail ministry to local soup kitchens. Parishioners have leadership roles in the local judicial system, law offices, hospitals, and schools.

A fourth aspect of Saint John the Evangelist's vision is a desire to be a parish that grows in faith. To accomplish this the congregation seeks out intergenerational circles of education, dialogue, and action for the purpose of learning about, witnessing to, and promoting the Gospel of Jesus Christ. Sacramental celebrations purposely involve people of different generations coming together to share the life that makes them Christian. The family penance services, offered twice a year, provide a setting of prayer to focus on the experience of forgiveness for families and households.

A New Organizational Stance

But how does a congregation with such a commanding vision move from vision to action? We believe that to move from faith vision to faith action calls for a new organizational stance—a shift in focus from seeing congregational life as something we do as humans to something God does and is doing. To make this shift and to facilitate this new stance, we advocate a vision-to-action strategy designed to open congregations to a collaborative approach. A key word in this strategy is not *control* but rather *relationships*.

Leaders in congregational renewal and transformation for ministry in the twenty-first century, like Bill Easum, Tom Bandy, Lyle Shaller, Leonard Sweet, David Anderson, and Mert Strommen, all stress organizational change within the leadership of a congregation from control to permission-giving. Jim Collins, in his book *Good to Great*, points out that in the secular world of business and also in nonprofit organizations, the key to moving from good to great is leadership and vision. The key focus is moving from control to relationships.[3]

This shift in viewpoint is described by Margaret J. Wheatley in *Leadership and the New Science*.[4] The new paradigm is based on discoveries made through quantum physics and the chaos theory—quite unlikely sources. Scientists have discovered that the smallest subatomic particles do not have a continuous existence that can be predicted and controlled. Rather, these particles change in composition as invisible fields of force affect them. These minute changes occur constantly. Though some phenomena appear to be chaotic, they remain within well-defined boundaries.

These discoveries have encouraged a movement away from a preoccupation with things (particles) to a focus on relationships. Why? Particles are in essence no more than a set of relationships that reach outward to other things. The quick appearance and disappearance of particles is the result of continual interactions among different fields of force. Each particle changes to become a different entity in a different place.

Fields of force encourage us to think of a universe that resembles an ocean, filled with interpenetrating influences and invisible structures that connect with one another. Interconnectedness is a characteristic of this quantum world, and space is no longer a lonely void. On the contrary, space is full of fields, invisible, non-material structures that are the basic substance of the universe. As a result of such findings, the world has changed for the scientist from predictable to surprising.

This new view of the universe serves as a useful analogy for what is occurring in real life. With respect to fields of force, we know our atmosphere is filled with electrical signals picked up by radio or television. Our emotional sensitivities can feel good customer service when we walk into a store. The atmosphere of a congregation can be sensed upon entering a church for a morning worship service. This is not imagination—it is reality.

One can go a step further and acknowledge the unique, invisible power of prayer. Two people can agree on something they ask of God and later see situations changed and people transformed. Within the Christian Church, changes brought about by the Holy Spirit are a fact of life. On the other hand there are "spiritual forces of evil in the heavenly places" (Ephesians 6:12, NRSV) that the Apostle Paul speaks about in his Letter to the Ephesians. Clearly, invisible fields of force change people and situations just as they change the nature of particles.

Leaders in business apply this analogy to how they administer their organization. They have come to recognize that ideas constitute a field of force that can change employee response even more than a manager's authority. For that reason business leaders seek to create fields of force by disseminating ideas to employees in all corners of the organization. For these ideas or plans to become real to employees, employees must interact with them.

As people are involved in clarifying and discussing the ideas and plans a company cares about, fields of force are developed that bring energy into form. Because of these ongoing conversations, an organization's vision grows.[5] That is why the process of bringing employees together for two- or three-day conferences is deemed an effective organizational strategy. The concepts that employees embrace shape an organization more than elaborate rules or structures do.

This emphasis on gaining the wide participation of people in discussing ideas related to the mission of an organization is developed through the vision-to-action process described in this chapter. This approach helps members of a congregation think about how their ministries can best strengthen family life and enhance the faith of their people. The process stresses the principles enunciated by Wheatley in her book:

- The role of participation: The discussion of ideas and plans are important to an organization because they create the fields of force that shape the lives of participants.
- The importance of relationships: The more people feel a part of an organization, the more they do and the more they contribute.
- The role of information: Ours is not a universe of things but a universe of information. Therefore, when information is freely generated and shared, it has generative properties.
- The importance of self-reference: Changes must be consistent with the history and identity of an organization. Its identity centers on the values, traditions, aspirations, competencies, and culture that guide an organization.[6]

In this new paradigm, the leaders of a congregation must ask members a series of questions: What is the gift you bring to the Body of Christ? How do we help you unwrap it and strengthen it? Where would you like to use that gift so the whole Body of Christ at this congregation grows? When people bring gifts that flow from the vision, they should be given permission to develop the vision and make it happen. The faith community must unleash them to the power of the Holy Spirit and support them with prayer.

The Action Side of a Vision

This book has presented a radical vision of a ministry of discipleship, evangelism, and congregational renewal. Youth and family ministry is about faith formation and passing on faith. It has

Figure 28

Conceptual Model of the Planning Process

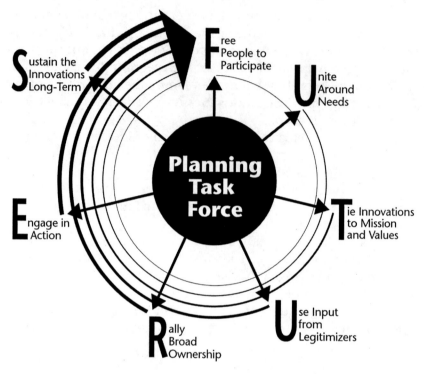

introduced what some congregations would consider a revolutionary concept. Because there is a natural resistance to anything that breaks with the traditional way of doing ministry, it is important to consider how this new paradigm can best be introduced into a congregation. The forms of resistance that may occur are identified in the book *The Innovative Church: Seven Steps to Positive Change.*[7] Also presented in this book is a conceptual model of how best to move from vision to action (see fig. 28).

F: Free People to Participate

The first essential in fostering a congregation's readiness to respond is an atmosphere that frees people to participate in effecting needed change. Such an atmosphere is engendered by a culture that seeks to develop the gifts of individual members and equip individuals for a ministry to others. This represents a break from the stance of seeking to organizationally control all that goes on in a congregation.

Leaders using this approach are evaluated in terms of their ability to create enthusiasm because they believe in the impossible. They are people who are committed to making whatever changes will improve the congregation's ministry. They treat people in an affirming, trusting, and supportive way, and they encourage creativity by fostering the freedom and flexibility of spirit needed for innovative thinking.

U: Unite Around Needs

Any attempt to introduce a significant change or innovation, however, courts failure if the people who are involved have no feeling of need for a change. For a need to become a driving force, it must be felt by all whose involvement is needed.

An inner persuasion to do something is enhanced when people see how the need is related to the Church's mission, to Christ's Great Commission. There are two kinds of needs. One kind is the evident needs of hurting people who are looking for help, families that are breaking up, or youth who show little interest in the Church. These are the kind of needs a congregation can most easily understand and address. The other kind is less evident to members. These needs center on the absence of spiritual interest, a willingness to reach out to others, a drive to serve, or a grace-oriented belief system. Such needs are often best identified through a carefully conducted survey.[8]

T: Tie Innovations to Mission and Values

Every congregation has a hierarchy of values shaped over time by its leaders, opinion makers, and founders. Its dominant values reflect the congregation's sense of mission, its defenses, and its cultural norms.

According to a five-year study of organizational dynamics entitled "Effecting Utilization," which began in 1977 and undergirds the conceptual model, the most powerful predictor of a readiness to respond is the value placed on congregational mission, the "why we exist." Therefore, linking an innovation to the congregation's mission encourages broad acceptance and support.

With a clear sense of mission come expectations that good will come in the future, that lives will be changed, that families will be strengthened, and that people will benefit. An expectation of results is clearly a motivating factor.[9]

U: Use Input from Legitimizers

Legitimizers are the gatekeepers in a congregation, the people whose approval and support are needed if a change is to be made. Legitimizers include not only the pastor and the formally elected leaders of a congregation but also the unofficial opinion makers whose position on a matter is influential.

These people can encourage resistance to a proposed change or help dissipate it. In every congregation there undoubtedly will be skepticism about anything new, a desire to protect the current situation, and a contentment with the status quo. A far more significant factor of resistance, however, is the presence of conflict or tension within the congregation.

The involvement of legitimizers is a first and essential step in coping with resistance and gaining support for a proposed innovation. A good generalization is that success is positively related to the extent one works through persons whose opinions are influential.[10]

R: Rally Broad Ownership

A good rule is to involve those who have a stake in the outcome of the plan, those who are affected by the plan, and those who will be asked to implement the plan. These people need to have a part in the final shaping of the innovation, to have the sense of having contributed in some way to its development. True involvement leads to a sense of ownership, a motivation to support and further the success of the new ministry.

The people who will be affected by the plan need to feel that the plan is necessary. They need to see how it ties into the Church's mission, and they need to participate in shaping the vision of what might be accomplished. Involvement leads to commitment. Commitment means more than simply being enrolled or being willing to be a part of something. Ideally commitment means feeling fully responsible for making the vision happen.[11]

E: Engage in Action

Creativity is thinking up new things. Innovation is doing new things. Great ideas need to be implemented. To ensure that action takes place, that something happens, the task of innovation should be placed in the hands of a task force that can think through how best to introduce the innovation and foster its acceptance over time.

A useful strategy is to test the innovation on a small scale or temporary basis. When people know something new is temporary and will be evaluated, they are far more likely to withhold judgment and cooperate. The important consideration is that careful preparation goes into the trial run so that it has the greatest likelihood for success.

Something more profound than careful planning needs to take place in the lives of task force members, however. They need to feel closer to their Lord as a result of the meetings. This means taking the time to lay all plans before the Lord in prayer, asking for his guidance, blessing, and empowerment; thus, meetings of the task force become a time for both learning and fellowship.[12]

S: Sustain Long-Term Innovations

The adoption of a recommended innovation should not be a finished act; it should be a continuing process that may lead to something much better than the original design. A common fallacy is the assumption that an innovation must succeed the first year. On the contrary, an innovation might need three or more years to become established.

A long-term approach views the launching of an innovation as a continuing process and not a finished act. That is why a task force is so important. It can stay with the innovation, evaluating it and making modifications that will enhance its effectiveness.

Because a sustained effort is involved, a task force becomes in truth a learning team. It learns to function as a team. It learns through the evaluations it makes from time to time. It learns through in-service training and the workshops and books made available for enhancing knowledge and expertise. Most of all the task force learns through seeking God's guidance and coming to understand what it means to enter into God's mission.[13]

What follows now is an example of a vision-to-action process that we, the authors, facilitated at Trinity Lutheran Church in Stillwater, Minnesota—a process that incorporated the principles of Wheatley and the collaborative approach of the innovative church.

A Vision-to-Action Process

Trinity Lutheran Church is a family of Christians whose mission is to "GATHER in worship, GROW in God's word, and GO forward in faith to serve their Lord Jesus Christ." Seventy-two of its members, drawn from all sectors of the congregation, assembled around eleven round tables for a two-evening workshop to begin the vision-to-action process.

Examining and Interpreting Information

In small groups of six or seven, the participating youth and adults first examined and interpreted information on the external and internal environment of their congregation. They became aware of societal trends that currently affect their church:

- mounting antichild attitudes
- the changing nature of the family
- the changing role of women
- increased secularization
- a growing moral vacuum
- an emerging spiritual interest
- an epidemic increase in hurting people
- growing minority populations

The participants identified what pleased or troubled them about their congregation's efforts to counter or take advantage of these trends. They became concerned as they saw what was lacking in their current ministry.

They then directed their attention to an evaluation of their internal environment as defined by four imperatives of a youth and family ministry defined in preceding chapters:

- faith-focused Christian education
- strong life-shaping families
- congregation as family
- Christian youth subcultures

Using information from a survey completed in the congregation a couple of months in advance, the workshop participants, both youth and adults, then evaluated how well their congregation was bringing about the imperatives. Items in these surveys assessed the importance respondents attributed to thirty-two outcomes related to the imperatives listed above. The survey also assessed people's perceptions as to how well each of these outcomes was being achieved. The results of these surveys were available in profile form for evaluation and discussion. The youth and adult participants used two questions to guide their analysis of the data: What do you see as strengths of Trinity Lutheran Church? and What would you like to see strengthened at Trinity?

When table groupings finished answering these questions, they reported to the entire group. As they gave their reports, the reality of Trinity congregation became apparent.

Following these group reports, each participant was asked to help establish the congregation's agenda for the next three to five years. They were to determine which three of the thirty-two possible outcomes should be given highest priority. The following outcomes received the highest number of votes:

- a personal relationship with Christ
- an interest in the Scriptures
- inspirational worship services
- a warm, welcoming atmosphere
- focused prayer

The deliberations had moved beyond viewing needs as problems to solve to seeing them as opportunities for growth and development. The workshop shifted from a focus on problems to a focus on possibilities. (The importance of this shift is demonstrated by the work of Dr. Ronald Lippitt, a former professor at the University of Michigan.)[14]

Figure 29

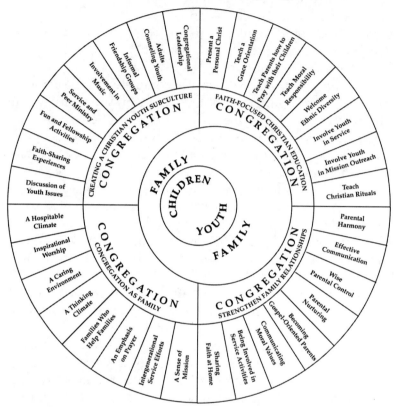

Priorities for Your Congregation

Creating a Shared Vision

After determining which outcomes should be given the highest priority (see fig. 29), the participants were asked to envision what they see God doing in their congregation three years from now. They were asked to create a picture of something that did not presently exist. The following are examples of some of the scenarios that participants envisioned:

- "I see Trinity Lutheran Church (TLC) having added additional facilities, offering three simultaneous worship services and parallel Sunday school shifts, each with different styles but all with a family emphasis. Family has become very inclusive. The 'adopt a

Sunday grandparent' program has really taken off. Prayer groups are now called families."

- "I see a single mom, struggling to keep afloat financially, emotionally, and spiritually being mentored, prayed for, and encouraged by another family in the church. This family is there for her when she has to work and when the kids need a ride somewhere and when she feels like she has come to the end of her rope and just needs someone to talk to. When she and the kids don't make it to church on Sunday, they are missed. She and the kids have a 'family' with whom they celebrate holidays."

- "I see TLC holding healing services following the Saturday evening services. Members recognize this as a time they can ask for mental, physical, or spiritual help, and supportive people in the congregation stay to give comfort and prayers. Members of prayer groups or ministry staff follow up and encourage people to share their faith stories."

- "I see TLC regarded as an outstanding congregation in organizing and fighting for social justice in the greater community. Our congregation will achieve this by heeding Christ's admonition to feed the hungry, clothe the naked, and visit the imprisoned. We will realize that as we have done these things for our neighbor we have done these things for Christ. I see TLC working cooperatively with other churches and secular organizations here in the Saint Croix Valley and through the expanded work with the Saint Paul Synod and similar organizations. Finally, we should be lifting our voices and prayers for the oppressed around the world as well as in our own country, to fight discrimination and truly treat all God's children as our brothers and sisters."

- "I see the annual Festival of the Family, a weekend where 150 groups celebrate the diversity of the family and reaffirm the weekly meetings they attend for devotion, support, and prayer on issues that concern them, taking place at TLC. During the year, some of these groups focus on maintaining their marriages, others are groups that support divorced parents and help them communicate civilly with their ex-spouse so they can raise healthier children. There are groups who focus on parenting issues for all ages, ranging from the day the child is born to the day the child loses his or her job and returns home at age thirty. Singles meet together and have fellowship with one another. Kids and parents

meet together for Bible studies that open them to topics important in both their lives. All the groups come together once a year
during the Festival of the Family to worship the God who, like a
shepherd, cares for them all as part of his flock."

At the end of this evening, we, as facilitators of the workshop,
had an engrossing task. We read each of the one hundred or more
scenarios and classified them by subject. We found these dreams
of the future focusing on the following topics (areas of congregational life that usually emerge when members dream about what
God could be doing at their congregation):

- new facilities
- variety of worship experiences
- mission-minded community of faith
- training-based ministry
- unwrapping spiritual gifts
- small-group involvement
- development of strong families
- prayer power at Trinity
- intergenerational learning
- creative educational approaches

Using the scenarios classified under each topic, we developed a
composite image for each of the topics given above. We duplicated
these so they could be handed to participants at the beginning of
the next evening's workshop. We also copied these ten composite
images on large sheets of newsprint and posted them on the walls
of the meeting room for participants to see when they entered the
room. The images were a description of ministries or activities people in the congregation might want to see happening three years
hence.

To establish priorities, participants were asked to review the
ten composite images and vote on the ones they felt were most
important. The votes, once counted, provided a strong indication
of which composite images commanded the greatest urgency. The
following composite images won the highest number of votes, becoming priority vision statements:

1. Prayer power at Trinity (214 votes). We see prayer becoming a high priority at every activity and meeting at Trinity Lutheran
Church. It has become a power that undergirds all of Trinity's ministries. It is being emphasized through the ever-increasing numbers

of prayer groups, the solicitation of prayer requests, prayer vigils, the location of a prayer chapel, a list of ongoing prayer requests, classes teaching families and individuals how to pray, and regular healing and prayer services. There is a growing awareness of God's ability to act and perform in our lives.

2. Developing strong families (155 votes). We see the results of Trinity Lutheran Church having embraced a lifelong learning approach to families that ranges from infants to grandparents. A learning sequence, introduced annually through a Festival of the Family, offers opportunities for classes, workshops, and home-learning events that deal with issues faced by children, adolescents, parents, singles, grandparents, and so on. There are learning opportunities that address issues such as faith sharing in the home, communication with one another, wise parental control, and parental accord. Classes are offered on premarriage, marriage, and nontraditional family issues. The focus is on developing strong, life-shaping Christian families.

3. Becoming a mission-minded community of faith (120 votes). It is the year 2001 and we see Trinity Lutheran Church filled with people of a variety of ethnic backgrounds. Every family has developed a mission statement and has attached it to its refrigerator. We see youth and adults of Trinity working hand in hand with local agencies and other congregations to focus on justice, peace, and family well-being issues in the Saint Croix community. We see children, youth, and adults of Trinity providing leadership for local mission projects, inner-city projects, and world mission projects. We hear the church staff and lay mission teams discussing the possibilities of starting worship and ministry missions in the area. We see an intentional outreach ministry to people of other ethnic backgrounds as Trinity welcomes and celebrates diversity as a gift of God.

(The remaining topics drew votes that ranged from eighty-nine to thirty-two.)

Defining Desired Outcomes

After determining priorities for the composite images, participants were organized into teams. Each team chose a composite image as its focus. Their assignment was to agree on a definition of the desired outcome that the activities in the composite image were to bring about. Their definition of the desired outcome was to become their shared vision.

Listening to teams trying to agree on a simple statement of outcome was a great learning experience for us. We began to realize that most people in a congregation do not think in terms of outcomes they hope to see as a result of a church's ministry. Rather, they tend to think in terms of programs—that is, how something might be done. To get the participants to describe an outcome, we asked them to complete every action statement with the words, "so that . . ." This moved them to describe a specific outcome of a specific action.

Even though the writing of the desired outcomes is one of the most difficult steps in the vision-to-action process, the groups arrived at clear statements of desired outcomes—statements that could provide a focus for their planning.

Committing to Action

The next step in the planning process was dedicated to planning for action. Meeting around tables, the participants worked on action plans to achieve their desired outcomes. This activity involved three steps:

1. Deciding what innovations were needed to move their congregation toward the desired outcome
2. Deciding what initial steps were needed to gain the support and approval of legitimizers, such as the pastor, officers, committee chairpersons, and opinion makers
3. Deciding who should do what when

The table groups devised the following plan to move the three priority vision statements into action:

Priority 1: Prayer Power at Trinity

Desired Outcome: Through Trinity's corporate and individual prayer, people come to know God as Lord and Savior and to recognize his power and grace.

- *Innovation 1.* Establish a prayer steering committee that commits itself to praying for guidance and learning how to establish a prayer ministry. This committee will plan, promote, and implement prayer as an accepted, expected behavior in our church culture.

- *Innovation 2.* Establish a prayer resource library, possibly as part of an enhanced prayer chapel. Make available to Trinity's individual groups resources dealing with prayer.
- *Innovation 3.* Establish a group of prayer mentors who would be available to Trinity's groups.

Prayer teams have been established and frequent prayer services are being conducted. Representatives of this task force have met with each of the other task forces to establish the habit that whatever they do is rooted in prayer.

Priority 2: Developing Strong Families

Desired Outcome: Trinity equips families of all types with tools for lifelong learning in order to develop strong, life-shaping, Christ-centered families that pass on the faith from generation to generation.

- *Innovation 1.* Establish a "Home As First Church" team to be keepers of the vision.
- *Innovation 2.* Develop a "Total Family Sunday School" ministry or worship service.
- *Innovation 3.* Create learning opportunities for families through a multimedia library, weekly Sunday morning family forums, family retreats, and recreational events in cooperation with the community.

One of the first action steps of this innovation was to restructure the church council from a control orientation to a permission-giving orientation. A leadership team on the church council has a primary task of evaluating and supporting ministries according to the vision of the home as the primary place to teach and nurture the faith.

A second action step was the establishment of the new position of congregational ministries coordinator. This person is responsible for connecting all the program ministries with the various milestones in the life of children, youth, and adults.

A third action step was to institute a midweek, family-oriented worship service. A new instrumental band has been created for this service and a format established that involves children, youth, and adults. It features thematic, nonlectionary-based sermons, dramas, interactive discussion opportunities, and solicitation of prayer requests.

Priority 3: Becoming a Mission-Minded Community of Faith

Desired Outcome: The Trinity family lives God's vision of the Gospel by doing justice and showing mercy through creative mission and outreach to all people in need.

- *Innovation 1.* Establish a mission outreach team.
- *Innovation 2.* Provide regular educational and informational forums to discuss mission and justice issues.
- *Innovation 3.* Encourage Trinity members to participate in a TLC mission activity.

Follow-Up

The final step of the planning process, sustaining long-term innovations, involved creating action teams to develop a plan for each innovation. Every innovation needs an action plan and every action plan needs an action team to create the plan and make certain it is carried out and evaluated. One of the facilitators of the vision-to-action process returned to the congregation to assist the action teams. They used a resource developed by The Youth & Family Institute called *VisionPak* to get through the process of implementation (see fig. 30). *VisionPak* is much like a day planner for carrying out a vision. *VisionPak* allows the action team to record what needs to be done, who is responsible to see that it gets done, and when the action is to be accomplished.[15]

Conclusion

We conclude by reiterating that the family is the most powerful institution in promoting faith in youth. The family atmosphere allows children to enter into a love relationship with God. We say this out of a conviction that congregations have erred in allowing the focus of faith development to shift from the home to the congregation or parish. In doing so congregations have institutionalized faith.

This book calls for a radical model in which families and congregations enter into a conscious partnership of faith development.

Figure 30

ACTION PLAN

Desired Outcome

Innovation

Already in Place (to build on)	Action Steps	Who Is Responsible Individual(s), Group(s)	When Show beginning and end of months, quarters, years X - - - - - X

Work Group Members:

Date:

The congregation assumes the role of helping parents carry out their God-given roles of passing on the faith. Parents, in turn, look to the congregation for assistance in giving doctrinal and intellectual structure to the faith they are seeking to nurture in their children.

In this partnership, the home as domestic church and the congregation as communal church form a community of faith. Together the home and the congregation seek to affect, even transform, their community, culture, and creation through acts of service and love.

The end result of this partnership of faith is a greater likelihood that our young people will graduate from high school reflecting the Ten Characteristics of Committed Youth. The youth will be committed to faith in Jesus Christ and living a life of witness and service to God.

Chapter Notes

Chapter 1

1. Search Institute was founded in 1958 to research the disparities between the "is" and the "ought" found in churches, schools, and communities. At that time, social scientists were largely ignoring religion and faith as research variables. This became evident in a review by fifty scholars of all published studies that included religion as a variable. This review was for the handbook *Research on Religious Development*. Of the tens of thousands of empirical studies they reviewed, less than 2 percent took religion seriously as a significant variable in accounting for a person's attitudes and behavior. Less than 2 percent included items that assessed the effect of religious values, beliefs, or commitments on how people respond to life's challenges (p. xx).

Search Institute has conducted scientific studies probing the effect of religious faith using comprehensive assessments and multivariate analyses. By taking the religious factor seriously, Search Institute has been able to present detailed and well-documented evidence regarding the effect of a religious faith.

2. See Christian Smith with Melinda Lundquist Denton, *Soul Searching: The Religious and Spiritual Lives of American Teenagers* (New York: Oxford University Press, 2005), pp. 148–154.

3. Ibid., p. 171.

4. See Merton P. Strommen and A. Irene Strommen, *Five Cries of Parents* (San Francisco: HarperCollins, 1993), p. 134.

5. See Peter L. Benson, *Catholic High Schools: Their Impact on Low-Income Students* (Washington, DC: National Catholic Educational Association [NCEA], 1986), p. 99.

6. See Peter L. Benson and Carolyn H. Eklin, *Effective Christian Education: A National Study of Protestant Congregations* (Minneapolis: Search Institute, 1990), p. 46.

7. Steve Farcas and Jean Johnson, *Kids These Days: What Americans Really Think About the Next Generation* (New York: Public Agenda, 1997), pp. 8–9.

8. Robert P. Stamschror, an unpublished research paper titled "Families Are the Foundational Setting in Which Children Receive Initial Faith and in Which Faith is Formed," p. 3.

9. Smith, *Soul Searching*, p. 261.

10. See Department of Education, *Renewing the Vision: A Framework for Catholic Youth Ministry*, (Washington, DC: United States Catholic Conference [USCC], 1997), pp. 1–8.

11. See John Roberto with Mariette Martineau, *Generations of Faith Resource Manual: Lifelong Faith Formation for the Whole Parish Community* (New London, CT: Twenty-Third Publications, 2005), p. 8.

12. See Diana R. Garland, "What Is Family Ministry?" *Christian Century* 113, no. 33 (November 13, 1996): pp. 1100–1101.

13. Marjorie Thompson, *Family: The Forming Center* (Nashville, TN: Upper Room Books, 1989), pp. 24–26.

14. See Wendy M. Wright, *Seasons of a Family's Life: Cultivating the Contemplative Spirit at Home* (San Francisco: Jossey-Bass, 2003) p. 11.

15. Stamschror, an unpublished research paper titled "Families Are the Foundational Setting in Which Children Receive Initial Faith and in Which Faith is Formed," p. 11.

16. For more information, see the DVD *Splashed with Promise* or the *Passing On Faith Leadership Manual,* both of which can be purchased from The Youth & Family Institute. See Resource List.

17. See United States Bishops, "Family Perspective," *Partners in Faith Newsletter* (Helotes, TX: Lady of Guadalupe Church, n.d).

18. See Cynthia Tejeda, "Partners in Faith," *Odyssey* 3, no. 2 (June 1995): p. 2.

19. Ben Freudenburg, "Touching People with Jesus Christ for Healing and Service," *Concordia Bulletin* (March 21 and 22, 1998): p. 1.

20. See Ben Freudenburg with Rick Lawrence, *The Family Friendly Church* (Loveland, CO: Group Publishing, 1998), pp. 30–94.

21. See John Roberto, *Becoming a Church of Lifelong Learners* (New London, CT: Twenty-Third Publications, 2006).

22. For more information on the *FaithLife in the Home Resource and Gift Guide,* contact The Youth & Family Institute. See Resource List. *FaithChest®* is a registered trademark of The Youth & Family Institute. You can download plans for making a *FaithChest* from the Institute's Web site.

23. See Richard P. Olson and Joe H. Leonard, *A New Day for Family Ministry* (Washington, DC: Alban Institute, 1996).

24. See Don Harting, "Starting Smart," *The Lutheran* (1999): p. 11.

25. See Willmar Thorkelson, "Crash-Proof Marriages," *Metro Lutheran* 12, no. 5 (1997): p. 1.

26. See Beth Azar, "Nursing Marriage from Sickness to Health," *Monitor* (June 1997): pp. 10–11.

27. See William Axinn and Arland Thornton, "The Relationship Between Cohabitation and Divorce," *Demography* 29 (1992): p. 358.

28. See Roland Martinson, "Work and Family," *Word and World* 17 (fall 1997).

29 Walter Brueggemann, "The Covenanted Family: A Zone for Humanness," *Journal of Current Social Issues* 14, no. 5 (1977): p. 18.

30. Martin Luther, "The Estate of Marriage," *Luther's Works* 45 (1958), p. 46.

31. See David W. Anderson, Paul Hill, and Roland D. Martinson, *Coming of Age: Exploring the Identity and Spirituality of Young Men* (Minneapolis: Augsburg Fortress, 2006), pp. 31–42.

32. See Wade F. Horn, "Why There Is No Substitute for Parents," *Imprimus* 26, no. 6 (1–4 June 1997): p. 1.

33. Laurie Hertzel, "Burden and Joy," *Minnesota Monthly* (January 1995): pp. 50, 132.

34. See "Family," *Minneapolis Star Tribune,* November 6, 1988.

35. See George Cadwalader, *Castaways: The Penikese Island Experiment,* (Chelsea, VT: Chelsea Green Publishing, 1988).

36. Knut Andresen, "Youth in the Church of Norway" (paper presented at the Lutheran World Federation Conference, Minneapolis, January 24, 1993), pp. 3–4.

37. See Strommen and Strommen, *Five Cries of Parents,* pp. 2–3. Information in this book is based on a national survey involving 8,156 young adolescents and 10,467 parents randomly selected from thirteen national Church bodies or organizations. These included Protestant church bodies, schools of the National Catholic Educational Association, 4-H Extension, and the National Association of Homes for Children.

38. See Alan C. Acock and David H. Demo, *Family Diversity and Well-Being* (Thousand Oaks, CA: Sage Publications, 1994), pp. 179–225.

39. See Les Parrott III and Leslie Parrott, *Relationships: An Open and Honest Guide to Healthy Connections* (New York: McGraw Hill, 1993), p. 58.

Chapter 2

1. See Merton P. Strommen, *Five Cries of Youth* (San Francisco: HarperSanFrancisco, 1993), p. 44. Using a software program called Automatic Interaction Detection, researchers were able to insert thirty-nine possible factors for family disunity into a computer. The computer then allowed all the factors to compete and determined that marital discord is the strongest contributing factor.

The results of this study are based on the responses of 7,050 church youth who described their values, concerns, beliefs, and behaviors by responding to 420 questions. The participants were randomly selected from congregations of the American Baptist, Southern Baptist, Roman Catholic (parochial school), United Methodist, Young Life, Lutheran, United Church of Christ, Evangelical Covenant, and Episcopal youth.

2. See Frank D. Fincham, John H. Grych, and Lori N. Osborne, "Does Marital Conflict Cause Child Maladjustment?" *Journal of Family Psychology* 8, no. 2 (1994): p. 134.

3. See Acock and Demo, *Family Diversity and Well-Being,* p. 189.

4. Ibid., p. 190.

5. Ibid., pp. 196–211.

6. Judith Wallerstein, "The Long-Term Effects of Divorce on Children," *Journal of the Academy of Child Adolescent Psychiatry* 30, no. 3 (1980): p. 354.

7. See Nicholas Zill, Donna Morrison, and Mary Jo Coiro, "Long-Term Effects of Parental Divorce on Parent-Child Relationships: Adjustment and Achievement in Young Adulthood," *Journal of Family Psychology* 7, no. 1 (1993): p. 96.

8. Retreats and marriage enrichment seminars that nurture parental understanding and accord are vital to family ministry. They provide an opportunity to deal with dynamics that subtly influence the way parents relate to one another and their children. When defenses can come down and the Spirit of God is given a chance to surface hidden dynamics, new and stronger relationships can form between husband and wife. A unique resource of a congregation's ministry is the reconciling work of the Holy Spirit. This transforming power can significantly alter the effects of hidden dynamics.

9. See Strommen and Strommen, *Five Cries of Parents,* p. 13.

10. Ibid., p. 17. This study of American Lutheran women was reported by Robert A. Reineke in 1981. It is based on a national survey of the one million women of the American Lutheran Church. A total of thirteen hundred randomly selected women responded to yield a 70 percent participation. A follow-up study of the remaining 30 percent who did not respond in the first study yielded a 50 percent response. The information is based on their responses to a questionnaire of 357 items.

11. See John P. Robinson and Geoffrey Gadbey, *Time for Life: The Surprising Ways Americans Use Their Time* (University Park, PA: Pennsylvania State University Press, 1997), p. 105.

12. See A. Hochschild, *The Second Shift: Working Parents and the Revolution at Home* (New York: Viking, 1989).

13. See Joan Bordow, *The Ultimate Loss* (New York: Beaufort Books, 1982), p. 52.

14. See Merton Strommen and Irene Strommen, *Five Cries of Grief* (Minneapolis: Augsburg Fortress, 1993), p. xii.

15. See Sanford L. Braver et al., "A Longitudinal Study of Noncustodial Parents: Parents Without Children," *Journal of Family Psychology* 7, no. 1 (1993): p. 9.

16. See Zill et al., "Long-Term Effects of Parental Divorce on Parent-Child Relationships," p. 100. Because of the difficulties for single parents to establish the climate needed for close family relationships, a congregation can help create a sense of family. It can provide opportunities for members to become the surrogate parent, uncle, aunt, or close friend of mothers and children in single-parent households. Children's scores on psychological tests reveal the positive effects of such support.

17. See Smith, *Soul Searching,* p. 281.

18. See Acock and Demo, *Family Diversity and Well-Being,* p. 196. Reference has been made in the previous section to the devastating effects of marital conflict. Equal to marital discord in effect are anger and conflict between members of a family. This includes the kinds of verbal disagreements and criticism that lead to physical aggression. In families that experience high levels of conflict, members suffer considerable distress and often become emotionally ill. Communication in such homes comes to a virtual halt. The more children are exposed to and involved in hostile and aggressive interactions, the fewer chances they have to learn adaptive ways of handling this anger and resolving disputes.

19. See Fred Kasischke and Audray Johnson, *Resources for Family Ministry* (La Sierra, CA: La Sierra University Press, 1993).

20. Fred Kasischke and Audray Johnson, "Mything the Point, Dealing with Denial, Getting the Facts," *Adventist Review: Seventh-day Adventist* (August 11 and 18, 1993).

21. See Acock and Demo, *Family Diversity and Well-Being,* pp. 134–136.

22. See H. D. Grotevant and C. R. Cooper, "Patterns of Interaction in Family Relationships and Development of Identity in Adolescence," *Child Development* 56 (1985): pp. 415–428.

23. See Eugene C. Roehlkepartain, *The Teaching Church* (Nashville, TN: Abingdon Press, 1993), p. 177.

24. See Peter L. Benson, *Growing Up Adopted* (Minneapolis: Search Institute, 1994), pp. 52–54. This adoption study involved 715 families randomly selected from the adoption files of four states: Wisconsin, Illinois, Minnesota, and Colorado. A four-year study, supported by the National Institute of Mental Health, this research focused on families that adopted infants between the years 1974 and 1980.

25. See Bridget Murray, "Parent's Role Is Critical to Children's Learning," *APA Monitor* (June 25, 1997): p. 25.

26. See Parrott and Parrott, *Relationships: An Open and Honest Guide to Healthy Connections,* p. 76.

27. Ibid., pp. 76–77.

28. Because communication between husband and wife is essential for parental harmony, efforts have been made to help overcome the gender differences and to help couples improve and deepen their communication. One notable program that originated in the Roman Catholic Church more than thirty-five years ago in Spain is entitled Marriage Encounter. This weekend event has helped more than one million couples build their marriage and faith. In the United States, there is also a strong Protestant version, National Marriage Encounter. It uniquely combines Christian values, sound psychology, and practical methods to improve communication between husband and wife. Its purpose is to help good marriages become better. Interestingly, its brochure makes it clear that Marriage Encounter is not marriage counseling, sensitivity training, or group therapy. Neither is it group sharing or group discussion. Personal sharing takes place only between partners. The remarkable success of Marriage Encounter in doing

just that commends this program to congregations wishing to enhance parental harmony among the people they serve.

29. See Strommen and Strommen, *Five Cries of Parents*, pp. 86–91.

30. Ibid., p. 87.

31. See Strahan, *Parents, Adolescents, and Religion* (New South Wales: Avondale College, 1994), p. 25.

32. See L. J. Walker and J. H. Taylor, "Family Interaction and the Development of Moral Reasoning," *Child Development* 62 (1991): pp. 264–283.

33. See Merton P. Strommen et al., *A Study of Generations* (Minneapolis: Augsburg Publishing, 1972), p. 134.

34. See Strommen and Strommen, *Five Cries of Parents*, p. 90.

35. See Strommen, *Five Cries of Youth*, p. 147.

36. A congregation needs to help young parents see the positive effects of clearly established rules and a flexible stance blended with good judgment. Our research shows that parents who use this kind of authoritative parental control are far more likely to find their children saying no to at-risk behaviors, reflecting healthy self-esteem, responding positively to the Gospel, and becoming involved in service activities. Classes in parental control represent an important ministry to parents, because wise parental control is such a strong contributor to close family relationships.

37. See V. Bailey Gillespie, *Valuegenesis Report* (Minneapolis: Search Institute, 1994), pp. 5, 127. Information in this report was gained through a national, stratified random sample of all students in Seventh-day Adventist parochial schools, grades six through twelve. More than eleven thousand youth participated, 40 percent of them from ethnic minority groups.

38. See Benson, *Growing Up Adopted*, p. 11.

39. See Strommen and Strommen, *Five Cries of Parents*, pp. 95–96.

40. See Strahan, *Parents, Adolescents, and Religion*, p. 36.

41. Ibid., pp. 94, 97.

42. See Roger L. Dudley, *Faith in the Balance* (La Sierra, CA: La Sierra University Press, 1992), p. 294.

43. Strahan, *Parents, Adolescents, and Religion*, p. 94.

44. David Anderson and Paul Hill, *Frogs Without Legs Can't Hear: Nurturing Disciples for Home and Congregation* (Minneapolis: Augsburg Fortress Press, 2003) pp. 171–176.

45. To teach parents how to listen and how to establish good communication with their children, this four-session training program builds on the principles used in peer helping as developed by Dr. Barbara Varenhorst. The program helps parents develop an awareness of the need for quality communication in the family setting, develop the skills they need to make conversation and share their feelings, and integrate this training with scriptural teaching to better communicate this dimension of caring as an expression of faith. The training program is available through The Youth & Family Institute. See Resource List.

46. This comparison is based on the selection of two samples from the sample of 10,467 parents who participated in the *Early Adolescent Study*. The samples were selected on the basis of the criteria indicated in the text.

Once selected, the children of these parents were found and assembled into the comparison groups A and B.

Chapter 3

1. See "Under Attack," *Minneapolis Star Tribune,* February 11, 1998.

2. See Ellen T. Charry, "Raising Christian Children in a Pagan Culture," *Christian Century* 111, no. 5 (February 16, 1994): pp. 166–168.

3. Peggy Johaningsmeir, "Report of Family Focus Groups," (Minneapolis: Minnesota Annual Conference, Family Ministries Initiative, 1996), pp. 5, 10.

4. Smith, *Soul Searching,* p. 57.

5. See Rebecca Clay, "Psychologists' Faith in Religion Begins to Grow," *APA Monitor* 27, no. 8 (August 1996): pp. 1, 48.

6. See Howard Rosenberg, "Divine Inspiration for 'Angel,'" *Minneapolis Star Tribune,* January 2, 1997.

7. Charles S. Anderson, *Readings in Luther for Laymen* (Minneapolis: Augsburg Publishing, 1967), p. 203.

8. Kenda Creasy Dean, *Practicing Passion: Youth and the Quest for a Passionate Church* (Grand Rapids, MI: Eerdmans, 2004), pp. 18–19.

9. Martin Luther, *Luther's Small Catechism* (St. Louis Concordia Publishing House, 1986), p. 15.

10. Anderson, *Readings in Luther for Laymen,* p. 122.

11. Sacred Congregation for the Clergy, *General Catechetical Directory* (Washington, DC: USCC, 1971), p. 29.

12. Congregation for the Clergy, *General Directory for Catechesis* (Washington, DC: USCC, 1997), pp. 74–75.

13. See Sharon Daloz Parks, *The Critical Years* (San Francisco: Harper and Row, 1986), p. 50.

14. Anderson, *Readings in Luther for Laymen,* p. 203.

15. See Strommen, *Five Cries of Youth,* pp. 133–135.

16. Dean, *Practicing Passion,* pp. 108–109.

17. See Strommen et al., *A Study of Generations,* pp. 100–151. Information in this study comes from the responses of more than five thousand randomly selected Lutherans, ages fifteen to sixty-five, in a stratified, random sample of 316 congregations. These Church members responded to 740 items dealing with values, beliefs, attitudes, behaviors, and issues of faith. The study made it possible to address such questions as the following:

What are the factors that most powerfully influence the values, beliefs, attitudes, and behaviors of church people? Are they sociological factors such as residence, income, and education? Are they psychological factors such as feelings of concern, self-esteem, and prejudice? Are they religious factors such as a personal faith, a life of service, and a lifestyle of Christian piety? Which of these most powerfully shapes a person's values, beliefs, attitudes, and behaviors?

Measures developed through various studies of Search Institute made it possible to find answers to these questions using complex computer analyses.

18. See Benson, *Catholic High Schools,* pp. 93, 97–98.

19. See Benson and Eklin, *Effective Christian Education,* p. 15. Information in this study was gained through a national study involving five Protestant denominations: Evangelical Lutheran Church in America, Christian Church (Disciples of Christ), Presbyterian Church (USA), United Church of Christ, and United Methodist Church. Randomly selected participants from within 561 randomly chosen congregations included 3,567 adults, 3,121 adolescents, 3,466 Christian education teachers, 399 coordinators of Christian education, and 519 pastors.

20. Ibid., pp. 15–16.

21. Margaret Krych, *Teaching the Gospel Today* (Minneapolis: Augsburg Publishing, 1987), pp. 143–144.

22. See Strommen et al., *A Study of Generations,* p. 287.

23. Ibid., pp. 103, 133.

24. Dolores Curran, "Family Ministry," in *Family Ministry* (Minneapolis: Winston, 1980), p. 17.

25. C. S. Lewis, *The Abolition of Man* (New York: Macmillan, 1947).

26. See Strommen and Strommen, *Five Cries of Parents,* pp. 113–114.

27. Peter L. Benson, *All Kids Are Our Kids,* second edition (San Francisco: Jossey-Bass, 2006), p. 6.

28. See Merton P. Strommen, "Project Youth: Training Youth to Reach Youth," *Character Potential* 6, no. 4 (February 1974): pp. 177–181. From this project one can conclude that training programs are powerful tools for transmitting values to high school youth, for enhancing self-esteem, and for creating greater openness, especially when college-aged youth have professional guidance.

29. Elizabeth Dole, *Tentmakers Newsletter* (Minneapolis: Tentmakers Youth Ministry, 1995), p. 2.

30. For more information about Via de Cristo, contact Via de Cristo National Lutheran Secretariat. See Resource List.

31. For more information about the *Good News Bearers* program, contact The Youth & Family Institute. See Resource List.

32. Strommen and Strommen, *Five Cries of Parents,* p. 127.

33. See Peter L. Benson, *Beyond Leaf Raking: Learning to Serve/Serving to Learn* (Nashville, TN: Abingdon Press, 1993), p. 27.

34. Ibid., p. 29.

35. Ibid., p. 11.

36. Ibid., p. 22.

37. See Peter L. Benson, *The Catholic High School: A National Portrait* (Washington, DC: National Catholic Educational Association [NCEA], 1985), p. 12.

38. Benson, *Effective Christian Education,* p. 57.

39. Used with permission from the *FaithLife in the Home Resource and*

Gift Guide of The Youth & Family Institute. For more information on the four keys, see David W. Anderson and Paul Hill, *Frogs Without Legs Can't Hear: Nurturing Disciples for Home and Congregation* (Minneapolis: Augsburg Fortress Publishers, 2003) pp. 96–150.

40. See David S. Schuller, ed., *Rethinking Christian Education* (St. Louis: Chalice Press, 1993), pp. 58–63.

41. J. Bradley Wigger, *The Power of God at Home: Nurturing Our Children in Love and Grace* (San Francisco: Jossey-Bass, 2003), p. 36.

42. *FaithTalk, FaithTalk with Children, FaithTalk* coasters, and *Faith-Chest* are registered trademarks of The Youth & Family Institute.

Chapter 4

1. Smith, *Soul Searching,* p. 57.

2. See Department of Education, "Renewing the Vision," p. 2.

3. See Anderson, *Readings in Luther for Laymen,* p. 122.

4. See *Harper's Encyclopedia of Religious Education,* s.v. "Sunday School Movement."

5. Ibid.

6. See Merton Strommen, "The Lutheran Sunday School in the 1980s," *Directors of Christian Education Bulletin* (January 1981). Published by the Board of Parish Education Lutheran Church–Missouri Synod, St. Louis.

7. Information based on reports made of each visit.

8. See Bruce Marshall, "Recovering a Christian College," *Lutheran Forum* 27, no. 2 (May 1993): pp. 66–67.

9. Rich Melheim, "Conformation (Sic!) Is Dead," *Lutheran Partners* (May–June 1993): p. 17.

10. See Benson and Eklin, *Effective Christian Education,* p. 25.

11. See Richard R. Osmer, "The Case for Catechism," *Christian Century* (April 23–30, 1997): pp. 408–409.

12. Ibid., p. 408.

13. Tex Sample, *U.S. Lifestyles and Mainline Churches* (Louisville, KY: Westminster/John Knox Press, 1990), pp. 25–26.

14. See Benson, *Catholic High Schools,* p. 4.

15. Merton P. Strommen, *Research on Religious Development: A Comprehensive Handbook* (New York: Hawthorn Books, 1971), pp. 277–280.

16. See George Barna, *What Americans Believe* (Ventura, CA: Regal Books, 1991), p. 157.

17. Martin E. Marty, "Christian Education in a Pluralistic Society," in *Rethinking Christian Education,* ed. David S. Schuller (St. Louis: Chalice Press, 1993), p. 20.

18. Ibid., p. 20.

19. Information based on conversations with Dr. Phil Bauman, a member of the staff of the Lutheran Seminary in Hong Kong.

20. Marty, "Christian Education in a Pluralistic Society," p. 54.

21. William H. Willimon, "Pastors As Teachers," in *Rethinking Christian Education,* ed. David S. Schuller (St. Louis: Chalice Press, 1993), p. 52.

22. See E. D. Hirsch Jr., *Cultural Literacy* (New York: Vintage Books, 1988), pp. 20–21. Hirsch documents an alarming decline in literate knowledge by using the National Assessment of Educational Progress. His assessment shows that between 1970 and 1980, seventeen-year-olds decreased in their ability to understand written materials, a decrease especially striking in the top group.

More precise quantitative data is found in scores of the verbal Scholastic Aptitude Test (SAT), a sensitive instrument for measuring levels of literacy. Its scores decreased dramatically over a fifteen-year period. Though recent reports show scores rising again, they rise from a very low base. Most significant is that fewer and fewer of the best and brightest students are making high scores on the test.

23. See Hirsch, *Cultural Literacy,* p. 34. Experiments with children have demonstrated the importance of background knowledge for general reading ability. This knowledge enables them to grasp the meaning of any piece of writing addressed to the general reader. The more a person knows, the more a person can learn.

24. Ibid., p. xvii.

25. See Meltzoff Gopnik and Alison Gopnik, *Words, Thoughts, and Theories* (Boston: MIT Press, 1997).

26. See Katherine Kersten, "Trinity School Is a Testament to the Vital Importance of Standards and Ideals," *Minneapolis Star Tribune,* December 11, 1996.

27. See Katherine Kersten, "Core Knowledge Curriculum Delivers Vision and Results," *Minneapolis Star Tribune,* May 6, 1998.

28. Osmer, "The Case for Catechism," p. 410.

29. See Richard R. Osmer, "Three 'Futuribles' for the Mainline Church," in *Rethinking Christian Education,* ed. David S. Schuller (St. Louis: Chalice Press, 1993), p. 134.

30. See Willimon, "Pastors As Teachers," in *Rethinking Christian Education,* p. 50.

31. *FaithLife in the Home Resource and Gift Guide* (Bloomington, MN: The Youth & Family Institute, 2006–2007), p. 7.

32. See Strommen, *Five Cries of Youth,* pp. 95–111.

33. See Strommen and Strommen, *Five Cries of Parents,* pp. 138–139.

34. For more information about the *Self-Portrait* survey, contact Immanuel Lutheran Church. See Resource List.

35. These items form the Justification Scale used in *Five Cries of Youth* and in the *Self-Portrait* assessment instrument. The scale was formed using the items that clustered together with a high degree of cohesiveness.

36. See Strommen, *Five Cries of Youth,* p. 75.

37. For more information about these stories, contact John Hancock

Youth and Family Center. See Resource List.

38. Stuart Tyner is pastor for family ministries at La Sierra University Church in Riverside, CA. See Stuart Tyner, *Searching for the God of Grace* (Oshawa, Ontario, Canada: Pacific Press Publishing, 2006), p. 19.

39. See Krych, *Teaching the Gospel Today*, p. 48.

40. Paul Tillich, *Theology of Culture* (New York: Galaxy Books, 1964), p. 201.

41. In the New Testament, the Greek word for *doubt* is used in two different ways. Most frequently it is translated "to discern, to discriminate, to make distinctions, to examine, to scrutinize." In other words, doubt can be a state of open-mindedness wherein one sees for oneself and becomes personally convinced.

This meaning stands in contrast to doubt that does not seek truth but rather reflects an obstinacy of the mind, an unwillingness to accept, a hatred of the truth.

It is significant that in the *Effective Christian Education* study a higher percentage of people show a mature faith whose congregation is characterized by a thinking environment. In such an environment, people feel free to raise questions, discuss two sides of an issue, and explore various possibilities.

42. Tony Campolo, "Will the Real Jesus Please Stand Up?" *World Vision* (October–November 1998): pp. 5–6.

43. See Philip Yancey, *The Jesus I Never Knew* (Grand Rapids, MI: Zondervan, 1995), p. 142.

44. For more information about *Walk Thru the Bible* (also known as *Walk Thru the Old Testament* and *Walk Thru the New Testament),* contact Lutheran Bible Institute. See Resource List.

45. For more information about the Bible story learning program and the weekday program, contact *Good News Bearers*. See Resource List.

46. For more information about *Catechesis of the Good Shepherd,* contact the Association of the Catechesis of the Good Shepherd in Oak Park, IL.

47. See Robert Coles, *Girl Scouts Survey on the Beliefs and Moral Values of America's Children: Executive Summary* (New York: Girl Scouts of the United States of America, 1989), pp. 4, 7.

48. See Roland Larson and Doris Larson, *Teaching Values* (La Sierra, CA: La Sierra University Press, 1992), pp. viii–ix.

49. See Thomas J. Everson, "Faith Development, Moral Development, and Conscience Formation," in *Pathways: Fostering Spiritual Growth Among At-Risk Youth* (Omaha, NE: Boys Town Press, 1993), p. 18.

50. Information based on personal interview of Richard Ross.

51. See Won K. Yoon, *The Asian-American Adventist Youth: A Valuegenesis Report,* (La Sierra, CA: La Sierra University Press, 1995), p. 39.

52. Donald Ng, "Multicultural Perspectives," in *Pathways: Fostering Spiritual Growth Among At-Risk Youth,* p. 13.

53. Ibid., pp. 14–15.

54. See Yoon, *The Asian-American Adventist Youths,* pp. 19–24.

55. See María-Elena Cardena, "Multicultural Perspectives," in *Pathways: Fostering Spiritual Growth Among At-Risk Youth*, pp. 5–14.

56. Buster Soaries, "Multicultural Perspectives," in *Pathways: Fostering Spiritual Growth Among At-Risk Youth*, p. 21.

57. Ibid., p. 24.

58. Reaves Nawhooks, "A Native American Perspective," in *Pathways: Fostering Spiritual Growth Among At-Risk Youth* (Omaha, NE: Boys Town Press, 1993), pp. 1–4.

59. See Strommen, *Five Cries of Youth*, p. 84.

60. See Benson and Roehlkepartain, *Beyond Leaf Raking*, p. 10.

61. Ibid., p. 22.

62. Ibid., p. 18.

63. Ibid., p. 26.

64. Ibid., pp. 10–11.

65. Ibid., pp. 19–20.

66. See David Ng, "Rethinking Youth Ministry," in *Rethinking Christian Education*, ed. David S. Schuller (St. Louis: Chalice Press, 1993), p. 95.

67. When I (Merton Strommen) served as national youth director for a Lutheran denomination, I was impressed by the sense of mission that motivated a small youth group in Silverton, Oregon. Though lacking a youth director and a pastor who was particularly good with youth, the fifteen or so young people reflected the value orientation of their homes. Their witness activities included visits to hospitals, nursing homes, and churches. When they graduated from high school and moved on to college, several of them brought their strong sense of mission to the campus of Willamette University. Here they helped form a Bible study group that viewed the campus, including faculty, as their mission field.

Their first focus was a popular political science professor who had been challenging them to be open to various political viewpoints. They adopted his stance by challenging him likewise to be open to the claims of the Christian faith. He accepted their challenge by responding to an invitation to attend their Bible studies. Through attendance at these Bible studies, this political science professor, Mark Hatfield, became a Christian. Later, as a distinguished senator from Oregon, Mark Hatfield acknowledged publicly that this group of mission-oriented young people was responsible for his conversion.

68. See Dr. Silvanna Quattrocchi Montanaro, "Understanding the Human Being: The Importance of the First Three Years of Life," in *The Good Shepherd and the Child: A Joyful Journey* (Chicago: Living Liturgy Training Publications, 1996), pp. 17–25.

69. See Thomas J. Everson, "What Do At-Risk Youth Say Helps Them to Grow Spiritually?" in *Pathways: Fostering Spiritual Growth Among At-Risk Youth*, pp. 1–2.

70. See Sofia Cavalletti, *The Religious Potential of the Child* (Chicago: Liturgy Training Publications, 1992).

See Sofia Cavalletti, *Living Liturgy: Elementary Reflections* (Chicago: Liturgy Training Publications, 1998).

71. Tina Lillig, *The Catechesis of the Good Shepherd in a Parish Setting* (Chicago: Liturgy Training Publications, 1998), pp. 3–4.

72. See Sofia Cavalletti et al., *The Good Shepherd and the Child: A Joyful Journey* (Chicago: Liturgy Training Publications, 1996), pp. 17–25.

73. See Kristine Goodrich and Josetta Walsh, *Faith-Full Families: Family Celebrations for the Seasons* (Bloomington, MN: The Youth & Family Institute, 1998).

74. See Robert J. Brancatelli, *Pilgrimage As Rite of Passage: A Guidebook for Youth Ministry* (New York: Paulist Press, 1998).

Chapter 5

1. Each of the research visitors submitted detailed reports of their visit. Of these, forty-nine were available to the senior author. These were read to identify what the reporter singled out as important or characteristic of the congregation visited. The comment made most often had to do with a strong sense of congregational family.

2. See Benson and Eklin, *Effective Christian Education,* p. 45.

3. See Peter Benson et al., *Congregations at Crossroads* (Minneapolis: Search Institute, 1995), p. 55.

4. See Strommen et al., *A Study of Generations,* pp. 256–257.

5. Ibid., p. 257.

6. David Luecke, *The Other Story: Lutherans in Worship* (Tempe, AZ: Fellowship Ministries, 1995), pp. 9, 19.

7. Ibid., p. 116.

8. See David Luecke, "Contemporary Worship in American Churches," *Your Church* (March–April 1994): p. 19.

9. Marva Dawn, *Reaching Out Without Dumbing Down* (Grand Rapids, MI: Eerdmans, 1995), p. 60.

10. Os Guinness, *Dining with the Devil* (Grand Rapids, MI: Baker Book House, 1993), pp. 28–29. Guinness's concern is a legitimate one. I attended the morning service of a congregation that lauds its success in reaching the crowds and boasts a membership of seven thousand. The sermon I heard from a pastor in casual clothes started with a nonsequitur joke, and then proceeded for fifteen minutes as a shallow exposition of parenting in relation to a Gospel text. The pastor used at least eight stories or illustrations, making it obvious that he wanted the sermon to be easy for the audience; he assumed that the audience would not want a heavier fare.

I wondered if the depth and content would be forthcoming in the adult Bible study that followed the service. Here an excellent study was presented by a layman, but less than fifteen people were there from this huge congregation. I looked at the brochure describing its drive to raise funds for a new church and noted that only a small percentage of the seven thousand members are contributors. I wondered if the attempt to make the Gospel so palatable and inviting was developing a congregation of people that does not know what it is to "take up their cross and follow Jesus."

11. See Martin Luther, *Luther's Works* 53 (1958): pp. 19–40.

12. Neil Postman, *Amusing Ourselves to Death* (New York: Penguin, 1985), p. 121.

13. Dawn, *Reaching Out Without Dumbing Down*, p. 145.

14. Ibid., p. 93.

15. Ibid., p. 264.

16. See Luecke, *The Other Story*, p. 24.

17. See Tim Celek and Dieter Zander, *Inside the Soul of a New Generation* (Grand Rapids, MI: Zondervan, 1996), pp. 115–116.

18. Marva Dawn, "Beyond the Worship Wars," *Christian Century* 114, no. 18 (June 4–11, 1997): p. 551.

19. The *Innovation and Change* study identified twenty factors that facilitate or hinder the asking of needed change. One of these factors, identified as internal tension, was found to have a devastating effect on a congregation or youth-serving organization. When tension was high, little could be innovated or introduced.

Added encouragement for fostering a caring climate comes from the *Effective Christian Education* study. It shows that for both youth and adults, an environment where members care about one another, especially those who are hurting, is associated with greater faith maturity. People in such congregations score higher on measures assessing evidences of faith.

20. See Dudley, *Faith in the Balance*, p. 294.

21. See Strommen, *A Study of Generations*, p. 126.

22. For more information about peer ministry training, contact The Youth & Family Institute. See Resource List.

23. For more information about Stephen Ministry, contact Stephen Ministry. See Resource List.

24. M. Pilisuk and C. Froland, "Kinship, Social Networks, Social Support, and Health," *Social Science Medicine* 12 (1978): p. 273.

25. See H. Peters-Golden, "Breast Cancer: Varied Perceptions of Social Support in the Illness Experience," *Social Science Medicine* 16 (1982): pp. 483–491.

26. J. R. Bloom, "Social Support, Accommodations to Stress and Adjustment to Breast Cancer," *Social Science Medicine* 16 (1982): pp. 1329–1338.

27. For more information about the parish nurse training program, contact Concordia College. See Resource List.

28. See Larry Dossey, *Healing Words: The Power of Prayer and the Practice of Medicine* (San Francisco: Harper, 1993), p. 205.

29. Thomas A. Droege, *The Faith Factor in Healing* (Philadelphia: Trinity Press International, 1991), p. 33.

30. See Harold G. Koenig, *Healing Power of Faith* (New York: Simon and Schuster, 1999).

31. See Benson, *Beyond Leaf Raking*, p. 28.

32. Ibid., p. 28.

33. Laurent A. Daloz et al., *Common Fire: Lives of Commitment in a Complex World* (Boston: Beacon Press, 1996), p. 193.

34. Ibid., p. 195.

35. Ibid., p. 206.

36. See Merton P. Strommen, *The Innovative Church: The Seven Steps to Positive Change in Your Congregation* (Minneapolis: Augsburg Fortress, 1997), pp. 101–102.

37. Dr. Richard Hardel attended this training event for human relations development (HRD) professionals, human resources (HR) practitioners, and line managers. It was sponsored by University Associates and held in Orlando, Florida, in January 1990.

38. See George Barna, *Turning Vision into Action* (Ventura, CA: Regal Books, 1996), p. 115.

39. See Darlene Pfister, "An Act of Passion," *Minneapolis Star Tribune,* April 8, 1988.

Chapter 6

1. See Peter L. Benson, *All Kids Are Our Kids* (San Francisco: Jossey-Bass Publishers, 1997), p. 58.

2. See F. G. Cressey, *The Church and Young Men* (Chicago: Fleming H. Revell, 1903), p. 85.

3. Frank Otis Erb, *The Development of the Young People's Movement* (Chicago: University of Chicago Press, 1917), p. 37.

4. See Charles Courtoy, "Historical Analysis of the Three Eras of Mainline Protestant Youth Work" (PhD dissertation, Vanderbilt University, 1976), p. 33.

5. Ibid., p. 33.

6. Ibid., p. 45.

7. Ibid., pp. 46, 50.

8. See Gerald Jenny, *The Youth Movement* (Minneapolis: Augsburg Publishing House, 1928), p. 139.

9. Ibid., p. 144.

10. Cressey, *The Church and Young Men*, p. 2.

11. Ibid., p. 44.

12. See Courtoy, "Historical Analysis of the Threes Eras of Mainline Protestant Youth Work," p. 67.

13. See Clarence Peters, "Development of the Youth Programs of the Lutheran Churches in America" (PhD dissertation, Concordia Seminary, 1951), pp. 33–34.

14. Ibid., p. 73.

15. See Courtoy, "Historical Analysis of the Three Eras of Protestant Youth Work," pp. 81–82.

16. Ibid., p. 34.

17. Ibid., p. 82.

18. Ibid., p. 84.

19. Ibid., pp. 85–87.

20. Ibid., pp. 91–92.

21. See John Roberto, *Early Adolescent Ministry* (New Rochelle, NY: Don Bosco Multimedia, 1991), pp. 86–87.

22. Ibid., pp. 77, 86, 97.

23. See Donald Ratcliff and James A. Davies, *Handbook of Youth Ministry* (Birmingham, AL: R.E.P. Books, 1991), p. 3.

24. See Jolene L. Roehlkepartain, *Youth Ministry: Its Impact on Church Growth* (Loveland, CO: Group Publishing, 1989), pp. 6–7.

25. See section 2 of the initial report of the study "The Study of Exemplary Congregations in Youth Ministry Qualitative Research: Spirit and Culture of Youth Ministry," by Dr. Roland Martinson, Luther Seminary, St. Paul, MN, and Dr. Wes Black, Southwestern Baptist Theological Seminary, Fort Worth, TX. The report can be found on the project Web site.

26. See Lynne Hybel and Bill Hybel, *Rediscovering Church* (Grand Rapids, MI: Zondervan Publishing House, 1995), pp. 30, 51, 130.

27. For more information about faith-sharing programs, contact The Youth & Family Institute. See Resource List.

28. See Steven Carter, *The Culture of Disbelief* (New York: Basic Books, division of HarperCollins, 1993), p. 25.

29. See Paul Vitz, "Religion and Traditional Values in Public School Textbooks" (abstract of an empirical study, part of an NIE grant, project no. 2-0099, 1995), p. iv.

30. See J. David Stone and Larry Keefauver, *Friend to Friend* (Loveland, CO: Group Publishing, 1983), p. 79.

31. See Barbara Varenhorst, *Real Friends* (San Francisco: Harper, 1983), pp. 182–183.

32. See Strommen, *Five Cries of Youth,* pp. 178–181.

33. See Donald C. Posterski and Reginald W. Bibby, *Teen Trends: A Nation in Motion* (Toronto, Canada: Stoddart Publishing, 1992).

34. Ibid., p. 32.

35. See Mark A. Holmen, "Discipline in the 90s," in *How to Be an Effective Leader* (Bloomington, MN: The Youth & Family Institute, 1996), pp. 4–7.

36. See Mark A. Holmen, *How to Be an Effective Youth Leader* (Bloomington, MN: The Youth & Family Institute, 1996), pp. 6–9.

37. See Joseph P. Tierney, Jean Baldwin Grossman, and Nancy L. Resch, *Making a Difference: An Impact Study of Big Brothers/Big Sisters* (Philadelphia: Public/Private Ventures, 1995).

38. See Peter L. Benson et al., *Adults Who Influence Youth: Perspectives From 5th–12th Grade Students* (Minneapolis: Search Institute, 1986), p. 15.

39. Smith, *Soul Searching,* p. 226.

40. See Les Parrott III, *A Counseling Guide: Helping the Struggling Adolescent* (Grand Rapids, MI: Zondervan, 1993), p. 21.

41. See Dr. Roland D. Martinson, *Effective Youth Ministry: A Congregational Approach* (Minneapolis: Augsburg Publishing, 1988), pp. 82–83.

42. See *The Spirit of Youth Ministry National Conference Participant's Manual,* section 3, pages 1–3.

Chapter 7

1. See Dale A. Blyth, *Healthy Communities, Healthy Youth* (Minneapolis: Search Institute, 1993), p. 8.
2. Ibid.
3. See Benson, *All Kids Are Our Kids*, pp. 2–4.
4. Ibid., p. 4.
5. See Steve Farkas and Jean Johnson, *Kids These Days*, p. 8.
6. Ibid., p. 12.
7. See Benson, *All Kids Are Our Kids*, p. 34.
8. Ibid., p. 42.
9. Ibid., p. 49.
10. Ibid., p. 63.
11. See *AGB Reports* (May–June 1987): p. 11.
12. See Victor Battistich et al., "Caring School Communities," *Educational Psychologist* 32 (summer 1997): pp. 137–151.
13. Ibid., p. 148.
14. Farkas and Johnson, *Kids These Days*, p. 9.
15. See Roman Catholic Bishops, *Renewing the Vision: A Framework for Catholic Youth Ministry* (Washington DC: National Conference of Catholic Bishops [NCCB]), pp. 6–7.
16. David J. Bodenhammer, "Initiatives in Religion," *Lilly Endowment* newsletter, (fall 1996): p. 5.
17. Farkas and Johnson, *Kids These Days*, p. 10.
18. See Blyth, *Healthy Communities, Healthy Youth*, pp. 6–7, 23.
19. Lynn Borud, "Lessons from Real Life," *Assets* (autumn 1996): p. 9.
20. Kate Tyler, "What's Your Mission Statement?" *Assets* (summer 1997): p. 6.
21. Ibid., p. 10.
22. See Joy G. Dryfoos, *Adolescents at Risk* (New York: Oxford University Press, 1990), pp. 228, 232.
23. For more information about peer ministry training, contact The Youth & Family Institute. See Resource List.
24. Kimberly Hayes Taylor, "The Power of Mentoring," *Minneapolis Star Tribune* June 6, 1997.
25. See Tierney et al., *Making a Difference: An Impact Study of Big Brothers/Big Sisters* (Philadelphia: Public/Private Ventures, 1995), p. 2.
26. Gary Walker, Meeting of the Funders of the Big Brothers-Big Sisters Study (November 15, 1995).
27. Dwight Hobbes, "Black Adults Must Reach Out, Mentor Failing Students," *St. Paul Pioneer Press* April 15, 1997.
28. Rebecca N. Saito and Dale A. Blyth, *Understanding Mentoring Relationships* (Minneapolis: Search Institute, 1992), p. 9.
29. Ibid., p. 60.
30. For more information about *A Mentoring Guide for Congregational Youth Ministry* and *One on One: Making the Most of Your Mentoring*

Relationship, contact General Conference Mennonite Church. See Resource List.

31. *General Directory for Catechesis,* no. 168.

32. John Roberto with Mariette Martineau, *Generations of Faith Resource Manual* (New London, CT: Twenty-Third Publications, 2005), p. 20.

33. See Steve Cornils, ed., *The Architect* 2, no. 3 (October 1997): p. 1. This monthly newsletter is published for Lutheran pastors and lay leaders and is supported by Lutheran Brotherhood. For more information, contact Steve Cornils. See Resource List.

34. See Dick Hardel and Jennifer Mull, *It's for L.I.F.E!* (Bloomington, MN: The Youth & Family Institute, 1995), p. 19.

35. Robert Coles, "On Raising Moral Children," *Time* (January 20, 1997): pp. 48, 51.

36. See Strommen, *Five Cries of Youth,* p. 123.

37. See Strommen and Strommen, *Five Cries of Parents,* p. 138.

38. See Strommen, *A Study of Generations,* pp. 164, 182, 189, 195, 199, 227.

39. See Eugene C. Roehlkepartain and Peter C. Scales, *Youth Development in Congregations: An Exploration of the Potential and Barriers* (Minneapolis: Search Institute, 1995), p. 53.

40. A characteristic of correlations is that one must assume that each factor is influencing the others. One cannot input causality where influence is credited as occurring in only one direction. This is shown in the fact, for instance, that youth who experience a caring climate reflect higher faith scores.

41. See Search Institute, *America's Promise: The Alliance for Youth* (Minneapolis: Search Institute, April 27, 1997).

42. Ibid.

43. See Cokie Roberts and Steven V. Roberts, "Colin Powell: Striking a Nerve," *USA Weekend* (November 14–18, 1997): p. 4.

44. Ibid.

45. Ibid.

Chapter 8

1. See Robert N. Bellah et al., *Habits of the Heart* (Berkeley, CA: University of California Press, 1985), p. 82.

2. Ibid.

3. See Robert N. Bellah et al., "Individualism and the Crisis of Civic Membership," *Christian Century* 113, no. 16 (May 8, 1996): pp. 510–515.

4. Christopher Lasch, *The Culture of Narcissism: American Life in an Age of Diminishing Expectations* (New York: Werner Books, 1979), p. 33.

5. Smith, *Soul Searching,* p. 171.

6. Steven Carter, *The Culture of Disbelief,* (New York: Basic Books, 1993), p. 3.

7. *Wall Street Journal,* Thursday, December 25, 1997, p. A16.

8. Allan Bloom, *Closing the American Mind,* (New York: Simon and Schuster, 1987), p. 374.

9. George A. Lindbeck, *The Nature of Doctrine: Religion and Theology in a Post-Liberal Age,* (Philadelphia: Westminster Press, 1994), p. 127.

10. See Sample, *U.S. Lifestyles and Mainline Churches,* pp. 14-19.

11. See Benson, *All Kids Are Our Kids,* p. 7.

12. See Ratcliff and Davies, *Handbook on Youth Ministry,* pp. 259–273.

13. See Ratcliff and Davies, *Handbook on Youth Ministry,* pp. 259–260.

14. See Strommen, *Five Cries of Youth,* p. 148.

15. See Rebecca Clay, "Children's TV Remains Steeped in Violence," *Monitor,* (June 1997): p. 36.

16. See Steven Stecklow. "Evangelical Schools Reinvent Themselves by Stressing Academics," *Wall Street Journal* LXXV, no. 148 (May 12, 1994): pp. A1, A8

17. H. Richard Niebuhr, *Christ and Culture* (New York: Harper and Brothers, 1951), p. 83.

18. Ibid., p. 89.

19. Ratcliff and Davies, *Handbook on Youth Ministry,* p. 261.

20. Ibid., p. 261.

21. Campolo, *Growing Up in America,* p. 79.

22. Charles Socarides et al., "Don't Forsake Homosexuals Who Want Help," *Wall Street Journal,* January 9, 1997, p. 1. One of these men, Jeffrey Satinover, gives the scientific evidence for this position in his book *Homosexuality and the Politics of Truth.* He identifies nine psychotherapists who counseled 341 homosexuals, reporting that 52 percent of the homosexuals gained sexual reorientation.

23. Carter, *The Culture of Disbelief,* p. 232.

24. Wade Clark Roof and William McKinney, *American Mainline Religion: Its Changing Shape and Future* (New Brunswick, NJ: Rutgers University Press, 1987), p. 242.

25. See Ellen T. Charry, "Formative Years: The Seminary Experience," *Christian Century* (November 19–26, 1997): p. 1069.

26. See Niebuhr, *Christ and Culture,* pp. 118–119.

27. Ibid., p. 122.

28. In Gibbs, "The Message of Miracles," *Time* (April 10, 1995): pp. 64–73.

29. Ibid.

30. Niebuhr, *Christ and Culture,* p. 156.

31. Ibid., p. 174.

32. Ibid., pp. 193–194.

33. Ibid., p. 227.

34. See Ratcliff and Davies, *Handbook on Youth Ministry,* p. 263.

35. Ibid., p. 270.

36. Campolo, *Growing Up in America,* pp. 99–100.

37. Ibid., pp. 201–210.

38. See Rosenberg, "Divine Inspiration for 'Angel.'"

39. Joseph Jaworski, *Synchronicity: The Inner Path of Leadership* (San Francisco: Berrett-Koehler Publishers, 1996), pp. 156–159, 166–169.

40. Ibid., p. 182.

41. Ibid., pp. 3, 182.

42. See Daloz et al., *Common Fire*, pp. 52–53.

43. Ibid., p. 141.

44. Ibid., pp. 219–220.

45. Campolo, *Growing Up in America*, pp. 207, 209.

Chapter 9

1. Norman Habel, *Seven Songs of Creation* (Cleveland: Pilgrim Press, 2004), p. 12.

2. David Rhoads, "Training Manual for the Green Congregation Program," (October 2006), p. 42, Web site, *www.webofcreation.org/FinishedCompleteGC.pdf*, accessed January 24, 2008.

3. Habel, *Seven Songs of Creation*, pp. 15–16. Dr. Habel notes that Earth is capitalized to emphasize Earth as a living subject, a planet that God has chosen to make a sanctuary.

4. See Kevin Giles, "A Vision of Earth in Crisis: Widespread Hunger, Drought, Floods, Death," in *Minneapolis Star Tribune*, April 7, 2007, pp. A1, A8.

5. Edward J. P. Hauser, "Caring for Creation Sunday—The Message" (2005), pp. 3–6, Web site, *www.nclutheran.org/pdfs/cfc/CFCSERM05.pdf*, accessed January 24, 2008.

6. See Richard Louv, *Last Child in the Woods: Saving Our Children from Nature-Deficit Disorder* (Chapel Hill, NC: Algonquin Books, 2006), pp. 120–121.

7. See Peter L. Benson, *All Kids Are Our Kids*, second edition (San Francisco: Jossey-Bass, 2006), pp. 34–36.

8. Louv, *Last Child in the Woods*, pp. 162.

9. Ibid., p. 31.

10. Ibid., p. 183.

11. Ibid., pp. 183–184.

12. See Ibid., pp. 294–297. More information about The National Religious Partnership for the Environment can be found on the organization's Web site, *www.nrpe.org*. The founding partners include the following: U.S. Conference of Catholic Bishops (USCCB), Coalition on Environment and Jewish Life, National Council of Churches, and the Evangelical Environmental Network.

13. Louv, *Last Child in the Woods*, p. 198.

14. The description of Hands-On Pastoral Education using Clergy Sustaining Agriculture (HOPE CSA) was provided by Jeff Hawkins. For more information contact Hope CSA, Inc., 10373 North 300 East, North Manchester, IN 46962, *www.hopecsa.org*, hope@hopecsa.org, (260) 982-4961.

15. Habel, *Seven Songs of Creation*, p. 12.

16. See Kevin W. Irwin, "Overview of General Norms for the Liturgical Year and the Calendar," in *The Liturgy Documents: A Parish Resource* (Chicago: Liturgy Training Publications, 1991), p. 170.

17. See Habel, *Seven Songs of Creation*, p. 14.

Chapter 10

1. George Barna, *Without Vision, the People Perish* (Glendale, CA: Barna Research Group, 1991), p. 11.

2. Leonard I. Sweet, *FaithQuakes* (Nashville, TN: Abingdon Press, 1994), front cover.

3. See Jim Collins, *Good to Great* (New York: HarperCollins, 2001).

4. See Margaret J. Wheatley, *Leadership and the New Science*, (San Francisco: Berrett-Koehler Publishers, 1994), pp. 32, 48, 50, 51.

5. Ibid., p. 56.

6. Ibid., p. 94.

7. Merton P. Strommen, *The Innovative Church: The Seven Steps to Positive Change in Your Congregation* (Minneapolis: Augsburg Fortress Publishing, 1997), pp. 60, 70–73.

8. Ibid., pp. 78, 89, 90.

9. Ibid., pp. 99, 108.

10. Ibid., pp. 117, 119–122.

11. Ibid., pp. 132, 138, 142.

12. Ibid., pp. 148, 149, 155.

13. Ibid., pp. 158, 159–165.

14. Dr. Ronald Lippitt, personal conversation with Merton P. Strommen. Lippitt tells how the limitations of a problem focus became dramatically evident in one of his studies. His graduate students made audio recordings of twenty-five different groups that were involved in problem solving, planning, and goal setting. The tapes revealed an increase of depression in voices from one fifteen-minute interval to the next. Furthermore, the tapes revealed an increase in the frequency of statements attributing the cause of the problems to sources outside the control of the group. A third finding was an increase in the frequency of words and phrases indicating feelings of impotence, futility, and frustration. The groups' decisions tended to be short-term, symptom-oriented goals aimed at getting away from the pain instead of moving toward positive, future-oriented goals.

These findings led Lippitt and his associates to experiment with "image of potentiality" exercises. Working with school boards, agency staffs, company managements, and families and individuals, he found that a focus on images of potential generated energy and excitement. Aspirations were generated by a focus on images of concrete feasible steps toward desirable goals. He discovered power was inherent in an approach that turns attention toward a desired future.

15. For more information about *VisionPak*, contact The Youth & Family Institute. See Resource List.

Resource List

The Alban Institute, Inc.
Herndon, VA

American Bible Society
New York, NY

American Youth Work Center
(secular, publishes *Youth Today*)
Washington, DC

Assets (a magazine of ideas for
healthy communities and
healthy youth)
Minneapolis, MN

Association for Women in Youth
Ministry (Evangelical Youth
Leadership/AWYM)
Minneapolis, MN

The Association of the Catechesis
of the Good Shepherd
Oak Park, IL

Augsburg College (BA program in
youth and family ministry)
Minneapolis, MN

Augsburg Fortress Publishing (Lutheran ELCA)
Minneapolis, MN

Baylor University Center for Fam-
ily and Community Ministries
(Baptist)
Waco, TX

Bethel University and Seminary
(MA program in youth ministry
in partnership with youth leadership)
St. Paul, MN

Black Methodists for Church
Renewal (training for youth and
adults)
United Community Centers, Inc.
Birmingham, AL

Boys Town Center for Adolescent
and Family Spirituality
Boys Town, NE

The Center for Children and Theology
Washington, DC

The Center for Children at Worship
Hollywood, MD

Center for Ministry
Development (Roman Catholic)
Naugatuck, CT

Center for Parent-Youth
Understanding (secular)
Elizabethtown, PA

The Center for Theology and Godly
Play
Houston, TX

Center for Youth As Resources
(secular)
Washington, DC

Center for Youth Ministries
Wartburg Seminary
Dubuque, IA

Child and Family Institute
Menlo Park, CA

Christian Education Conference
(Episcopal)
The School of Theology at the University of the South
Sewanee, TN

Christian Family Movement Booksource (Roman Catholic)
Ames, IA

Concordia College
Parish Nurse Program
Moorhead, MN

Concordia Publishing House
(Lutheran, LCMS)
St. Louis, MO

Stephen Cornils
Mount Olivet Lutheran Church
Minneapolis, MN

Creating Youth Friendly Worship
(Roman Catholic)
Catholic Education and Formation
Ministries
St. Paul, MN

Department of Child Ministry
Lutheran Church-Missouri Synod
St. Louis, MO

Department of Youth Ministry
Lutheran Church–Missouri Synod
St. Louis, MO

DevoZine (a devotional magazine
for youth—United Methodist)
Upper Room
Nashville, TN

Director of Youth Ministries
Evangelical Lutheran Church in
America (ELCA)
Chicago, IL

Faith and Life Resources (Mennonite)
Newton, KS

Faith Inkubators
Stillwater, MN

Family Based Youth Ministry
Nashville, TN

Family Ministry Action Team
(United Methodist)
Minnesota Annual Conference of
the United Methodist Church
Minneapolis, MN

Family Ministry Journal
Louisville Presbyterian Seminary
Louisville, KY

Family Research Council
(evangelical)
Washington, DC

Family Shield Ministries, Inc.
St. Louis, MO

Family Time Training
Littleton, CO

Family University (nondenominational, publishes *Smart Families*
newsletter)
Murrieta, CA

Fellowship of Christian Athletes
Kansas City, MO

Focus on the Family (evangelical)
Colorado Springs, CO

Forum for Adults in Youth Ministry
(FAYM, Methodist)
Methodist Theological School of
Ohio
Delaware, OH

*Foundations: A Newsletter for Newly
Married Couples* (Roman Catholic)
Portland, ME

General Conference Mennonite
Church
Winnipeg, Manitoba

Getting Ready (secular monthly
magazine for teens)
Northwest Media, Inc.
Eugene, OR

Good News Bearers
The Youth & Family Institute
Bloomington, MN

Group Publishing, Inc. (nondenominational)
Loveland, CO

Group Workcamps (nondenominational)
Loveland, CO

Huntington University Graduate
School of Christian Ministry (MA
program in youth ministry, United Brethren in Christ Church)
Huntington, IN

Intentional Intergenerational
Ministry
Points of View Incorporated
Orono, MN

International Bible Society
Colorado Springs, CO

InterVarsity Christian Fellowship
Madison, WI

John Hancock Center for Youth
Ministry (Seventh-day Adventist)
Riverside, CA

Leader Resources (Episcopal Journey to Adulthood)
Bethesda, MD

Life Innovations Inc. (nondenominational)
Minneapolis, MN

LifeStories
Game by Talicor, Inc.
Plainwell, MI

Life Teen, Inc.
Mesa, AZ

Liturgical Conference (Roman
Catholic)
Silver Spring, MD

Lutheran Education Association
River Forest, IL

Lutheran Institute on Aging and
Family
Concordia University
Seward, NE

Luther Seminary (graduate program in youth and family ministry)
St. Paul, MN

Men Marked with the Cross of Christ
Highland Ranch, CO

Mentor Guide and One on One
Faith & Life Press
Newton, KS

Midland Lutheran College (BA program in youth and family ministry)
Fremont, NE

National Association for the Education of Young Children (NAEYC) (catalog of resources)
Washington, DC

National Association of Catholic Family Life Ministers (Roman Catholic)
University of Dayton
Dayton, OH

National Council on Family Relations (secular)
Minneapolis, MN

National Federation for Catholic Youth Ministry (Roman Catholic)
Washington, DC

National Network of Youth Ministries (Fundamentalist and Conservative Evangelical Youth Ministries)
San Diego, CA

National Peer Ministry Training Center
The Youth & Family Institute
Bloomington, MN

National Study of Youth and Religion
The University of North Carolina at Chapel Hill
Chapel Hill, NC

NavPress
Colorado Springs, CO

Paulist Press (Roman Catholic)
Mahwah, NJ

Perkins School of Theology Youth Ministry Institute (January, week-long training of youth workers—United Methodist) Continuing Education
Perkins School of Theology
Southern Methodist University
Dallas, TX

Prepare/Enrich Training
Minneapolis, MN

Presbyterians for Renewal Youth Ministry (PCUSA)
Chattanooga, TN

Presbyterian Youth Connection (PCUSA)
Louisville, KY

Princeton Theological Seminary Institute for Youth Ministry (PCUSA)
Princeton, NJ

Rock the World Youth Mission Alliance (Episcopal)
Ambridge, PA

Saint Mary's Press
Winona, MN

Search Institute
Minneapolis, MN

Seraphim Communications, Inc.
St. Paul, MN

Southwestern Baptist Theological
    Seminary
Fort Worth, TX

Stephen Ministries
St. Louis, MO

Study of Exemplary Youth Ministry
Luther Seminary
St. Paul, MN

Tentmakers (evangelical training in
    youth ministry leadership)
New Hope, MN

Tirosh, TEC, or Chrysalis
Tucson, AZ

Trinity Lutheran College (BA
    program in youth and family
    ministry)
Issaquah, WA

True Love Waits
Nashville, TN

Twenty-Third Publications
New London, CT

Via de Cristo National Lutheran
    Secretariat
Fort Dodge, IA

Walk Thru the Bible Seminars
Atlanta, GA

Wheat Ridge Ministries
Itasca, IL

Young Life (evangelical)
Colorado Springs, CO

The Youth & Family Institute
Bloomington, MN

Youth Encounter
St. Paul, MN

Youth for Christ/USA (evangelical)
Englewood, CO

Youth Leadership
St. Paul, MN

Youth Ministry and Spirituality
    Project (PCUSA)
San Francisco Theological Seminary
San Anselmo, CA

Youth Policy Institute
Los Angeles, CA

Youth Specialties, Inc. (nondenom-
    inational, evangelical)
El Cajon, CA

Youthworks
Minneapolis, MN

Selected Bibliography

Anderson, David W., and Paul Hill. *Frogs Without Legs Can't Hear: Nurturing Disciples for Home and Congregation*. Minneapolis: Augsburg Fortress Publishing, 2003.

Anderson, David W., Paul Hill, and Roland D. Martinson. *Coming of Age: Exploring the Identity and Spirituality of Younger Men*. Minneapolis: Augsburg Fortress Publishing, 2006.

Azar, Beth. "New Theory on Development Could Usurp Piagetian Beliefs." *Monitor* (June 1997): p. 9.

Bellah, Robert N. et al. "Individualism and the Crisis of Civic Membership." *Christian Century* 113, no. 16 (May 8, 1996).

Benson, D. Marshall. "An LF Symposium on the Church and Higher Education: A Response to Robert Benne's article, 'Recovering a Christian College,'" 1993.

Benson, Peter L. *Developmental Assets Among Youth*. Minneapolis: Search Institute, 1996.

Benson, Peter L., and Eugene C. Roehlkepartain. *Youth in Single-Parent Families*. Minneapolis: Search Institute, 1993.

Benson, Peter L., M. A. Galbraith, and Pamela Espeland. *What Kids Need to Succeed*. Minneapolis: Free Spirit Press, 1995.

Black, Wesley. *An Introduction to Youth Ministry*. Nashville, TN: Broadman Press, 1991.

Bodenhammer, David J. "Initiatives in Religion." *Lilly Endowment* newsletter (fall 1996).

Center for Early Adolescence. "Living with 10- to 15-Year-Olds: A Parent Education Curriculum." Minneapolis: Search Institute, 1992.

Dean, Kenda Creasy. *Practicing Passion: Youth and the Quest for a Passionate Church*. Grand Rapids, MI: Eerdmanns, 2004.

De Vries, Mark. *Family-Based Youth Ministry*. Downers Grove, IL: InterVarsity Press, 1994.

Durka, Gloria, and Joanmarie Smith. *Family Ministry.* Minneapolis: Winston, 1980.

Durkheim, Emile. *The Elemental Forms of the Religious Life.* New York: Free Press, 1985.

Encyclopaedia Britannica, 9th ed., s.v. "family."

Erickson, Judith B. *Directory of American Youth Organizations.* 2nd ed. Minneapolis: Center for Youth Development and Research at the University of Minnesota, 1983.

"Faith and Longevity: Is There a Link?" *Harvard Men's Health Watch* newsletter (September 1997): p. 6.

Farkas, Steve. "Adults' Views of Youth: Pretty Dim." *Minneapolis Star Tribune* (June 26, 1997).

Feldmeyer, Dean, and Eugene C. Roehlkepartain. *Parenting with a Purpose.* Minneapolis: Search Institute, 1995.

Garland, Diana. *Sacred Stories of Ordinary Families.* San Francisco: Jossey-Bass, 2003.

Gillespie, V. Bailey. *Perspectives on Values.* La Sierra, CA: La Sierra University Press, 1993.

Gobbi, Gianna. *Listen to God with Children.* Trans. by Rebekah Rojcewicz. Loveland, OH: Treehaus Communications, 1998.

Hardel, Dick, and Roland Martinson. *It Takes More Than Love.* Bloomington, MN: The Youth & Family Institute, 1995.

Harris, Maria. *Portrait of Youth Ministry.* New York: Paulist Press, 1981.

Hetherington, E. Mavis. "An Overview of the Virginia Longitudinal Study of Divorce and Remarriage with a Focus on Early Adolescence." *Journal of Family Psychology* 7, no. 1 (June 1993): pp. 39–56.

Jacobson, James R. *Hope for Tomorrow's Families' Family Education.* Peoria, AZ: Family Education, 1995.

Jacox, Lisa H., and Rena L. Repetti. "Conflict in Families and the Psychological Adjustment of Pre-adolescent Children." *Journal of Family Psychology* 7, no. 3 (December 1993): pp. 344–353.

Karim, Reed. "Grand Forks: The City That Won't Give Up." *USA Weekend* (December 19–21, 1997): pp. 4–5.

Kehrwald, Leif, editor. *Families and Faith: A Vision and Practice for Parish Leaders.* New London, CT: Twenty-Third Publications, 2006.

———. *People of Faith: Generations Learning Together.* Orlando, FL: Harcourt, 2005.

Lee, W. Jerry, and Gail Taylor Rice. "Portrait of the Adventist Family: Actions and Outcomes." Report 5. La Sierra, CA: La Sierra University, 1995.

Little, Sara. *Youth, World, and Church.* Richmond, VA: John Knox Press, 1968.

Lynn, David, and Kathy Lynn. *HomeGrown with Faith.* Nashville, TN: World Publishing, 2006.

Murray, Bridget. "Home Schools: How Do They Affect Children?" *Monitor* 27, no. 12 (December 1996): pp. 1, 43.

Nichols, Michael P. *The Self in the System: Expanding the Limits of Family Therapy.* New York: Brunner/Routledge, 1987.

Pilisuk, M., and C. Froland. "Kinship, Social Networks, Social Support, and Health." *Social Science Medicine* 12 (1978): p. 273.

Roberto, John. *Becoming a Church of Lifelong Learners.* New London, CT: Twenty-Third Publications, 2006.

Roberto, John, with Mariette Martineau. *Generations of Faith Resource Manual.* New London, CT: Twenty-Third Publications, 2005.

Roberts, Cokie, and Steven V. Roberts. "Colin Powell: Striking a Nerve." *USA Weekend* (November 14–18, 1997).

Robinson, Anthony B. "Campus Morality." *Christian Century* 114, no. 27 (October 8, 1997): pp. 862–863.

Roehlkepartain, Eugene C. *Building Assets in Congregations.* Minneapolis: Search Institute, 1997.

———. *The Teaching Church.* Nashville, TN: Abingdon Press, 1993.

Roehlkepartain, Eugene C., and Peter C. Scales. *Youth Development in Congregations: An Exploration of the Potential and Barriers.* Minneapolis: Search Institute, 1995.

Roehlkepartain, Eugene C., and Peter L. Benson. *Youth in Protestant Churches.* Minneapolis: Search Institute, 1993.

Ross, Richard, and G. Wade Rowatt. *Ministry with Youth and Their Parents.* Nashville, TN: Convention Press, 1986.

Sacred Congregation for the Clergy. *General Catechetical Directory.* Washington, DC: United States Catholic Conference (USCC), 1971.

Satinover, Jeffrey. *Homosexuality and the Politics of Truth.* Grand Rapids, MI: Baker Books, 1996.

Scales, Peter C. *Boxed in and Bored: How Middle Schools Continue to Fail Young Adolescents and What Good Middle Schools Do Right.* Minneapolis: Search Institute, 1996.

————. *A Portrait of Young Adolescents in the 1990s*. Minneapolis: Search Institute, 1995.

————. *Working with Young Adolescents and Their Families*. Minneapolis: Search Institute, 1996.

Shapiro, Joseph P., et al. "Invincible Kids." *U.S. News and World Report* (November 11, 1996): p. 10.

Smith, Christian, with Melinda Lundquist Denton. *Soul Searching: The Religious and Spiritual Lives of American Teenagers*. New York: Oxford University Press, 2005.

Stafford, Tim. *Sexual Chaos*. Downers Grove, IL: InterVarsity Press, 1993.

Stoop, David. "My Family and Me." In *Relationships: An Open and Honest Guide to Healthy Connections*. San Francisco: McGraw Hill, 1993.

Strommen, A. Irene. *Faith and Skills for Parenting*. Bloomington, MN: The Youth & Family Institute, 1997.

Strommen, Merton P. "Ministering to Families in the Twenty-first Century." In *Life-Changing Events for Youth and Their Families*. Nashville, TN: Convention Press, 1995.

Strommen, Merton P., and Dick Hardel. *Youth and Family Ministry: Four Imperatives*. Bloomington, MN: The Youth & Family Institute, 2002.

Sweet, Leonard I. *Quantum Spirituality: A Postmodern Apologetic*. Dayton, OH: Spirit Venture Ministries, 1994.

Tyner, Stuart. *Surrounded by Strangers*. Riverside, CA: Hancock Center Publications, 1997.

U.S. Bishops. "Family Perspective." *Partners in Faith* newsletter. Helotes, TX: Lady of Guadalupe Church.

Varenhorst, Barbara B. *Peer Ministry Training*. Bloomington, MN: The Youth & Family Institute, 2003.

Wallis, Claudia. "Faith and Healing." *Time* 147, no. 26 (June 24, 1996): pp. 58–64.

Welter, Paul. *Learning from Children*. Wheaton, IL: Tyndale Press, 1983.

Wigger, J. Bradley. *The Power of God at Home: Nurturing Our Children in Love and Grace*. San Francisco: Jossey-Bass, 2003.

Wright, Wendy M. *Seasons of a Family's Life: Cultivating the Contemplative Spirit at Home*. San Francisco: Jossey-Bass, 2003.

Woodward, Tom. "Darwin in Decline?" *Minneapolis Star Tribune*, December 6, 1997.

Acknowledgments *(continued)*

Many people supported us with their prayers, insights, and gifts. We are sure that in listing some we will forget to list others.

We are most grateful for Craig Dykstra and the Lilly Foundation, whose grant made the research for the writing of this book possible.

We thank God for Fr. Bob Stamschror and the people of Saint Mary's Press for their willingness to publish this book and to work with The Youth & Family Institute. We'd like to give a special thanks to Ron Klug for his editorial skill in bringing clarity to this manuscript.

We would not have been able to write this book without the support of the staff of The Youth & Family Institute.

Our critical reviewers helped us make substantial changes in the final draft to benefit the readers. Thank you:
Dr. Kenda Creasy Dean
The Rev. Dr. Nathan Frambach
Dr. Diana Garland
The Rev. Dr. Paul Hill
The Rev. Dr. Roland Martinson
John Roberto

The following are some of the thirty-five directors of youth and family ministry in congregations throughout the United States whose insights and comments encouraged us to write seven drafts of this book:
The Rev. Pat Fletcher
Dr. Nancy Going
Mark Holmen
Heather Hultgren
Sally Mancini
Kent L. Smith
The Rev. Deb Stehlin

The figures on pages 36, 68, and 92 are from *Young Adolescents and Their Parents: A National Portrait.* Copyright © 1984 by Search Institute®, Minneapolis, MN, *www.search-institute.org.* Reprinted with permission of Search Institute®. All rights reserved.

The figure on page 52 is from *Five Cries of Parents,* by Merton P. Strommen and A. Irene Strommen (San Francisco: Harper and Row, 1985), pages 75. Copyright © 1985, 1993 by The Youth & Family Institute. Used with permission.

Index

Figures are indicated with "fig." following the page number.

A

AAA (Triple A) parents, 71–72
The Abolition of Man (Lewis), 91
abstinence pledges, 147–148
abuse, 43, 46, 49
Acock, Alan, 37, 41, 48
acquired immune deficiency syndrome (AIDS), 49
activism, 287
Ada Bible Church (Ada, Michigan), 107
Adolescent-Parent study (Search Institute), 98, 263
adolescents: adult views of, 17, 224; advisers and mentor choices of, 53, 227; Bible-centered discussions for, 209–213; biblical ignorance of, 115–116, 140; caring awards for, 225; caring environments for, 70–73, 71 fig., 178–181, 356; church affiliation decline surveys, 35–36, 206; church attendance and lifestyle, 229, 230 fig.; committed youth, characteristics of, 20, 22 fig., 73–74, 74 fig., 105 fig., 214; counseling for, 224–229; decision-making education, 146–147; developmental assets statistics, 250; disciplinary approaches to, 62–66; ethnic minorities, 148–153; faith-formation influences, 20–21, 78, 90; faith-sharing experiences of, 35, 213–216; family discussions on faith studies, 15–16; on family unity, 36, 36 fig.; friendship groups for, 223–224; as full laity, 203, 204; fun and fellowship activities for, 216–217; godparenting program for, 73; identity formation of, 56, 241, 243; intergenerational service efforts toward, 189–191; justification by faith survey, 138; with law orientation, 98; leadership training of, 154–155; leaving congregations, 170, 171; in mission outreach, 156–159; moral orientations of, 143–145; moral values and, 90–99, 92 fig.; musical connection to, 221–222; parental bonding with, 66–68, 68 fig., 70; parent communication with, 52–54, 52 fig.; in peer ministry, 93–94, 219–221; personal relationships with God, 132–135; and service, 100–101, 153–155, 217–218, 264; worship programs for, 177–178. *See also* at-risk youth; children; high school students
adopted children, 56, 67
Adoption Study (Search Institute), 56, 67
adoptive family, 23
adults: Bible, interest in, 140–141; in Bible-centered discussions, 210–211; on Bible's importance, 120 fig.; in caregiving ministries, 180–181, 224–226; Christian education programs for, 128–129; communication styles of, 58–59; faith maturity of, 88; in intergenerational service, 189–191; as mentors, 226–227; surveys of, on youth, 17, 224. *See also* fathers; mothers; parents
affection, demonstrative, 67–68, 68 fig., 98
African American congregations: choirs of, 222; music styles of, 176; prayer emphasis in, 131; teachers in, 134; welcoming atmosphere of, 170
African Americans: and evangelical education, 278; faith maturity of, 151; and

mentoring, 254–256; welcoming strategies for, 151–152
aggression, 47, 343
AIDS (acquired immune deficiency syndrome), 49
alcohol abuse: adolescent studies on, 92 fig.; and developmental assets, 245 fig.; and disciplinary approaches, 64; family survey statistics of, 49; mentoring programs' effect on, 226; and moral orientation, 145; Seventh-day Adventist surveys, 276 fig.; stress contributing to, 47
Alegent Health (formerly Immanuel Medical Center), 259–260
Aleshire, Daniel, 280–281
Alliance for Youth, 265–266, 290
All Kids Are Our Kids (Benson), 196, 239, 265, 272–273
All Saints Church (Phoenix, Arizona), 50–51
All Saints Episcopal Church (Minneapolis), 284
American communities. *See* communities
The American Crime Factory: How It Works and How to Slow It Down (Lykken), 34
American Indians, 152, 172, 189, 254, 284–286
American Institute for Church Growth, 206
American Mainline Religion: Its Changing Shape and Future (Roof and McKinney), 280
American Medical Association, 239
American Psychological Association, 79, 229, 279
America's Promise: The Alliance for Youth, 265–266, 290
Amish, 275
Amman, Jacob, 275
Amusing Ourselves to Death (Postman), 174

Anderson, David W., 28, 32, 33, 71, 162, 306
Andreson, Knut, 35
animal ethics, 309
Apollo 17 (spacecraft), 300
Arapahoe tribe, 254
Area Agency on Aging (Corvallis, Oregon), 259
Asian Americans, 130, 148–150
assets paradigm. *See* developmental assets
Astin, Alexander, 153
at-risk behaviors: and church attendance, 229, 230 fig.; in deteriorating communities, 239; developmental assets impact on, 241, 244, 264–265; gang involvement, 284–286; and home schooling options, 277–278; law orientation impact on, 98, 276, 276 fig.; mentoring impact on, 226, 254–255; moral value erosion and, 91–93, 92 fig.; and parental bonding, 67; self-fulfillment ethics and, 273; service project impact on, 100
at-risk youth: and American culture, 273; born out of wedlock, 34; counseling for, 227–228; fellowship groups for, 196–197; mentoring for, 226–227; mission outreach impact on, 157–159; peer ministry to, 219–221; in Protestant denominations, 214; service programs for, 190; studies on, 35, 273
attachment theory, 66–70, 68 fig., 69 fig.
Attitudes and Behaviors survey, 250–251
autocratic discipline, 62–64
Automatic Interaction Detection software program, 341
Axinn, William, 31

B

baby boomer generation, 117, 272

banquets, recognition, 217

Baptist Sunday School Board, 202

Baptist Training Union, 202

Baptist Young People's Union, 202

Baptist Youth Fellowship, 201

Barna, George, 191–192, 318

Barna Research Group, 119, 191

Bartholomew, Patriarch, 305

Baumrind, Diana, 62

Bear Clan youth group, 284–286

Being There: Culture and Formation in Two Theological Schools (Jackson, Wheeler, Aleshire, and Long), 280–281

Bellah, Robert N., 270

Bellevue, Washington, 251

Benne, Robert, 289

Benson, Peter, 101, 153, 155, 196, 239–240, 265, 272–273

Bergen, Abe, 256

Berryman, Jerome, 107, 142

Bethany Covenant (Minneapolis), 152–153

Bethlehem Congregation (Grand Marais, Minnesota), 109–110

Bethlehem Lutheran Church (Aberdeen, South Dakota), 28, 110

Beyond Leaf Raking: Learning to Serve/Serving to Learn (Benson and Roehlkepartain), 155

Bibby, Reginald, 221, 223

Bible: age and importance of, 120 fig.; discussion groups on, 210–213; as educational priority, 124, 130; encouraging adult interest in, 140–141; on family relationships, 17; family rituals of, 32; grace orientation education and stories of, 137; income and importance of, 119, 119 fig.; intellectual approach to, 181–182; programs for reading and studying, 96–97, 100, 139–140; values expressed in, 91; youth's unfamiliarity with, 115–116, 119. *See also* Bible study programs; biblical verses; Gospel

Bible camps, 220, 232, 309–310

Bible-centered discussion groups, 210–213

The Bible for Today's Families, 137

Bible schools, 220, 231

Bible study programs: Christian education priorities and, 130; combined with service, 100, 129, 156; to encourage interest, 139–142; at Willamette University, 350

biblical verses: commitment to Christ, 18, 197; congregational family, 165–166, 179; creation and human stewardship, 299, 301, 304; faith, 81, 89; faith-based vision, 317–318; forces of evil, 322; healing through prayer, 282; heavens and humans, 297; literal acceptance of, 281–282; parental roles, 18, 31, 102, 106; passion, 81; personal relationships with Christ, 132, 299; rituals, 159; service, 85, 99, 153; struggle and prayer, 185; supporting youth fellowships, 201; support within culture, 197; world culture views, 273–274, 275

Big Brothers and Big Sisters, 226, 254–255

Bishop's National Catholic Welfare Conference, 118

Bishop's Task Force for Caring for Creation, 304

blessings, as rituals, 162

Bloom, Allan, 271

Bloom, J. R., 184

Bloomington Covenant (Minneapolis), 152–153

Blyth, Dale, 256
Bodenhammer, David, 249
bonding: for faith formation, 18; parent-child model, 18, 66–71, 68 fig., 69 fig.; through mission outreach, 191
The Book of God (Wangerin), 141
Booth, Connie, 33
Borud, Lynn, 250
Boston Couples Study, 58
boundaries, 66, 241, 242, 275–276
Boy Scouts, 200, 216, 309
Brancatelli, Robert J., 162
Brokering, Lois, 170
Brown, Dan, 79
Brown, Harold O. J., 271
Brueggeman, Walter, 31–32
Buddy System, 256
Burke, Weir, and Harnson study, 58
Bush, Barbara, 225
Busters, 169–170, 177

C

Cadwalader, George, 35
Calvary Church Newport Mesa (Costa Mesa, California), 169
Calvary Lutheran Church (Golden Valley, Minnesota), 176
Calvin, John, 287
Cambridge, England, 289–290
Camp Fire Girls, 200
Campolo, Anthony, 138–139, 275, 278–279, 287, 294
Campolo, Bart, 287
Canaan Presbyterian Church (Chicago), 130
Canadian Mentor Strategy National Training Leaders Organization, 256–257
cancer patients, 183–184
Cardena, María-Elena, 150
caring environments: of communities, 247–249; of congregations, 178–181; creation of, 180–181; for faith

formation, 70–72, 71 fig.; faith maturity correlation with, 352; teacher recruitment and training for, 133–134; as vision-mission component, 320; and youth counseling, 224–226
Caring Youth Award, 225
Caring Youth Day, 225
Carnegie Council on Adolescent Development, 206
Carter, Steven, 77, 215, 271, 280
Castaways: The Penikese Island Experiment (Cadwalader), 35
The Catechesis of the Good Shepherd in a Parish Setting (Lillig), 161
Catechesis of the Good Shepherd program, 107, 142
catechetical teaching: case for return to, 125; and CCD movement, 118; family-centered, 24–25; *Passing On Faith* model of, 24. *See also* Christian education
Catholic denominations: Christian education in, 117–119; faith-assets correlation with, 263–264; faith-based vision of, 319–320; faith-formation goals of, 112; family discussions on faith in, 16; Gospel *versus* law orientation of, 87. *See also* Roman Catholic Church
The Catholic High School: A National Portrait study, 101
Catholic High Schools: Their Impact on Low-Income Students, 87
Catholic Office of Indian Ministry, 286
Cavalletti, Sofia, 160
CCD (Roman Catholic Confraternity of Christian Doctrine), 118
Celek, Tim, 169, 175
Center for Health Research (Loma Linda University), 49

The Center for Ministry
Development (Roman Catholic
Church), 106–107
Center for the Study of Religion,
Spirituality, and Health (Duke
University), 186
Central Christian Church
(Decatur, Illinois), 129–130
chaos theory, 321
Charismatic congregations, 282
Charry, Ellen T., 78
Chicago Christian Church,
181–182
Child and Family Institute, 162
child care centers, 259
children: abandonment of, 33;
adopted, 56, 67; adult views
of, 17, 224; Bible-reading
programs for, 96–97, 140, 141,
142; born out of wedlock,
34; caring environments
for, 71–73; cultural illiteracy
of, 122–123, 174; death of,
impact, 47, 58; disciplinary
approaches to, 62–66; divorce
and, 47–48; faith and, 81;
family support networks for,
183; in fatherless families, 33;
grace education for, 137; of
incompetent parents, 34–35;
mentors chosen by, 53, 227;
mission outreach supporting,
193; moral orientations of,
144–145; newspapers developed
by, 109; and outdoor recreation,
307–310; parental bonding with,
66–71, 68 fig., 69 fig.; parental
communication with, 51–57;
and parental harmony, 41–43;
and parent's behavior, 43–46;
parents praying with, 142–143;
and rituals, 160; and service
projects, 100, 101; stepparenting
and, 48; and values, 90, 93–98;
and worship services, 168, 170–
171, 177. *See also* adolescents;
at-risk youth

Children and Family Institute
(Menlo Park, California), 107
choirs, 221–222
Christ and Culture (Niebuhr), 274
Christ Clown College, 261
Christ Clown Connection, 261
Christian Copyright and
Licensing, 175
Christian education: adult
programs of, 128–129;
biblical emphasis of, 130;
biblical illiteracy in, 123–124;
congregation's role in, 126;
ethnic minorities in, 148–153;
as faith enhancement, 121–122;
faith-formation tasks of, 85;
and faith sharing, 102; grace
orientation, 135–142; mission
outreach of, 156–159; moral
values instruction, 143–148;
objectives of, overview, 131–132;
personal relationship with
Christ, 132–135; pluralism's
challenge to, 120–121; prayer
emphasis of, 131, 142–143; by
Protestant denominations, 113–
117; ritual instruction, 159–163;
by Roman Catholic church,
117–119; service orientation
for, 101, 126–127, 129–130,
153–156; sources for, 112–113;
teacher recruitment and training
for, 127–128, 133–134; youth
fellowships tied to, 201. *See also*
catechetical teaching
Christian Endeavor Society,
198–200
Christian Formation and Youth
Ministry, 73
Christianity: accommodation
stance of, 278–281; against
culture, 275–278, 276 fig.;
culture in paradox with, 271,
283–286; environmental
responsibility of, 304–306;
high culture associations with,
172; pluralism's challenge to,

120–121; synthesis stance of, 281–283; transformation stance of, 286–290

Christian Reformed World Relief Committee, 289

Christian Youth Fellowship, 201

Christian youth subculture: contemporary importance of, 196–197; historical development of, 197–199; Protestant eras of, 199–206. *See also* youth ministry

The Church and Young Men (Cressey), 200

churches: accessible facilities at, 171; attendance at, and lifestyle correlation, 229, 230 fig.; music at, 172–173, 175–176, 222; seating and parking at, 170; trends in worship services at, 172

church members: Gospel *versus* law orientation of, 87–88; lifestyle *versus*, 306–309; mature faith statistics, 88; Search Institute's study of, 86–87; as teachers, 126–128; in vision-to-mission process, 324–325, 326. *See also* congregations

CIT (*Counselors in Training*), 232

CitySongs, 261–262

civic humanist morality, 144, 145

"Civil Rights Issues Facing Asian Americans in the 1990s," 149

Clark, Francis E., 198, 199

clergy, 50, 121, 310–311

Clinton, Bill, 265

Clinton, Hillary Rodham, 225

Closing the American Mind (Bloom, A.), 271

clown ministry troupes, 216, 261

cohabitation, 31

Coleman, Lyman, 32, 109, 110, 311

Coles, Robert, 262

Collins, Jim, 321

Coming of Age (Anderson, Hill, and Martinson), 33, 306

Coming of Age ministry, 110

commitment, 200, 292–293

commitment cards, 147

committed youth, 20, 22 fig., 73–74, 74 fig., 105 fig., 214

Common Fire: Lives of Commitment in a Complex World (Daloz, Parks, Keen, and Keen), 292–294

communication: with ethnic minorities, 148–153; faith sharing and, 103; gender differences in, 56, 58–59; with Generation X, 169–170; listening guidelines, 60–61; marital discord impact on, 343; nonverbal, 59, 72; personal relationships with God and, 135; stress factors and, 47. *See also* communication, parent-youth; faith sharing

communication, parent-youth: adoption studies on, 56; age and decline in, 36, 36 fig., 51–52, 52 fig.; and child development, 51, 57–58; child's desire and suggestions for, 54–55; as Christian parenting facet, 72; deterrents to, 59–60; listening guidelines for, 60–61; of moral values, 93–98; of past experiences, 44; research studies on, 52–54, 55, 57–58; training programs for, 56; verbal and active types, 56–57

communities: asset-building approach of, 240–247; caregiving ministries in, 180–181; caring quality of, 247–249; church-sponsored parenting courses in, 286; congregation's ministry to, 249–252; cultural transformation role of, 288–290; definition, 247; deterioration in, 239; developmental assets of, 242–244 fig.; family as first, 23; health assessments of, 238, 239–240; intergenerational programs in, 257–259; mentoring programs in, 254–257; music programs in, 261–262; national effort toward building, 265–267; peer helping programs in, 252–254; vision-mission statements of, 251; wellness programs in, 259–261

Concordia College (Moorhead, Minnesota), 184, 289

Concordia Lutheran Church (Kirkwood, Missouri), 26–27

"Conformation (Sic!) Is Dead" (Melheim), 116

Congregational Christian Church, 201

congregations: caring environments of, 178–181; Christian education role of, 128; community role of, 238, 249–252, 262–263; creation celebrations, 313; cultural transformation by, 289; disciplinary guidance of, 65–66; early youth fellowships of, 201–202; and ethnic minorities, 152–153; faith-assets goals of, 233–235; faith-formation roles of, 29, 78, 173–174; faith-sharing examples in, 106–110; as family, 165–167, 320–321; family ministry of, 37–38, 74–75, 342; family's partnership with, 19, 23–24, 28, 112; family support groups in, 183–185; grace *versus* law orientation of, 179; hospitality of, 168–171, 168 fig.; intergenerational service efforts of, 189–191; leadership training role of, 232–233; lifestyle conflicts with, 306; loyalty and commitment to, 154, 167; marriage ministries, 30; mission outreach programs of, 157–159, 191–194; music and, 172–173, 175–176; parental harmony promotion of, 48–51;

prayer emphasis and instruction, 131, 143, 185–187; reasons for joining, 206–207; reasons for leaving, 25, 170, 171; rituals instruction by, 161–163; self-evaluation of, 74–75; service dimension of, 129–130; teacher recruitment and training in, 126–128, 133–134, 146; thinking atmosphere of, 181–183; vision-to-action strategies for, 318, 320–321; wellness programs of, 182, 184. *See also* church members; worship services

Connecting Generations, 258

conventionalist morality, 144, 145

Cooper, C. R., 56

core knowledge schools, 124–125

counseling: caregiving types of, 224–226; clergy families and, 50; limitations of, 36–37; malpractice, 229; mentoring types of, 226–227; pastoral, 50; by trained counselors, 228–229; by youth ministers, 227–228. *See also* mentoring programs

Counselors in Training (CIT), 232

Courtoy, Charles, 198–199, 201

crack cocaine epidemics, 33

creation, circle of: animal ethics, 309; celebration and worship of, 312–314; Christian stewardship of, 304–306; environmental wellness programs, 310–311; and faith formation, 312–314; God's nature in, 299–300; humanity's relationship with, 300–304; and outdoor recreation, 306–310; theology of the cross, 297–299

credo, 83

Cressey, F. G., 200–201

crime, 34–35, 64

critical edge moments, 258

The Critical Years (Parks), 84

cross, theology of the, 297–299

Crossways (Bible study program), 100, 130
Cultural Literacy (Hirsch), 122–123
culture: of baby boomer generation, 117, 272; Bible's perspective on, 273–274; Christianity accommodation of, 278–281; Christianity against/separation from, 275–278, 276 fig.; Christianity associations with high, 172; Christianity in paradox with (dualism), 283–286; Christianity synthesis of, 281–283; Christianity transformation of, 286–290; in contemporary America, 153, 270–272, 290–295; counteracting influences of, 196; definition, 269; and faith sharing, 215
The Culture of Disbelief (Carter), 77, 215, 271, 280
The Culture of Narcissism: American Life in an Age of Diminishing Expectations (Lasch), 270–271
Curran, Dolores, 90
Cursillo retreat, 96, 214–215

D

Daloz, Laurent A. Parks, 292–294
Davies, James A., 206
The Da Vinci Code (Brown), 79
Davis, Sam, 261
Dawn, Marva, 173, 174, 176
Dean, Kenda Creasy, 80
death: of child, 47, 58; of parent, 44–45, 48
"Declaration on the Environment" (Roman Catholic Church), 305
Demo, David, 37, 41, 48
democratic discipline, 65, 344
depression, 46, 245 fig.

developmental assets: adult-child relationships as, 185; and at-risk behavior, 245 fig., 264–265; and community health, 238, 239–240; considerations for building, 249; definition, 238; external-internal categories of, 240–241, 242–244 fig.; mission statements on, 251; music's creation of, 261–262; peer ministry training in, 253; personal faith linked to, 262–265; positive consequences of, 246 fig.; video series on, 72–73; youth's average number of, 250
The Development of the Young People's Movement (Erb), 198
devotions, 17, 55, 103
Devries, Mark, 217
Diocesan Directors of Religious Education, 118
Disciples of Voluntary Effort (DOVE), 129
discipline, 62–66, 98, 344
discrimination: of ethnic minorities, 148–149, 151; of religious traditions, 271
Divine Drama (Bible study course), 130
divorce: citywide marriage agreements impact on, 30; cohabitation and statistics of, 31; effects of, on children, 47–48; factors contributing to, 47; family life survey statistics on, 49; marriage agreement's response to, 30; ministries counteracting, 30
Dole, Elizabeth, 95
domestic abuse, 43, 46, 49
Donahue (television program), 148
"Don't Forsake Homosexuals Who Want Help," 280
Dossey, Larry, 186
Dostoyevsky, Fyodor, 139
doubt, meanings of, 349

DOVE (Disciples of Voluntary Effort), 129
Droege, Thomas A., 186
drug abuse: child abandonment due to, 33; developmental assets impact on, 245 fig.; and disciplinary approaches, 64, 65; family survey and, 49; mentoring impact on, 226; Seventh-day Adventist surveys, 276 fig.
Dryfoos, Joy G., 252
dualism, 283–286
Duke University, 186
Durkheim, Emile, 285

E

Early Adolescent Ministry (Roberto), 206
Early Adolescents and Their Parents study, 104
Early Adolescent Study (Search Institute): disciplinary approaches, 63; family relationships, 53, 73–74; induction and moral values, 97; parent-child bonding, 68
Earth, 300–304. *See also* creation, circle of
Eden Prairie High School, 252
education: as Asian value, 149; childhood development rituals as, 160; content-oriented, 124–126; cultural illiteracy and, 122–123, 174, 348; evangelical education benefits, 278; home schooling, 277–278; and mentoring, 255–256; parochial schools, 117–118; service-learning, 155–156. *See also* Christian education; public education
"Effecting Utilization" study, 325–326

Effective Christian Education study (Search Institute), 56; adult caregiving, 224; at-risk behavior, 214; Bible-reading studies, 97; caring environments, 352; congregational family, 166–167, 168, 181; education as priority, 125, 127, 131; ethnic minorities, 131, 134, 148, 151; faith maturity, 88, 116, 121, 214; friendship impact, 223; Gospel *versus* law orientation, 87–88; music impact, 222; service projects, 100, 101, 153; worship services, 171
Effective Youth Ministry: A Congregational Approach (Martinson), 232
The Elemental Forms of the Religious Life (Durkheim), 285
Elkind, David, 56–57
Emmanuel Baptist Church (San Jose, California), 125–126
Emmaus Walk retreat, 96
empowerment, 240, 242
engaged couples, 30, 51
environmental responsibility, 302–310. *See also* creation, circle of
Episcopal Diocese of Central Florida, 215
Era of Societies and Leagues, 199–201
Era of Sunday Evening Fellowships, 201–203
Era of Youth Ministry, 203–206
Erb, Frank, 198
"The Estate of Marriage" (Luther), 32
ethnic minorities: Bible study programs of, 130; Christian education teachers, 134; congregations with thinking atmospheres, 181; cultural overviews and welcoming strategies, 148–153; literacy programs for, 189–190; loyalty

and congregations of, 167; and mentoring, 254–255; and prayer emphasis, 131
Evangelical Lutheran Church (Omaha, Nebraska), 259–260
Evangelical Lutheran Church (Southeastern Minnesota Synod), 159
Everson, Thomas, 146–147, 157
Explorers, 216
expressivist morality, 144, 145

F

Fairview Behavioral Services, 72
faith: content and adherence aspects of, 319–320; cultural accommodation approach to, 279–281; definition overview, 79–86, 81 fig., 82 fig., 84 fig., 86 fig.; developmental assets linked to, 262–265; grace (Gospel) versus law orientation, 86–90; healing power of, 79, 186; institutionalization of, 19; justification by, 138; morality tied to, 85; nurturing, 103; renewed interest in, 79; service enhancing, 129; vision-mission based on, 317–319; as whole-person response, 89. See also faith formation; faith sharing; maturity of faith
Faith and Skills for Parenting program, 56, 72
FaithChest, 29
The Faith Factor in Healing (Droege), 186
faith formation: caring environments for, 70–72, 71 fig.; child development and, 160; Christian education's role in, 85; in Christian subculture, 196–197; congregation's role in, 29, 78, 173–174; contemporary worship impact on, 29; family-centered models of, 22–28; family conferences for, 106;

father's role in, 32–33, 88–89; friendship's ties to, 93–94, 221, 223–224; Generations of Faith approach to, 23; goals for adolescents in, 112; influences on, 20–21, 78, 90; intergenerational programs for, 28, 29, 106–109; in Jewish versus Christian homes, 102, 121; marriage strengthening and, 31; nature connection with, 307, 312–314; and outdoor recreation, 312–314; paradigms for, 18–19, 21–22; parental roles in, 19–20, 31–33, 78; resources for, 106–110; service correlated with, 100, 156
Faith-full Families: Family Celebrations through the Seasons, 107
Faith-Full Families program, 162
FaithLife in the Home Resource and Gift Guide, 29, 108
FaithQuakes (Sweet), 318–319
faith sharing: in Catholic homes, 16, 319; in Jewish homes, 102; and parents, 102–106, 104 fig., 105 fig.; in Protestant homes, 16–17, 102–103; resources on, 106–110; of youth ministry, 213–216
FaithTalk, 108, 135
FaithTalk Coasters, 135
FaithTalk with Children, 29, 108, 135
Faith Trainers, 226
families: adoptive models of, 23; American Indian definition of, 152; Bible-reading programs for, 96–97; biblical focus on, 17–18; of committed youth, 74–75, 75 fig.; communication vital to, 51–60; congregational ministries to, 37–38, 74–75; congregation as, 165–166, 320–321; congregation's partnership with, 19, 23–24, 112; definitions of, 20; faith-formation role

of, 19–20, 23–28, 31–32; faith sharing in, 16–17, 35, 102–106, 104 fig., 105 fig.; family support networks for, 78, 183–185; fatherless, 33; father's spiritual leadership in, 32–33; healthy, traits of, 38; marital discord impact on, 42, 47, 48; mission statements of, 108–110; and outdoor recreation, 306–310; parental discipline in, 62–66, 98; parental nurturing in, 66–73; parents' self-descriptions of, 43; and rituals, 32, 159–163; service as activity of, 101; Seventh-day Adventist survey of, 48–49; single-parent, 32, 47, 226; stress impact on, 78; unity surveys, 36, 36 fig.; vision-to-action plans on, 333; well-being, variables affecting, 37–38; and worship services, 29. *See also* adolescents; children; parents

Family: The Forming Center (Thompson), 23

Family Diversity and Well-Being (Acock and Demo), 37

The Family-Friendly Church (Freudenburg), 27

Family Ministries Initiative (Methodist Church), 78

Family Ministry Committee (Southeastern California Conference of the Seventh-day Adventist Church), 48–49

Family Ministry (Curran), 90

Family Ministry (Garland), 312

"Family Perspective" (United States Bishops), 24

Family Time Training, 107

fathers: Bible on, 17–18; child care roles of, 51; demonstrative affection and, 68, 68 fig.; faith sharing with, 17, 102; feelings of failure by, 45–46; self-descriptions of, 43; spiritual leadership roles of, 32–33, 88–89; and time usage surveys, 46. *See also* parents

Feldman, Dean, 154

fellowships: for at-risk youth, 196–197; fun activities in, 216–217; and prayer, 185; youth, model development of, 201–203

The Fifth Quarter, 217

Fire on the Mountain retreat, 312

First Bilingual Baptist Church (Pico Rivera, California), 127–128, 155–156

First Chinese Baptist Church of China Town (Los Angeles), 126–127

First Christian Church (Pine Bluff, Arkansas), 180

First Lutheran Church (Carson, California), 131

First Lutheran Church (Duluth, Minnesota), 141, 211–212

First Presbyterian Church (Bend, Oregon), 109

First Presbyterian Church (Maitland, Florida), 216

First Presbyterian Church (Nashville, Tennessee), 227

First United Methodist Church (San Diego), 128

Five Cries of Grief (Strommen and Strommen), 47

Five Cries of Parents (Strommen and Strommen), 341

Five Cries of Youth (Strommen and Strommen), 134, 214, 229, 263

For Everything a Season: 75 Blessings for Daily Life (Nilsen Family), 163

Fostering Spiritual Growth Among At-Risk Youth (Everson), 157

4-H Clubs, 200, 309

Fourth Presbyterian Church (Bethesdsa, Maryland), 30

Freedom of the Christian (Luther), 113

Freud, Anna, 262

Freudenburg, Ben, 26–27

Friendly Village, 261

friendships, 93–94, 150, 221, 223–224

Friend to Friend (Stone and Keefauver), 219

Frogs Without Legs Can't Hear (Anderson and Hill), 71–72, 162–163

Froland, C., 183

Fullerton Longitudinal Study, 58

fun activities, 216–217

G

gangs, 284–286

Garland, Diana, 23, 312

gender differences: in communication, 56, 58–59; and divorce impact, 47–48; and faith maturity studies, 88

General Catechetical Directory, 83

General Directory for Catechesis, 83, 257

General Norms for the Liturgical Year and the Calendar, 313

Generations of Faith program, 23, 28, 257

Generations Together program, 258

Generation X, 169–170, 177

Gibson, Mel, 79

Girl Reserves of the YWCA, 201

Girl Scouts, 200, 309

glaube, 83

global warming, 303–304

God. *See* personal relationships with God

Godbox, 19

Godly Play program, 107, 142

godparenting programs, 73

Going, Nancy, 217

Good News Bearers, 97, 141

The Good Shepherd and the Child: A Joyful Journey, 161

Good to Great (Collins), 321

Gopnik, Meltzoff and Alison, 124

Gorman, Paul, 309

Gospel: African American

identification with, 151; on commitment to Christ, 197; communication and understanding of, 138; on congregational family, 23; cultural transformation through, 287; orientation to, 86–90; personal testimonies of, 96; on value of service, 99. *See also* Bible; biblical verses

Gospel orientation. *See* grace (Gospel) orientation

Governor's Conference on Youth (Montana), 101–102

grace, defined, 137

grace (Gospel) orientation: Bible's role in, 137; caring congregations with, 179; character of, 138; to communicate values, 98; education goals of, 135–139; law orientation *versus*, 86–88, 135, 179, 276; teaching approaches to, 137–142

Grace Lutheran Church (Evansville, Indiana), 222

Grand Forks, North Dakota, 288–289

grandparents, 21, 33, 134

Grand Persons arts program, 258

Greeks, ancient, 125

Greeley, Andrew, 118

grief, 44–45, 47, 58, 184

Gries, Cheryl, 162, 220

Grotevant, H. D., 56

Group Publishing, 108, 154, 207

Growing Up in America (Campolo, A.), 288, 294

Grow Series (memorization cards), 205

Guinness, Os, 173

H

Habel, Norman, 300, 312, 313

Habits of the Heart (Bellah), 270

Handbook of Youth Ministry
  (Ratcliff and Davies), 206
Hands-On Pastoral Education
  using Clergy Sustaining
  Agriculture (HOPE CSA), 311
happiness, as religious value, 16
Happy Feet (movie), 303
Hardel, Richard, 232–233
Harris Scholastic Research study,
  144
Hart, Betty, 57
Hastings, Minnesota, 248
Hatfield, Mark, 350
Haugen, Doug, 110
Haugk, Kenneth C., 181
Hauser, Edward J. P., 204
Hawkins, Jeff, 310–311
Healing Homosexuality (Nicolosi),
  279
Healing Words (Dossey), 186
health and healing, 79, 183–184,
  186, 282
Healthy Youth Initiative (Nampa,
  Idaho), 250
Heart Ignite, 108
Helping the Struggling Adolescent
  (Parrott), 229
Hennepin County, Minneapolis,
  34–35
high school students: Bible
  study programs for, 141–142;
  intergenerational programs
  with, 259; leadership training
  for, 232; moral orientation
  of, 136, 145; as peer ministry
  leaders, 220–221. *See also*
  adolescents
Hill, Paul, 33, 71, 162, 306
Hirsch, E. D., Jr., 122
Hispanics, 150–151
"Historical Analysis of the Three
  Eras of Mainline Protestant
  Youth Work" (Courtoy), 198
HIV (human immunodeficiency
  virus), 49
Hobbes, Dwight, 255
Hochschild, A., 46–47
Hoge, Dean, 117, 174

Holmen, Mark, 225–226
Holy Trinity Episcopal Church
  (Menlo Park, California), 162
HomeGrown Faith (Lynn and
  Lynn), 107
home schooling, 277–278
home support services, 50, 259
homosexuality, 145, 279–280,
  357
*Homosexuality and the Politics of
  Truth* (Satinover), 357
hope, 61, 228, 320
HOPE CSA (Hands-On Pastoral
  Education using Clergy
  Sustaining Agriculture), 311
Horn, Wade F., 33
Hosea (prophet), 303
hospitality, 148–153, 168–171,
  170, 293–294, 320
House of Blues, 221–222
House of Hope, 261
Hovel, Lee, 259
human immunodeficiency virus
  (HIV), 49
humanist morality, 144
Hussey, Grant, 252
Hybel, Bill, 212–213

I

identity, personal, 56, 241, 243
"I Have a Dream" program, 247
illiteracy: biblical, 123–124,
  174–175; cultural, 122–123, 174;
  religious, 174–175
illness, 183–184, 186
Immanuel Lutheran Church
  (Minneapolis), 134
Immanuel Medical Center (now
  Alegent Health), 259–260
incest, 49
inclusive language, 271, 280–281
An Inconvenient Truth (movie),
  303
individualism, 269, 270, 272
induction, 97–98, 99
innovation, introducing, 324–
  328

Innovation and Change study, 178

The Innovative Church (Strommen), 191, 324

Inside the Soul of a New Generation (Zander and Celek), 169

intergenerational programs: Bible-focused, 140; of communities, 257–259; for family-centered faith formation, 28, 29, 106–110; prayer teams as, 180; for ritual instruction, 159; for service, 189–191; as vision-mission component, 320–321; for welcoming, 170; of youth ministry, 23

International Council of Religious Education, 201

IQ scores, 57–58

Irwin, Kevin, 313

Isaiah, 315, 317–318

It Takes More Than Love (video), 72–73

J

Jackson, Carroll, 280–281

James (Apostle), 273

Jaworski, Joseph, 290–292

Jenny, Gerald, 200

Jernigan, Betsy and Leonard, 282

Jesus Christ: adoptive family model of, 23, 165; caring environment model of, 179; commitment to, 197, 214–215; false characterizations *versus* biblical, 138–139; on family priorities and commitment to, 18; grace orientation and focus on, 138–139; mission's proclamation of, 191; personal relationships with, 132–135; service-oriented ministry of, 99–100, 153, 220; transforming power of, 287; on the world's culture, 274. *See also* personal relationships with God

The Jesus I Never Knew (Yancey), 139

Jews, 30, 102, 121, 198, 276–277

Johaningsmeir, Peggy, 78

John (Apostle), 274

John Hancock Youth and Family Center (La Sierra, California), 137

John Paul II (Pope), 305

Johnson, Audray, 49, 50

Johnson, Benton, 117, 174

Jung, Carl, 84

Junior Achievement, 201

Junior Red Cross, 200–201

justification by faith, 138

Justification Scale, 348

K

Kaplan, David M., 47

Kasischke, Fred, 49, 50

Keefauver, Larry, 219

Keen, Cheryl H., 292–294

Keen, James P., 292–294

Kennedy, Robert F., Jr., 310

Kersten, Katherine, 124

Kids Clubs, 193

Kids These Days: What Americans Think About the Next Generation study, 17, 224

Kivnick, Helen, 261

Koenig, Harold G., 186

Kolb, David, 155

Korean congregations, 130, 181

Krych, Margaret, 88–89, 137

L

La Canada Presbyterian Church (La Canada, California), 286

Lamport, Mark, 207

Lang, Eugene, 244–247

language, inclusive, 271, 280–281

Larson, Roland and Doris, 146, 225

Lasch, Christopher, 270–271

Last Child in the Woods (Louv), 307–308, 310

Latinos, 150–151
law orientation: and at-risk behavior, 98, 276, 276 fig.; church member profiles with, 87; and disciplinary approaches, 64; grace (Gospel) orientation *versus*, 86–88, 135, 179, 276; lifestyles of, as response to culture, 275–276, 276 fig.
leadership: faith maturity and parental roles of, 88; men's ministries in, 109; parental roles of, 31–33; pastoral, as faith asset, 234; task-force training for, 231–232; in twenty-first century, 291–295; in vision-to-action process, 321; youth training in, 154–155, 204, 205. *See also* peer leadership
Leadership and the New Science (Wheatley), 321
learning: commitment to, as developmental asset, 241, 243; service-, 101–102, 155–156. *See also* Christian education; education; public education
Learning the Language of Faith in the Home (video), 54–55
learning theories, 124–126
Lee, Kai Cho, 130
legitimizers, 326
Leonard, Joe, 30
lesbianism, 279–280
Lewis, C. S., 91
Liberty Baptist (Alabama), 157
Liberty Chapel United Church of Christ (Monncure, North Carolina), 222
Licensing Parents: Can We Prevent Child Abuse and Neglect? (Westman), 34
Life, 114
Life in Christ Circus, 261
Life Teen program, 177–178
Lillig, Tina, 161
Lindbeck, George A., 272
Lippitt, Ronald, 329
listening guidelines, 60–61

Liturgy Training Publications, 161
Living Liturgy: Elementary Reflections (Cavalletti), 160
Living Well in Christ ministry, 182
Logos program, 223–224
Loma Linda University, 49
Long, Penny, 280–281
Los Angeles Times, 288
Louv, Richard, 307–308, 310
loyalty: and caring adults, 224; as commitment to Christ, 197; congregation's promotion of, 166–167; and friendships, 223; service activities promoting, 100, 154
Luecke, David, 172, 175
Luidens, Donald, 117, 174
Luke (Apostle), 165–166
Luther, Martin: on Earth's sacramentality, 301; on faith, 79, 81, 82–83, 84–85; faith formation and congregation, 173–174; on faith sharing, 113; on parental roles, 32
Lutheran Brotherhood (now Thrivent), 260, 289
Lutheran Church–Missouri Synod, 114, 168, 202
Lutheran congregations: Christian education in, 116, 130, 131, 141; on faith-assets correlation, 264; in flood-damaged communities, 289; Gospel *versus* law orientation, 87; youth support groups of, 200, 202
Lutheran Men in Mission, 110
Lutheran Social Services (Minnesota), 72
Luther Leagues, 200, 204
Lykken, David, 34
Lynn, David and Kathy, 107

M

Mancini, Sally, 177

Manly, Isaac, 282
marriage: citywide agreements
  on, 30–31; cohabitation before,
  31; discord within, 42, 47,
  48, 343; events to improve
  communication, 343–344;
  and mentoring, 30, 31, 50–51;
  ministries for, 20
Marriage Encounter, 343–344
Marriage Marathon Retreat, 51
"Marriage Savers" movement, 30
Marshall, Bruce, 115
Martinson, Roland D., 28, 31, 33,
  232, 306
Marty, Martin, 120
Mather, Cotton, 197–198
maturity of faith: adult statistics,
  88; caring environment
  influence on, 179, 179 fig.,
  180, 352; contributing factors
  to, 121; and ethnic minorities,
  151; gender differences, 88; and
  personal relationships with God,
  88; Protestant teacher studies
  on, 133; thinking environments
  promoting, 349; youth statistics,
  116, 214
Maurice, F. D., 287
Mazakute Memorial Church, 286
McGregor, Wynn, 107
McKinney, William, 280
McKnight Foundation, 256
McManus, Mike and Harriet, 30
Meaningful Differences (Hart and
  Risley), 57
media: faith as public interest
  in, 79, 147–148; individualism
  promoted in, 91; influence on
  culture, 269, 272; violence in,
  277
"Meet You at the Pole" prayer
  rallies, 200
Melheim, Rich, 116
memorization, 123–124, 205
Men Marked with the Cross of
  Christ, 32–33, 109, 311–312
Mennonite congregations, 256

Men of Heart, Soul, Mind, and
  Strength, 110
men's ministries, 32–33, 109, 110,
  311–312
A Mentoring Guide for
  Congregational Youth Ministry
  (Bergen), 256
mentoring programs: for at-risk
  youth, 226–227; in Canada,
  256–257; for children, 192–193;
  in communities, 254–257; for
  engaged couples, 30, 50–51; and
  ethnic minorities, 254–255; and
  men, 33, 110; prayer partner
  programs as, 227; research
  studies on, 254–255, 256;
  types of, 256; World Wide Web
  resources on, 257; for youth, 226
Methodist congregations, 78, 115
Methodist Youth Fellowship, 201
Milestones Blessing Bowls, 108,
  135
Milestones Ministry, 109, 110,
  141
Milestones Ministry Manual, 29,
  162, 177
Milestones Ministry Visitation
  Teams, 110
Minneapolis Star Tribune, 192,
  252
Minnesota Literacy Council, 190
minorities. See ethnic minorities
miracles, 282–283
mission outreach: to at-risk
  children, 157–159; bonding
  effects of, 191; community's
  statements of, 251; vision-
  to-action plan on, 333; ways
  to create, 192–194; youth
  involvement in, 156–159
mission statements: of churches,
  27, 319, 325–326, 328; of
  communities, 251; of families,
  109–110
modeling, 94–95, 112
molestation, 133
Monitor (journal), 279
Monroe, Washington, 251

Montana, state of, 101–102
Montanaro, Silvanna
    Quattrocchi, 160
Moody, Dwight L., 200
Moralistic Therapeutic Deism,
    16, 271
Morality and the Adolescent
    (Shelton), 146
moral values: from Bible, 91;
    Christian education and, 145–
    148; disciplinary approaches
    and, 63, 64; erosion of, in youth,
    17; faith linked to, 85; modeling
    of, 94–95; motivations for,
    90–91; orientations to (moral
    compasses), 143–145; parental
    communication of, 90, 93–99;
    self-centered values *versus*,
    91; sin *versus* sins, 98; vision-
    mission tied to; youth ministries
    and, 93–94
Morning Star Lutheran Church
    (Monroe, Washington), 251
Moses, 31
mothers: Bible on, 17–18;
    child abandonment by, 33;
    communication with children,
    51, 57; divorce and, 47; faith
    sharing with, 17, 102; feelings
    of failure by, 45–46; marital
    happiness of, affecting children,
    41; multiple-role stress of,
    46–47; self-descriptions of, 43; as
    spiritual leadership roles of, 32;
    in stepfamilies, 48; time usage
    survey, 46. *See also* parents
Mount Calvary (Phoenix,
    Arizona), 257
multiple-role stress, 46–47
music: asset-building success of,
    261–262; engaging youth, 221–
    222; as faith-sharing experience,
    216; Passion story presentations,
    192, 262; trends in, at worship
    services, 172–173, 175–176

N

narcissism, 271
National and Community
    Service Act, 101
National Assessment of
    Education Progress, 348
National Catholic Education
    Association (NCEA), 118
National Catholic Youth
    Council, 202–203
National Center for Fathering, 32
National Conference of Diocesan
    Directors of Religious
    Education (NCDD), 118
National Council of Churches,
    203
National Fatherhood Initiative,
    32, 33
National Institute of Mental
    Health, 220, 343
National Marriage Encounter,
    343
National Religious Partnership
    for the Environment, 309
National Survey of Youth and
    Religion, 112
National Youth Leadership
    Council, 101
Native Americans, 152, 172, 189,
    254, 284–286
Nativity of Mary Catholic
    Church (Minneapolis), 253
nature. *See* creation, circle of
Nature-Deficit Disorder, 307–308
*The Nature of Doctrine: Religion
    and Theology in a Post-Liberal
    Age* (Lindbeck), 272
Nawhooks, Reaves, 152
NCDD (National Conference of
    Diocesan Directors of Religious
    Education), 118
NCEA (National Catholic
    Education Association), 118
Neitzel, Julie, 252
Nelson, Franklin, 108
New Beginnings retreat, 215

A New Day for Family Ministry (Olson, R. and Leonard), 30
New Hope Community (Portland, Oregon), 192–193
New Song Church (Covina, California), 169
Newsweek, 147
New York Times, 148
Ng, Donald, 148–149
Nicolosi, Joseph, 279
Niebuhr, H. Richard, 274, 278, 281, 283, 286
Nightline with Ted Koppel (television program), 148
nonverbal communication, 59, 72
North Heights Lutheran Church (St. Paul, Minnesota), 192, 262

O

offerings at worship service, 97–98
Olson, Clara, 192–193
Olson, David, 50
Olson, Richard, 30
One Day to Live retreat, 312
One on One: Making the Most of Your Mentoring Relationship (Bergen), 256
openness, spirit of, 138
Oprah Winfrey (television program), 148
Oregon State University, 259
Osmer, Richard R., 116, 125
The Other Story: Lutherans in Worship (Luecke), 172
Our Lady of Guadalupe (Helotes, Texas), 24–26
Our Savior Lutheran Church (Saint Petersburg, Florida), 185–186
Our Savior's Lutheran Church (Minneapolis, Minnesota), 189–190
outdoor recreation, 306–309
out-of-wedlock children, 34
Overstreet, Bonaro, 226
Owens, Pat, 289

P

Parental Bonding Instrument and Model, 68–69, 69 fig.
parental harmony: and children's well-being, 41–42; congregation's promotion of, 48–51; deterrents to, 43–46; dynamics eroding, 42–43; as happiness variable, 37; Marriage Encounter for, 343–344; parenting experience correlation with, 36; stress impacting, 46–48
parenting: Bible on, 17–18; Christian, 72; inclusive, 73; intentional, 72; nurture-centered, 73; value-centered, 72
parents: Bible reading roles of, 96–97, 140, 142; bonding and attachment, 66–71, 69 fig.; caring (Triple A), 71–72; chosen as advisers, 53–54; Christian parenting training for, 72; communication responsibility of, 51–54, 58–61; death of, 44–45, 48; demonstrative affection of, 68 fig.; disciplinary approaches of, 62–66, 98, 344; divorce impact on, 47; faith-formation roles of, 19–20, 31–33, 78; faith-sharing roles of, 16–17, 102–106, 104 fig., 105 fig.; on family unity, 36, 36 fig.; feelings of failure, 45–46; gospel-oriented, 86–90; incompetent, 34–35; licensing of, 34; past experiences affecting, 44–45; rituals training for, 159–163, 319; self-descriptions of family, 43; stepparenting, 48; stress and, 46–48; time usage comparisons, 46; unfulfilled personal needs and, 45; unhealthy behavior patterns of, 43–44; value-centered, 72–73, 90, 93–99, 112. *See also* families; fathers; mothers
Parents of Promise rally, 106
parish nurse ministries, 184

Parks, Sharon Daloz, 83–84, 292–294
parochial education, 117–118
Parrott, Les, III, 228–229
Passing On Faith conference, 106
Passing on Faith Conference Participant's Manual, 32
Passing On Faith model: Bible story programs, 142; family-friendly worship services, 177; milestone strategies and faith formation guidance, 28–29; overview, 24; resources for, 29
passion, 80–81, 86
The Passion of the Christ (film), 79
Passion story presentations, 192, 262
pastor, word origins, 311
Pathways: Fostering Spiritual Growth Among At-Risk Youth (Everson), 146–147
Paul (Apostle), 17–18, 166, 196, 197, 283, 322
peer leadership: for Bible-centered discussion groups, 211–213; for Bible study programs, 141–142; counseling objectives of, 228; selection processes for, 212; training programs for, 231–232
peer ministry: to at-risk youth, 219–221; benefits of, 253–254; Bible-centered discussion groups in, 211–213; Bible-reading programs and, 97; at Bible schools and camps, 220; congregation programs in communities, 252–253; to public school children, 219–220; questions to use in, 219; research on, 220–221; training programs for, 93–94, 180, 221
Peer Ministry Training, 253
peers, 53–54, 90
Penikese Island experiment, 35
Pentecostal congregations, 282
People of Faith: Generations Learning Together, 106–107
permissive discipline, 64–65

personal relationships with God: biblical concept of, 132, 299; children's programs for, 107; as Christian education task, 132–135; cognitive relationship *versus*, 83–84; developmental assets tied to, 262–265; faith as, 85; and faith maturity, 88; humanity *versus* creation and, 300–304; recruiting teachers with, 133–134; theology of the cross, 297–299; youth studies on, 132–133, 134, 135
Peters-Golden, H., 183
Pfister, Darlene, 192
Piaget, Jean, 124
Pilgrimage As Rite of Passage: A Guidebook for Youth Ministry (Brancatelli), 162
Pilgrim Fellowships, 201
Pilisuk, M., 183
Pioneers of the YMCA, 201
Placentia Presbyterian Church (Los Angeles), 223–224
Planning Youth Ministry: From Boot-up to Exit (Ross), 232
pluralism, 120–121
Pocket Testament Movement, 139
poor *vs.* rich future scenarios, 291–292
Posterski, Donald, 221, 223
Postman, Neil, 174
potentiality, image of, 359
Powell, Colin, 190, 265, 266, 290
Practicing Passion (Dean), 80
prayer: as congregational emphasis, 185–187; as education priority, 131; fellowship through, 185; and grace orientation, 138; healing power of, 186, 192, 282–283; invisible power of, 322; mentoring programs using, 227; parent-child instruction in, 142–143; requests for, 180, 187, 313; as vision-mission component, 320; youth rallies for, 200
premarital intercourse, 92 fig. *See*

also sexual activity
Prepare and Enrich Inventory,
50–51
President's Summit for America's
Future, 101–102, 190, 265
Prince of Peace Lutheran Church
(Burnsville, Minnesota), 222
Progress from Relationships
scale, 221
Project L.I.F.E! (Lifestyle
Improvement for Excellence),
259–260
Promise Keepers, 32
Protestant denominations:
alternative lifestyle controversies
in, 279; at-risk behaviors in, 214;
Christian education in, 19, 113–
117; cultural accommodation
of, 278–279, 280; early youth
organizations of, 198–199;
environmental responsibility,
305; faith-assets correlation
in, 263–264; faith maturity
surveys of, 88, 116, 133; family
faith-sharing experiences
in, 16–17, 102–103; Gospel
versus law orientation of, 87;
institutionalized faith in, 19;
men's retreats of, 312; National
Marriage Encounter events of,
343; personal witness retreats of,
96; service projects and youth
in, 153–154; youth support
group eras, 199–206
"Psychologists' Faith in Religion
Begins to Grow," 79
public education: in content-
oriented schools, 124; cultural
illiteracy and, 122–123,
174–175; home schooling
as alternative, 277–278; peer
ministry's work in, 219–220;
religion ignored in, 215; religion
opposed in, 77

Q

quantum physics, 321–322

R

Rainbow Bags, 170
"Raising Christian Children in a
Pagan Culture" (Charry), 78
Ratcliff, Donald, 206
Ray of Hope (Decatur, Georgia),
156
Reaching Out Without Dumbing
Down (Dawn), 173
Ready, Click, Grow for Families,
109
reconciliation, 305
"Recovering a Christian College"
(Marshall), 115
recycling, 305
reducing, 305
Reformed Church of Youth
Fellowship, 201
Reineke, Robert A., 342
Rejoice Church (Omaha,
Nebraska), 162
Rejoice Lutheran Church
(Omaha, Nebraska), 186
The Relationship Between
Cohabitation and Divorce
(Axinn and Thornton), 31
relationship building: divorce
and, 48; family, 17–18; past
experiences affecting, 44–45;
through outdoor recreation,
307–309; unhealthy behavior
patterns affecting, 43–44; in
vision-to-action process, 321–
322
Religion and Society Report
(Rockford Institute), 271
The Religious Potential of the
Child (Cavalletti), 160
Renewing the Vision: A
Framework for Catholic Youth
Ministry, 22, 112, 249
reparative therapy for
homosexuality, 279

repentance, 305
Research on Religious Development, 339
resiliency, 244
Resources for Family Ministry (Kasischke and Johnson), 49, 50
restoration, 305
Rethinking Christian Education (Osmer), 125
retreats: Bible-focused, intergenerational, 140; Bible study, high school, 141–142; faith-sharing, 216–217; for men, 32–33, 109, 110, 311–312; for parental harmony, 51, 342; personal witness, 96
reusing, 305
Rhoads, David, 301, 312
Rhodes, Sun, 254
Richardson, Bev, 216
rich *vs.* poor future scenarios, 291–292
Risley, Todd, 57
rituals: Bible on, 159; Durkheim on functions of, 285; faith-sharing, 103; family instruction and practice in, 32, 159–163, 319; and Latino culture, 150
Roberto, John, 23, 24, 28, 206, 257
Roberts, Cokie and Steven, 266
Robinson, John, 46
Rockford Institute, 271
Roehlkepartain, Eugene, 101, 153, 155
Rojas, José, 190–191
"The Role of Work and Family in the Faith and Value Formation of Children" (Martinson), 31
Roman Catholic Church: asset-building focus of, 249; Christian education in, 117–119; creation celebration promotions by, 313; environmental responsibility, 305; on faith, 83; faith formation and role of family, 19; faith-sharing programs of, 107; intergenerational emphasis of,

257; Marriage Encounter event of, 343–344; personal witness retreats in, 96; retreats of, 32–33, 109, 311–312; youth group development of, 202–203, 206; youth ministry programs of, 22, 214–215. *See also* Catholic denominations
Roman Catholic Confraternity of Christian Doctrine (CCD), 118
Roof, Wade, 280
Rose, Rob, 217
Rosenberg, Howard, 288
Ross, Richard, 147–148, 231–232
Royal Dutch Shell, 290

S

Saint Andrew Lutheran Church (Eden Prairie, Minnesota), 252–253
Saint John Lutheran Church (Winter Park, Florida), 161–162, 182, 261
Saint John's Lutheran Church (Mound, Minnesota), 184
Saint John the Evangelist Church (Rochester, New York), 319–321
Saint Louis Park, Minnesota, 225
Saint Luke's Lutheran Church (Bloomington, Minnesota), 142
Saint Mary Catholic Community (Helena, Montana), 73
Saint Paul's Lutheran Church (Grand Island, Nebraska), 220
Saint Timothy Catholic Church (Mesa, Arizona), 177–178
Saito, Rebecca, 256
Sample, Tex, 117, 272
San Diego Christian Studies, 128
Satinover, Jeffrey, 357
SAT (Scholastic Aptitude Test), 348

SATs (Stanford Achievement Tests), 278
scavenger hunts, 161–162
scenario planning, 291–292
Scholastic Aptitude Test (SAT), 348
schools, 117–118, 124–125, 247–248. *See also* education; public education; Sunday schools
Scriptures. *See* Bible
Scripture Talk, 108, 135
Searching for the God of Grace (Tyner), 137
Search Institute: adoption studies, 56, 67; asset development research, 72–73, 185, 224, 242–244 fig., 263; at-risk behavior studies, 93, 250–251; Bible-reading studies, 97; Christian education studies, 56, 115; church members studies, 86–87; church participation studies, 170, 206; committed youth studies, 16; congregational family studies, 167; cultural transformation goals of, 290; faith maturity studies, 88, 100, 264; God and morality research, 85; innovation-change studies, 178; mentoring research studies, 226–227, 256; mission outreach studies, 191; parent-youth studies, 52–53, 63, 64, 67, 73–74, 98–99; peer ministry research, 220; personal relationship with God studies, 132–133; religious commitments studies, 89–90; research focus, 339; service and bonding studies, 100. *See also* *Early Adolescent Study*; *Effective Christian Education* study; *A Study of Generations*
Seasons of a Family's Life: Cultivating the Contemplative Spirit at Home (Wright), 23–24
Seasons of Faith program, 25
Seattle, Washington, 251

seder meals, 32
Seeler, David, 35
self-disclosure, 58
self-fulfillment/gratification, ethic of, 143, 269, 272
Self-Portrait survey, 134, 135
senior citizens, 23, 28, 131, 185, 257–258
Seraphim Communications, 72
service: benefits of, 100; Bible study with, 100, 129, 156; bonding effect of, 191; Christ as model for, 99; Christian education and, 129–130, 153–156; faith's correlation with, 84–85, 99–100, 264; as faith sharing, 103; intergenerational, 189–191; as leadership criteria, 231–232; learning combined with, 101–102, 155–156; loyalty to church and, 154; national-level, 190–191; public sector emphasis on, 101–102; teaching as, 126–127; as welcoming strategy, 150–151; work camps for, 108; youth participants in, 100, 217–218, 287, 350
Service-Learning Cycle, 155–156
Seventeen, 148
Seventh-day Adventist Church: adolescent faith studies of, 70–71, 71 fig.; at-risk youth programs of, 190; congregational atmosphere of studies by, 169; counseling for clergy families of, 50; ethnic minority studies of, 149; family life surveys of, 48–49; grace-oriented curriculums of, 137; law-oriented lifestyles of, 275–276, 276 fig.; parent-child studies of, 69–70; service programs of, 190–191
sexual activity: abstinence pledges, 147–148; cultural influence on, 279; and developmental assets,

245 fig.; moral orientation and, 145; premarital, opposition percentages, 92 fig.; Seventh-day Adventist surveys, 276 fig.

Shaller, Lyle, 177

Shelton, Charles, 146

silent generations, 23

Silverman, Robin, 289

Silverton, Oregon, 350

sin, 98, 137, 298, 302–304, 309

Sinai Christian Church (Brooklyn, New York), 131, 186

single-parent households, 32, 47, 226, 342

Smidt, Donald D., 258

Smith, Christian, 16, 80, 112, 174, 227, 271

Soaries, Buster, 151

social competencies, 241, 243

Sonnenberg, E. Steven, 191

Soul Children of Chicago, 222

Soul Searching (Smith), 16, 174, 227, 271

Sounds of Grace, 222

Southern Baptist Convention, 202, 231

Southern Cross constellation, 297

Spears, Melanie, 284

Spirit of Youth Ministry National Conference, 233

St. Edward's Catholic Church (Bloomington, Minnesota), 109

St. Paul Pioneer Press, 255–256

St. Peter's Church (Mesa, Arizona), 109

Staats, Linda, 50

Stamschror, Robert, 19, 24

Stanford Achievement Tests (SATs), 278

Star Tribune, 303

"The Statement on the Environment" (Episcopal Church), 305

Stecklow, Steve, 278

Steindal, Yvonne, 232–233

stepfamilies, 31, 48

Stephen Ministry, 180–181, 224

Stone, J. David, 219, 224

Stoop, David, 38

Strahan, Bradley, 63, 70

stress, 46–48, 78

Strommen, Irene A., 47, 72

Strommen, Merton, 47, 321

Student Volunteer Movement, 200

Study of Exemplary Youth Ministry in Congregations, 233

A Study of Generations (Search Institute): on disciplinary approaches, 64; on faith-assets correlations, 264; on grace (Gospel) *versus* law orientation, 86–88, 179; on relationships with God, 89, 214

suicide, 49, 245 fig.

Sunday schools: age of children and, 24; as family-centered catechesis option, 25; history of, 113–115; newspapers developed by, 109; teachers of, 127–128, 133

Sundberg, Paul, 251

support groups and networks: as developmental asset, 240, 242; families for families, 183–185; for family crises, 50; for parents, 193; for youth, 196–197. *See also* caring environments

Sweet, Leonard I., 318–319

Synchronicity: The Inner Path of Leadership (Jaworski), 291

T

TalkPoints discussion tool, 108

task-force leadership training, 231–232

Taylor, J. H., 63

teachers, Christian education, 126–128, 133–134, 146, 153

Teaching the Gospel Today (Krych), 88–89, 137

Teaching Values (Larson and Larson), 146
teenagers. *See* adolescents
Teens Encounter Christ (TEC), 96, 215
Teen Trends: A Nation in Motion (Posterski and Bibby), 221, 223
Tejeda, Cynthia, 25, 26
Ten Characteristics of Committed Youth: family relationships and, 73–74, 74 fig.; list of, 20, 22 fig., 77; parental faith sharing and, 105 fig.
Tender Loving Care, 193
testimonies and witnessing, personal, 96, 110, 216
theist morality, 144, 145, 147–148
Theology of Culture (Tillich), 138
theory theory, 124
thinking atmospheres, 181–183, 349
Thompson, Marjorie, 23, 24
Thornton, Arland, 31
threshold people, 293
Thrivent (formerly Lutheran Brotherhood), 260, 289
Tillich, Paul, 138
Time, 79, 147, 215, 282
time management, 46, 78, 241, 242–243
tobacco abuse, 245 fig.
Today (television program), 148
Tolstoy, Leo, 139
Touched by an Angel (television series), 79, 288
Treatise on the Freedom of the Christian (Luther), 82–83
Tres Dies retreat, 96
Trinity Lutheran Church (Mission, Kansas), 259
Trinity Lutheran Church (Stillwater, Minnesota), 328–336
Trinity Lutheran Church (Town and Country, Missouri), 217
Trinity School (Bloomington, Minnesota), 124
The Troubled Journey study, 100

True Love Waits program, 147
Tulip Grove Baptist Congregation, 147
Turning Vision into Action (Barna), 191–192
20/20 (television program), 148
Twin Cities Community Marriage Policy, 30
Tyner, Stuart, 137

U

Ulschmid, Terri, 253–254
unchurched societies, 27
unchurched youth, 141, 212–213, 221, 229
"Understanding the Human Being: The Importance of the First Three Years of Life" (Montanaro), 160
United Church of Christ (Iglesia Evangelica Unida de Puerto Rico), 128
United States Catholic Conference (USCC), 22
The Uniting Word (Bible reading guide), 139, 205
U.S. Lifestyles and Mainline Churches (Sample), 117, 272
USA Today, 148
utilitarian morality, 144, 145

V

Vaagenes, Morris, 192
Valley Interfaith Coalition to Recovery (VICTORY), 289
Valuegenesis study, 149, 179
values: of congregation, 325–326; as developmental assets, 241, 243, 248–249; peer ministry affecting, 254; as primary American concern, 249; self-serving, 91; surveys ranking, 248. *See also* moral values

Values and Faith (Larson and Larson), 146

Vander Ark, Brian, 107

Vanishing Boundaries: The Religion of Mainline Protestant Baby Boomers (Hoge, Johnson, and Luidens), 117

Varenhorst, Barbara, 56, 180, 219, 253

Veggie Tales (videos), 142

verbal sharing, 95–96

Via de Cristo retreat, 96

VICTORY (Valley Interfaith Coalition to Recovery), 289

violence, 245 fig., 277

vision: community's mission statements of, 251; equated with mission, 191–192; faith-based, 317–319. *See also* vision-to-action process

A Vision of Youth Ministry, 22

VisionPak, 336, 337 fig.

vision-to-action process: action commitments of, 334–336; collaborative approaches to; defining outcomes, 333–334; evaluation phase of, 328–329; planning process of, 324–328; priority vision of, 330–333, 330 fig.; resources for, 336, 337 fig.; science-based principles of, 321–323; task force's role in, 327–328

Vision-to-Action workshop, 55

Vitz, Paul, 215

Vogue, 148

W

Walker, Gary, 255

Walker, L. J., 63

Walk Thru the Bible retreat, 140

Wallerstein, Judith, 42

Wall Street Journal, 278, 280

Walther League, 202, 204

Wangerin, Walter, Jr., 141

Wanstall, David, 254

Washington Post, 148

The Way of the Child (McGregor), 107

Weaver, Kirk, 107

welcoming environments, 148–153, 170, 320

wellness programs, 182, 184, 259–261, 310–311

Wendt, Harry, 100, 130

Westburg, Granger E., 184

Westman, Jack, 34

Westminster Youth Fellowship, 201

Westwood Lutheran Church (Minneapolis), 225

Westwood United Methodist Church, 128, 133

Wheatley, Margaret J., 321–323

Wheat Ridge Ministries (Itasca, Illinois), 225

Wheeler, Barbara, 280–281

Willamette University, 350

Williamson, Martha, 288

Willimon, William, 121–122, 125

Willow Creek Community Church (South Barrington, Illinois), 212–213

"Will the Real Jesus Please Stand Up" (Campolo, A.), 138–139

Wind River Reservation (Wyoming), 254

Without Vision, the People Perish (Barna), 318

witnessing and testimonies, personal, 96, 110, 216, 350

Woman's Day, 148

Woodbury Baptist Church (Woodbury, Minnesota), 108

Words, Thoughts, and Theories (Gopnik and Gopnik), 124

work camps, 108

World Wide Web mentoring information, 257

worship services: contemporary trends in, 172, 173–174; creating inspirational, 171–178; creation celebrations in, 312–314; family-friendly faith formation, 29; of inclusive communities, 130; music at, 172–173, 175–176; offerings at, 97–98; prayer requests at, 187; welcoming children, 168, 170–171, 177

Wright, Wendy, 23–24

WWJD (What Would Jesus Do?), 200

Wynn, Joan, 250

X

X Factor program, 141

Y

Yancey, Phillip, 139

Yellowstone National Park, 300

YMCA (Young Men's Christian Association), 198, 200

YMHA (Young Men's Hebrew Association), 198

Young Adolescent-Parent National Survey, 43, 45

Young Adolescents and Their Parents study, 16

Young Life, 205–206

Young Men's Hebrew Association (YMHA), 198

Young Men's Christian Association (YMCA), 198, 200

Young People's Association, 198

Young Women's Hebrew Association (YWHA), 198

Young Women's Christian Association (YWCA), 198

Your Church (magazine), 173

Youth Connection, Building Leaders for Our Church (Steindal and Hardel), 233

Youth Encounter (Minneapolis), 216

The Youth & Family Institute: Bible-reading programs, 97; communication training programs, 56; faith-formation conferences, 106; faith-formation ministries of, 24, 28; faith-formation resources of, 29, 107, 108, 109, 135, 162; family-friendly worship resources, 177; ministries for men, 32–33, 110; peer ministry training, 180; principles of, 130; vision-to-action planning resources of, 336

YouthFirst (Hastings, Minnesota), 251

Youth for Christ, 205–206

Youth in Mission, 205–206

"Youth in the Church of
Norway" (Andreson), 35
youth ministry: Bible-
centered discussions for,
209–213; components
for successful, 208–209;
counseling programs
in, 224–229; of cultural
Protestantism, 278–279;
cultural transformation goals
of, 287; current concerns of,
207; early organizations for,
198–199; eras of, 199–206;
faith-assets goals of, 235–236;
faith-sharing experiences in,
213–216; friendship training
and groups, 93–94, 223–224;
fun and fellowship activities
in, 216–217; goals of, 206;
godparenting programs for,
73; importance of, 206–207,
208; leadership selection and
training for, 232–233; music
involvement of, 221–222;
peer ministry programs,
219–221; reformation of,
22; service projects for,
217–218; task-force approach
to, 231–232; term origins,
204; worship programs for,
177–178. *See also* adolescents;
children; high school
students
The Youth Movement (Jenny),
200
Youth Reaching Youth **project,**
93–94
YWCA (Young Women's
Christian Association), 198
YWHA (Young Women's
Hebrew Association), 198

Z

Zander, Dieter, 169, 175
Zimmerman, Ginny, 192
Zion Lutheran Church
(Anoka, Minnesota), 107–
108, 217–218
Zion Lutheran Church
(Puerto Rico), 131
Zuzek, Elaine, 251